Understanding Soviet Politics

About the Book and Author

To what extent did the Russian revolution of 1917 bring about the changes wanted by the Bolsheviks? Why did many of these changes fail to materialize? How has the Russian heritage adapted to the challenges facing all modernizing societies? What does Russia's past tell us about the present role of the USSR in world affairs?

In this collection of essays, which includes new part and chapter introductions, Dr. Black discusses these questions, examining the major issues that shape our understanding of Soviet politics. Beginning with a general exploration of the ways the traditional heritage of the Russian empire has both helped and hindered the adaptation of Soviet society to the contemporary world, he illustrates the extent to which the Russian empire was already evolving into a modern society before World War I. The author analyzes the modernization of the USSR, emphasizing the interaction of tradition and modernity and the ways the Russian heritage of institutions and values has been adapted since 1861 to the needs of political development, economic growth, and social integration. Comparisons are made with a wide range of societies, first in 1967—the fiftieth anniversary of the Russian revolution—and again in the 1980s.

The book considers the past and present relations of Russia/USSR with the outside world in the context of universal societal changes. Dr. Black discusses such questions as the differences between the foreign policy objectives of Czarist Russia and the Soviet Union; the degree to which Russia/USSR has been able to influence other countries through means other than military power; and, drawing on his experience in Bulgaria, the origins of the cold war. The book concludes with Dr. Black's personal interview with Nikita Khrushchev, a discussion that provides rare insights into the thought processes of a leading Soviet statesman at the height of his power.

Since the 1940s, Cyril E. Black has figured prominently in the study of Russian history and politics. At Princeton University, he inaugurated the study of Russian history and played a leading role in the development of regional studies. From 1968 to 1985 he was director of the Center of International Studies at Princeton, where he is currently James S. McDonnell Distinguished University Professor of History and International Affairs.

Written under the auspices
of the Center of International Studies,
Princeton University

A list of other Center publications
appears at the back of this book

UNDERSTANDING SOVIET POLITICS

The Perspective of Russian History

Cyril E. Black

Routledge
Taylor & Francis Group
LONDON AND NEW YORK

First published 1986 by Westview Press, Inc.

Published 2019 by Routledge
52 Vanderbilt Avenue, New York, NY 10017
2 Park Square, Milton Park, Abingdon, Oxon OX14 4RN

Routledge is an imprint ofthe Taylor & Francis Group, an informa business

Library of Congress Cataloging-in-Publication Data
Black, Cyril Edwin, 1915-
Understanding Soviet politics.
A collection of previously published essays.
Includes index.
1. Soviet Union—Politics and government. 2.Soviet Union—History. 3. Soviet Union—Social conditions. 4. Soviet Union—Economic conditions. I. Title.
DK43.B52 1986 947 86-15783

ISBN 13: 978-0-367-21270-4 (hbk)
ISBN 13: 978-0-367-21551-4 (pbk)

To Corinne
this book is affectionately dedicated

Contents

Preface

When Fred Praeger invited me to prepare these essays for publication, I decided to organize them into three sections. The first section deals with the continuities and discontinuities between the Russian Empire and the Union of Soviet Socialist Republics—one of the main focuses of the book. This distinction led me to adopt the somewhat awkward but nevertheless useful term *Russia/USSR* to indicate the continuities between the two regimes.

The second group of essays centers on modernization, an interest of mine since the 1950s. Modernization studies as they relate to Russia/USSR are concerned with the ways that the Russian heritage of institutions and values has been adapted—both before 1917 and since then—to the functions of political development, economic growth, and social integration that are common to all modernizing societies. This type of analysis involves comparisons both between the Soviet Union and Russia and between Russia/USSR and other countries.

The last group of essays examines the question of how the relations between Russia/USSR and other countries have been affected by the changes involved in modernization. To what extent is the contemporary role of the Soviet Union in world affairs unique in the country's history? To what extent does this role continue themes that have deep roots in Russia's past? How has Russia/USSR influenced the institutions and values of other countries, and how has this influence fluctuated over time?

While all twelve essays have been reprinted in their original form, a few titles have been changed to emphasize the major themes of the book.

I would like to express my appreciation to my wife, Corinne, for her thoughtful suggestions on organization and style. Her experience in editing and university teaching proved invaluable in these matters.

Cyril E. Black
Princeton, N.J.

PART ONE

Russian History: A Window on Soviet Politics

The four essays in this section deal with Russian history as it illuminates our understanding of current Soviet politics. Russian history, analyzed and interpreted by Western historians, gives us valuable and sometimes surprising insights into the limits the Russian heritage placed on any reform movement. It also helps to explain why the revolution of 1917 failed to produce the sweeping changes that its rhetoric espoused.

In 1917 Lenin and his colleagues led a revolution that, at the level of its legislative program and rhetoric, was the most radical the world had known. It sought nothing less than the abolition of all the inequities that had characterized imperial Russia—and most other countries—and the establishment of a society based on equality and justice for all. Yet some seventy years later, despite changes in institutions and values no less dynamic than those that have occurred in other advanced societies, much of the old Russia is still in evidence, especially in the political sphere. Despite a very significant development of political participation through institutions and organizations, the centralized and autocratic government of the 1980s bears much more than a passing resemblance to the institutions of imperial Russia. This and other elements of continuity raise the question of whether revolution is possible. Can a society be transformed overnight? Can a revolution accomplish any more than bringing to power a new group of leaders who can set a society moving in a new direction but who must work within the constraints of the old system?

A socialist society as envisaged by Marx—to use his terminology—was supposed to emerge in developed capitalist societies in which industrial workers had already gained substantial political influence. Among the West European countries, England and Germany in particular might be said to have met this criterion at the time of World War I. Lenin and his colleagues were well aware that Russia was still predominantly agrarian and by no means ready for a socialist revolution as defined by Marx. Indeed, Lenin was convinced that his revolution would fail if it did not receive the support of socialist revolutions in the West. He feared that if capitalism survived in the countries of Western Europe, they would attack and destroy the revolutionary movement in Russia. Capitalism did survive, and there were limited efforts to support the counterrevolutionary forces in Russia, but at the end of World War I the Western countries were in no mood for another major military effort.

Lenin's revolution retained power after considerable civil strife. The Bolsheviks then faced the problem of implementing their program in a country not only quite unprepared for socialism but also devastated by war, revolution, and civil war. It was not until 1928—a loss of fifteen years—that the Soviet Union achieved the 1913 level of per capita production in agriculture and industry. Under these circumstances, the old regime weighed heavily on the new. After Lenin's death in 1924 most of the Bolsheviks who came to power under Stalin's leadership were individuals whose outlook was formed as much by the old mentality as by the new. The society that emerged from these beginnings was one that Marx would not have recognized as "socialist." Indeed, most West Europeans who consider themselves to be socialists in the Marxist tradition do not regard the Soviet Union as an examplar of their political philosophy.

The disparity between the actual economic and social conditions in the Soviet Union and the claims of the new regime to be in the process of creating the most advanced form of society was the source of many anomalies. Important among these was the self-image of the new leaders as expressed in historical writing. Their rhetoric required that they renounce their roots in the past, but as they gained experience in the Stalin era they came to recognize the significance of continuities with the past and to make use of them in their effort to mobilize domestic support. Among the top leaders, Khrushchev was the last of the romantics, who thought that the Soviet Union could bypass the evolutionary processes of societal transformation. Not until Gorbachev's revised Communist Party Program of 1986 was it officially recognized that socialism was still beyond the horizon.

CHAPTER 1

Russian History and Soviet Politics

This first chapter takes the rather bizarre form of a statement made at a hearing before the Subcommittee on Strategic Arms Limitation Talks of the Committee on Armed Services of the U.S. Senate in March 1970. My invitation to appear before the subcommittee arose from the belief of its chairman, Senator Henry W. Jackson, that "the salient themes of Russian history that bear on her contemporary foreign and defense policy should be explored by the subcommittee." The hearing offered me an opportunity to discuss some of the aspects of Russian history that have continuing relevance to Soviet society and politics. These include in particular the relatively unchallenged role of the state, which under the empire scarcely less than after the revolution may be held accountable for both the achievements and the excesses of public policy. Of comparable significance is the international environment in which Russia/USSR has always found itself, with undefined frontiers and neighbors perceived as real or potential enemies. Similarly, the ethnic complexity of the country, in which Russians have been a bare majority of the population, has been a continuing formative condition.

THE INTERPRETATION OF RUSSIAN HISTORY

In seeking to draw conclusions of contemporary significance from the long historical record of the peoples of Russia, it is important to identify the recurring patterns of behavior that give evidence of the characteristic conditioning of peoples with a common historical experience. To the extent that such patterns can be identified with some assurance, they can provide guidelines of significant value to the evaluation of policy.

Reprinted from *Hearings Before the Subcommittee on Strategic Arms Limitation Talks of the Committee on Armed Services, Ninety-First Congress, Second Session, March 18, 1970* (Washington, D.C.: U.S. Government Printing Office, 1970), 3–18.

Just as a mature person can alter the habits of many years with difficulty, even in the face of a challenge that may threaten his very existence, so nations with deeply ingrained ways of conducting their affairs change only gradually under the impact of new experiences. In this sense, history is always with us. The leaders of a nation can modify historically evolved institutions and values only to a limited degree, and at any given moment the genuinely new elements in a nation's life are relatively few and those that have deep roots in the past are inevitably much more influential. This very substantial degree of historical continuity in all societies is perceived as an obstacle by those seeking rapid political, economic, and social change, and as a powerful support by those concerned with the stability of institutions and values in times of stress and strain.

Historians who wish to determine the range of variation that a given society is likely to undergo must seek to identify those salient characteristics that are not likely to change very substantially in a decade or a generation, and to distinguish these from the more or less ephemeral policies that men and women in positions of great political authority may be able to change drastically in a short time. To say this is not to minimize the role of individuals in history, but simply to place this role in its social context. Individuals may have great influence in decisions that can be directly implemented, but even a totalitarian government can hope to effect only gradual change when the internalized habits and attitudes of many millions of people are concerned.

It is significant in this connection that Russia is one of the few countries whose peoples have lived together for several centuries as independent states within approximately their present territorial confines. Among the major countries, England, France, Japan, and China share this experience, but most of the other one hundred and fifty in which the peoples of the world live today have been formed rather recently. Most European countries emerged in their present form only in the nineteenth century and several did not gain their independence until after the First World War. In other parts of the world, no less than seventy countries have taken their present form only in this century. In this sense the United States, which will soon celebrate the 200th anniversary of its independence, is one of the oldest and most firmly established countries in the modern world. To the extent that the peoples of a country have a long experience of facing problems together, one can with greater confidence identify those institutions and values that have enduring significance by virtue of having stood the test of time.

While Russia is thus different from most other countries in the age and continuity of its institutions and values, it shares with most other countries the experience of having undertaken the profoundly difficult task of transforming an established agrarian society consisting predominantly of peasants and led by a small minority of landowners, merchants, and government officials, into an urban, industrial society.

Americans seeking to interpret Russian history bring to this subject important advantages, but also serious handicaps. The advantages arise from the relative detachment of a country which has never confronted Russia in war and which in fact has been an ally in the two major wars of our era; which is strong enough to deal with the Russians as an equal at the international level; and which also has the resources and talents to become the principal foreign center for the study of Russian history and institutions. In seeking to understand the Russian historical experience, in other words, Americans do not suffer the handicaps of neighbors who have been engaged in a bitter struggle with the Russians, or of those within the Soviet political orbit who are unable to express themselves freely, or of more distant peoples who have not been able to accumulate libraries of Russian books and journals and train a generation or two of scholars to use them.

At the same time we have some handicaps, and these stem from some of the same sources as our advantages—our historical experience has been so different from that of the Russians, that we have great difficulty in seeing things from their point of view, of overcoming the feeling that we are right and they are wrong. Most of the peoples of the world, from England clear across to China, have faced the problem of transforming deeply imbedded traditional societies in modern times under the impact of the scientific and technological revolution. That is the hard way to do it, but they had no choice except to start with what they had.

We did it the easy way. We started with an empty continent, with bountiful resources, and filled it with vigorous immigrants from across the oceans. We know that some came here unwillingly, but a very significant majority came to the new world for the specific purpose of breaking away from their traditional institutions and starting all over again to achieve a modern way of life. It would of course be going too far to say that they came without traditional institutions and values, but the important point is that we started with a self-selected group of leaders and without a traditional society of landowners and peasants who had lived in the country for centuries. The only other countries that have shared this experience are Canada, Australia, and New Zealand. We are in many respects the most successful country in the world, but the process by which we achieved this success cannot very well be repeated by others.

For reasons such as this there is a sense in which it may be easier for Englishmen, or Poles, or Indians, or Chinese, to understand the process by which contemporary Russian institutions have evolved. Their experience to this extent at least has been closer to the Russian than ours. This is not a fatal handicap for us, but simply one we should be aware of and seek to overcome. So long as we recognize the differences between the way we have developed and the way they have developed and are wary of transferring our assumptions and values to their history, there is no reason we should not study them with confidence that we can reach useful conclusions.

SALIENT THEMES IN RUSSIAN HISTORY

In seeking to identify the salient themes over a period of more than a thousand years in the history of the diverse peoples who comprise the USSR today, a useful approach is to analyze a major turning point in their history as a reflection of both the heritage of historically formed institutions and the legacy that may have a bearing on contemporary problems. Such a major turning point was represented by the emancipation of the serfs by Emperor Alexander II in 1861, which was compared by contemporaries with Lincoln's emancipation of the slaves. Together with related reforms in the 1860's the emancipation was one of the most important efforts at government-administered social change up to that date. This is a useful vantage point from which to view both the historical antecedents of the political, economic, and social patterns characteristic of mid-nineteenth-century Russia and the subsequent transformation of the country from an agrarian to an industrial way of life.

The emancipation and related reforms directly affected no less than 42 million Russian citizens in the 50 provinces of European Russia, of whom about half were held as serfs by some 600,000 gentry landowners, and the balance were held in bondage by the state and the crown. The serfs and state peasants were freed from their obligation to till the soil and perform certain other services for their owners, but the emancipation was not an unmixed blessing. The settlement left the peasants with somewhat less land than they had tilled on their own account under serfdom, it burdened them with quitrents and redemption payments which in the end proved too heavy for them to bear, and it required them to share these burdens collectively within the framework of the village commune so that their individual freedom was still restricted.

The gentry kept more than their fair share of the land and received compensation for the balance, but they too had their problems. Less than 5 percent of the gentry were major landowners who held 45 percent of the serfs. The great majority of them had not owned enough serfs to support them, and had earned their living predominantly as government officials, officers, or professional men. Many of them had been in debt before the emancipation, and many more failed to adapt themselves to the commercialization of agriculture.

The 42 million serfs and state peasants ultimately affected by this settlement comprised 70 percent of the population of the 50 European provinces of Russia, which also had another 12 million rural and 6 million urban inhabitants. The Russian Empire included in addition at this time 16 million inhabitants in the Caucasus, the Steppe region, Siberia, Finland, and Poland for a total of about 76 million.

The circumstances in which this momentous body of reforms in the 1860's was carried out, reflect characteristic features of the historical development of Russia that help to explain contemporary Soviet attitudes and policies. These circumstances may be summarized in terms of five themes: the predominant role of the state; values that stress collective at the expense of individual interests; a purposeful economic policy; a multinational society; and an international position of relative insecurity. Since we are particularly concerned with understanding the features of contemporary Russia that seem alien to the experience of the West-European and English-speaking countries, the brief discussion of these themes will emphasize the relatively unique features of Russian developments.

It is a striking feature of the emancipation and the accompanying reforms that they were undertaken by the state for reasons of national policy as determined by the emperor and his bureaucracy. Although the Russian autocracy as it existed in the 19th century was not a totalitarian government in the modern sense of the term, for it administered directly only a small share of the gross national product and did not seek to regulate in detail the lives of most of its citizens, it nevertheless played a larger role than any other major government in the 19th century. The Russian emperor could decide on his own authority to change fundamentally the status of 42 million peasants and 600,000 landowners, and possessed the legal and administrative institutions necessary to give effect to this decision. The emperor did not run the country like a dictator, and the bureaucracy was very modest in size by modern standards, but neither was there any alternative political authority in the country that could counterbalance the emperor. There were by this time no regional princes, or leaders of political, economic, or social interest groups, who could challenge the authority of the imperial government, and its power was limited primarily by a customary allocation of authority that left most provincial administrative matters in local hands.

The relatively unchallenged position of the state is perhaps the most distinctive feature of Russian society, and may be held to account for both the achievements that have made Russia great among nations and for the excesses that have made it an object of fear at home as well as abroad. It would doubtless be an oversimplification to say that historical experience has taught the Russians that unless they are united under a strong state they will be plundered by foreigners, but to a greater extent than most other peoples the Russians have seen themselves as facing the choice of unity under an autocrat or subjugation by a foreign power.

The political and geographical environment within which the modern Russian state was formed confronted it with harsher alternatives than those prevailing in Western Europe, and the models on the basis of which the Russian rulers constructed their political system were also different. The first and most influential of these models was the Byzantine Empire, from which the concept and practice of autocracy were derived. Although both Russia and the West have a common heritage in the traditions of the ancient world as transmitted by Greece and Rome, the rulers of Russia received this tradition through a Byzantium in which the state played a preponderant role with the church as its principal ally. Byzantine writings were the principal source of political guidance for the princes of Moscow until the 18th century, and other political lessons gained from association with the Mongol and Ottoman empires likewise stressed the importance of centralized authority.

The development of autocratic institutions in Russia was based as much on practice as on theory. The Kievan principalities to which the origins of modern Russia can be traced, flourished between the ninth and thirteenth centuries in the river systems stretching from the Baltic to the Black seas. The security of these principalities depended less on their own efforts than on the larger international security system which was managed by the Byzantine Empire. When the empire declined, the defenses of the entire orbit were weakened, including those of Kiev, and the Mongol invasion in the thirteenth century virtually destroyed these early Russian principalities.

It was in a less hospitable geographical and political environment to the northeast that the remnants of these early principalities gradually formed a new state under the leadership of Moscow. In the face of oppressive Mongol rule and the petty bickering of a dozen or more little principalities, the rulers of Moscow gradually beat their fellow princes into submission. Vasily II (1425–62) was known as the Blind because of an injury received in civil strife; Ivan III (1462–1505) as the Great because of his services in extending the lands and prestige of Moscow; Ivan IV (1533–84) as the Terrible, or the Dread, because of his violent confiscation of much of the property of his landowners in his efforts to assert his authority over them; and Peter I (1689–1725) was Great because he borrowed successfully from Western models for the purpose of strengthening the authority of the state over society. In the course of this process the traditional autonomy of princes, church, landowners, towns, and peasants was eroded. The country exploded into civil strife in the first decade of the seventeenth century, but when order was restored it was at the expense of local rights. When the peasants were finally enserfed in the mid-seventeenth century it was an act designed to ensure order and revenue under conditions which free men would not tolerate.

Autocracy and serfdom were thus modern institutions in Russia. One normally thinks of the West-European and English-speaking countries as having moved in modern times toward a broadening of participation in political decisions. In Russia the trend between the sixteenth and nineteenth centuries was in the opposite direction. Even after 1906, when new fundamental laws that included a parliament were in effect, the Russian political system was described not inaccurately as "a constitutional monarchy under an autocratic tsar." Granted that a vigorous political life was finally achieved with a variety of organized parties and a modicum of civil liberties, it is significant that this limited form of a pluralistic society lasted only one decade.

Values are more difficult to discuss than political systems, because they are inevitably more imprecise and less easily defined. At least by comparison with the experience of the West-European and English-speaking peoples, the dominant outlook of both state and society was one that stressed collective welfare at the expense of individual welfare. Not only did the very act of emancipation in 1861 demonstrate the subordination to authority of the individual, whether peasant or gentry landowner, but the social structure of the country also supported this attitude. The principal social groups recognized by law—gentry, clergy, townspeople, and peasants—were organized as corporate bodies, in some cases with tax-assessing and tax-collecting responsibilities. Persons with grievances took action through corporate bodies rather than as individuals, and it was not until after 1900 that political parties representing like-minded individuals replaced these traditional institutions.

Similarly the Russian Orthodox Church supported the authority of the state. Its theology drew on Byzantine and Muscovite traditions which saw a state-oriented Orthodoxy as the true Christian faith in contrast to the individualism of the heretical Roman Catholics and Protestants. The important trend of Slavophile thought among Russian intellectuals likewise contrasted the traditional values of Russian social institutions, especially the village commune, to those of the West. To be sure there were also countervailing trends which included the widely popular dissenting sects, as well as the Westernizers who opposed the Slavophiles, but most of the adherents of these views were against traditional authority rather than in favor of individualism.

Among the political parties which emerged at about the turn of the century, the preponderant trend despite their great diversity was toward collective values. This was, of course, the case with the Bolshevik and Menshevik branches of the Social Democratic Party who espoused Marxist socialism; and it was also true of the Socialist Revolutionaries, whose populism rested on the strong belief in some form of agrarian socialism. A more conservative political trend, including the views of the emperor and his immediate supporters, favored corporate forms of society in which different social strata ran their own affairs along traditional lines. Of all the political doctrines, only those of the Western-oriented liberals, represented particularly by the Constitutional Democrats, believed that Russia should and would abandon its traditional institutions and adopt the norms then prevalent in Western Europe. Western liberals both then and since have found it difficult to understand why liberalism in Russia was so weak, and have tended to attribute it primarily to the late development of a middle class. Yet Russia had socialism without a large working class, and liberalism like socialism is an ideology and not simply the reflection of an interest group. The answer should rather be sought in the historical experience of the Russian people, in which the values of collective interest have predominated.

The reforms of the 1860's also mark the watershed between a relatively stagnant serf economy and one of the most rapidly industrializing economies that the world has known. The state did not emancipate the serfs in order to clear the way for industrialization, but rather with the more limited objective of commercializing agriculture in the belief that this would provide a better basis than serfdom for a stable society. The political and social reforms that accompanied the emancipation drew significantly on Western models and laid the basis for a society in which merit, education, and equality under law gradually came to predominate over the traditional system of privilege. These reforms were nevertheless all made within the context of an agrarian and autocratic system, and were not designed at the time as a step toward an industrial society of the Western type.

When industrialization finally came to be recognized in the next generation as necessary and desirable, it took an institutional form significantly different from that in the countries that had industrialized earlier. In the West-European and English-speaking societies, capital, entrepreneurial skills, and markets had been provided largely by the rapidly growing middle class. In Russia they were provided to a much greater extent by the state, or under its auspices. Mining and manufacturing, frequently on a large scale, had a tradition in Russia that went back in some instances to the 17th century, and in both the earlier and the more modern periods there were strong-minded and affluent entrepreneurs with great industrial achievements to their credit. Yet the role of the state in economic growth was always large and tended to become relatively larger in the last decades of the empire. The foreign loans administered by the state were a critical source of capital, and the state also used its authority to mobilize the export of grain and other raw materials which maintained the international position of the currency.

Once industrialization got underway, it proceeded more rapidly in Russia than in most other countries. The average annual rate of growth of industry in Russia for the entire period from 1885 to 1913 was greater than in any other major country except the United States and Sweden. To be sure, this rate of growth can be explained in part by the relatively low level from which Russia started, but by the First World War it was the fifth in rank in terms of gross production, and was surpassed only by the United States, Germany, Britain, and France. Its per capita level was lower than any of the West-European states, but the direction and rate of its development were clear to all. As industry grew, society was also transformed apace. Some 13 million peasants moved into the cities in the four or five decades before the First World War, enrollments in schools and universities multiplied rapidly, and children of peasants and workers began to enter the ranks that had formerly been reserved for the privileged.

One must thus accustom oneself to thinking about the Russian empire in its last phase as being autocratic in politics, collective in social values, and at the same time dynamic in economic growth. This is an incongruous mixture by Western standards, and there were many both within Russia and abroad who believed that politics and values would soon have to adapt themselves to the imperatives of industrialization as understood in the West if they were to survive. Subsequent developments have not borne out this view, however, and our minds should not be closed to the possibility that societies may be successfully modern within quite a diversity of institutions and values.

It has been noted that the emancipation of the serfs applied only to the 50 provinces of European Russia, and this draws attention to the fact that Russia was a multinational empire the different parts of which retained their distinctive character. It is difficult to avoid referring simply to "Russia" and "the Russians," yet at the end of the 19th century only 43 percent of the population of the country was Great Russian. Another 22 percent were Ukrainians and Byelorussians, differing to some extent in language and political and social traditions but nevertheless members of the linguistic family of Eastern Slavs. The numerous minorities comprising the remaining 35 percent of the population were much more distinctly foreign. These included Finns and Swedes in the Grand Duchy of Finland; the Estonians, Latvians, and Lithuanians in the Baltic provinces; the 6 million Poles and 4 million Jews living in the territories acquired in the partition of Poland; the Armenians, Georgians, Azerbaijani, and numerous smaller minorities in the Caucasus; the native peoples of Siberia; and a substantial population of Turkic and Persian-speaking Moslems in the areas of Central Asia annexed in the 1860's.

What was significant about these non-Russian peoples was not only that they comprised such a large proportion of the population, but also that they lived for the most part in contiguous groups on the borderlands around the Great Russian core, and adjacent to Russia's neighbors. Only the Poles among these minorities had had their own independent state in modern times, and initially Russia placated these various peoples by letting them retain their traditional institutions. In the course of the 19th century many of these peoples were aroused by the dominant nationalist trend, however, and came to feel that their interests would be better served by autonomy or even independence than by Russian rule. The Russian government met this trend with a policy of centralization and Russification that greatly intensified the discontent prevalent among the minority peoples. The Jewish minority in the Western territories was particularly discontented because of the discriminatory policies of the government which prevented them from leaving the territorial "pale" to which they were confined except under special circumstances, and discontent turned to hatred when the government adopted a policy of savage anti-Semitic pogroms in the later years of the empire.

As a country of diverse peoples Russia bore a strong resemblance to Austria, Turkey, and the United Kingdom. Until the 19th century it was common for different ethnic groups to live together under the rule of dynasties, and in the traditional context there were compensating considerations of security and economics which made these arrangements acceptable. In an age of nationalism, however, those minority peoples that had a possibility of establishing viable independent states saw liberation as their highest goal. As a consequence of defeat in the First World War, the Austrian and Turkish empires exploded under these pressures, Russia lost its Polish, Finnish, and Baltic territories, and even the relatively stable United Kingdom lost part of Ireland. The significance of the minorities problem for foreign policy lies in its relationship to the international system. In the case of Russia, the leaders of many of the national minorities were not only among the most vociferous advocates of political, economic, and social change, but were also prepared to seek the assistance of Russia's enemies in achieving their goals.

In evaluating the foreign policy of a country, one may distinguish between policies more or less directly concerned with territorial and economic security. and those involving more general theoretical and ideological considerations. In the case of Russia, the policies in the first category might be considered to include the concern for adjacent territories that an enemy might preempt for hostile purposes, the search for warm-water ports, and the desire to incorporate peoples traditionally regarded as "Russian."

Finland and the Baltic provinces were considered to be important initially because they flanked a major commercial outlet, and the establishment of the national capital at St. Petersburg early in the 18th century made the region politically sensitive as well. The region most vital to Russian security since the 16th century has been Eastern Europe. All the wars that have threatened the security of Russia have been fought in this region, and in this context even the partition of Poland may be seen from the Russian standpoint as a measure designed to counterbalance the power of Prussia and Austria. It is significant that at the time of the First World War both liberal and conservative statesmen in Russia proposed to establish a sphere of influence in Eastern Europe resembling in significant ways the Warsaw Pact organization today. Russia's interest in this region was also related to its desire to regain from Poland and later from Austria the territories occupied by Eastern Slavs who had once formed a part of Kievan Russia.

Russia expanded toward the region of the Black Sea and the Caucasus initially in the course of its campaigns against the retreating Mongols, and later in the course of numerous wars with Turkey involving considerations relating both to security and to the desire for a commercial outlet through the Turkish Straits to the Mediterranean and the Atlantic. In the 18th and 19th centuries the Christian minority peoples in the Balkans and in the Caucasus looked to Russia as a liberator from Turkish rule. The Russian expansion into Central Asia in the second half of the 19th century, on the other hand, reflected primarily a concern that Britain might gain influence in this power vacuum if Russia did not move in first.

The Russian position in Central and East Asia followed Russian expansion into the vast and virtually unpopulated expanses of Siberia in the 16th and 17th centuries. There was no substantial presence in this region until the 19th century, and the construction of the trans-Siberian railroad and the establishment of a warm-water port at Vladivostok paralleled in some respects the American conquest of the West. The search for fur-bearing animals led the two countries to mutually profitable arrangements in the northern Pacific until Russia withdrew from Alaska in 1867. Russia also participated with Britain, France, Germany, Italy, and Japan in the establishment of extraterritorial rights in China, and in addition it gained a position of influence in northern Korea. By the turn of the century Russia had over-stepped the limits of its strength in this region, and it retreated under the pressure of Japan in 1905. In the Arctic region it met with no foreign opposition, however, and with the establishment of Archangel in 1584 and Murmansk in 1915 it obtained sea outlets which were useful when others were blockaded.

The foreign policy considerations that were generally of a more theoretical and ideological character were associated initially with the view that Moscow, succeeding Rome and Constantinople, was the center of the true Christian faith; and in a nineteenth-century version, that Russia was to become the eleventh (and final) civilization destined to replace Western Europe in the forefront of the progress of mankind. Ideological motivations of this type, reinforcing more practical considerations, led Russia to seek influence among the Western and Southern Slavs, the Rumanians, Greeks, Georgians and Armenians who were Orthodox but not Slavs, and also the distant Ethiopians.

A more effective ideological concern was reflected by Russia's leadership in the various coalitions that sought to stem the tide of revolution emanating from France. As the most active member of the Quadruple Alliance, Russia sought in the first half of the nineteenth century to preserve the territorial settlement of 1815, and it intervened in Greece and Hungary to defend the authority of the legitimate monarchs. Until almost the end of the nineteenth century Russia cooperated with Germany and Austria to defend the traditional institutions that it saw threatened by French ideas and British power. As a modern Germany came to occupy a dominant position in Central and Southeastern Europe, however, Russia turned to cooperation with France and Britain to restore the balance, and it was as their ally that she entered the First World War.

It would be difficult even for a well-programmed computer to calculate the many complex interactions of domestic and international forces that affected the equilibrium of the political, economic, and social system of Russia at the end of the nineteenth century. That it was a delicate balance, we can judge from the fact that even the relatively minor defeats in the Crimea in 1856 and in East Asia in 1905 were enough to release domestic forces that led to major reforms in the 1860's and a revolutionary crisis in 1905–6. Although the experience of Russia in the First World War through 1916 did not technically constitute a defeat, the strain on the resources of the country was immeasurably greater than anything that Russia had experienced since the Napoleonic wars, and the collapse when it occurred was correspondingly cataclysmic.

The empire had gone a long way in finding its characteristic solution to the challenges of modernization, but even under the most enlightened leadership at least another generation of peace was needed to make the transition from a predominantly agrarian to a predominantly industrial way of life. Under the strains of war, the grievances of many sectors of society broke through the political restraints that could barely contain them in times of peace: the peasants demanding more land, the workers demanding better compensation, the national minorities demanding equality or independence, the intellectuals demanding that Russia adopt one or another of the European ideologies perceived to be more appropriate to the modern era, and the various revolutionary movements with their non-negotiable demands.

THE USSR IN HISTORICAL PERSPECTIVE

One may well ask whether the collapse of the empire in 1917 was not a sign that the salient themes of Russian history that had characterized the empire had by now run their course, and that the revolution marked a sharp break with the past. A revolution there certainly was, in fact, two revolutions: the first in the spring of 1917 which brought to power the moderate provisional government, and the second in the autumn which was in many respects the most radical that the world has known.

The Russian revolution was radical in the sense both that it represented the opposite end of the political spectrum from the imperial government which it succeeded within 240 days, and because it sought to institute a nation-wide program of economic and social planning with public ownership of the means of production in place of the traditional system of property, rank, and privilege. Civil strife in many forms had to be resolved before this doctrine could be given effect, but when the Soviet system in its contemporary form began to emerge in the late 1920's it became apparent that in many significant respects the salient themes that characterized the empire continued to retain their vitality.

The predominant role of the state, the prevalence of collective values, and an emphasis on policies in support of rapid economic growth are so characteristic of the Soviet system that one often thinks of them as essentially "Soviet" rather than "Russian" features. The USSR is likewise confronted by the problems of a multinational society similar to those faced by the empire, and its international position has reflected significant elements of insecurity despite the great military power that it commands. In what respects are the historical themes characteristic of the earlier period still valid today, and to what extent can they help us to gauge the temper of contemporary Soviet policy? In seeking to judge the attributes of a potential partner in a treaty that involves vital issues of national security, one can best evaluate specific foreign policies in the context of a comprehensive view of its society.

If one may judge the priorities of political leaders by the way they allocate the resources at their disposal, one may conclude that the Soviet leaders are primarily concerned with three interrelated objectives: the preservation of the Communist Party and the Soviet state in more or less the form in which they have emerged in recent years; the economic and social transformation of Soviet society; and the maintenance of the national security of the USSR through the strength of its own military power and through treaty relations with other countries.

The dual system of party and state in which the party directs and supervises and the state administers, appears to have achieved a relatively stable form since the mid-1950's. The process of legitimizing the political power which the Bolsheviks achieved in 1917 was a long and agonizing one. It included a struggle involving civil war and foreign intervention that lasted until 1921, and a much longer struggle to gain control over Russian society. Throughout the 1930's the efforts of the party-state to mobilize the peasants and the urban manual and nonmanual workers, and of the rival leaders of the party to gain control over its membership and policies, led to greater losses of life and liberty than anything Russia had known since the sixteenth and seventeenth centuries. Even today the restrictions on individual freedom are such that one may question whether they do not reflect a lack of confidence in the people on the part of their leaders rather than the continuation of a traditional view of the proper relationship of state and society. Yet if one compares the experience of the peoples of Russia in the two world wars, it is clear that they bore the greater strains of the second war far better than those of the first. It ended not in revolution but in a society that has shown much more cohesion and purposefulness in the 1950's and 1960's than in the 1920's and 1930's.

The Soviet party-state in its contemporary form exercises immeasurably greater control over the resources and skills of the peoples of Russia than did the empire that preceded it, and its solution to the universal problems of extracting revenue from and allocating resources to conflicting interest groups is significantly different both from that of the empire and from that of most other contemporary societies. A comparison of the party to the central nervous system and of the state to the human structure of bones, muscles, and organs, conveys an idea of how the system works—and like human systems it is subject to nervous as well as structural breakdowns.

The conflicting views of interest groups are expressed through the agencies of the party rather than through elections and lobbies, and the negotiations by means of which these conflicts are aggregated take place within the party apparatus that staffs the Central Committee of the party and its Politburo. Diversities of opinion and interest are no less characteristic of Soviet than other societies, but they are resolved within the administrative system rather than by electoral campaigns and parliamentary debate.

There is sufficient stability of leadership at the higher party levels to afford considerable assurance regarding the continuity of basic policy. Indeed, if the welfare of the Soviet system were one's primary interest, one might be concerned whether Soviet leadership is not too set in its ways to meet new problems imaginatively. At the same time the procedures for selecting the party leaders who manage this vast enterprise are not as public or as well established as those of other modern states. This absence of institutional precedents is more apparent than real, however, and in practice the new leaders who have succeeded the old have come from a rather small elite and reflect a rather narrow range of views regarding national objectives.

The stated goal of the Communist party leaders is to bring to the peoples of Russia the benefits of the scientific and technological revolution, and one may judge their progress toward this goal over a period of half a century by comparison with the record of other countries developing at the same time. On the basis of gross national product as estimated in the United States in the mid-1960's, the USSR ranks 20th among the countries of the world on a per capita basis. A comparable estimate made at about the same time by the Central Statistical Administration of the USSR, based on a somewhat different calculation of national income per capita, ranks the USSR 14th.

While such calculations do not reflect as much accuracy as one might wish, the fact that they are relatively close gives one confidence in their general validity. It is also significant that, so far as one can judge from the limited information available, the countries that rank ahead of Russia today also ranked ahead of it in 1900 and 1917. To conclude from this that Russia's position relative to other countries has not changed, however, would be to overlook the fact that many gaps have been significantly narrowed and that with respect to individual indicators the USSR has moved ahead in some cases.

More specifically, one may estimate the balance of achievements and costs in the Soviet pattern of development by noting the indicators with respect to which it ranks relatively high or relatively low. In economic growth; in the shift of the labor force from agriculture to industry, and from manual to nonmanual and elite strata; in enrollments in secondary and higher education; in expenditures for research in science and technology; and in life expectancy and the ratio of physicians to population, for instance, the USSR ranks higher per capita than some of the West-European countries.

In other respects, such as the proportion of the labor force remaining in agriculture, the growth of purchasing power in hourly wages in terms of food, the burden of taxation borne by the lower income groups, and enrollment in primary schools, the USSR ranks relatively low by West-European standards. The pattern reflected by these rankings is one of relatively heavy investments in selected aspects of development, such as heavy industry, higher education, and public health, essentially at the expense of the level of income of peasants and workers. Whether one views such a pattern of development in positive or negative terms, and how one weighs the human costs represented by purges and deprivation that must be entered into the balance sheet, depends upon one's evaluation of the alternatives available to Soviet leaders and of the pressures of the international environment, as well as on the value one places on individual human beings.

In their efforts to maintain the national security of the USSR, Soviet leaders have pursued a policy that reflects considerable stability when viewed in the perspective of the pre-revolutionary record. From a territorial standpoint, it has secured its position in the Baltic through a bilateral treaty with Finland, and by reannexing the Baltic states which had formed a part of European Russia from 1721 to 1917. Its frontier with Europe is substantially further to the East than it was before the revolution, and it is about as close to the ethnic line between the Eastern Slavs and the Western Slavs, Hungarians, and Rumanians, as is possible given the mixed character of the region. In the Caucasus and in Central Asia the frontier remains unchanged, and in East Asia the USSR annexed Tannu Tuva (1944) from Mongolia, and in 1945 regained Southern Sakhalin lost to Japan in 1905 and also annexed the South Kuriles as well. In the Arctic region, the USSR has been more active than the empire in developing the northern sea route and in taking possession of the islands that fall within the portion of the Arctic region embraced by a frontier that extends to the North Pole.

The USSR is also in a stronger position than the empire with respect to the important security interests represented by its relations with its immediate neighbors: Norway, Finland, Poland, Czechoslovakia, Hungary, Rumania, Turkey, Iran, Afghanistan, Pakistan, India, China, Mongolia, Korea, and Japan. A number of factors contribute to this increased security. The defeat of Germany, and to a lesser extent that of Japan, has greatly increased the relative security of Russia in areas of great importance to it. Of the non-Slavic nationalities, which now represent 20 percent of the population, probably only the Baltic peoples represent minorities that would, if it were possible, vote for secession with a reasonable prospect of establishing viable independent states.

It is also significant that since 1945 the USSR has received general recognition as an industrial state of the first order, with the capability of achieving parity with the United States in the new military technology.

It now commands a respect for its knowledge as well as for its power that is unprecedented in Russian history. This new position lends authority to the security system represented by the Warsaw Pact, and permits the USSR to play an influential role in the affairs of the United Nations.

These developments, that tend to enhance the security of the USSR and that might lead other countries to expect it to be more concerned with preserving than with changing the status quo, must nevertheless be evaluated in terms of the theory and practice of world revolution. The rhetoric of world revolution continues to play a vital role in the Soviet view of the world, and will doubtless continue to do so because it is logically an integral part of Marxism-Leninism. Like the law of gravity, Marxist-Leninist theory applies equally to all parts of the world. If the view were accepted that historical materialism was valid only so far and no farther, and stopped at the frontiers of the USSR, or at those between Communist and non-Communist countries, the ideology would become meaningless. The question is to determine what resources the USSR is prepared to allocate to world revolution and what risks to Soviet security it is likely to take to promote the expansion of Communism.

It is significant in this connection that of the thirteen states in which Communist parties have gained power since the Bolshevik revolution, in only five (Albania, China, Cuba, North Vietnam, and Yugoslavia) have they been successful without direct Soviet military assistance, and of these China and Yugoslavia have become major rivals and potential enemies. Indeed, China is the only one of the many neighbors that Russia has dealt with through the centuries which is today raising serious claims that might lead to prolonged hostilities. In an era in which over a hundred countries have gained their independence under circumstances conducive to revolution, this is not a very impressive record.

This is not of course the whole story. Within the past decade alone, the missile crisis in Cuba, the support provided to North Vietnam, and the occupation of Czechoslovakia, indicate that the USSR is prepared to allocate very substantial resources to Communist requirements abroad. There are also a number of effective Communist parties in Europe, Asia, and Latin America that are available to take advantage of opportunities for revolution when they arise. This challenge to international security by Soviet-backed Communist movements is at the same time limited by the reluctance of the USSR to commit its own armed forces beyond its frontiers, except in the countries of the Warsaw Pact organization which Soviet leaders consider the cornerstone of their defensive system.

In an era in which a dozen or more revolutions are likely to occur each year for the foreseeable future in the less developed countries, the availability of Communist parties with substantial if limited Soviet support is a challenge that must be met at its own level by other countries. Modernizing revolutions represent a significant arena of conflict as a result of which countries and groups of countries can change sides from one alliance system to another without a shot being fired by a major power. It is also an arena in which Communists have not been notably more successful than others in solving the complex problems of modernization.

It is ironic that just at the point in Russian history when the country had recovered from its greatest test in war, and for the first time occupied a leading position in science and technology, a security problem arose that differed from all others in the vast disproportion between the resources it consumed and the nature of the challenge. Unlike the potential menace of a German-led Europe which depends on the complexities of European politics, or the confrontation with a China whose leaders are deeply aggrieved by Russian actions over a period of a century which they perceive as hostile, the nuclear challenge comes from a rival which is not a historical enemy and which has developed its strategic arms primarily to deter the USSR. The components of the problem are remarkably incongruous in the sense that the possibility of the devastation of two great countries arises from an issue which does not have deep roots in history or popular feeling, which may have arisen in considerable measure from an absence of good communications, and which is capable of reasonable discussion between governments that have the authority to keep the danger within bounds.

In evaluating the policies of foreign states, the perspective of history provides a basis for estimating how their leaders are likely to perceive their security and allocate their resources. To the extent that one can tell which precedents are considered to be relevant, history is a better guide than dictionaries to the meaning of official statements, and to theory in the evaluation of motives.

In reviewing the domestic and international factors that constitute the record of Soviet policy, several are particularly impressive: the continuing pace of economic and social development, despite occasional setbacks; the security of its territories by conventional standards, despite the challenge of China; the relatively stable policies of its leaders, even though individual statesmen may come and go for reasons not clear to foreigners; and the limits within which armed force has been employed abroad, despite a number of dramatic incidents.

The change as compared with the record of the empire has not been as radical as one might expect from the half-century of revolutionary upheavals and rhetoric, but neither is the country being driven to desperate measures by domestic and foreign setbacks. The USSR is not likely either to gamble its military forces in reckless aggression, or to reduce its strength at a sacrifice to security. In a situation such as that prevailing at present, in which vast resources are being expended primarily to deter another power that finds itself in a parallel position, one may anticipate that Soviet leaders will find it in the interest of their country to explore the possibilities of negotiation and compromise.

The United States and the Soviet Union are separated by profound differences in historical experience and in institutions and values, but they both bear the heavy burden of mutual deterrence systems that concern the two of them more than they concern any other state or group of states. At the same time, both have a large backlog of human problems whose solution awaits the availability of adequate resources. Problems of this magnitude call for a most serious consideration of the opportunities offered by the mutual limitation of strategic arms.

CHAPTER 2

The Nature of Imperial Russian Society

Many conservatives as well as radicals often assume that Russia was backward and undeveloped when the Bolsheviks came to power in 1917. This chapter argues that this was by no means the case and that by World War I Russia was on the way to becoming an industrial society. When war came, however, Russia was still in an unsettled intermediate stage resulting from the dislocations of rapid industrialization in a still predominantly agrarian economy. In addition, political development had not kept pace with economic growth and social integration, and the autocracy refused to recognize the need for broader political participation.

One can only speculate as to what might have happened if the strains of war had not undermined the rather fragile stability of the empire. Some scholars maintain that revolution in some form was bound to occur even if the war had not intervened. One can also speculate that, given its rate of development, imperial Russia might have equaled or surpassed the economic and social achievements of the Soviet Union over the long run if it had not been for the war. The experience of Japan suggests that evolutionary processes of change can be no less successful than revolutionary policies. Yet one must not be distracted by such speculations.

I

How does one go about describing briefly a large and complex society in the process of rapid change? The problems involved are not only of space but also of conceptualization. To be comprehensive yet succinct one must fall back on generalizations, which always run the danger of concealing the very nuances that make up the richness and diversity of a culture. Moreover, the nature and direction of change in modern societies is a matter of continuing controversy, and a common basis of

Reprinted with permission from the *Slavic Review*, 20 (December 1961), 565–582.

theory and terminology cannot be taken for granted. No society in modern times has been more subject to conflicting assumptions and interpretations than that of Russia. Under these circumstances, perhaps the best solution is to adopt an approach sufficiently general to do justice to the complexities involved and at the same time definite enough in its point of view to offer a consistent interpretation—as well as a reasonably clear basis for controversy.

The interpretation suggested here is one which sees the world as composed of well over one hundred politically organized societies, each with its own deep-seated traditional institutions, undergoing at different stages a process of change which has certain universally common features. This process of change, which can be traced to the revolutionary expansion of knowledge originating in Western Europe in the Middle Ages, tends to affect in one degree or another all aspects of human activity. It seems likely to result eventually in a world of modern societies which will be essentially similar in function but which will retain for the foreseeable future significant features of their diverse traditional structures of institutions and values. There is no set pattern which guides the interaction of the modern and the traditional, and indeed in any society there are innumerable ways in which traditional institutions can be adapted to modern functions. The course of change therefore depends to a considerable degree on the nature of leadership, and in practice an important element in the history of a society consists of arguments, conflicts, rivalries, and struggles among individual leaders and groups of leaders representing a wide variety of points of view and interests. Chance, in the form of the presence or absence of far-sighted and effective leaders at critical moments, has an important share in this process.

Russia is one of these societies, differing from others in her traditional culture as others differ from each other, but also undergoing like them the characteristic interaction of the traditional and the modern. It is not possible in brief scope—if it is possible at all—to describe the intricacies of this subtle and many-faceted process of change. What will be attempted here is something much more limited: a brief description of certain distinctive features of traditional Russian society as it existed in the eighteenth and early nineteenth centuries, an indication of the principal ways in which that society was changing under the impact of modern ideas and institutions, and finally some suggestions as to the significance of this interaction of the traditional and the modern. It is scarcely feasible to document these observations in any detail, for there is an enormous body of literature which deals with this period, but a few references will be made when they seem to be called for in regard to specific matters of interpretation.

II

A brief statement of the features that distinguished Russian imperial society must of necessity be highly selective and impressionistic, and it is proposed here to touch on only five characteristics: the physical setting, the autocratic state, the system of social stratification, the agrarian economy, and the multinational structure.[1]

The most significant features of the physical setting of imperial Russia were its size, its location, and its poverty. The conquest of Siberia in the sixteenth and seventeenth centuries resulted in a vast increase in the territory under the rule of Moscow. This large territory inherited by Peter nevertheless lacked either well-defined frontiers or suitable maritime outlets for commerce, and at the same time was subject to many pressures on the long frontier with Europe and Western Asia. In the course of the many wars of the eighteenth and nineteenth centuries the frontiers of the empire were further extended, and indeed throughout this period Russia was by all odds the largest country in the world in terms of territory. At the same time the number of inhabitants grew from 14 to 170 million, with the result that Russia was by 1917 inferior in population only to China and India. As significant as its size was its location, bordering as it did on Europe and on the broad sweep of Asia stretching from the Bosporus to the Kuril Islands. In earlier centuries Byzantine influences, and to a much lesser extent Mongol and Ottoman, had played a vital role in the culture of Muscovite Russia. To this extent Russia, like Byzantium itself, could be said to have cultural roots in both Europe and Asia. In the period of the empire, which was one of almost exclusively European influences, the principal significance of geographical location lay in the realm of foreign policy. In an age in which Europe was embracing the world, a country of Russia's size and position could not well avoid being drawn into the affairs of the many countries on its borders and beyond.[2]

Economic poverty was also an important element in the Russian setting. The vast size of the country was to a considerable degree illusory, since only a small part of it was suitable for agriculture, and much of that had a poor soil or climate. It is now known to be rich in natural resources, but before the First World War only its petroleum and a few other minerals had been adequately developed. In per capita terms Russia was very poor by the standards of the European countries which were her principal competitors. Perhaps the best way of expressing the problem confronting the statesmen of the empire was that they had to find a means of converting her rather meager and scattered resources into effective national power. This is no doubt a rather abstract formulation, yet Peter the Great must have looked at things somewhat in this fashion when he undertook to strengthen the administrative apparatus of a state which already had a claim to autocratic power well established in theory if not in practice.

It would probably not be going too far to say that in no other major society in the eighteenth and nineteenth centuries did the sovereign and the state play as great a role as they did in Russia. Prussia in the eighteenth century and China and Turkey in earlier times are among the first examples that come to mind of centralized political systems which had a comparable role in the life of the country. In the nineteenth century, at any rate, the Russian empire stood alone as a society in which a great many aspects of human activity were to a large extent administered or at least regulated by the state. The Russian government was formally an autocracy in the sense that all political authority was vested in the autocrat. The theory of autocracy came from Byzantine political thought and, modified by adaptations from Tatar and Ottoman administrative practices, it became a reality in the course of the fifteenth and sixteenth centuries as the princes of Moscow succeeded in consolidating the political power which had been shared since the thirteenth century by the various principalities of northeastern Russia and their Tatar overlords. What was in theory an autocracy was often for all practical purposes an oligarchy, however, for the princes of Moscow had great difficulty in establishing effective and orderly control over the ruling families whose lands they successively incorporated into the new state. The reigns of the principal architects of the Muscovite political system—Vasilii II the Blind, Ivan III the Great, and Ivan IV the Terrible—were marked by continual internecine strife culminating in the Time of Troubles. After the establishment of the Romanov dynasty in 1613 it was half a century or more before the central administrative system was sufficiently effective to permit the sovereign to free himself from the assembly of notables which had established the dynasty and guided its early fortunes. It was this system which Peter the Great reshaped and rationalized on the basis of Swedish and other European models to form the "regulated state" which, with significant changes to be sure, lasted until 1917.[3]

Under the system established by Peter the emperor was more of an autocrat than the tsars had ever been, yet the oligarchy composed of high civilian and military officials and leading families of noble landowners continued to play an independent role throughout the eighteenth century during the reigns of eight rulers who were relatively weak for reasons of youth, sex, or mental disability. Paul, the last of these rulers, is generally portrayed as mad—but there was a method in his madness. He took the first measures in the direction of reaffirming the authority of the autocrat, and this authority was further consolidated by his successors.[4] Despite the many political changes which occurred during the last century of the empire, the sovereign remained an autocrat in theory and to a considerable extent in practice, although only in the reign of Nicholas I did he in fact approximate the theoretical model.[5]

A more fundamental question than the relationship of the autocrat to the oligarchy is that of the role of the state in society. No less than two-fifths of the forty million peasants in European Russia were directly administered by the state before emancipation, as were many economic enterprises as well. Through its administration of the Holy Synod, the Academy of Sciences, all higher education, and most primary and secondary education, and through the censorship, the state had a direct and permeating influence on the intellectual life of the country. The rapid economic and social changes which occurred after the emancipation of the serfs did not have the effect of reducing the role of the state. On the contrary, the state played a leading role in this process. There were few phases of Russian life in which it was not directly interested, and over many of the most important it had a virtual monopoly through direct administration and a decisive influence in policy-making.

One of the most significant consequences of the "omnicompetence" of the Russian state, to borrow Sumner's felicitous term,[6] was its influence on the position of social strata. It was as though the autocrat could imagine no other way to assure the state of the support of its leading citizens and a regular income from the rather backward agrarian economy than by binding all individuals to its service. In a purely formal sense, all citizens of the empire were divided into three general categories: natives, non-natives, and Finns (who were a separate category by virtue of inhabiting an autonomous Grand Duchy). The native citizens in turn were divided by statute into four estates or strata—nobility, clergy, townsmen, and peasants—but these categories were not very meaningful. There were important differences between hereditary and personal nobles; townsmen were separated into four quite distinct categories—notable citizens, merchants, tradesmen, and artisans; the clergy were an occupational group rather than a social stratum, for both those who left the clergy and children of clergymen in general were legally regarded as townsmen of the rank of notable citizens; moreover a nobleman could also be a member of the clergy. Perhaps only the peasants were a legally homogeneous class, although there were significant differences between state peasants and serfs as well as those imposed by the widely varying customs of the diverse regions of Russia.[7]

More fundamental than these formal distinctions was that which prevailed substantially until the revolution of 1905 between the privileged and the unprivileged. The privileged were not subject to direct taxes or corporal punishment and could travel freely within the country. Only the nobles and townsmen of the rank of notable citizens, totaling between 1 and 2 per cent of the population, enjoyed these privileges. The nobles also had the privilege until 1861 of owning serfs. Moreover, the privileged had access to political power, if they did not actually share it, while the unprivileged bore the burden of supporting the privileged as well as the heavy superstructure of the state. The unprivileged were subjected to severe restrictions as to movement, along with other forms of personal and social discipline, and had virtually no access to the ranks of the privileged before the middle of the nineteenth century. Indeed the gap between the two groups tended to widen during much of this period, as the privileged gained in education and influence while the position of the peasants in particular became more depressed. These hardships weighed even more heavily on the nonnatives—the Jews, the Moslems, and the various indigenous peoples of Siberia. The grosser inequities were relaxed in the latter part of the nineteenth century and were largely removed after 1905, but the government yielded reluctantly and only under great pressure. The growth of civil liberties in the last decades of the empire thus released accumulated tensions which could be contained only by a political system whose authority was not weakened by economic distress or foreign defeats.[8]

The system of social stratification also had the effect of inhibiting the development of a sense of political responsibility. This was in part the result of the corporative organization of the social strata, which tended to isolate them from each other. Thus the hereditary nobles, three categories of townsmen (the merchants, the tradesmen, and the artisans), and the peasants were organized in corporative associations by province, town, or village. These associations were collectively responsible for the conduct of their members, and in the case of the townsmen and the peasants had important fiscal and disciplinary functions. This form of social organization encouraged these groups, which formed the bulk of the population, to negotiate directly with the government rather than to seek common cause against it. This attitude was further encouraged by contradictory prevailing trends of political thought which maintained either that the autocratic state was good, or that it must be eliminated, or that it should be ignored as a necessary evil. It was not until the end of the nineteenth century that the possibility of effective political action against the state within the framework of the empire was widely accepted.[9]

The system under which the peasants were bound to the soil and to the noble landowner is known as serfdom, and it existed in its most rigorous form between 1649 and 1861. Russian serfdom must be distinguished from feudalism as it existed in Western Europe. Feudalism was a political system characterized by a contractual relationship between lord and vassal, whereas in serfdom the relationship was primarily economic and was based not on contract but on the edict of the sovereign. There had been elements of the lord-vassal relationship earlier in Russian history, but these had disappeared with the rise of serfdom.[10] The state created serfdom as a means of assuring itself of a reliable source of revenue in a situation in which land was plentiful but labor was scarce, and agriculture was the principal source of income. The conditions of peasant life were so hard in Russia in the fifteenth and sixteenth centuries, because of the endemic civil strife and the increasing need of the state for revenue to meet the requirements of national defense, that the peasants tended constantly to escape to the south or east to avoid oppression. Various efforts were made to restrict the freedom of movement of the peasants, and these finally culminated in the middle of the seventeenth century in the imposition of a form of serfdom noted for its oppressiveness.[11]

There were numerous and large-scale peasant revolts both before and after the imposition of serfdom, but in every case they were repressed. In the course of the two centuries during which serfdom was in force, the machinery of government underwent a fundamental transformation, the noble landowners won a substantial relaxation of their obligations to the state, and modest beginnings were made in the development of an industrial system. There was no comparable improvement in the status of the peasants, whether under the state, the crown, or the landlords, however, and in the case of the latter it tended to become more oppressive. This is not to say that the nobles benefited by the system either, for most of them were persons of limited means and they were increasingly going into debt during the first half of the nineteenth century.

Serfdom had been established principally for the benefit of the state, and no doubt it provided the basis for a type of stable administrative and fiscal control over the peoples and the resources of the country which could not readily be achieved by other means. Stability was achieved at the price of stagnation, however, for there was no Russian counterpart of the rapid economic and social change which the societies of Western and Central Europe experienced during the period in which serfdom prevailed in Russia. Serfdom tended to discourage initiative on the part of peasant and noble landowner alike, and in a variety of ways inhibited the growth of industry. It may be argued that the real obstacle to social and economic change in Russia was in the minds of its leaders, and that much could have been done even within the framework of serfdom to stimulate technological improvements in agriculture and to encourage industry. In any event, as the conception of a modern society began to gain adherents among Russian leaders, a process in which the defeat in the Crimea appears to have had a large influence, serfdom was the first institution which they undertook to reform.[12]

The attempt to present a brief characterization of a complex society runs a particular danger in the case of Russia, since only 43.3 per cent of the population was Great Russian at the end of the nineteenth century, and the many minority peoples enjoyed a wide diversity of traditional institutions. What has been said about the decisively centralizing character of the administration must be modified to the extent that the Ukraine, the Baltic provinces, and Congress Poland all enjoyed a degree of autonomy during parts of the period under consideration, and the Grand Duchy of Finland had substantial privileges except for the short period between 1903 and 1905. Similarly as regards social stratification and the agrarian system, there were many differences in the position of the various minority peoples. Indeed, it was long the practice of the imperial government to respect the diverse institutions of the peoples annexed in the course of the expansion of the empire, and it was only toward the end of the nineteenth century that a rigorous policy of administrative and cultural Russification was attempted.[13]

The multinational character of imperial Russian society also had grave consequences in the realm of foreign policy. The chief concern of Russia in annexing these peoples, located almost entirely on her borders with Europe and Western and Central Asia, was for her own security. The territories they inhabited either blocked Russian access to the Baltic and Black seas; or, as was the case with Poland and Central Asia, might have come under the rule of other great powers to the detriment of Russia's interests; or again, as was the case with the Ukraine and Georgia, actually sought Russian protection against neighbors they feared more. It would doubtless be going too far to say that Russia had no imperialist ambitions, for numerous proposals for annexing noncontiguous territories can be found in her diplomatic records. The ambitions of Russia's statesmen were nevertheless limited, by the standards of the time, and were concerned principally with adjacent territories of strategic significance for commerce or defense. In this sense Russian statesmen favored a continental policy, resembling perhaps that of China in earlier times and of the United States in the nineteenth century, and did not undertake to create an extensive overseas empire such as those carved out by the seafaring societies of Western Europe.

III

It has already been noted that the institutions of imperial Russian society underwent many changes in the course of two centuries, and indeed the history of this period is punctuated with numerous reforms, revolts, assassinations, wars, territorial issues, and social conflicts reflecting the continuing readjustments in the structure of Russian society as well as the idiosyncrasies of its leaders. At the same time it was undergoing a more fundamental transformation, which was stimulated primarily by the example of the societies of Western and Central Europe. These societies were in the forefront of a revolutionary process intellectual in its origins and political in its initial impact, accompanied by economic growth and social change of unprecedented proportions. The levels of achievement attained in the course of this revolutionary transformation, which may be referred to in general terms as "modern" or at least "modernizing," were the prototypes of those which were eventually to become the goal of virtually all societies.

The initial reaction of Russia's political leaders to this momentous development was to adopt, or at least adapt, those modern institutions which seemed best suited to preserving the traditional Russian society from the increasingly threatening competition of its neighbors. This reaction is represented typically by the reforms of Peter the Great, which rationalized the civil and military structure of the central government and tightened the control of the state over the noble landowners and the townsmen, and of the landowners over the peasants. No attempt was made, however, to adapt to Russian society the economic and social institutions which were being developed in the more modern societies. Peter's reforms were explicitly defensive in their motivation and implications, and they were successful in preserving the traditional social structure of the country with relatively few changes for a century and a half. In the course of time the gap between a relatively static Russia and an increasingly dynamic West grew to a point where it could not fail to cause concern to Russian leaders, and during the reigns of Alexander I and Nicholas I many plans and proposals for reform were considered and some actually undertaken. Nevertheless, human nature being what it is, they preferred the certainty of problems which they understood and felt confident in handling to the uncertainties of a thorough going social transformation. It took the defeat in the Crimea to shift the balance of official opinion in favor of reform, and it has become customary to regard the emancipation of the serfs in 1861 as the turning point between the passive and the active phases of the attitude of Russia's political leaders towards modern ideas and institutions. It will of course be recognized that 1861 is in most respects simply a symbolic date, since some segments of Russian society felt the breath of reform a generation or more earlier, while others were relatively unaffected until a good deal later. Indeed, it was not until the end of the nineteenth century that Russian society as a whole was gripped by thoroughgoing change.

It has already been noted that the modern revolution was intellectual in its origins, resting as it did on the phenomenal expansion of knowledge which had its roots in the Middle Ages, and its initial impact on Russia was similarly intellectual. This impact may be traced back to the movements favoring the revision of religious texts and doctrine in the fifteenth and sixteenth centuries, and to the appearance in the seventeenth century of isolated nobles with a Western outlook.[14] It was nevertheless not until the eighteenth century that there was a general turning to the West on the part of the state and the nobility, and only in the nineteenth century did the problem of "Russia and Europe" come to absorb the full attention of Russian intellectuals. The diversity and brilliance of Russian political and literary thought concerning the relationship of traditional to modern values and institutions is probably matched only by that of China and Japan among non-European peoples. It produced a wide spectrum of interpretations, ranging from the strongest reaffirmation of the rightness and sanctity of the Russian way of doing things to the view that the imperial state was a form of "oriental despotism" which must be destroyed to make way for the socialist society toward which mankind was alleged to be moving ineluctably.

This rich body of thought moved in two currents, which were continually intermingling but which remained reasonably distinct. The first was represented by the political leaders and high officials, starting with Peter the Great and ending with Witte and Stolypin, who sought to adapt imperial Russian society in one degree or another to the requirements of the modern world. Their views were set forth in speeches, reports, memoranda, and statutes, and perhaps in deeds more than in words. The second source of intellectual activity was that represented by the intelligentsia, who almost by definition were disassociated and not infrequently alienated from the governing circles. The intelligentsia left a fascinating heritage of speculation and interpretation which reflected a broad understanding of European society and a deep concern for the destiny of the Russian people. They had a profound influence on the development of Russian society during the period of the empire, since their works were read and discussed by all educated people. They nevertheless remained until the end alienated from official Russia, which bore the burden of responsibility and deserves much of the credit for the extent to which Russian society was transformed by the time of the First World War. The intelligentsia as a group did not gain access to political power until the fall of the empire, and this access was terminated for all but a few when the Bolsheviks began to suppress deviations from orthodoxy in the early 1920's. In the realm of scholarship Russia joined the world of modern knowledge in the course of the eighteenth and nineteenth centuries and made distinguished original contributions.

The history of Russian thought in the nineteenth century as a general phenomenon has yet to be written. Much able work has been done on individual writers and on the leading intellectual movements, such as the Decembrists, the Slavophiles, the Populists, and the Marxists. The thought of the reforming officials has not, however, received comparable attention. Neither the prerevolutionary intelligentsia nor the writers of the Soviet Union have been attracted to this subject, for reasons which are not hard to find, and Western scholars are only now beginning to explore it. Interest in intellectual history seems to have been concerned principally with a desire to study the background of the political revolution of 1917, and this has resulted in a serious neglect of the fundamental process of political, economic, and social change as a central issue in Russian thought.[15]

In the political sphere the adoption of modern institutions in Russia can be seen in the many reforms which had the purpose of rationalizing the system of law and administration, integrating the various territories and social strata, and establishing a closer rapport between state and society to the end that political decisions could be effectively formulated, communicated, and implemented. The reforms of the eighteenth century had performed a similar function for the state itself, and it was now a question of extending this process to the entire society. The codification of the laws by Speransky was the first significant step in this second phase, and it was followed in the 1860's by an extensive reform of the judiciary and local government and of the administrative system of the central government. As late as 1905, however, the state had relatively few direct administrative contacts with the peasants except for a rather scanty police force and the land captains established in 1889. Peasant affairs were handled largely by the peasants themselves. The administration of the Stolypin land settlement required the government for the first time in its history to establish organs for administering directly at the local level policies ultimately affecting a large proportion of the population and involving the co-ordination of several ministries.[16] This was a very late development, however, and the weakness of the imperial bureaucracy was soon revealed in the harsh test of war.

The effort to transform the political system of imperial Russia along the lines pioneered by the societies of Western Europe provoked a struggle among several trends of thought. One was that of the supporters of the traditional system as it had been consolidated in the eighteenth and early nineteenth centuries. This was the view of the imperial family and its immediate entourage, and it had strong support in the army and bureaucracy and in the cabinet, even when that body was headed by a reforming minister. The reforms of the 1860's had indeed been launched by the emperor himself, but more in the Petrine spirit of trying to achieve a new conservative stability than with a view to a thoroughgoing social reconstruction. This approach continued to have strong official support until the end, and one may well attribute the catastrophic character of the fall of the empire to the stubbornness with which one group of its leaders resisted change.

Another main trend was the very large one represented by those both in the government and among the intelligentsia who favored fundamental change by evolutionary means and looked to models ranging from England and France to Prussia and Japan. The diversities of their various programs make it difficult to contain these many groups in a single category, but the Fundamental Laws of 1906 provided them with a more or less acceptable basis for action and there was a significant degree of continuity from the four successive Dumas to the Provisional Government. Included also in this category were the leaders of the national minorities who demanded a degree of self-government. Only the Poles insisted unconditionally on independence. This issue has been beclouded by war, revolution, and civil war, but it appears that under "normal" circumstances the leaders of the other minority peoples would in all likelihood have been satisfied on the eve of the First World War with some form of federalism.

A third trend was composed of those who had no faith in evolutionary changes within the framework of the empire. This was the view of the Bolsheviks and many Socialist Revolutionaries, who saw their political role principally as a destructive one so long as the empire survived. The final arbiter among these various approaches, as it turned out, was the First World War. The strains of the conflict eroded the political structure of the empire, and in so doing undermined the prospects for evolutionary change within its framework. The collapse of the empire opened the way for a revolutionary approach, and the revolutionaries were much more at home than the liberals in the ensuing chaos.[17]

Among the changes which occurred during the last half-century of the empire, those in the intellectual and political realm have attracted the most attention, but the remarkable economic growth in its later decades deserves equal emphasis. Agricultural production, which had not been able to keep up with the growth of the population during the first half of the century, increased much more rapidly, especially after the 1880's. Not only did agricultural production surpass the rate at which the population was growing, but it was also significantly diversified to include industrial crops and potatoes. The expansion of industrial production was of course much more rapid, with an annual average rate of growth of somewhat over 5 per cent for the period 1885–1913.

The rate for the 1890's, the period of most rapid growth, was surpassed only by that of Japan, the United States, and Sweden. Underlying the increased rates of growth in agriculture and industry was the construction of an extensive railroad network, which grew from 1,000 miles in 1860 to 40,000 miles at the time of the First World War. In terms of national income, the Russian rate of growth for the period as a whole was higher than that of the United Kingdom, France, and Italy, somewhat below that of Germany, and considerably below that of the United States and Japan. On a per capita basis Russia's position was of course less favorable, owing to the rapid growth of her population. By the time of the First World War real income per capita was about the same as that of Italy, which means that it was still a great deal lower than that of the advanced industrial societies.[18]

Although Russia had thus in no sense attained a leading position as an industrial society at the time of the First World War, what is significant is that by the 1880's it was launched on a pattern of economic growth comparable in rate and dimensions to that of the more advanced societies. It should also be noted that this was very largely the achievement of the imperial government, which took the initiative and bore the main burden of building railroads and supplying capital to industry, and also provided the principal market for the output of heavy industry. No doubt the sovereign and the conservative-minded courtiers and ministers, like Peter the Great in his day, still thought of industrialization principally as a means of bolstering the autocratic system. The leading cabinet members and high officials, however, had a vision of a Russia transformed into a modern industrial society. Their goal may be said to have been of a West European character, but their methods were quite different. Little attention was devoted to agriculture, and such income as it normally provided was channeled into industry. Railroads and heavy industry were favored as against consumer goods. Modern technology was imported from the West to make up for deficiencies in skilled labor, and economies were made in management and supervision by concentrating production in large plants. A not inconsiderable role in this growth was played by private entrepreneurs and small businessmen, but the pace was set by the government and by the large enterprises which it controlled or patronized. Indeed, it was the role of the government as planner, investor, entrepreneur, and consumer which distinguished economic growth in Russia from that in the societies which started earlier.[19]

This economic growth was accompanied by fundamental social changes. The urban population grew from 7 to 20 million during the last fifty years of the empire, the rigid system of social stratification disintegrated rapidly, and the foundations were laid for a new stratum of professional people, businessmen, and officials. This "middle class" was drawn from all of the traditional strata. The nobles, clergy, and townsmen were naturally the principal sources of recruitment for this new stratum at the start, but the peasantry and workers were gradually drawn into it and represented in the long run its principal reserve of manpower. The nobles lost much of their distinctive position in the last decades of the empire and, with the exception of the relatively few families of great wealth, did not gain much advantage from their remaining formal privileges in the evolving industrial society. At the same time the industrial working class grew apace, and numbered some 3.5 million at the end of this period. In 1913, according to the official classification, 70.2 per cent of the population were farmers, 16.7 per cent were wage and salary workers, 7.2 per cent were craftsmen, 3.6 per cent were self-employed townsmen, and 2.3 per cent were military and others.[20]

The institutions of higher education were the chief training ground for this new class, and their enrollment in proportion to the population increased more than nine times between 1885 and 1914. The increase in secondary-school enrollment was even greater, and by the time of the First World War Russia had made substantial progress toward a system of universal elementary education. The social mobility accompanying the growth in higher education is reflected in the fact that the proportion of children of peasants, craftsmen, and workers enrolled in the universities grew from 15.7 per cent in 1880 to 38.8 per cent in 1914, and in the higher technical institutes was 54 per cent in the latter year.[21] The officer corps was no doubt the most conservative branch of the bureaucracy, but it appears that by the end of the empire a majority of the new officers came from non-noble families as did some of the leading generals in the First World War.[22] In recording these changes it should be noted that this rapid growth in educational opportunities and social mobility was not achieved without a momentous struggle. In the central government the reformers waged a constant battle with the traditionalists, and were strongly aided by the increasingly effective support which they received from the local government institutions, the municipalities, and the Duma. At the time of the First World War, Russia was still a country where 78 per cent of the population was agricultural and rural illiteracy was high. The changes of the last half century had been so rapid, however, that contemporary reforming statesmen could look forward with confidence to the day when the empire would attain the level of achievement of Western societies.

Something should also be said about the personality changes which may have accompanied this general process. National character in the sense that it is used by the social psychologists is a controversial concept which is still in an early stage of formulation, and one hesitates to venture into a territory so ridden with pitfalls. Yet it is clear that the personality of the individual reflects the character of his upbringing in the family setting, which in turn depends on the larger social context. When the latter undergoes the drastic changes represented by urbanization, one would expect the family and its individual members to be vitally affected. In the case of the Great Russian people, for example, it has been maintained that the characteristically patriarchal peasant family tended to produce a personality which was markedly ambivalent. This is to say that the Great Russian personality contained simultaneously elements of great vitality and serious depression, which may be explained as resulting from a family setting in which an awesome father was both feared and resisted. As a peasant society with these characteristics is urbanized, with the mother as an urban worker gaining a position of authority more nearly equal to that of the father, an altered family setting is produced in which the children are exposed to somewhat different influences and will develop correspondingly different personalities. This example suggests what is meant by the effects of social change on personality, and it also reveals the difficulties which confront one in trying to deal with Russia in these terms. Russia was a vastly complex empire with many traditional cultures, of which the Great Russian was only one. Moreover, the available studies deal principally with the Soviet period, and there is little factual data from earlier decades to draw on. One may argue that Chekhov, Gorky, and their literary colleagues did a pretty good job of reporting social change at the family level without benefit of professional training in the behavioral sciences, but it is difficult for a historian to generalize on the basis of their findings. It is also clear that the impact of social change on personality was at its very earliest stages in the last decades of the empire, and that one would not expect to find general manifestations of a transformation of national character in Russia until well into the twentieth century. Under the circumstances the best one can do is to call attention to this important aspect of social history and to regret that one cannot do it justice.[23]

IV

The interaction of traditional and modern institutions and values in imperial Russian society should be considered in terms both of its general implications and of its particular significance for the crisis provoked by the collapse of the empire in the First World War.

The prevailing Western approach between the two world wars to Russian developments was to assume that the institutions characteristic of the more advanced societies of the West represented the model which other societies were destined to follow. There was therefore a tendency to judge the empire as well as its successors by the extent to which they adopted the Western pattern in such matters as civil liberties, representative government, education, and the role of the state in economic growth. By this standard the empire was reactionary, the Provisional Government had liberal aspirations, and the Soviet Union represented a bewildering combination of modern and traditional elements. In the course of the past quarter of a century many other societies have entered and some have completed the experimental phase of adapting the traditional to the modern, and the process of transformation can now be seen as a much more complex matter than one of simply duplicating Western institutions. It seems clear that there are certain functions which all modern societies must perform—political decision-making effective for the entire population, sufficient savings to permit a reasonable rate of economic growth, education, social mobility, and so on—and perhaps most important of all, a value system compatible with the necessary institutional changes. It is also clear, however, that there is a wide degree of variety in the extent to which the diverse traditional institutional systems are adaptable to the functions of modern societies. No society can avoid very profound changes as it modernizes, but some traditional institutions are much more adaptable than others.

What is significant in the case of Russia is that its traditional institutional system was different from those of the societies of Western Europe, as indeed it was from those of non-European societies as well. In Western Europe modern political institutions, for example, evolved from those of feudalism into a characteristic form of liberal government in which political power was shared by elected representatives and a permanent civil service. In Russia, by contrast, the starting point was not a feudal system but an autocratic state which had characteristically exercised very extensive political functions. It was not difficult for this state, in the generation after the defeat in the Crimea, to initiate a very fundamental reorientation of national life. Between 1861 and 1917 the autocracy in Russia put into effect a series of reforms which resemble in many respects those achieved by very different methods in France between 1789 and 1848—if one may risk an historical analogy.[24] To extend the analogy a step further, one may suggest that the autocratic state in Russia played a role similar not only to that of the middle class and the Napoleonic empire in France but also to that of the samurai in Japan, the Young Turks in the Ottoman Empire, the army officers in Egypt, and the European-educated politicians in Africa today. Modernizing political leadership may take many forms, and the alternatives available to political leaders cannot fail to be profoundly affected by the traditional political institutions which a society has inherited from earlier centuries. This is not to assert an institutional or a cultural determinism. It is rather to suggest that, however similar the ultimate functional goals, political leaders in different societies are likely to proceed by different routes.

It would be outside the limits set for this paper to venture beyond the fall of the empire in February/March, 1917, but it is relevant to discuss the bearing on subsequent developments of the changes which the empire was undergoing in its final decades. It is well enough to attribute the fall of the empire to the strains of the First World War, for the connection between the two is clear, but it is also necessary to note that the crisis was not so great that a more effective government might not have been able to cope with it. The vital struggle in the last decades of the empire was that which was going on within the government between those who supported the traditional autocracy to the bitter end, and those who favored the transformation of Russia into a modern bureaucratic and constitutional state. The Wittes and Stolypins were still separated by a wide gap from the liberals, but the gap was perhaps no wider than that which separated them from the emperor. The lines dividing the various conservative and liberal conceptions of an evolutionary constitutionalism were becoming increasingly blurred in the last years of the empire, and much would have depended on the leadership which might have emerged.

The war came at a time when these conflicts between the emperor and his critics within the government were still unresolved, and in fact it only served to make them more bitter. The fragmentation of Russian politics at this stage was such that the collapse of the autocracy in 1917 resulted in a situation in which no alternative had any wide support. There was of course a significant group of leaders favoring parliamentary democracy who had gained political experience in the Duma and in local government, but the political methods which they favored were not generally understood or accepted. Where parliamentary democracy has been successful it has in fact been a value system widely supported by many elements of a society rather than one reflecting the interests of a particular social stratum. The vast majority of Russians—whether peasants, workers, bureaucrats, officers, or professional people—were not generally familiar with the values and techniques of parliamentary democracy. To this extent the task of leaders favoring parliamentary methods in 1917 was infinitely more difficult than that of those prepared to rely on force. This does not necessarily mean that the empire might not under other circumstances have developed into a political democracy of the type familiar in the West, or even that something resembling such a system may not yet develop in Russia at some future time. It means only that, at the time the empire collapsed, the balance of domestic political experience weighed heavily in favor of those leaders who were prepared to employ authoritarian methods.

NOTES

1. Boris Brutzkus, "Die historischen Eigentümlichkeiten der wirtschaftlichen und sozialen Entwicklung Russlands," *Jahrbücher für Kultur und Geschichte der Slaven*, X (1934), 62–99, and Rushton Coulborn, "Der europäisch-russische Gegensatz," *Die politische Meinung*, II (February, 1957), 13–26, offer suggestive interpretations of imperial Russian society.

2. George Vernadsky, "The Expansion of Russia," *Transactions of the Connecticut Academy of Arts and Sciences*, XXXI (July, 1933), 391–425, provides a succinct account. The very extensive development of the lands beyond the Urals after 1861 is described in Donald W. Treadgold, *The Great Siberian Migration: Government and Peasant in Resettlement from Emancipation to the First World War* (Princeton, 1957).

3. B. I. Syromiatnikov, *"Reguliarnoe" gosudarstvo Petra Pervogo i ego ideologiia* (Moscow, 1913) offers what is probably the most perceptive discussion of Peter's reforms.

4. M. V. Klochkov, *Ocherki pravitelstvennoi deiatelnosti vremeni Pavla I* (Petrograd, 1916) develops this theme.

5. Nicholas V. Riasanovsky, *Nicholas I and Official Nationality in Russia, 1825–1855* (Berkeley, 1959), and Sidney Monas, *The Third Section: Police and Society in Russia under Nicholas I* (Cambridge, Mass., 1961) present in graphic detail the theory and practice of autocracy in the reign of Nicholas I and offer a valuable guide to the large literature on this subject.

6. Benedict H. Sumner, *A Short History of Russia* (New York, 1943), pp. 84–85.

7. N. M. Korkunov, *Russkoe gosudarstvennoe pravo* (2 vols.: St. Petersburg, 1913), I, 274–368, provides the best analysis of the formal system of stratification; the historical background is discussed in V. O. Kliuchevskii, *Istoriia soslovii v Rossii* (3rd ed.; Petrograd, 1918).

8. The structure and functioning of the stratification system are discussed in K. Kocharovskii, *Sotsialnyi stroi Rossii* (Prague, 1926); G. B. Sliozberg, Dorevoliutsionnyi stroi Rossii (Paris, 1933), pp. 78–108, 258–79; Robert A. Feldmesser, "Social Classes and Political Structure," *The Transformation of Russian Society: Aspects of Social Change Since 1861*, ed. Cyril E. Black (Cambridge, Mass., 1960), pp. 235–52 (hereafter cited as *Transformation of Russian Society*); and Robert C. Tucker, "The Image of Dual Russia," *Transformation of Russian Society*, pp. 587–605.

9. Leopold H. Haimson, "The Parties and the State: The Evolution of Political Attitudes," *Transformation of Russian Society*, pp. 110–45.

10. For a discussion of this important question see Mare Szeftel, "Aspects of Feudalism in Russian History," *Feudalism in History*, ed. Rushton Coulborn (Princeton, 1956), pp. 167–82; and Rushton Coulborn, "Russia and Byzantium," ibid., pp. 344–63. The extensive controversy in Russian historiography on this

issue is reviewed by Mare Szeftel in ibid., pp. 413–19. A similar conclusion is reached in George Vernadsky, "Feudalism in Russia," *Speculum,* XIV (July, 1939), 300–323.

11. Jerome Blum, *Lord and Peasant in Russia from the Ninth to the Nineteenth Century* (Princeton, 1961), provides a comprehensive account of the origins and development of serfdom.

12. G. Pavlovsky, *Agricultural Russia on the Eve of the Revolution* (London, 1930), and Gerold T. Robinson, *Rural Russia Under the Old Regime* (New York, 1932).

13. These developments are reviewed in L. I. Strakhovsky, "Constitutional Aspects of the Imperial Russian Government's Policy Toward National Minorities," *Journal of Modern History,* XIII (December, 1941), 467–92.

14. Dmitrij Cizevskij, *History of Russian Literature from the Eleventh Century to the End of the Baroque* (The Hague, 1960), chaps. vi and vii, provides a valuable discussion of early European influences.

15. The literature on this subject is virtually inexhaustible. Among recent American contributions, Theodore H. Von Laue, "The Industrialization of Russia in the Writings of Sergej Witte," *American Slavic and East European Review,* X (October, 1951), 177–90, and Marc Raeff, *Michael Speransky: Statesman of Imperial Russia, 1772–1839* (The Hague, 1957), are examples of a renewed interest in the thought of reforming bureaucrats.

16. This subject has been studied recently in George L. Yaney, "The Imperial Russian Government and the Stolypin Land Reform," unpubl. Ph.D. diss. (Princeton, 1961).

17. The adaptation of Marxism to the Russian environment is a matter of particular interest. See especially Adam Ulam, "The Historical Role of Marxism and the Soviet System," *World Politics,* VIII (October, 1955), 371–401; and Karl A. Wittfogel, "The Marxist View of Russian Society and Revolution," *World Politics,* XII (July, 1960), 487–508.

18. Alexander Gerschenkron, "The Rate of Industrial Growth of Russia Since 1885," *Journal of Economic History,* VII, Supplement (1947), 144–74; and Raymond W. Goldsmith, "The Economic Growth of Tsarist Russia, 1860–1913," *Economic Development and Cultural Change,* IX (April, 1961), 441–75.

19. See Alexander Gerschenkron, "Problems and Patterns of Russian Economic Development," *Transformation of Russian Society,* esp. pp. 42–61, for a discussion of the underlying economic policies of the imperial government.

20. Warren W. Eason, "Population Changes," *Transformation of Russian Society,* pp. 72–90, summarizes and interprets Russian statistical materials; Valentine T. Bill, *The Forgotten Class: The Russian Bourgeoisie from the Earliest Beginnings to 1900* (New York, 1959) has performed a useful service in calling attention to the role of the entrepreneur; Gaston V. Rimlinger, "Autocracy and the Factory Order in Early Russian Industrialization," *Journal of Economic History,* XX (March, 1960), 67–92, discusses the status of the workers in the last decades of the empire.

21. Nicholas Hans, *History of Russian Educational Policy (1701–1917)* (London, 1931), pp. 229–42, provides a convenient summary of educational statistics.

22. Raymond L. Garthoff, "The Military as a Social Force," *Transformation of Russian Society*, pp. 326–27, reviews the available evidence on the changing social status of the officer corps.

23. A valuable introduction to this subject will be found in Clyde Kluckhohn, "Recent Studies of the National Character of Great Russians," *Human Development Bulletin* (February 5, 1955), pp. 39–60; Henry V. Dicks, "Some Notes on the Russian National Character," *Transformation of Russian Society*, pp. 636–52; and Alex Inkeles and Daniel J. Levinson, "National Character: The Study of Modal Personality and Sociocultural Systems," *Handbook of Social Psychology*, ed. Gardner Lindzey (2 vols.; Cambridge, Mass., 1954), II, 977–1020.

24. Theodore H. Von Laue, "Die Revolution von aussen als erste Phase der russischen Revolution 1917," *Jahrbücher für Geschichte Osteuropas*, IV (1956), 138–58, stresses the differences between the Russian and French Revolutions, in contrast to Isaac Deutscher, "The French Revolution and the Russian Revolution: Some Suggestive Analogies," *World Politics*, IV (April, 1952), 469–81.

CHAPTER 3

History and Politics in the Soviet Union

In the Soviet Union, history is the most political of academic disciplines. The Soviet leaders have made a special effort to define their identity and legitimize their authority with reference to earlier Russian history. Chapter 3 is an introduction to a volume of essays that describes specific examples of this practice and the changes in interpretation called for by the changing needs of the government. Generally speaking, the Soviet authorities started out by denigrating all aspects of imperial Russian society and stressing the redress of all grievances that would result from the establishment of socialism. In the later 1920s, this view was expressed more formally in Marxist terms following long debates as to how "feudalism" and "capitalism" should be periodized in the Russian context. In the 1930s, as Stalin began to mobilize Soviet society as a prerequisite to his program of rapid industrialization, an effort was made to instill pride in the past. This refocusing on the past served as a means of reinforcing governmental authority at a time when a supreme effort was being demanded of the educated public and the industrial sector. The glorious past was evoked not only through historical writing but also through literature and drama. Held up as precedents for Stalin's harsh rule were Ivan III, who extended Muscovite authority over the neighboring Russian principalities, and Ivan IV (known in the West as "The Terrible," but more accurately as "The Dread"), who asserted centralized control over the noble landowners. A particularly interesting example was the reinterpretation of the role of Peter the Great to meet changing needs. His image was changed over a period of two decades from that of a dissolute agent of merchant capital to a heroic defender of Russia against foreign enemies. Finally, during and after World War II, the military leaders of the empire who had repelled foreign invaders were elevated to heroic stature.

Reprinted with permission from *Rewriting Russian History: Soviet Interpretations of Russia's Past*, ed. by C. E. Black (New York: Praeger Publishers, 1956), 3–31.

The relationship between historical writing and the Communist party line offers some valuable insights into the workings of the Soviet system. It touches on the role of Marxism in Soviet policy, and on the question whether Marxism as a working philosophy can be said in fact to offer a guide to historical interpretation. This relationship also illustrates the nature of the controls exercised by the party and state over scholarship, and the uses to which history can be put in propaganda and education. Perhaps most significantly, it provides an example of the extent to which scholars can oppose, evade and counterbalance the massive power of party and state—the extent to which they can, in dealing with the authorities, use the bargaining power represented by their training and knowledge.

A thorough study of these problems should properly cover an area as broad as scholarship itself, and in recent years considerable attention has been devoted to this subject.[1] The essays in this volume are limited to history, and in fact to a select field of history: the Russian state and its policies, principally before the nineteenth century. This is the field that has occupied the main attention of historians in the Soviet Union, and it is one in which the changes in the party line and the conflicts between scholarship and politics can best be illustrated. Similar trends can also be observed, however, in the fields of general non-Russian history, the history of the non-Russian peoples of the U.S.S.R., the history of the people's democracies of Eastern Europe and of China, and particularly in the history of the Communist party of the Soviet Union.

I

Russia entered the First World War with a rich heritage of historical scholarship which was an integral part of the European school that had created the modern historical method. The great tradition of social and economic history of Klyuchevsky, who died in 1911, was at its height. For another generation or more Russian historical work was dominated by his students, among whom were such diverse figures as the liberal Milyukov and the Marxist Pokrovsky. The rich creativeness of Russian historiography likewise included trends such as that represented by Presnyakov, who emphasized the political role of the state, and the influential school of legal historians led by Sergeevich. The members of these two schools were also students of Klyuchevsky, although they did not share his predominant interest in social history.

Within this community of Russian historians only the very few Marxists such as Pokrovsky and Rozhkov challenged the accepted tenets of historical scholarship. The great majority devoted themselves to the publication of sources, the production of monographs and the writing of broader interpretive syntheses. Historians who were not politically active were in large measure free from government control, for the regime did not systematically use historical scholarship as a direct and continuous means of implementing its policies. At the same time historians of such opposing views as Milyukov and Pokrovsky were both banned from teaching because of their political activities.[2]

Russian historical scholarship was deeply affected by the revolution of 1917 and the civil war that followed, but the disruption caused by these events was more a result of the chaotic conditions of life than of the policies of the Soviet government. Many of the leading historians chose to remain in Soviet Russia, and during the first post-revolutionary years their scholarly activity was relatively unimpeded, although the government gave them only limited funds for publication. This was indeed a major difficulty, for between 1917 and 1924 at least half a dozen scholarly journals founded by this group were forced to cease publication for lack of funds, and for another decade many manuscripts were left unpublished for the same reason.[3]

At the same time, historical scholars continued to occupy important positions in the profession. Thus the Institute of History, founded in 1921 under the auspices of the University of Moscow, was initially headed by a group of non-Marxists. Even when this Institute was transferred in 1925 under Communist auspices to the newly-organized Russian Association of Scientific Institutes for Research in the Social Sciences, generally known as RANION from its Russian initials, the non-Marxist historians played a very active role in its work. Some of the smaller research organizations, such as the State Historical Museum and the Society for History and Russian Antiquities, remained in their hands for as much as a decade. Under these circumstances it was possible for such leading representatives of Russian historical scholarship as Bakhrushin, Bogoslovsky, Gotye, Likhachev, Lyubavsky, Platonov, Presnyakov and Tarle to continue until about 1928 as active scholars, despite the fact that they suffered from discrimination on political grounds and experienced great difficulty in obtaining funds for the publication of major works.

Parallel to this group of scholars dedicated to the scientific method as applied to history there grew up an official school of Marxist historians under the leadership of Pokrovsky, seconded by Adoratsky, Olminsky, Piontkovsky, Ryazanov and Volgin. As the official historians of the Soviet regime, this group organized a series of commissions and institutes dedicated to the study of such subjects as the diplomatic background of the war, the October revolution, the Communist Party, trade unionism and the pre-Bolshevik revolutionary movement. In addition to publishing several series of documents, of which the most notable was the multi-volume edition of the diplomatic documents of the tsarist and provisional governments, this group also edited several historical journals devoted to these predominantly revolutionary subjects. A Marx-Engels Institute and a Lenin Institute were also established to collect and edit the writing of the Communist theorists. In 1922 Pokrovsky founded *Krasnyi Arkhiv* [Red Archives], which until its demise in 1941 published 106 volumes of documentary materials.

Of more direct consequence for the future of historical scholarship was the establishment in 1918 under Pokrovsky's supervision of a Socialist Academy for the Social Sciences, soon to be renamed the Communist Academy. This organization became the fountainhead of official doctrine in a number of fields of study, although it was not until the Institute of History was transferred from RANION in 1929 to the Academy that the latter became a dominant force in historical research. The training of scholars in the Marxist doctrine was the task of the Institute of Red Professors, founded in Moscow in 1921. The ubiquitous Pokrovsky was in charge of the work in history at this institute, a position which gave him a dominant influence over the younger members of the profession. He also headed the Society of Marxist Historians, founded in 1925, as a branch of the Communist Academy, and edited its journal, the *Istorik-Marksist* [Marxist Historian] (1926–41), which became the official organ of the Communist Party in the field of history.

It was thus almost a decade after the revolution before the Bolsheviks were in a position from the point of view of staff and organization to exert a decisive influence on the historical profession, although throughout this period they occupied the "commanding heights" in this field as in others through their control of budgetary allocations, publication outlets, research and training institutions, as well as of the police. The traditional historians were not only tolerated during this period, but in fact remained the principal source of scholarship except in those fields connected with the war and revolution in which the Communist Party was particularly interested. The coexistence of these two groups appeared to be feasible as late as 1928, when they appeared together at a special conference of Russian historians organized in Berlin by the Deutsche Gesellschaft zum Studium Osteuropas,[4] and at the Sixth International Congress of Historical Studies at Oslo.

This situation came to an end in 1929, when the Communists began to take decisive steps to liquidate their "bourgeois" colleagues. In that year several leading historians were forbidden to teach and deprived of access to research facilities, and such distinguished figures as Gotye, Platonov, Likhachev, Lyubavsky, and Tarle, among others, were arrested and sent into exile. At the same time the Academy of Sciences was formally taken over by the Communists, and non-party members were generally purged from academic institutions. Although as late as 1928 the Communists had pointed to the relative freedom of their "bourgeois" colleagues as evidence of the tolerant attitude of the Soviet regime, these same colleagues were now castigated as enemies of the working class and as potential saboteurs. This about-face was by no means limited to the historical profession, but was in fact part of a general policy of the party to wipe out "class enemies" with a view to strengthening the body politic for the efforts of the first Five-Year Plan. This new line had been heralded at the fifteenth congress of the Communist Party in 1927, and it was implemented gradually in the ensuing years in the various walks of Soviet life. From now on all historians were required to forsake objectivity and follow the party line, and the adherents of traditional scholarly methods were censured for eclecticism and pluralism when they were not accused of treason.[5]

II

Pokrovsky now emerged as the unchallenged leader of the Soviet historical profession, but his victory was short-lived. He died in 1932, and within two years he was being vilified by former students and colleagues alike as a falsifier of Marxism. What is the explanation of these strange events?

To judge from contemporary Soviet publications, it was primarily a question of the interpretation of Marxism. Pokrovsky himself had of course always been a Marxist. He had gone so far as to assert that "Marx is one of the greatest representatives of the historical method in world literature. Marx is historical to the core, Marxism—is historism."[6] In reviewing the work of the Society of Marxist Historians in 1930, he noted the continued presence of non-Marxist personnel and urged the desirability of "an ideological check on our specialists." And he added: "The most important task is to relate the historical work that we are doing to the struggles of the proletariat against wage slavery. Where this connection is not made, there is no contemporary Leninist history."[7] The even more violent attacks of Pokrovsky's Marxist colleagues against the non-Marxist scholars were likewise made in the name of Marxism.[8] Yet when the time came for Pokrovsky's posthumous liquidation, he too was accused of "anti-Marxist conceptions."

One could continue citing accusations and counteraccusations in the name of Marx throughout the twenty years since Pokrovsky's fall, and there are many examples of this in the chapters that follow, without discovering precisely what is the true Marxist interpretation of history. As a matter of fact, it may well be questioned whether Marx's historical materialism, taken literally, contributes anything substantial to an understanding of history. To say this is not to belittle the position of Marx as one of the pioneering sociologists of the nineteenth century, for his insights concerning the impact of industrialization on modern society have served to stimulate several generations of thinkers. The issue is rather whether Marx's historical materialism provides any more than a series of broad generalizations subject to a wide variety of interpretations, and indeed whether Marx himself regarded historical materialism as anything more binding or prophetic than a general attitude towards history.[9]

Non-Marxist thinkers who have devoted serious study to historical materialism, tend to agree that it is speculative and utopian rather than scientific. They recognize its appeal to human aspirations for progress, but note that it is illogical and incoherent in many of its details. They are skeptical about the division of history into fixed periods, and especially about predictions regarding the future which fail to take into account the possibility of unforeseen discoveries and developments. They can also cite well-documented examples of the failure of Marx's predictions to come true, if predictions he indeed intended them to be. It has moreover been amply demonstrated that in areas subject to universally accepted standards, such as mathematics and the natural sciences, neither in the U.S.S.R. or elsewhere has dialectical materialism become a principle of research.[10]

The Central Committee has for years been calling upon Soviet historians to provide a Marxist interpretation of Russian history, but the historians are no nearer to a solution of this problem than they were in 1917. What is demanded of them is that they identify in Russian history the evolving economic relations that Marx regarded as the "substructure" of society, define the social and political institutions constituting the "superstructure," and then demonstrate their relationship and interaction. Even if one assumes that Marx and Engels intended their theories to be used in this fashion, which is most unlikely, the problem is paradoxical for they bequeathed no formula for its solution. They were by no means clear as to the relationship between "substructure" and "superstructure," although Marx, at least, expressed his theories as though he were a fairly consistent economic determinist who admitted only secondary influence on the part of institutions and ideas. If Soviet historians have failed to agree on a Marxist interpretation of Russian history in this narrow and "scientific" sense, it is not for any lack of intelligence or zeal. It is because the task is impossible. Marxism provides not a scientific law of history but simply a general approach, a point of view, a spirit, and nothing more.[11]

If Marxism is not a scientific guide to the past, present and future, then what is the source of the policies of the Communist Party and the Soviet state? This is a question which has not been adequately studied and to which there is no simple answer. Communist leaders are doubtless sincere in considering Marxism as a guide to action, yet Marxism provides no such guide, and was not intended to, beyond the broadest outlines. As a body of theory which dealt with some of the fundamental problems of industrialization and which seemed to promise abundance for all in the foreseeable future, Marxism was capable of inspiring great enthusiasm among persons dedicated to the modernization of society and was in many respects transformed and adapted by them to suit their various needs. The Bolsheviks added to Marxism a strong dose of the Russian revolutionary tradition in its most uncompromising form, and this intoxicating blend has continued to inspire two generations of leaders. When it comes to policy decisions, however, whether strategic or tactical, it seems pretty clear that the Bolshevik's have been guided by what they considered necessary for the modernization of Russian society and for the preservation of their own political power. These practical decisions have always been presented in Marxist terminology, but the latter is more a means of expression than a source of ideas.

The motives that led first to the establishment of Pokrovsky as the dean of Soviet historians and later to his posthumous liquidation, should thus probably be sought not in the writings of Marx and Engels but in the needs of the party and the state. In the first phase of Stalin's struggle for power, he of necessity concentrated on his major rivals and permitted such peripheral fields of state activity as scholarship and the arts to continue along the relatively unrestricted lines established by Lenin and reflecting the spirit of the New Economic Policy. As Stalin became more sure of his power and prepared to launch the economic revolution of the five-year plans, he felt the need to gain further control over scholarship and the arts. This need was reflected in the policy of removing non-Marxist historians from positions of influence in the profession and of giving party members under the leadership of Pokrovsky full control in this field.

The order of the day after 1928 was the monopoly of the party in all phases of cultural life, but this did not resolve the question as to who would control the party. The tightening of the party's grip on the country was accompanied by a tightening of Stalin's grip on the party. The motives and purposes of Stalin's various purges are still a matter of dispute, but in general it was the bureaucratic politicians who replaced the ideologists. This involved a much more direct subordination of scholarship and the arts to the immediate purposes of the party and the state. The ideologists had been interested in ideas, derived primarily from the European tradition of Marxism, and they exercised a good deal of individual judgment in their work even though they were frequently intolerant of non-Marxists. The bureaucrats were more interested in loyalty to their leader and in the implementation of his program of industrialization, and were prepared to use any means to achieve their ends.

A policy of this type required pliant instruments, and Pokrovsky was not such a man. A second upheaval in the historical profession starting in 1934 was therefore needed to remove the vestiges of Pokrovsky's independence and to enforce a more universally compliant attitude on the part of the scholars. Pokrovsky's name appears many times in the chapters which follow, and he emerges as a rather naive economic determinist who tended in his interpretation to see only the pervasive and rather mechanical influence of the productive forces and class relationships which form Marx's "substructure." He was at the same time a great organizer and editor, whose oversimplified sociological schemes did not prevent him from planning and executing a great deal of valuable documentary and archival work. What nevertheless distinguished him most of all, and what ultimately led to his posthumous condemnation, was his relative independence from manipulation by the bureaucrats of the Central Committee apparatus.

Pokrovsky's general interpretation was evolved before the revolution, it had received Lenin's approval, and it came close to being the official party interpretation of history for a decade and a half or more. Pokrovsky's history was also party history in the sense that his interpretation was designed to demonstrate the soundness of Marxism and the inevitability of the Soviet regime, but it was an interpretation that he evolved independently. He was not a party historian in the Stalinist sense of being willing to adapt his views to every zig and zag of the party line, for his loyalty was more to the spirit of Marxism as he understood it than to the policy of any particular clique of Central Committee bureaucrats. It is significant that Pokrovsky, although officially proclaimed as dean of Soviet historians, was in fact pretty much of a figurehead for several years before his death in 1932. Some of his principal ideas were attacked and discarded by his colleagues, and he in fact admitted in 1931 that his interpretation had not been well expressed. He nevertheless continued to maintain that his history was sound Marxism, and to cite the public approval that Lenin had accorded his work.[12] The elevation of Pokrovsky thus resembled what later came to be known as a united-front operation: the prestige of his name was used to facilitate the expulsion of non-Marxist historians, but once this was accomplished he was the next on the list of those to be discarded.

It is not difficult to understand why this was done, given the aims and methods of the Central Committee. Pokrovsky had portrayed all pre-Soviet institutions and personalities in a sarcastic vein, and had presented his materials in a theoretical and schematic form. This did not meet the needs of a regime that wished to stimulate patriotism by rehabilitating selected personalities, and to present Russian history in an interesting narrative form suited to secondary school education. This concern was well stated in the decree of May 16, 1934, which announced the new line:

> Instead of the teaching of civic history in an animated and entertaining form with the exposition of the most important events and facts in their chronological sequence and with sketches of historical personages, the pupils are given abstract definitions of social and economic formations, which thus replace the consecutive exposition of civic history by abstract sociological schemes.
>
> The decisive condition of the permanent mastery of history is the observance of historical and chronological sequence in the exposition of historical events, with a due emphasis in the memory of the pupils of important historical facts, the names of historical persons and chronological dates. Only such a course of historical teaching can assure the necessary understanding, fidelity of presentation and real use of historical material; correct analysis and correct presentation of historical events leading pupils to the Marxist conception of history, are possible only on this basis.[13]

The new party line stressed history as indoctrination, and in the years after 1934 a variety of themes were given positive approval. These are set forth in a recent Soviet manual on the teaching of history: "The correct teaching of history must create in the students the conviction that capitalism will inevitably perish. . . . Through the study of history, students become convinced that everywhere, in all spheres of science and art, industry and agriculture, in the work of peace and on the battlefields the Soviet people march in the forefront of other nations, and have created values which are unequalled anywhere in the world. . . . The study of history helps students to form their patriotic feelings and to find an external expression for them. . . . Historical material pertaining to wars and military questions is very important for the cultivation of Soviet patriotism."[14]

III

The manner in which Pokrovsky and his associates were first given a monopoly in the field of history and were then removed from power within half a dozen years, is illustrative of the mechanisms by which scholarship is manipulated in the Soviet system. The key to this manipulation lies in the concentration of decision-making and power at the summit of the Communist Party, and the implementation of its policies by the party bureaucracy. Such negative controls as the various kinds of censorship and of course the ubiquitous police are too well known to require comment. More significant are the positive controls which center in the budgetary allocations on the part of the Ministry of Higher Education and the Academy of Sciences, and more particularly the manipulation of personnel and ideology by the party bureaucracy.

The chain of command through which the control is exerted has its point of departure in the Central Committee of the Communist Party, and more particularly in the Politburo, renamed the Presidium in 1952. The directives which establish the themes for historical interpretation and indicate the types of work which the party wishes to see accomplished are formulated by the Propaganda and Agitation Department of the Central Committee, which was headed by Zhdanov from 1938 until his death in 1948. On very important matters the leaders of the party may announce a new line of policy, as in 1934 when a series of instructions on the teaching of history were issued in the name of Stalin, Zhdanov and Kirov. More commonly, the views of the Central Committee are set forth in the leading party publications in unsigned editorials or in articles signed by secondary officials. The initiative in implementing these views is generally taken by the party cells in the research institutes and educational establishments. The personnel for this work is trained in the Higher Party School, which stresses administrative problems, and more recently also in the Academy of the Social Sciences of the Communist Party, founded in 1946, which is devoted to theory and ideology. Both of these institutions are directly under the Central Committee, and hence distinct from the state system of higher education. Both include general and Russian history in their curricula.[15]

In the field of history, as in most other fields of scholarship, the Academy of Sciences of the U.S.S.R. has been the principal agency of party supervision since 1936, when the Institute of History was transferred to it from the defunct Communist Academy. The Academy of Sciences is ostensibly an autonomous institution, subordinated directly to the Council of Ministers and governed by a General Assembly that meets periodically and a Presidium with interim powers. Party control resides principally in two mechanisms: the Scientific Secretariat of the Academy, which exercises the real executive power, and the party organization. The latter, subordinated to the Moscow district of the party, has its own secretary and operates through party units at all levels of the Academy organization. With both direct management and indirect supervision in its hands, the party thus has a firm control over all aspects of the Academy's work. The Academy also maintains branches in twelve of the constituent Soviet republics.

The Department of Historical Sciences is today one of the eight principal divisions of the Academy of Sciences, and in turn includes eight semi-autonomous scholarly organizations of which the most important is the Institute of History. Also within this Department are institutes devoted to ethnography, material culture, Oriental studies, history of the arts, and Slavic studies, as well as the Archives of the Academy and a museum of the history of religion. The Institute of History itself is a complex organization. It includes twelve Sectors divided by historical fields, ranging from History of the U.S.S.R.: Feudal Period to World History; two Commissions, on the history of historical sciences and the history of agriculture; and five Auxiliary Sections, devoted to post-graduate training, editing and publishing, reference and bibliography, the library, and manuscripts and archives. The Department of Historical Sciences has some fifteen academicians, out of a total of about 140 in the Academy, and an undetermined number of scholars of lesser rank.[16]

The functions of the Institute of History embrace research at a scholarly level, the training of scholars for the two advanced Soviet degrees of Candidate and Doctor, and a wide variety of adult education and propaganda activities. The latter include the compilation of popular encyclopedias and handbooks, patriotic and exhortative lectures intended for a wide audience, and participation in meetings at the Academy and elsewhere designed to lend dignity to the various propaganda campaigns of the party. The scholarly work of the Institute of History may be followed in the general publications of the Academy, especially the *Izvestiya* [News], in its various series, from 1928 to 1952; and since 1931 the *Vestnik* [Journal]. Among earlier periodicals devoted to Russian and general history, *Krasnyi Arkhiv* [Red Archives] and *Istorik-Marksist* [Marxist historian] were both discontinued in 1941. The work of the Institute of History has been reflected more directly in *Borba Klassov* [Class warfare] from 1931 to 1936, *Istoricheskii Zhurnal* [Historical journal], from 1936 to 1945, and in *Voprosy Istorii* [Problems of History], which has been the principal historical journal since 1945. The Institute has also published *Istoricheskii Arkhiv* [Historical archives], since 1936, *Istoricheskie Zapiski* [Historical notes], since 1937, and *Doklady i Soobshcheniya* [Reports and Communications], since 1954. The Academy has gradually been given a virtual monopoly of historical scholarship, but some historical work also appears in the learned journals of the larger universities.

As is the case with other branches of the Soviet elite, the political loyalty of scholars is assured by a characteristic system of incentives and controls. The incentives include a relatively high base pay, in addition to substantial fees for administrative duties at the Academy, for teaching at one of the higher educational institutions of the party or state, for supervising the training of graduate students, for editorial work on scholarly journals, for advising government departments, and in some cases for such political activities as membership in the Supreme Soviet. The academicians are the aristocrats in this society of scholars, with many privileges relating to housing, transportation and consumer goods. They are followed in rank by corresponding members, senior and junior research associates, technical assistants and graduate students. In addition there is a clerical and maintenance staff some two to three times more numerous than the scholars. Scholars rank high in the Soviet hierarchy, and membership in this group offers rare privileges and opportunities. These are indeed so great as to constitute in themselves a major source of discipline, for by denying or threatening to deny one or more of these various sources of privilege and income the party can bring many subtle pressures to bear on a scholar and his family.

In addition to these incentives, there are of course many direct controls. There are the general restrictions of party and police which affect all levels of Soviet society and probably constitute the most all-pervading system of supervision that the world has known. There are other controls more particularly adapted to work of scholarship. These include a wide variety of restrictions relating to topics of research; consultation of archival materials, which since 1938 have been controlled by the police; consultation of foreign literature; and of course foreign travel and research. The party also censors research at various stages before and after publication, requires certain set forms and procedures in relating all research to Marxism-Leninism, and limits discussion among scholars to certain set topics approved in advance or more often recommended. Publications surprised by a changing party line may be withdrawn from circulation, and in at least one instance a Doctor's degree has been revoked. Historians must not only adhere strictly to all party directives, but must repeat and elaborate them with marked enthusiasm in print and at public meetings called for this purpose. Through the yearly and five-year plans required of the Academy and its subdivisions, the historians are instructed as to which themes of research are of interest to party and state. The party also designates which students will be allowed to do graduate work, and with which scholars.[17]

IV

Many of the Soviet methods of control are present in some form in other societies, and indeed no large state operation can proceed without plans, budgets, boards of review, priorities and personnel management. What characterizes the Soviet system is the lengths to which these measures are carried and the concentration of all controls in the hands of a highly centralized party. With all these instruments of pressure in its hands, the party should long since have converted the historical profession into a willing tool of the party line. Yet, this is not the case. The historical journals and the publications of the Academy have in recent years contained frequent and sharp criticism of the Institute of History, reflecting a general failure on its part to follow party dictates. The Institute has been criticized for negligence in preparing adequate histories for general use, especially textbooks; for the poor organization of its research resulting in a lack of attention to contemporary history and to problems of theory; for failure to elaborate a satisfactory Marxist periodization of Russian history; and for non-fulfillment of the plans of research, with delays of a decade or more on individual projects.[18] After a generation of party activity since the death of Pokrovsky, is it not strange that party control meets with such resistance? How is this to be explained?

A good deal of the criticism of the Institute of History is certainly a reflection of the party's method of operation. The party tends to set impossible tasks and obscure theoretical standards for scholars, and then goes through a ritual of "criticism and self-criticism" designed to keep the scholars on their toes and to demonstrate to higher officials the vigilance of party agents. A totalitarian system seems to require synthetic measures to take the place of the incentives provided by a freer society, for these exercises are very characteristic of the Soviet system of controls. The sudden shifts and inequities of party policy may also be explained by differences of opinion and maneuvering for power on the part of party leaders at the summit of the Central Committee. At the same time it appears that the insubordination of the Institute of History reflects something much more interesting: the training and knowledge of the scholars give them a certain bargaining power with the party.

In the 1930's a majority of the scholars were non-Marxist, and even today party members may still be in a minority in the upper echelons. It has been estimated that in the late 1930's no more than five percent of the academicians and corresponding members of the Academy of Sciences belonged to the party, while at the junior research level about one-half were party members.[19] A totalitarian regime—one that wishes to manipulate all phases of human activity to achieve its ends—must inevitably come to terms with those possessing technical skills. There is perhaps no better indication of the nature of Communism than the concessions the party is willing to make to opposing points of view if they can be accommodated to the party line. Many examples of the tug of war between party and scholarship will be seen in the chapters that follow, and indeed this is the main theme of these chapters.

The sudden zigs and zags of the party line frequently call into question the integrity of the scholars concerned, who may be required to attack in uncompromising and humiliating terms their own major work of scholarhip within a few years after it is published. It should, therefore, be recognized that the explanation does not lie in any particular fickleness on the part of the individuals concerned, but in the extraordinary pressures to which they can be subjected in the Soviet system. Individual scholars may in fact be confronted with the alternative of adjusting their views to the party line or of losing their privileges as members of the Soviet elite, their jobs, their freedom of movement, and in some cases their lives. A number of historians died in prison or exile in the early 1930's and others disappeared in the great purges, although there is no case on record of a formal trial and liquidation on grounds of historical interpretation alone. It is rather the milder and more flexible pressures which are most frequently used, and these gain their effectiveness from the total control exerted by the party over all elements of the scholar's environment.

From the individual scholar's point of view, it is a question of finding a compromise between his physical security and his personal views. Each person faces this problem in his own way, but in a surprisingly large number of cases the scholar has been able to make a concession in form to the party line while in substance retaining much of his personal integrity. The distinction between the non-Marxist historian and the party historian is clear enough in the published monographs and textbooks. The former usually present the results of their research in the traditional manner, but within a light framework of party-oriented interpretation. In fact a number of excellent monographs have appeared since the 1930's in which there was little trace of the party line, and even less of Marxism, between the introduction and the conclusions. Only at the outset and at the end were references made to appropriate statements of the party leaders and to the Marxist "classics." By contrast the party historians, who have in fact been relatively few in number, devote themselves primarily to revolutionary and party history. In this category, which lies beyond the scope of the present volume, the most extreme forms of historical revision and suppression of well-known facts and personalities have been employed. When the party historians explore the deeper past, it is chiefly to draw upon secondary materials to illustrate some phase of the current party line.[20]

It was the desire of the party in the later 1930's to use Russian history as a means of creating in Soviet opinion several attitudes designed to strengthen the regime. This policy gave historical scholarship, and in particular non-Marxist historians, an opportunity to regain a position of influence in research and publication. Since 1934 the party has stressed such historical themes as the repulsion of foreign invasions, the heroic efforts of Ivan the Terrible and Peter the Great in defeating domestic enemies and in centralizing the government, and the territorial growth of Russia. These themes serve to provide justification in Russian history for certain policies of the regime, and help to base these policies on the common historical experience of the Russian people rather than on Marxist doctrine. These developments in the field of history in the 1930's were thus part of the general trend in Stalinist political thought away from the theoretical determinism of Marxism and in the direction of a voluntarism which as yet has an uncertain theoretical basis. This new emphasis on human consciousness was still expressed in Marxist terms, but non-Soviet scholars are generally agreed that it marks a fundamental departure from Marxist doctrine as understood in the West.[21]

In terms of their knowledge and skills it was the older generation of non-Marxist historians who were best able to implement this new line, and they seized the opportunity with vigor. Their names figured prominently in the new collaborative textbook for university students, and under the cover of the new party line they published a number of works which testified to the continued existence of important historical scholarship in the Soviet Union. Some of the most significant of these works were by deceased scholars whose manuscripts could not have been published under Pokrovsky's regime. Others were clearly the result of more recent and continuing research. Any monograph or compilation of documents could be fitted into the new party line so long as it was not unpatriotic in tone, and avoided all discussion of the achievements of the tsarist government in the century after the Napoleonic invasion. The party historians, who included now a number of reformed adherents of Pokrovsky's Marxism, had in general a somewhat separate sphere of activity. They wrote the textbooks at the secondary school level, and they concentrated more particularly on certain phases of economic history and on the revolutionary movements of the nineteenth century. The more immediate history of Bolshevism tended to be written by public relations officials specializing in "agitation and propaganda" rather than by professional historians, and research in this field involved political risks which few were willing to take. In those aspects of their work where they did not go far beyond the documents, the party historians also produced some valuable scholarship.

The influence of the non-Marxist historians reached its height during the Second World War, when many controls were relaxed and the conflicting elements in Soviet society were temporarily united in the struggle against the common enemy. The historical profession was freer than it had been at any time since the revolution, and doctrinal issues were submerged in the upsurge of patriotism. The end of the war nevertheless confronted both state and party with new problems, and the resulting changes in the party line soon made themselves felt in the field of history. The party apparently believed that, once the pressure of German aggression had been removed, the inherent centrifugal forces in Soviet society would again make themselves felt. The friendly relations with the Western allies, the hopes stimulated by the regime for a more relaxed atmosphere after the war, and the extensive personal contacts with the West on the part of Russian soldiers and civilians, all had to be counteracted if the security of the regime was to be safeguarded. The formal launching of a cold war against the West in 1946 was the general policy that the party adopted to meet this crisis, and within this framework it singled out certain existing or imagined trends in Soviet historiography for vigorous attack.

Thus all indications of respect for the West and acknowledgment of Western influence in Russia were attacked as "cosmopolitanism," defined as "a reactionary bourgeois ideology, which rejects national traditions and national sovereignty, advocates an indifferent attitude towards the fatherland and the national culture, and seeks the establishment of 'world government' and 'world citizenship,'"[22] On the other hand, failure to pay lip service to Marxist terminology was attacked as "bourgeois objectivism," defined as "an interpretation of the conformity of the historical process designed to justify and immortalize the capitalist system."[23] More specifically, the historians were criticized for failure to praise the successes of tsarist foreign policy, for neglecting the advantages derived by the peoples of Central Asia through incorporation into the Russian empire, for ignoring the superiority of Russian culture both before and since the revolution, for admitting that foreign ideas or institutions may have been adopted in Russia at any period in its history, and for failing to emphasize the leading role of the Great Russian people within the Soviet Union.

The historians also had to take cognizance of the unusually obscure theoretical statements of Stalin in his essays *Concerning Marxism in Linguistics* (1950) and *Economic Problems of Socialism* (1952). The burden of these statements, despite certain inconsistencies and contradictions, was to emphasize the ability of the state to manipulate the economic substructure and to transform society. The active role of the state, and hence of the party, had of course long been a fact in Soviet society. This adjustment of theory to practice served to strengthen the hand of the party in its postwar effort to reassert its influence. Indeed, since 1949 there has been a very significant tightening of party control over the writing of history. The general patriotic line initiated in 1934 has not been changed, but the ways in which it can be expressed have been greatly limited. Both Marxist and non-Marxist historians have been brought to task for minor infractions of the party line, and the party has relied much more heavily than before on such devices as requiring historians to participate in formal discussions of periodization, or of the significance for historiography of Stalin's essay on linguistics.[24]

The party has now channelized the writing of history very largely into the preparation of textbooks and of multi-volume collaborative histories. The stated purpose of all this work is to demonstrate, at various levels of popularization, that the future belongs inevitably to the Soviet type of socialism. It is claimed that 87,500,000 copies of history textooks at the elementary and secondary school level have been published since the Second World War, and 1,775,000 copies of history textbooks designed for higher educational institutions. The multi-volume collaborative histories now in preparation include general treatises on the history of the U.S.S.R. (7 volumes), on world history (10 volumes), on the history of Moscow (6 volumes), on the history of Leningrad (3 volumes), and on the history of Russian historiography (3 volumes). Histories of the people's democracies are also being prepared. At the same time there has been a marked decline since 1949 in the publication of scholarship based on primary research. The quality of individual chapters and sections in these multi-volume treatises is frequently high, reflecting the vast amount of research that has been done on many aspects of Russian history during the past century. The heavy hand of the party is always in evidence, however, whether in the general interpretation or in the neglect of such important problems as foreign influences in Russia. The official patriotic tone in these works tends to be characteristic of government-sponsored histories all over the world, but the exclusive restriction of an important body of scholars to this type of writing has now gone well beyond anything heretofore known even in the U.S.S.R.[25]

The historians have adopted various devices to frustrate party controls. They have tried to concentrate their work in the Kievan and Muscovite periods, where Marxism has relatively little relevance. They have devoted attention to the publication of documents and to annotated editions of important sources, where problems of general interpretation can be avoided. They have taken advantage of the emphasis on patriotism to publish manuscripts which might not otherwise have seen the light. When impossible theoretical tasks have been assigned to them, such as providing a Marxist periodization of Russian history in a narrowly literal fashion, they have discussed and procrastinated for years before reaching the conclusion that their knowledge was not yet adequate for the task. When asked to prepare a seven-volume history of Russia under circumstances in which many important things cannot be said, one suspects that the historians are hinting at its shortcomings when they entitle it *Essays*. There are doubtless many other methods, hidden from outsiders, by which party agents can be guided or argued into supporting sound scholarship. All these subterfuges have their limits, for the ultimate power is in the hands of the party, but that they have been so stubbornly employed testifies as to the bargaining power of the non-Marxist specialists.

V

The interplay of history and politics in the Soviet Union is no doubt an extreme example of the way in which scholarship can be turned to political uses in a totalitarian system. History belongs to a category of subjects, which includes law, political economy, literature and the arts, peculiarly suited to the propagation of the party line. Mathematics and the natural sciences, with the notable exceptions of biology and genetics, have on the whole been relatively free from ideological controls in this narrow sense. What has saved history from being completely subverted is that the party line, though ideological in form, is in fact very largely political in content. Since the Marxist language as employed by Soviet ideologists consists of little more than abstractions, non-Marxist scholars have found that the political content of the party line frequently provides sufficient leeway to permit the publication of a considerable amount of non-political scholarship.

It appears that one must attribute the survival of scholarly history in the Soviet Union very largely to the astuteness of the great majority of the leading historians who have been non-Marxists. This older generation is now rapidly dying out, and there is some reason to doubt whether the younger historians, even when they are not party members, possess either the scholarship of the independence of the older generation. The quality of the Soviet participation in the Tenth International Congress of Historical Sciences at Rome in September, 1955, was illustrative of the extent to which history has now been subordinated to politics.[26]

One may nevertheless question whether this effort to use historical scholarship for political purposes will not in the end defeat itself. The very controls which seek to guarantee that historians will be ready servants of the party line, tend to destroy the conditions under which historians can be trained.

At the Twentieth Congress of the Communist Party in February, 1956, criticism was voiced of the distortions of history which took place under Stalin's regime.[27] The interpretation of such themes as the role of the individual and the relationship of the peoples of the U.S.S.R. has been changed since Stalin's death, and a somewhat less hostile approach to the work of non-Soviet historians and even of Pokrovsky and his associates is now recommended.[28] These are nevertheless changes in the party line rather than a relaxation of controls, and the new regime appears to be as determined as the old to make the interpretation of history conform to the needs of party and state.

NOTES

1. Carl J. Friedrich, ed., *Totalitarianism* (Cambridge, 1954), proceedings of a conference held at the American Academy of Arts and Sciences, Boston, March 1953; *Science and Freedom* (Boston, 1955), proceedings of a conference convened by the Congress for Cultural Freedom, Hamburg, July 1953; *Academic Freedom Under the Soviet Regime* (Munich, 1954), proceedings of a conference held by the Institute for the Study of the History and Culture of the U.S.S.R., New York, April 1954.

2. Anatole G. Mazour, *An Outline of Modern Russian Historiography* (Berkeley, 1939); Michael Karpovich, "Klyuchevski and recent trends in Russian historiography," *Slavonic Review*, XXI (March, 1943), 31–39; Alfred A. Skerpan, "Modern Russian historiography," *Kent State University Bulletin, Research Series I*, XL (October, 1952), 37–60; the best Soviet accounts are N. L. Rubinshtein, *Russkaya istoriografiya* [Russian historiography] (Moscow, 1941), and M. N. Tikhomirov, ed., *Ocherki istorii istoricheskoi nauki v SSSR* [Essays in the history of historical scholarship in the U.S.S.R.], Vol. I (Moscow, 1955), the first of a projected three volumes.

3. A. Presniakov, "Historical research in Russia during the revolutionary crisis," *American Historical Review*, XXVIII (Jan., 1923), 248–57.

4. Otto Hoetzsch, ed., *Aus der historischen Wissenschaft der Soviet-Union*, in *Osteuropäische Forschungen*, N. F. VI (1929).

5. Fritz Epstein, "Die marxistische Geschichtswissenschaft in der Soviet Union seit 1927," *Jahrbücher für Kultur und Geschichte der Slaven*, N. F. VI (1930), 78–203; P. Vostokov, "Les sciences historiques en Russie," *Le Monde slave*, n. s. VII (Sept., 1930), 438–68; (Oct., 1930), 79–98; (Nov., 1930), 294–311; (Dec., 1930), 437–60; n. s. VIII (Feb., 1931), 265–94; Hans Jonas, "Die Entwicklung der Geschichtsforschung in der Soviet Union seit dem Ausgang des Weltkrieges," *Zeitschrift für osteuropäische Geschichte*, V (1931), 66–83, 386–96; R. Salomon, "Zur Lage des Geschichtswissenschaft in Russland," *ibid.*, VI (1932), 385–402; Paul Gronski, "La littérature historique Soviétique," *Bulletins d'Information des Sciences historiques en Europe Orientale*, IV (1931), 38–50; Antoine Florovsky,

"La littérature historique Soviétique-Russe. Compte-rendu 1921–1931," *ibid.*, VI (1934), 120–86; VII (1935), 5–111; Josef Pfitzner, "Die Geschichtswissenschaft in der Sowjetunion," in *Bolschewistische Wissenschaft und "Kulturpolitik"* (2nd ed., Königsberg and Berlin, 1942), 163–218; the leading Soviet accounts of this period are M. V. Nechkina, "Nauka russkoi istorii" [Scholarship in Russian history], in *Obshchestvennye nauki SSSR, 1917-1927*, ed. by V. P. Volgin, G. O. Gordon and I. K. Luppol (Moscow, 1928), 126–62; *Trudy pervoi vsesoyuznoi konferentsii istorikov-marksistov* [Proceedings of the first all-union conference of Marxist historians] (2 v.; Moscow, 1930); and V. P. Volgin, E. V. Tarle and A. M. Pankratova, eds., *Dvadsat pyat let istoricheskoi nauki v SSSR* [Twenty-five years of historical scholarship in the U.S.S.R.] (Moscow, 1942).

6. M. N. Pokrovsky, "Marks—kak istorik; doklad" [Marx as an historian; a report], *Vestnik sotsialisticheskoi Akademii*, No. 4 (April–July, 1923), 374.

7. M. N. Pokrovsky, "O zadachakh marksistskoi istoricheskoi nauki v rekonstruktivny period" [On the tasks of Marxist historical scholarship in the period of reconstruction], *Ist.-Marks.*, XXI (1931), 7.

8. See for example G. Zaidel and M. Tsvibak, *Klassovyi vrag na istoricheskom fronte: Tarle i Platonov i ikh shkoly* [The class enemy on the historical front: Tarle and Platonov and their school] (Moscow, 1931); and Sergei A. Piontkovsky, *Burzhuaznaya istoricheskaya nauka v Rossii* [Bourgeois historical scholarship in Russia] (Moscow, 1931).

9. Karl Korsch, *Karl Marx* (London, 1938), 167–8; Isaiah Berlin, *Karl Marx: His Life and Environment* (2nd ed., London, 1948), 143–4.

10. Important recent contributions to the large literature on this subject are Karl Popper, *The Open Society and its Enemies* (rev. ed.; Princeton, 1950); M. M. Bober, *Karl Marx's Interpretation of History* (rev. ed., Cambridge, 1950); Herbert J. Muller, *The Uses of the Past* (New York, 1952); and H. B. Acton, *The Illusion of the Epoch: Marxism-Leninism as a Philosophical Creed* (London, 1955).

11. See especially Chapter Two in *Rewriting Russian History: Soviet Interpretations of Russia's Past*, ed. by C. E. Black (New York: Praeger Publishers, 1956).

12. See the Preface and first Appendix in the 10th edition of Pokrovsky, *Russ. ist. v samom szhatom ocherke.*

13. "O prepodavanii grazhdanskoi istorii v shkolakh SSSR" [On the teaching of civic history in the schools of the U.S.S.R.], *Direktivy VKP(b) i postanovleniya sovetskogo pravitelstva o narodnom obrazovanii za 1917–1947 gg.* (Moscow, 1947), 170–1; trans. in *Slavonic and East European Review*, XIII (July, 1934), 204–5.

14. M. A. Zinoviev, *Soviet Methods of Teaching History* (Washington, D.C., 1952), 84–92, trans. from the Soviet edition of 1948; see also Paul Olberg, "The teaching of history under Stalin," *Contemporary Review*, CLV (1937), 464–69; and Frederic Lilge, "The political control of history texts in the Soviet Union," *School and Society*, LXVII (May 29, 1948), 393–7.

15. Louis Nemzer, "The Kremlin's professional staff: the 'apparatus' of the Central Committee, Communist Party of the Soviet Union," *American Political Science Review*, XLIV (March, 1950), 64–85; Mark G. Field, "The Academy of the Social Sciences of the Communist Party of the Soviet Union," *American Journal of Sociology*, LVI (Sept., 1950), 137–41.

16. Alexander Vucinich, *The Soviet Academy of Sciences* (Stanford, 1956), 21–41.

17. *Ibid.*, 81–124; see also A. A. Avtorkhanov [Aleksandr Uralov], "Polozhenie istoricheskoi nauki v SSSR" [The position of historical scholarship in the U.S.S.R.], *Materialy konferentsii nauchnykh rabotnikov (emigrantov) sostoyavsheisya v Myunkhene 11–14 yanvarya 1951 g.* [Materials of the conference of émigré scholars convened in Munich on 11–14 January 1951] (Munich, 1951), III, 5–53; "Thought control in the Soviet Union," *Department of State Bulletin*, XXV (Nov. 5, 1951), 719–22; (Nov. 26, 1951), 844–51; V. P. Marchenko, *Planirovanie nauchnoi raboty v SSSR* [The planning of scholarly work in the U.S.S.R.] (Munich, 1953); Alexander P. Ohloblyn, "Soviet historiography," *Academic Freedom Under the Soviet Regime: A Symposium* (Munich, 1954), 69–77; and, of related interest, Merle Fainsod, "Censorship in the USSR—A documented record," *Problems of Communism*, V (March-April, 1956), 12–19.

18. Characteristic of recent criticisms of the Institute of History are: Z. Mosina, "O rabote Instituta istorii Akademii nauk SSSR" [Concerning the work of the Institute of History of the Academy of Sciences of the U.S.S.R.], *Vop. Ist.*, IV, 11 (Nov., 1948), 144–49; A. Pankratova, "Nasushchnye voprosy sovetskoi istoricheskoi nauki" [The vital questions of Soviet historical scholarship], *Kommunist*, XXX (April, 1953), 55–69; and "O nauchnoi deyatelnosti i sostoyanii kadrov Instituta Istorii" [Concerning the scholarly activity and status of the personnel of the Institute of History], *Vestnik Akademii Nauk SSSR*, XXIII (April, 1953), 77–9.

19. Vucinich, *Soviet Academy of Sciences*, 38.

20. The distortions in the history of the Communist Party are graphically described in Bertram D. Wolfe's "Operation rewrite: The agony of Soviet historians," *Foreign Affairs*, XXI (Oct., 1952), 39–57, and "Totalitarianism and history," in *Totalitarianism*, ed. by Carl J. Friedrich (Cambridge, 1954), 262–73.

21. The developments in this period are treated in Stuart R. Tompkins, "Trends in Communist historical thought," *Slavonic and East European Review*, XIII (1934–35), 294–319; B. H. Sumner, "Soviet History," *ibid.*, XVI (1937–38), 601–15; XVII (1938–39), 151–61; E. F. Maximović, "Doctrine marxiste-léniniste appliqué a l'étude concrète de l'histoire," *Bulletin de l'Association russe pour les Recherches scientifiques à Prague*, VII, No. 46 (1938), 219–63; Georges Kagan, "La crise de la science historique russe," *Revue Historique*, LXV (1940), 1–35; G. B. Carson, "Changing perspectives in Soviet historiography," *South Atlantic Quarterly*, XLVII (April, 1948), 186–95; Georg von Rauch, "Die Grundlinien der sovietischen Geschichtsschreibung im Zeichen des Stalinismus," *Europa Archiv*, V (1950), 3383–88, 3423–32, 3489–94; and Klaus Mehnert, *Stalin Versus Marx: The Stalinist Historical Doctrine* (London, 1952.

22. "Kosmopolitizm" [Cosmopolitanism], *Bolsh. Sov. Ents.* (2nd ed.), XXIII, 113.

23. "Obyektivizm burzhuaznyi" [Bourgeois objectivism], *ibid.*, XXX, 442; "Protiv obyektivizma v istoricheskoi nauke" [Against objectivism in historical scholarship], *Vop. ist.*, IV, 12 (Dec., 1948), 3–12, trans. in *C.D.S.P.*, I, 6 (March 8, 1949), 11–17.

24. Sergius Yakobson, "Postwar historical research in the Soviet Union," ***Annals of the American Academy of Political and Social Science***, CCLXIII (May, 1949), 123–33; R. Schlesinger, "Recent Soviet historiography," ***Soviet Studies***, I (1949–51), 3–21, 138–62, 265–88; Horst Jablonowski, "Die Lage der sowjetrussischen Geschichtswissenschaft nach dem zweiten Weltkriege," ***Saeculum***, II (1951), 443–64; Anatole G. Mazour and Herman E. Bateman, "Recent Conflicts in Soviet Historiography," ***Journal of Modern History***, XXIV (March, 1952), 56–68; G. Shtakelberg, "Otrazhenie politiki SSSR v smene sovetskikh istoricheskikh kontseptsii" [The repercussions of the policy of the U.S.S.R. on the change in the Soviet conception of history], ***Vestnik Instituta po Izucheniyu Istorii i Kultury SSSR***, No. 2 (Munich, 1952), 34–53; M. Miller, "Postwar historical science in the U.S.S.R.," ***The U.S.S.R. Today and Tomorrow*** (Munich, 1953), 111–18; Anatole G. Mazour, "Party line history," ***American Scholar***, XXII (Summer, 1953), 293–303; Valentin Gitermann, "The study of history in the Soviet Union," ***Science and Freedom*** (Boston, 1955), 202–11.

25. A. L. Sidorov, ***Soviet Historical Science: Its Problems and Achievements*** (Moscow, 1955).

26. Peter Geyl, "New orthodoxy for old: Shackled Soviet historians," ***Nation***, CLXXXII (April 14, 1956), 299–301.

27. Speech by Anna M. Pankratova at the Twentieth Congress of the Communist Party, ***Pravda*** (Feb. 22, 1956), trans. in *C.D.S.P.*, VIII (May 2, 1956), 9–11; "XX syezd KPSS i zadachi issledovaniya istorii partii" [The twentieth congress of the Communist Party of the Soviet Union and the problems of research in party history], ***Vop. Ist.***, XII, 3 (March, 1956), 3–12, trans. in *C.D.S.P.*, VII (June 20, 1956), 6–9, 18.

28. "Ob izuchenii istorii istoricheskoi nauki" [Concerning the study of the history of historical scholarship], ***Vop. Ist.***, XII, 1 (Jan., 1956), 3–12; see also Alexander Dallin, "More rewriting of history," ***New Republic***, CXXXIV (June 11, 1956), 26–30.

CHAPTER 4

Russian and Soviet Interpretations of World History

This chapter describes the views set forth in three prominent world histories written in the nineteenth and twentieth centuries, those of Danilevsky, a natural scientist; Rozhkov, an independent Marxist; and Zhukov and his colleagues, who represent the views of the ruling Communist Party. Despite many differences, all three conclude in effect that the Russians are a chosen people whose civilization represents the culmination of world history and who in a foreseeable future will provide not only a model, but a final model, for all other societies.

To be sure, most professional historians in Russia before 1917 and most political leaders held the then-conventional view that Russia would in due course follow the path of political, economic, and social development characteristic of Western and Central Europe after the French Revolution. The interpretations of Danilevsky and Rozhkov may therefore be dismissed as the idiosyncratic views of two individuals, although Danilevsky had a considerable following in the late nineteenth century among Panslavs and other nationalists. The interpretation of Zhukov and his colleagues, however, represents the official view of the Soviet government that all societies are bound by the immutable laws of history to evolve from feudalism and capitalism to socialism and communism. This view is set forth in a wide variety of textbooks in history, political economy, and Marxist philosophy used in Soviet educational institutions.

I

All countries in the modern era face a problem of identity. This is particularly true of those countries that were not among the first to achieve a modern way of life and that do not have a glorious past on

Reprinted with permission from *The Analysis of International Politics*, ed. by James N. Rosenau (New York: The Free Press, 1971), 371–390. An earlier version of this paper was presented as the Henry Wells Lawrence Lecture of History at Connecticut College.

which to build their self-confidence. Under modern conditions the state demands so much of its citizens in terms of taxes, military service, and other forms of loyalty—and is under such pressure from the competition of other countries—that its leaders are profoundly aware of the need to justify this loyalty and to demonstrate the correctness of current policies and the ultimate hope for a better way of life.

Efforts to establish the identity of a nation must inevitably be made primarily in terms of similarities and differences between it and other nations and groups of nations. In discussing the cognitive aspects of man-milieu relationships, Harold and Margaret Sprout have noted that one must study the ways in which peoples perceive of their environment in order to understand their purposive responses to it.[1] In the case of the peoples of Russia, their central problem in developing a sense of who they are and where they are going has been to define their relationship to the states of western and central Europe that throughout modern times have been seen both as models to be imitated and as rivals to be overtaken and surpassed. The essential element of this challenge has been whether Russia should adopt European institutions to the exclusion of its own traditional heritage, or alternatively should create its own unique modern culture in which those elements of European culture that were of universal significance would be creatively adapted to Russia's needs and values. Many books and essays have been written in Russia on the subject of "Russia and Europe," and numerous works of scholarship have been produced by authors from the West European and English-speaking countries devoted to interpreting and reinterpreting the Russian interpretations.[2]

One form of this debate that has grown in importance through the years is that which has been concerned with finding Russia's correct place in the stream of world history. These efforts are devoted to identifying the main trends in world history, to describing the rise and fall of empires, civilizations, and cultures, and to assessing the relationship of Russia to these developments.

World histories can be many things. They can be, as is too often the case, simply histories of all the countries of the world laid end to end. They can be comparative histories, seeking to discover what is universal and what is unique in the evolution of countries and civilizations. They can be histories that seek in the past a pattern that will have predictive value for the future. They can also be academic histories, usually the most useful and the least exciting of these efforts—that seek in a cautious and balanced fashion to put all that is known about the past into an organized narrative without reaching any conclusion at all.

The three Russian interpretations of world history that will be discussed here share in some measure all of these characteristics. The first, by a nationalist, had as its purpose to elaborate a program for Russia's future greatness. The second, by a Marxist, was primarily concerned with exploring the past in terms of Marx's interpretation of history. The third, by a team of Marxist-Leninists, is a propaganda vehicle for the Communist Party of the Soviet Union in the form of an academic history.

II

Nikolai Iakovlevich Danilevsky was born in 1822 in the province of Orlov. His father was an army officer who had fought in the Napoleonic wars, and during his childhood the family was constantly on the move from one army post to another. Danilevsky was an unusually gifted child, and as a student of natural sciences at the University of St. Petersburg he was an outstanding success. His early concern with problems of social change was reflected in his interest in Fourier, and he was associated briefly with the socialist discussion group led by Petrashevsky. He was in fact held in prison for a few months in 1849 in connection with the investigation of the Petrashevsky group, of the members of which Dostoevsky was destined to become the most noted.

Upon his release in the following year, Danilevsky was sent in administrative exile for three years to Vologda and later to Samara, where he served as a clerk and translator. Having completed his advanced education before his arrest, Danilevsky now entered government service as a natural scientist. He had a distinguished career as a specialist in fisheries, heading numerous scientific expeditions, and at the time of his death in 1885 he was a high official in the Ministry of State Domains. In the course of his career Danilevsky published 46 articles and books. Most of these were reports of his expeditions, but they also included a two-volume critique of Darwinism and a number of polemical articles on political subjects. He is remembered, however, not for his professional work but for his political hobby which resulted in the publication of *Russia and Europe.*[3]

The view of world history set forth by Danilevsky in his *Russia and Europe,* first published serially in 1869 and later issued in book form, was both an interpretation of the past and a program for the future.[4] The driving force of Danilevsky's interpretation was his reaction against the view, generally held in Europe in the mid-nineteenth century and widely accepted in Russia, that European culture and institutions were of universal validity, and that the principal problem of other societies was to become as much like Europe as possible. The science and technology of Europe were in Danilevsky's lifetime gaining universal acceptance, and it seemed to many that the absorption of Russia into European civilization was only a matter of time. Danilevsky believed this view to be fundamentally mistaken, and in support of his opinions he pointed to the widespread antagonism of the European states toward Russia, which had reached its climax in the Crimean War. We know that the juxtaposition of "Europe" and Russia was in fact by no means as clear-cut as Danilevsky believed it to be, and that on this issue as on so many others the European states were deeply divided. Danilevsky nevertheless took this supposed antagonism of Russia and Europe as a point of departure for his theory of world history.

The central feature of Danilevsky's theory was his analysis of the historical record in terms of "cultural-historical types," of which he distinguished ten: (1) Egyptian, (2) Chinese, (3) Assyrian-Babylonian, (4) Indian, (5) Iranian, (6) Hebrew, (7) Greek, (8) Roman, (9) Arabic, and (10) Germano-Roman, or European. History, in his view, did not move in a unilinear fashion but rather through this succession of cultural-historical types.[5] These types developed in accordance with five laws: (1) they had to have common linguistic bonds, and (2) political independence as a state or federation of states; (3) their cultures as a whole were not transmissable, although individual aspects might influence other civilizations; (4) they flourished best if they encompassed a diversity of peoples; and (5) after many centuries of development each cultural-historical type achieved a relatively brief period of four to six centuries in which all of its creative resources were put to full use, and thereafter it became sterile or was dissolved into other cultural-historical types.[6]

While maintaining that his cultural-historical types were self-contained and essentially incompatible, Danilevsky nevertheless recognized that scientific knowledge developed without regard to such artificial compartments. In a lengthy discussion of the history of science, he stressed the evolutionary process by which the various branches of science had developed from the initial collection of data to the eventual formulation of general laws, and the contributions made in each case by scientists from a variety of cultural-historical types. He concluded from this analysis that scientific knowledge was not necessarily a monopoly of the Germano-Romans, i.e., the Europeans, but could continue to evolve under Slavic auspices.[7] In Danilevsky's view, the essential qualities that determined the success of a cultural-historical type were not its productivity in the realm of scientific knowledge, but its ability to perform creatively in four spheres of activity: religious, cultural, political, and social-economic. He maintained that in the original primary civilizations—Egypt, China, Assyria-Babylonia, India, and Iran—these spheres of activity were not clearly differentiated. Religion, politics, and science were at such an elementary level that they formed part of a single value system. Other cultural-historical types were one-sided in their creativity—thus, the

Hebrew was primarily religious; the Greek primarily cultural and aesthetic; and the Roman primarily political.[8]

This whole argument served as a background for Danilevsky's critique of the European cultural-historical type, which he considered to be nearing the end of its creativity. He recognized the unprecedented achievements of Europe in the spheres of politics, of art and science, and of industry, but he found many faults in the quality of its civilization. These he summarized in terms of a threefold anarchy: religious anarchy resulting from the efforts of Protestantism to establish religious truth on the basis of personal authority; philosophical anarchy, arising from a negativistic materialism that was beginning to preempt the role of religious convictions; and political-social anarchy, based on the contradiction between political democracy and economic feudalism. Thus the European cultural-historical type must, according to Danilevsky, be regarded as a failure in religious, philosophical, and social-economic terms despite its success in other respects.[9]

In contrast to this crippled and declining European cultural-historical type, Danilevsky wrote a glamorous account of the Slavic cultural-historical type which in his view was destined to take the place of the European—if the Slavic peoples understood their destiny and adapted their policies accordingly. It is perhaps not surprising, in view of his general outlook, that Danilevsky found the Slavic peoples to be capable of outstanding contributions in all four of the essential spheres of activity, and he discussed these at some length. Two quotations will serve to illustrate the tone of his argument. As regards religious qualities, he asserted that "From an objective, factual point of view, the Russians and most of the other Slavic peoples were destined by history to be, along with the Greeks, the principal guardians of the living tradition of religious truth—orthodoxy, and by virtue of this to be the continuers of the great work stemming from Israel and Byzantium—to be peoples chosen by God."[10]

So much for the past. As to the future, Danilevsky predicted that "Russia is virtually the only government that has never had (and in all probability will never have) a political revolution, that is to say a revolution having as its goal the limitation of the extent of power, the acquisition of all power or a portion thereof by any social stratum or by the whole mass of citizens— the expulsion of the legal ruling dynasty and the substitution of another."[11]

Danilevsky thus believed that the Slavic peoples were endowed with special virtues and predicted that their cultural-historical type, which was only at the start of its creative phase, was destined to supersede the Germano-Roman- or European-type. "The mainstream of universal history," he declared in his concluding paragraph, "originates in two sources on the banks of the ancient Nile. One, celestial, divine, flows through Jerusalem and Constantinople and reaches Kiev and Moscow in undisturbed purity; the other, earthly, human, divides its course into two main political and cultural channels—and flows past Athens, Alexandria, Rome—to the countries of Europe, temporarily drying up, but again being replenished by new, ever more abundant waters. On Russian soil a new spring breaks through, guaranteeing to the popular masses a just social-economic order. On the broad plains of Slavdom all these streams must flow together into one vast reservoir."[12] He then concluded his volume with a verse entitled "The Spring," published in 1835 by the Slavophil A. S. Khomiakov, which sings the praises of the spring in the bosom of Russia that is destined to allay the spiritual thirst of foreign peoples.[13] Khomiakov also left incomplete but voluminous notes on universal history to the middle ages, in which he sought to counteract European-centered historiography by exploring the religious and literary antiquity of the Slavic and Near Eastern peoples. A fragment of these notes was published in 1860 but a full edition was not issued until 1872, and it does not appear that Danilevsky was influenced by this work.[14]

The mixed metaphors and unnatural hydrography that characterize the tortured course of this bifurcated mainstream flowing from the banks of the Nile, reflect in an extreme form the logical confusion that characterizes some of Danilevsky's thinking. His *Russia and Europe* also includes so much emotional misinformation both about general history and about European politics that one is inclined to dismiss it as the irrational ramblings of a rabid nationalist or at least as a dire warning to natural scientists that they should stick to their last. Yet interest in Danilevsky's ideas has grown because he touched on certain themes that have been of continuing concern to later thinkers.

In the realm of historical theory, Danilevsky's conception of cultural-historical types, or of "civilizations" as we would call them now, has become one of the important structural features of recent efforts to interpret world history. There is an unresolved controversy as to the origin of this concept, but it appears to have been original with him to a considerable degree. Heinrich Rückert used the terms "cultural-historical" and "type," separately in this *Lehrbuch der Weltgeschichte in organischer Darstellung* (2 vols.; Leipzig 1857), and his typology of civilizations was somewhat similar to Danilevsky's. It is possible that Danilevsky adopted Rückert's terminology, but there is no definite evidence that he had ever read the German's work. There is also considerable doubt whether Spengler knew of Danilevsky's work, despite certain striking similarities in their conceptions of the structure of historical development and the destiny of European civilization.[15]

The significance of Danilevsky's work in this respect thus lies not as a predecessor of the twentieth-century historians who have based their work on the comparative study of civilizations. It lies rather in the fact that, in all likelihood independently of earlier students of civilization and without direct influence on later historians, he formulated a conception of civilizations that has proven to be useful as a means of organizing the complex materials of history. Not only Spengler, but more recently Arnold J. Toynbee, Alfred L. Kroeber, Pitirim A. Sorokin, Walter Schubart, and Rushton Coulborn, have all based their interpretations on "cultures" and "civilizations"—although none have employed these terms in the same way or reached the same conclusions as Danilevsky.[16]

Another of Danilevsky's themes that has come to fruition in the twentieth century, although again not as a direct result of his influence, is his advocacy of the formation of a Russian sphere of influence in Eastern Europe. He devoted two chapters of *Russia and Europe* to elaborating his conception of an all-Slav union comprising the Slavic and Orthodox peoples of Eastern Europe, with Constantinople as a kind of federal capital. Russia was to be the dominant member of this union, with its capital transferred to Moscow. It was this union of Slavic (and non-Slavic) peoples that was to constitute the cultural-historical type that would inherit from the Germano-Roman the role of dominant world culture.[17]

It is easy to ridicule this all-Slav union as a goal of Russian foreign policy, for none of Russia's intended partners were interested either then or later in entering into such a relationship and all looked to Western Europe—as indeed did Russia itself—for the basic models in their effort to achieve a modern way of life. Moreover the Poles, Czechs, Slovaks, Croats, and Slovenes, although Slavs, were Catholic or Protestant; the Rumanians and Greeks were Orthodox but not Slavs; and the Hungarians and Albanians, along with numerous other minorities, were neither. Yet as the early course of the First World War revealed the full danger to Russia of the coalition of Germany and Austria-Hungary, and as the vast costs of the war came to demand war aims of a commensurate order of magnitude, the Allies acceded to Russia's request for a territorial settlement that was not very different from what Danilevsky had in mind. In 1915 Constantinople and adjacent territories were assigned to Russia in a secret treaty, and on the very eve of the March revolution in 1917 the Allies acceded to Russia's request for a dominant role in the postwar frontier settlements in Eastern Europe. No one can say how a victorious Tsarist government might have sought to reorganize Eastern Europe after a defeat of Germany and Austria-Hungary, but the predominant view among Tsarist policy-makers was that the peoples of this region should be given their independence or autonomy under some form of Russian hegemony.[18]

At the end of the Second World War, Russia came much closer to achieving this goal. As a result of its occupation of Eastern Europe, and in a large measure with the agreement of its allies, the U.S.S.R. gained effective influence over all of this region and made a strong claim for the right to establish military bases in the Turkish Straits in the vicinity of Constantinople, now Istanbul. This latter claim was firmly rejected, but the underlying goal of denying access to this region to any other military power or alliance system has been effectively maintained since 1945.[19] What in Danilevsky's day were the dreams of an extreme nationalist, have thus become realities of European politics.

Danilevsky's conception of a future world order likewise seems less visionary in the light of the subsequent evolution of international relations. His theory of history was cast in universal terms, but his central concern—reflected in the title of his work—was the danger that Russia would be engulfed by a worldwide European civilization. It is interesting to note in this connection that Danilevsky regarded the United States as occupying a unique status. It was a country that possessed great natural resources and it had never been burdened by the need to defend itself against powerful enemies. It could therefore devote its resources to technological progress and did not require a highly structured political system. This freedom to concentrate on technology at the expense of political and military needs, which was not possible under European conditions, let alone under Russian, was nevertheless bought at a price, according to Danilevsky, for if the United States had possessed a powerful standing army it would have been able to solve promptly and in an orderly manner the political differences that led to a costly civil war.[20]

Although the United States—and the other English-speaking outposts in the new world—should logically have been incorporated in some form into the Germano-Roman historical type, Danilevsky did not discuss the question in these terms. The importance of the United States in his scheme of things was as a third center of power, collaborating with Slavdom to keep Europe in its place. The world order that he envisaged was thus one in which Europe, the United States, and Slavdom would be the three centers of power, and to these he assigned spheres of influence that encompassed the world: to Europe—Africa, Australia, and the southern peninsulas of Asia; to the United States—The Americas; to Slavdom—western, central and eastern Asia.[21]

Many things have changed since Danilevsky's day, and a United Nations now provides a common forum for all peoples. Yet the idea of a regional organization of the world has not been without responsible advocates, and it continues as one of the realities of international relations.

Churchill's original conception of a postwar world order envisaged a number of regional units—the United States, United Europe, the British Commonwealth and Empire, the Soviet Union, South America, and several others undefined in Asia and Africa—that would in turn send representatives to a Supreme Body.

The United Nations itself recognizes the principle of regionalism in its provision for permanent and nonpermanent membership in the Security Council. Moreover the United States, the United Kingdom, and Russia did in fact cooperate to contain an Axis Europe during the Second World War; the European Union movement seeks to create a continental organization that would in a significant degree counterbalance the United States and the Soviet Union; and China is evolving its own sphere of influence.

To note these various ways in which some of Danilevsky's conceptions have evolved is not to trace these developments to his influence or to attribute to his theories a predictive value that they did not possess. The list of his views that were totally erroneous is much longer, and arose from his fundamental misunderstanding of European politics and especially his identification of Germany with "Europe."

III

Nikolai Aleksandrovich Rozhkov, unlike Danilevsky, was a professional historian. He was born in 1860 in the province of Perm, his father was a schoolteacher who eventually rose to be inspector of schools in Ekaterinburg (now Sverdlovsk), and he studied history at the University of Moscow. As a typical student of the 1880's he participated in political demonstrations, and in his student years he became acquainted with Marxism. While completing his professional training he taught classical languages, and from 1898 to 1906 he was a lecturer in history at the University of Moscow. He taught at a number of other institutions in the course of his career.

In the course of the revolution of 1905 Rozhkov became actively involved in politics, joining the Social Democratic party and associating himself with its Bolshevik wing. For a while he was close to Lenin, seeing him frequently and participating with him in political activities, although they were never in complete agreement as to policy. During these turbulent years Rozhkov devoted himself largely to journalism and organizational work, and in 1907 he attended the second congress of the Bolshevik party in London and was elected to its central committee. In the following year he was arrested, however, and after two years in jail he was exiled to Siberia.[22]

In Siberia Rozhkov continued to engage in journalism, but he gradually moved away from the extremist point of view represented by Lenin. He now contributed articles to the Menshevik press that emphasized the profound changes that Russia was undergoing and advocated evolutionary reforms rather than violent revolution. This infuriated Lenin, who now regarded him as a renegade, and in a public address in Paris in November 1911 he singled out Rozhkov for attack as a "liberal" and a "liquidator."[23] These were two of the harshest epithets in Lenin's vocabulary, the latter term referring to those who wished to "liquidate" revolutionary violence and substitute in its place evolutionary reforms.

Rozhkov returned to the capital as a Menshevik immediately after the fall of the Romanov dynasty, and served for a few months as assistant minister of posts and telegraph in the Provisional Government. His differences with Lenin were intensified during this period, and he was jailed twice in the early 1920's. Lenin never forgave him his defection, and in 1922 insisted that his Politburo reverse a decision to permit Rozhkov to reside in Moscow.[24] Only after Lenin's death was Rozhkov permitted to resume a more or less normal career.

Rozhkov must have been a man of enormous energy, for despite his political activity his bibliography lists no less than four hundred titles. Many of these were short articles and reviews, but they included a number of substantial works of scholarship. His principal works of conventional history were *The Peasant Economy of Muscovite Russia in the Sixteenth Century* (1899), and *The Origins of Autocracy in Russia* (1906). Many of his briefer writings reflect an interest in sociology, and his *Survey of Russian History from a Sociological Point of View* (1905), to the middle of the seventeenth century, anticipates some of the characteristic views of his later work.[25] Not until he withdrew from politics after 1917 did Rozhkov produce another major work. He left the Menshevik party in 1924, and during the remaining three years until his death in 1927 he was politically inactive. For four years after the revolution he was rector of the Second Pedagogical Institute in Leningrad, and he continued to be active in historical circles. The twelve volumes of his principal work, *Russian History from a Comparative-Historical Viewpoint (Fundamentals of Social Dynamics)*, appeared in Moscow between 1919 and 1926.[26]

In the period between Danilevsky and Rozhkov, the only Russian historian who devoted serious attention to the problem of mankind as a subject of history was N. I. Kareev. Kareev was the leading Russian historian of modern Europe, and is best known for his seven-volume *History of Western Europe in Modern Times* (1892–1916). He was also interested in the theoretical aspects of history, and his doctoral dissertation was concerned with *Fundamental Problems of the Philosophy of History*

(1883; 3rd ed., 1897). In this early work he was concerned with mankind and with the idea of progress, which he interpreted in the conventional liberal sense of his day. His later theoretical works developed these themes further.[27] Although he did not write a world history, he published two short handbooks which set forth a scheme of world history.[28]

Kareev saw history as evolving from a diversity of national histories to a worldwide unity under European hegemony resulting from Western technical progress. He believed that Russia was rapidly being Europeanized, especially as a result of the reforms of Peter the Great and the emancipation of the serfs, and that it was destined to attain a European level of development and to participate as one of the great European powers in the establishment of a worldwide European civilization. He was therefore sharply critical of the Slavophils, and especially of Danilevsky, for maintaining that Russia was developing along non-European or anti-European lines and was evolving a civilization distinct from and superior to that of Europe.[29]

Rozhkov was a contemporary of Kareev's, and came under many of the same influences, but from early in his career he leaned more toward a sociological, and particularly a Marxist, approach. What is nevertheless striking about Rozhkov's historical work, and his political career as well, was his independence of mind. His changes from academic life to politics, and in politics from Bolshevism to Menshevism and later to a nonparty status, appear to have been the result not of indecision but of significant developments in his conception of history and politics. His final work on comparative world history represented the culmination of this process.

In this work Rozhkov referred to himself as a Marxist, and he was widely respected by professional historians in the Soviet Union in the 1920's. He has the further distinction, moreover, of being the only professional historian, Russian or otherwise, to have elaborated a general interpretation of world history along Marxist lines between the two world wars. It is important to recognize, in this connection, that in Rozhkov's lifetime Marxism did not represent a fixed or rigid set of categories, but rather a general point of view which individual scholars were free to develop as they saw fit. In other words, it was not the practice in his lifetime to draw a sharp line between orthodox Marxists and "deviationists." From the point of view of the ruling party in the Soviet Union in the 1930's, Rozhkov was a deviationist by virtue of having left the Bolshevik party before the First World War. From the point of view of European Marxism, there is no reason not to accept Rozhkov's self-evaluation as a Marxist.

Rozhkov's interpretation differed from Danilevsky's in two significant respects: it was structured in terms of traditional politically organized societies, or countries, rather than in terms of "cultural-historical types"; and the course of development of these societies was one involving a number of specific stages rather than a more general life-cycle. Indeed it was Rozhkov's scheme of stages that is the most characteristic feature of his interpretation. He believed that all countries passed through nine stages before reaching socialism: (1) primitve society, (2) savage society, (3) prefeudal, or barbaric society, (4) the feudal revolution, (5) feudalism, (6) the gentry revolution, (7) gentry rule (the old regime), (8) the bourgeois revolution, and (9) capitalism.[30]

In his work Rozhkov placed special emphasis on what he called social statics and social dynamics, terms borrowed from physics that reflected the scientism that was popular in his day. By social statics Rozhkov meant the interrelationship of social phenomena considered in a state of equilibrium. Social dynamics, by contrast, was concerned with the process of change. Rozhkov's social statics was derived from the necessities of economic life that affect social relations and in particular class structure. Political structure and culture in turn reflect the interests of the dominant class. He also believed that each class had a psychological character—what behavioral scientists today would call a "style" or "value system"—that was reflected in their policies. His view of social dynamics was not as well formulated, and indeed at one point he remarked that it was too early to describe the nature of social change. At the end of his work, however, he hinted that change in history is like change in nature, which is to say that it is evolutionary in character.

Rozhkov's periodization did in fact represent an alternation between static and dynamic periods. Thus his feudal period—the tenth to fourteenth centuries in England, and the thirteenth to mid-sixteenth centuries in Russia—was preceded by a feudal revolution against barbaric society and followed by a gentry revolution. The succeeding static period of gentry rule— James I and Charles I in England and 1725 to 1861 in Russia—was followed by a bourgeois revolution and another static period of capitalism.[31]

Rozhkov's theory of world history met with a good many criticisms on the part of his colleagues, despite their respect for his scholarship. Their principal objection was that it was not Marxist, it did not relate historical events closely enough to the class struggle, and in this sense was not dialectical. They pointed out, for example, that his period of the gentry revolution from the beginning of the reign of Ivan IV to the end of the reign of Peter I lasted 192 years, whereas the stable period of gentry rule lasted only 136 (1725–1861). For the later Soviet Marxists, revolution was supposed to be a short period of the violent transfer of power from one class to another, between long periods in which there was gradual development. They also objected to the fact that he regarded the state as inherently above parties, and concerned with the general welfare, whereas conventional Soviet Marxism regarded the state as an instrument of the dominant class.[32]

In considering these criticisms there is of course no reason to regard the later Soviet Marxists as exclusive authorities on the Marxist interpretation of history. Marx himself, and his contemporaries and imitators in England, France, and Germany, were much more broadminded and flexible in their view of history. They did not take Marx's writings as a narrowly defined dogma, but regarded them rather as a general guide which each historian could elaborate as he saw fit within the general spirit of economic determinism. What is significant about Rozhkov's interpretation for our purposes is that he saw changes evolving as a result of economic processes acting on society and ultimately on politics, on political institutions. He believed that this was an inevitable development that required no particular initiative on the part of political leaders. Although he himself had been active in politics, he did not advocate a political program. He simply wrote as an historian, developing the situation as he saw it from where he sat.

Yet he sat in a Russia that had just undergone a revolution marking the transition from the ninth stage—capitalism—to the tenth and presumably final stage of socialism. In this sense he was not immune to the events of his time and he regarded Russia as being in the forefront of historical development. "In this manner the Russian revolution of 1917 and the succeeding years," he wrote in his concluding volume, "represent an endeavor that was completely unavoidable and necessary for the victory of the socialist, proletarian revolution over the old order in Russia. Obliged by virtue of its origins in the combination of Russian economic and social forces united with ideological and practical scientific socialism, the Russian revolution and the state created by it constituted factors of highest importance in the task of achieving the victory of socialism throughout the world. To the question posed to the Russians by Vladimir Solovyov, what kind of an East do you wish to be—the East of Xerxes or the East of Christ— we can now reply that there is a third solution—history has made Russia the East of Marx, Engels, Plekhanov, and Lenin, a model of the confluence of the traditions of the West and of the East for the solution of the most important question of the contemporary era."[33]

IV

The third original history of the world written in Russia is the *Universal History* in ten volumes, prepared by an editorial committee under the chairmanship of Evgenii Mikhailovich Zhukov.[34] This is thus a collaborative work, written by some 400 authors, editors, consultants, and assistants. To this extent the biography of its editor-in-chief is not as significant for an understanding of this work as are those of his predecessors. Zhukov's life is nevertheless of interest since he is a typical Soviet "organization man" and is today the principal organizer of historical work in the Soviet Union. Born in 1907, he was trained as a diplomatic historian and his principal work is a collaborative history of international relations in the Far East from 1870 to 1945 which he edited. He joined the Communist Party in 1941 and since 1957 he has occupied the critical position of Scientific Secretary of the Department of History of the Academy of Sciences of the U.S.S.R.—a position that makes him the principal administrative officer and party guide for historical research in the Soviet Union. In addition to being chairman of the editorial committee of the *Universal History,* he is the leading historian of the Academy of Social Sciences of the Central Committee of the Communist Party of the Soviet Union, a member of the editorial board of the *Large Soviet Encyclopedia,* and a member of the boards of directors of the All-Union Society for the Dissemination of Political and Scientific Knowledge, the Soviet Committee for the Defense of Peace and the Soviet Committee for the Solidarity of Afro-Asian Countries.[35]

It is interesting to note that the introduction of modern organizational methods into the writing of history has also added to the length of the product. Danilevsky's book was 557 pages in length, or about 200,000 words by rough count; Rozhkov's 12 volumes add up to 4,195 pages and about 1,260,000 words; and Zhukov and his colleagues wrote ten much larger volumes of about 2,400,000 words.

The organization of the *Universal History* reflects the interpretation of Marxism-Leninism that has been elaborated in recent years by Soviet ideologists. As compared with Rozhkov's version of Marxism, that of Zhukov not only provides a more rigid and clear cut periodization of historical developments but also relates history more closely to contemporary international affairs and to a program of future action.

In organizing his world history, Zhukov rejects the concept of "cultural-historical complexes," or civilizations, on the ground that they tend to emphasize the achievements of the more civilized peoples at the expense of others who are treated as nonhistorical peoples outside the range of history. "World history," he has written, "is the history of all nations."[36] The terminology that Zhukov and his colleagues use to describe the development of human society will be familiar to those acquainted with Marxism. The basis of change in history is the production of material goods, the development of productive forces, and the productive relations of peoples. Thus change takes place not through the automatic influence of economic laws but through individuals, classes, and the popular masses. The superstructure of institutions is altered as a result of changes in the economic base, but the superstructure may also influence the development of society.

"Universal history is a progressive process. Its movement forward is determined primarily by the productive forces of society, the development and perfection of the implements and means of production."[37] Historical development is presented in terms of five main progressive periods—the primitive communal system, slavery, feudalism, capitalism, and socialism. These periods are of long duration and they are separated by shorter periods of revolutionary transition. The main periods are defined in terms of the relatively more advanced countries of each epoch—and in effect slavery, feudalism, and capitalism correspond roughly to the traditional periods of ancient, medieval, and modern history. It is nevertheless recognized that no two peoples make these various transitions at the same time, and indeed some have never advanced beyond the primitive or slave-owning stage. Thus the modern era in general starts with the "bourgeois revolution" in England in the mid-seventeenth century, and in France in 1789, and these two countries are still capitalist. In Russia the transition from feudalism to capitalism was not made until 1861, but there capitalism lasted only until 1917 when Russia made the transition to socialism.[38]

The new Soviet *Universal History* represents a rather incongruous combination of features. It is in many respects a scholarly and thorough account, with many illustrations and excellent maps. Much of the narrative concerning specific issues is conventional by Western standards, and the traditional periodization of ancient, medieval, and modern history is not only retained but extended from Europe to the entire world. Superimposed on this framework, however, is a Marxist-Leninist interpretation that sees all of history as moving inevitably toward communism. This higher interpretation rests on propositions that are assumed, and no effort is made to demonstrate them or argue the Marxist-Leninist case in comparison with other interpretations.

This version of world history appears to have the propaganda mission of arguing the inevitability of the victory of communism throughout the world. The general tendency of this propaganda line is reflected in a major doctrinal article written by Zhukov in 1963. In this article he argues that, as a result of the Second World War, the basis of socialism has grown from an isolated U.S.S.R. to a "world socialist system" consisting of fourteen states under communist governments and their allies in other countries. "The character and content of the world revolutionary process in the contemporary epoch," Zhukov maintains, "consists of the merging of the struggle against imperialism of peoples building socialism and communism, of the revolutionary movement of the working class in capitalist countries, and of the national-liberation struggle of oppressed peoples, into the single stream of the movement toward general democracy."[39] He illustrates the inevitability of the world socialist system by asserting that, whereas in 1917, 77 per cent of the territory and 69 per cent of the peoples of the world were colonial, today only 7.6. per cent of the territory and 1.5 per cent of the peoples are under colonialism. This, Zhukov asserts, "is a result of the 45-year support by the U.S.S.R., and more recently of other socialist countries, of the national liberation movements."[40]

Zhukov sees as the main problem in the years immediately ahead the growth of the world socialist system until it encompasses all the peoples of the world. This he envisages as taking place primarily by peaceful means, the precise nature of which will differ from country to country. In the more advanced countries, including the United States, it is a question of the working class gradually taking power from the bourgeoisie. In the case of the less developed societies, it will take the form of a conflict between "capitalism" and "socialism," with domestic revolutions being a frequent occurrence. He also envisages the possibility that in some instances revolutionary wars may be started by peoples seeking to liberate themselves from colonialism. He maintains that when this occurs the Soviet Union is prepared to support such wars in a comprehensive fashion since these are just wars. In general, however, the current Soviet view asserts that the spread of socialism will take place not by war, and certainly not by international nuclear war, but by the steady pressure exerted at all levels on the part of those favoring the Soviet form of socialism. It is significant that in presenting his case, Zhukov is particularly concerned with the argument of the Chinese Communists that force should be used more often. It is his view that "the international Communist movement on the basis of a profound analysis of the relationship of the class strength in the countries being liberated and of the international arena, has reached the conclusion that the further development of these countries is possible in a noncapitalist manner, specifically by means of the creation of national democratic governments. Advancement in this manner will safeguard the struggle of the working class, the peasantry, and all democratic forces for bringing to a conclusion the anti-imperialist democratic revolution and as an end result can lead to socialism."[41]

The ten-volume history concludes on a similar note of confidence. It sees victory for "socialism"—in the Marxist-Leninist sense—as being achieved by revolutions of national liberation with the active participation of all progressive forces. The course of contemporary international affairs is described in terms of a duel between the democratic and progressive peoples under the leadership of the Communist and workers' parties, and the rightwing bourgeois forces supported by England and the United States. "The conflict between these two tendencies has taken on the character of a struggle for political leadership, for the hegemony of the national-liberation movements."[42]

A postscript is devoted to a review of the materialistic interpretation of history. It sees the fundamental course of historical development as the transition from lower to higher social and economic formations. Only the materialistic interpretation of history understands the nature of the laws governing this development, and appreciates that it is a development that can be carried out only through revolutionary action. To this extent the fate of peoples is in their own hands. In this effort, the more advanced peoples can help the less advanced. "In the end, the main result of universal history is mankind itself and the contemporary world in all the complexity and contradictions of its development which, in spite of exceptional diversity of forms and variations, nevertheless distinctly reveals its dominant and definite tendency—the movement toward communism."[43]

V

The most striking feature of these interpretations of world history is that they all reach the same conclusion: Russian institutions and values as they are evolving and are likely to evolve in generation or two after the writers' lifetimes represent the culmination of world history. If changes continue to occur after the culmination is achieved, they would have to take place within the framework of the Russian-led civilization, for there is nothing to indicate that some further or better civilization will succeed that of Russia at some future time.

Danilevsky was the least deterministic of the three, for he foresaw that his eleventh "cultural-historical type" would emerge only if the Russian government succeeded in carrying out the policies that he advocated. Rozhkov was a scholar who believed in the inevitability of socialism and in the primacy of Russia in achieving socialism first in 1917, but his eyes were turned toward the past rather than toward the future. Zhukov and his colleagues for their part, are fighters on the frontiers of a world socialist movement which they see as already having turned the corner toward worldwide acceptance.

There is much of value in all three accounts, for they represent the work of vigorous and active minds seeking to understand the past and the role of their country in that past. Yet their efforts must also be recognized as distortions of world history and of the age-old effort of man to understand his destiny. They are distortions because of their parochial ethnocentricity and their insistence that one chosen people is destined to lead the world for all future time. A good world history seeks to overcome parochialism rather than to sustain it, to base its interpretation on the entire experience of mankind rather than on just one part of it, and to formulate hypotheses about this experience rather than to present conclusions that claim the authority of immutable laws.

The interest in these three world histories lies less in their contribution to scholarship than in their reflection of certain main trends in the perception of their international environment on the part of Russia's leaders. Danilevsky was an isolated individual, and his ideas were more idiosyncratic then representative of the main trends of Russian thought in the latter half of the nineteenth century. He nevertheless expressed views which won wide support in the 1870's and 1880's, especially among leading elements of the Russian political elite. Similarly Rozhkov, although he broke with Lenin in the course of the revolution, and was out of tune with the later Stalinist historiography, was the first and for 30 years the only historian to offer an interpretation of world history that gave a key position to the Russian revolution from a Marxist standpoint. The *Universal History* edited by Zhukov, for its part, provides an official interpretation in the formal sense and reflects the views of the Central Committee of the Communist Party of the Soviet Union.

What the interpretations conveyed by these accounts suggest is that the sacrifices required by a society engaged in the effort to modernize can be sustained more easily if accompanied by a belief that this effort will achieve an honored place in "world history." Just as countries in the throes of a great war come to believe that right is on their side, and have no difficulty in attracting scholars to the task of writing history in support of this view, so in the heat of rapid political, economic, and social change it is not uncommon for expressions of confidence in the future to take the form of new interpretations of history. World histories represent the ultimate form taken by such interpretations, since they serve to relate individual peoples to their total environment in time and space.

World histories are most likely to be written in countries which combine a pride in their history and a traditional sense of destiny with a somewhat retarded position by comparison with societies most advanced in the process of modernization. Turkey, China, and Japan, among others, share these characteristics with Russia. They started the process of rapid political, economic, and social change somewhat later than the West European and English-speaking countries, so they must work all the harder to overtake and surpass. This phenomenon is not limited to countries such as these, however, for what is Toynbee's message if it is not that Western Christendom must learn from the mistakes of the past if it is to fulfill its destiny? A milder and less distorted form of such interpretations is represented by the course in "Western Civilization" commonly offered to college students to convey the message that the "West" is in the forefront of mankind and that the destiny of the "non-West" is to become as much like the West as possible if it wishes to be "in." The related doctrine of "Westernization" is similarly biased.

To say that such views expressed in the form of world history are closely related to the psychological needs of the readers for whom they are intended, is not to suggest that the authors are not sincere or scholarly. The problems to which historians apply their scholarship are normally those to which they are led by their own life experience. As is the case with political and religious leaders, it is only the exceptional scholar who can lift himself above immediate concerns and seek to formulate generalizations that depart from the conventional wisdom of his contemporaries. We may not have a high regard for the theoretical qualities of the historical interpretations developed by Danilevsky, Rozhkov, or Zhukov and his colleagues, but they are of great interest for the study of the perceptions of Russian leaders.

NOTES

1. Harold and Margaret Sprout, *The Ecological Perspective in Human Affairs* (Princeton 1965), pp. 117–123.

2. Good recent interpretations of the dialogue between Russia and Europe are available in Alexander von Schelting, *Russland und Europa im russischen Geschichtsdenken* (Bern 1948) and V. V. Zenkovsky, *Russian Thinkers and Europe* (Ann Arbor 1953), and more generally in Thomas G. Masaryk, *The Spirit of Russia* (2nd ed., 2 vols.; London: 1955); Dmitrij Tschizewskij and Dieter Groh, in their *Europa und Russland: Texte zum Problem des westeuropäischen and russischen Selbstverständnisses* (Darmstadt 1959), have brought together thirty-six statements of the problem of Russia and Europe ranging in time from G. W. Leibniz to B. H. Sumner.

3. The fullest accounts of Danilevsky's career and ideas, apart from that of N. N. Strakhov (see footnote 4), are J. J. Skupiewski, *La doctrine panslaviste d'après N. J. Danilevsky* (Bucarest: 1890); Konrad Pfalzgraf, "Die Politisierung und Radikalisierung des Problems Russland und Europa bei N. J. Danilevskij." *Forschungen zur osteuropäischen Geschichte*, Vol. I (1954), pp. 55–204; and Robert E. MacMaster, *Danilevsky: A Russian Totalitarian Philosopher* (Cambridge: 1967). Briefer accounts are available in Frank Fadner, *Seventy Years of Pan-Slavism in Russia: Karazin to Danilevskii, 1800–1870* (Washington, D.C. 1962), pp. 314–338; Boris Mouravief, "L'histoire a-t-elle un sens? La doctrine de Danilevski et son developpement possible," *Schweizerische Zeitschrift für Geschichte*, Vol. IV (1954), pp. 449–477; Pitirim A. Sorokin, *Modern Historical and Social Philosophies* (rev. ed., New York 1963), pp. 49–71, 205–243; and Edward C. Thaden, *Conservative Nationalism in Nineteenth-Century Russia* (Seattle 1964), pp. 102–115.

4. *Rossia i Evropa* [Russia and Europe] was first published serially in 1869 in the journal *Zaria,* and in the book form in 1871. Four further editions were published between 1888 and 1895. The book carried the subtitle *Vzgliad na kulturnyia i politicheskiia otnosheniia Slavianskago mira k Germano-Romanskomu* [An inquiry into the cultural and political relations between the Slavic world and the Germano-Roman]. The version cited here is the third edition (St. Petersburg 1888), with an extended biographical foreword by N. N. Strakhov, v–xxxii.

5. *Danilevsky,* pp. 38–94.

6. *Ibid.,* 95–118.

7. *Ibid.,* 119–171.

8. *Ibid.,* 516–522.

9. *Ibid.,* 523–525.

10. *Ibid.,* 525.

11. *Ibid.,* 534.

12. *Ibid.,* 556–557.

13. "Kliuch," *Polnoe sobranie sochinenii Alekseia Stepanovicha Khomiakova,* Vol. IV (8 vols.; Moscow 1900), pp. 216–217.

14. "Zapiski o vsemirnoi istorii" [Notes on universal history], *Ibid.,* Vols. V–VII; the view of history reflected in these notes is discussed in A. Gratieux, *A. S. Khomiakov et le mouvement slavophile* (2 vols., Paris 1939), Vol. II, pp. 50–101; Orest Miller has treated the relationship of Khomiakov and Danilevsky in "Evropa i Rossia v vostochnom voprose" [Europe and Russia in the Eastern Question], *Slavianstvo i Evropa* (St. Petersburg 1877), pp. 264–315.

15. This is discussed in Robert E. MacMaster, "The question of Heinrich Rückert's influence on Danilevskij," *American Slavic and East European Review,* Vol. XIV (1955), pp. 59–66; and also in Pfalzgraf, pp. 194–202; N. Strakhov, "Istoricheskie vzgliady G. Riukherta i N. Ia. Danilevskago" [The historical views of H. Rückert and N. Ia. Danilevsky], *Russkii Vestnik,* Vol. CCXXXIV (October 1894), pp. 154–183; and A. L. Kroeber and Clyde Kluckhohn, *Culture: A Review of Concepts and Definitions* (New York 1963), 53–54, 286–288.

16. On this question, see Hans Joachim Schoeps, *Vorläufer Spenglers: Studien zum Geschichtspessimismus im 19. Jahrhundert* (Leiden 1953), 50 n.31; Robert E. MacMaster, "Danilevsky and Spengler: A new interpretation," *Journal of Modern History,* Vol. XXVI (June 1954), pp. 154–161; Hans Meyer, "Oswald Spengler und Seine Vorläufer," *Stimmen der Zeit,* Vol. CLXIX (October 1961), pp. 33–45; and Klaus von Beyme, *Politische Soziologie im zaristischen Russland* Vol. 52 (Wiesbaden 1965), pp. 52, 100–101. Useful earlier interpretations are Arthur Luther, "Ein russischer Vorläufer Oswald Spenglers," *Alere Flammam* (Leipzig 1921), 51–59; and M. Shvarts, "Shpengler i Danilevskii (Dva tipa kulturnoi morfologii)" [Spengler and Danilevsky (Two types of cultural morphology)], *Sovremennyia Zapiski,* Vol. XXVIII (1926), pp. 436–456.

17. Danilevsky, pp. 398–473.

18. On Russian war aims in Eastern Europe, see especially Alexander Dallin, and others, *Russian Diplomacy and Eastern Europe, 1914–1917* (New York 1963).

19. John A. Lukacs, *The Great Powers and Eastern Europe* (New York 1953), pp. 569–677, summarizes these developments.

20. Danilevsky, pp. 543–545.

21. *Ibid.*, p. 463.

22. The principal accounts of Rozhkov's career are in two series of articles, one in the journal *Katorga i Ssylka*, No. 32 (1927), including Rozhkov's brief autobiography (pp. 161–165), and sketches by L. S. Fedorchenko (pp. 165–172), N. Chuzhak (pp. 172–183), N. Teterin (pp. 183–189), and V. Bogoiavlensky (pp. 189–191); and a second series in the *Uchenye Zapiski Instituta Istorii RANION*, Vol. V (1928), including E. A. Morokhavets, "Kratkie biograficheskie svedeniia o N. A. Rozhkova" [A brief biographical account of N. A. Rozhkov] (pp. 7–14), N. Stepanov, "Politicheskaia deiatelnost N. A. Rozhkova" [The political activity of N. A. Rozhkov] (69–128), M. M. Bogoslovsky, "Iz vospominanii o N. A. Rozhkova" [From recollections of N. A. Rozhkov] (pp. 129–145), V. I. Nevsky, "N. A. Rozhkov—Revoliutsioner" [N. A. Rozhkov as a revolutionary] (pp. 146–156), and A. A. Gaisinovich, "Rozhkov—Uchitel" [Rozhkov as a teacher] (pp. 157–163).

23. V. I. Lenin, "Manifest liberalnoi rabochei partii" [The manifesto of the liberal workers' party], *Polnoe Sobranie Sochinenii*, Vol. XX (5th ed.; Moscow 1961), pp. 396–410.

24. Louis Fischer, *The Life of Lenin* (New York 1964), pp. 631, 634, 636.

25. *Obzor russkoi istorii s sotsiologichskoi tochki zreniia* (2 vols.; Moscow 1905).

26. *Russkaia istoriia v sravenitelno-istoriicheskom osveshchenii (Osnovy sotsialnoi diamiki)* (12 vols.; Moscow 1919–26).

27. Kareev's principal theoretical works are *Osnovnye voprosy filosofii istorii* [Fundamental problems of the philosophy of history] (Moscow 1883; 3rd ed., 1897); and *Lektsii po obshchei teorii istorii* [Lectures on the general theory of history] (2 vols.; Moscow 1913–15), of which the first volume is on the theory of historical knowledge and the second on the theory of historical process. Kareev's position in Russian historiography is discussed in M. N. Tikhomirov, M. V. Nechkina, and others, *Ocherki istorii istoricheskoi nauki v SSSR* [Essays on the history of historical studies in the USSR] (3 vols.; Moscow 1955–63), Vol. III, pp. 260–262, 474–487.

28. *Glavnyia obobshcheniia vsemirnoi istorii* [The main themes of universal history] (Moscow 1903; 2nd ed., 1905); and *Obshchii khod vsemirnoi istorii* [The general course of universal history] (Moscow 1903).

29. See especially the concluding chapter on Russia's position in universal history, in *Obshchii khod vsemirnoi istorii*, pp. 278–299; and Kareev's critique of Danilevsky in "Teoriia kulturno-istoricheskikh tipov" [The theory of cultural historical types], *Sobranie sochinennii* (3 vols.; St. Petersburg 1912–13), Vol. II, pp. 67–107.

30. Rozhkov, *Russkaia istoriia*, Vol. I, pp. 21–22.

31. *Ibid.*, Vol. VII, pp. 3–171; and Vol. X.

32. The principal Soviet critiques of Rozhkov are R. A. Averbukh, "Evoliutsiia sotsiologicheskikh vozzrenii N. A. Rozhkova" [The evolution of the sociological views of N. A. Rozhkov], *Uchenye zapiski Institute Istorii RANION*, Vol. V (1928), pp. 15–68; A. L. Sidorov, "Istoricheski vzgliady N. A. Rozhkova" [The historical views of N. A. Rozhkov], *Istorik-Marksist*, Vol. XIII (1929), pp. 184–220; and

N. A. Rubinshtein, ***Russkaia istoriografia*** [Russian historiography] (Moscow 1941), pp. 559–575.

33. Rozhkov, ***Russakaia istoriia,*** Vol. XII, p. 347.

34. E. M. Zhukov, editor-in-chief, and others. ***Vsemirnaia Istoriia*** [Universal History] (Moscow, 10 vols.; 1956–65); there is a German translation (Berlin, 10 vols.; 1961–68). A briefer world history, ***Kratkaia Vsemirnaia Istoriia*** [Short universal history] (Moscow, 2 vols.; 1966), written by a team headed by A. Z. Manfred, includes many of the same collaborators as the ten-volume work and reaches the same conclusions.

35. ***Prominent Personalities in the USSR*** (Metuchen, N.J., 1968), p. 723.

36. E. Joukov, "Des principes d'une 'Histoire Universelle,'" ***Journal of World History,*** Vol. III (1956), pp. 529.

37. ***Ibid.,*** pp. 530–533.

38. ***Ibid.,*** 533.

39. E. Zhukov, "Natsionalno-osvoboditelnoe dvizhenie na novom etape" [The national-liberation movement at a new stage], ***Kommunist,*** Vol. XL (August 1963), p. 23.

40. ***Ibid.,*** p. 24.

41. ***Ibid.,*** p. 30.

42. ***Vsemirnaia Istoriia,*** Vol. X, p. 608.

43. ***Ibid.,*** X, p. 709.

PART TWO

Modernization: How Russia/USSR Differs from Other Countries

Modernization studies are concerned with the transformation of social values and institutions from traditional-rural-agrarian to rational-urban-industrial under the impact of the scientific and technological revolution, which can be traced back at least to the sixteenth century. From this perspective, the engine of history is the advancement of knowledge. Over time, all of the various premodern societies face the task of accepting and using knowledge and then adapting, each in its own way, to modern functions.

This perspective is different from that of doctrinaire Western liberalism, which tends to see the search for political freedom as the engine of history and regards the modern West as the model for other societies. This perspective also differs from that of the Marxists and Marxist-Leninists—and therefore also from that of the world system theorists—for whom the class struggle is the engine of history and who regard the Soviet Union or an idealized socialist society as the universally valid end product of modern change.

These distinctive approaches ask different questions and get different answers, but at the same time they are dealing with a common subject, share many conclusions, and have much to learn from each other. One should also note that modernization should not be confused with "progress." Societal transformation arises from the enhancement of the human capacity to exploit the environment. This enhanced capacity can be used equally to promote human welfare, as it has been by and large, or to destroy all human life.

There is no simple way to describe the vast complexity of modern change, but a few salient features of this process may be noted. Certainly one feature is the acceptance of modern knowledge. It also seems clear that political development has been characterized by an enhancement of the role of the state and the population's increased participation through electoral and other procedures. Economic growth spurred by industrialization is doubtless the most readily recognized feature of the process of modern change and is accompanied by increased literacy and education, urbanization, and a demographic transition to low birth and death rates.

The question of how societies evolve from traditional to modern forms and functions is equally complex. Many Western theorists, and to their own detriment leaders of the later-developing societies as well, used to maintain that modernity replaces tradition. This view implies that modern institutions and values are essentially West European and American achievements and that other societies throughout the world must simply repress or abolish their diverse cultural heritages and adopt Western institutions and values. This view was implicit in Peter the Great's effort to transform Russian society in the first quarter of the eighteenth century. Peter and his followers literally believed that the old Muscovite Russia with its Byzantine heritage must be destroyed and replaced by institutions borrowed from Western Europe. This outlook is symbolized by the great equestrian statue of Peter erected in St. Petersburg (now Leningrad) in 1782 during the reign of Catherine II. Peter faces the West, while the rear hoofs of his steed crush a serpent representing the evil ways of the past. In some respects Peter's reforms were more sweeping than Lenin's, but the basic institution of serfdom was retained until a second wave of reform under the administration of Alexander II freed the serfs in 1861.

Experience has shown, however, that in fact, tradition and modernity interact over the decades and centuries. The past is always with us, although it takes new forms. Many, perhaps most, traditional forms can be adapted to modern functions. An obvious example is the evolution of the British parliament from the Magna Carta in 1215 to the extension of the electorate in 1948 to all citizens age 18 or over. The underlying conception of no taxation without representation evolved, to be sure with considerable lag, with changing political, economic, and social circumstances.

CHAPTER 5

The Modernization of Russia/USSR

This essay concluded a rather awesome symposium in which thirty-eight specialists in six disciplines discussed the salient features of societal transformation in Russia and the Soviet Union in the century after the reforms of the 1860s. The essay compares the ways in which political development, economic growth, and social integration in Russia and the Soviet Union have followed the pattern established by the earlier modernizers. Because Russia entered the modern era with a cultural heritage significantly different in various respects from those of Western societies, this essay also explores the extent to which the features that distinguish the Soviet Union today from other advanced industrial societies can be explained in terms of this heritage.

It would be preposterous, of course, to maintain that there is some sort of automatic "transformation of societies from traditional-rural-agrarian to rational-urban-industrial institutions and values." This transformation involves intense political controversy and takes place as a result of the myriads of conflicting and contradictory choices and policies of leaders, political parties, and interest groups. No two parties, and for many purposes no two leaders, agree as to how this transformation should take place. Until very recent decades, there was little understanding on anyone's part as to what was involved. Much has therefore depended on chance, which one dictionary defines as "the unpredictable and unwilled element of an occurrence." If Nicholas II had been a less tradition-bound and more perceptive individual, the autocracy might have adapted more subtly to the processes of change that confronted it. If Lenin had died before 1917, the Bolshevik movement would have been much less dynamic, and its leaders in all likelihood would not have sought to seize power when they did. Thus both tradition and chance must be taken into account

Reprinted from "The Modernization of Russian Society," *The Transformation of Russian Society: Aspects of Social Change Since 1861*, Cyril E. Black, ed. (Cambridge, MA: Harvard University Press, 1960), 661–680: with the permission of the President and Fellows of Harvard University.

in seeking to understand the processes of transformation in Russia and the Soviet Union.

I

In interpreting the transformation of Russian society since 1861, it is useful to think in terms of the broad pattern of social change which is now commonly known as "modernization." Modernization is the process of change from an agrarian to an industrial way of life that has resulted from the dramatic increase in man's knowledge of and control over his environment in recent centuries. In Europe this process has been evolving for half a millennium or more, and in modern times the influence of European knowledge and institutions has spread to most other parts of the world.

Modernization in this general sense has come to be accepted as a desirable, if not indeed inevitable, change in human affairs. Yet it must be recognized that the transformation of traditional societies has been in many ways a vastly destructive process. Not only have governments, ruling classes, and systems of knowledge and belief been destroyed, but social institutions, personal values, and not infrequently the psychological security of the individual have been undermined. Even in the societies which were the first to modernize, where change took place gradually over a period of many generations, the destructive aspects of modernization have been apparent. In societies that have modernized more recently, under great pressure to compete with the earlier modernizers, one frequently has the impression that traditional institutions and values have been destroyed before their modern replacements were available. Now that mankind has discovered the means to destroy itself, many will no doubt question to what extent modernization can be equated with progress. In any event, it is clear that what is involved is a vastly complex and universally pervasive process of change.

What concerns us here, however, is not the destiny of mankind but the much more limited question of social change in Russia in the century since the emancipation of the serfs in 1861. It is significant that Russia was not one of the early modernizers, and that the new ideas and institutions came to Russia from Central and Western Europe in forms which the Russian government believed to be as much a threat to its security as an opportunity for the development of the peoples under its rule. The influence of the more modern societies was felt in Russia with rapidly increasing force from the seventeenth century on, and to the extent that their institutions were adopted it was rather for the purpose of protecting the traditional Russian way of life against foreign intrusions than for undertaking a fundamental modernization of Russian society. Indeed, in Russia as elsewhere, modernization seems to have come in two phases: the first defensive and superficial, and the second aggressive and more thoroughgoing.

Insofar as borrowings from the West could contribute to strengthening the autocracy and increasing state power, they were accepted with alacrity. The armed forces and bureaucracy were reconstructed, mines and factories were established, an academy of sciences was created, and the nobility was transformed into a class of higher civil servants. But care was taken not to disturb the condition of the great mass of the peasants, who lived in some form of service to the state or bondage to the nobility—and on whose labor, directly or indirectly, the welfare of their owners was based. Even the emancipation in 1861 was not intended to inaugurate an era of thoroughgoing modernization, although it very soon became clear that this would be its effect. The significance of 1861 for Russia, as far as such comparisons are valid, was thus somewhat similar to the change of pace which took place in Central Europe in the first half of the nineteenth century, in France and the United States at the end of the eighteenth century, and in England somewhat earlier. To the extent that one can construct a general pattern of modernization as a yardstick for social change in Russia, it must be based primarily on the European and American experience. Something can doubtless also be learned by comparing Russian developments with those in Japan and Turkey, which modernized at about the same time and under somewhat similar circumstances, the former at first more rapidly and the latter more slowly.

Although any generalizations about the course of social change in Russia must be regarded as highly tentative at this stage, in view of the shortcomings both of our knowledge about Russia and of the theoretical bases available for the interpretation of such knowledge, it nevertheless seems worthwhile to attempt answers to three rather general questions. To what extent has the course of social change in Russia since 1861 followed more or less universal trends, as far as these can be established on the basis of what we know about other societies? To what extent can Russian deviations from such universal trends be explained by certain historically formed traditions of Russian society? And, finally, to what extent can the course of modernization in Russia be attributed to contingent circumstances, and more specifically to individual leaders, political parties, and state policy?

Any attempt to suggest brief answers to sweeping questions must of necessity omit much of the detail which provides the richness and variety of history. Such an attempt also runs the risk of neglecting important distinctions of degree and emphasis which may account for significant contrasts within superficially consistent trends. This risk is particularly great when one is discussing general trends in a very controversial period of Russian history. Indeed, some maintain that Tsarist autocracy and Soviet totalitarianism are so different that any attempt to find continuities will meet with insuperable obstacles, whereas others see them as essentially similar. In any event, a particular burden is placed on the reader to distinguish between the secular trends under consideration here and the short-term developments which are equally important and were no doubt much more real to the participants. For these essential distinctions one must look to the more detailed discussion of individual aspects of social change. The reader will also recognize that "Russia" is used here as a general term embracing the wide variety of nationalities and cultures within the changing boundaries of the Russian Empire and the USSR. It is a measure of the shortcomings of our understanding of this country that it is so difficult to give due weight to the differences which characterize its many peoples.

II

In measuring social change in Russia by the yardstick of universal trends, it is useful to start with the area of government, since so many of the changes characteristic of modernization have taken place within a framework of political action.[1] In this realm, the most characteristic feature of modernization has no doubt been the growth of the functions and scope of authority of governments. Governments which once performed no more than a few political and military functions are now engaged in a vast number of activities involving not only the maintenance of order on the provincial and local levels, but also the education and welfare of the individual, the administration of communications, and the regulation of commerce and industry, wages and prices. If it were possible to construct a table showing the proportion of the gross national product that has been administered more or less directly in recent centuries by governments, it would no doubt reflect the growth in the functions which they perform. Even in the United States, which started out with a very decentralized federal structure, a main theme of its political and legal history has been the accumulation by the federal government of a wide variety of functions. Although the American political system is still relatively decentralized, the federal budget is now equivalent to about one fifth of the gross national product.

This growth in the role of government has been accompanied by an increasing identification of the government with the people, and this has been reflected in the development of political democracy in those societies where the prerogatives of the government traditionally have been limited and the dignity of the individual has been held in high respect. In these countries the rule of law, equality before the law, and representative government have been accepted as the goal of political development. This identification of government with the people has been accompanied by sentiment favoring national self-determination, particularly in the dynastic empires, and movements for national independence and unification have been a dominant theme of modern history.

Russia had a long tradition of autocracy at the time the serfs were emancipated, but there also the functions of the government grew rapidly after 1861. The areas of local administration which had been left to the landowning nobility under serfdom were now assumed in part by the government, and in addition it soon became involved in general education, the regulation of labor, economic development, and many other activities. Until 1917 important aspects of local affairs were left to the zemstvos, the local government organizations created in 1864. The central government kept a sharp and jealous eye on the zemstvos, but the latter expanded their activities steadily until 1917 when local authority was swept away in all but name. What had been an autocracy, in considerable degree restrained by custom and by circumstance, now became a totalitarian government concerned at least in theory with every aspect of Russian life. With the inauguration of the five-year plans and the increasing urbanization of Russian life, theory has been converted into practice. The Soviet government has now achieved a more total control over society than has any other modern government and in fact administers more or less directly some three quarters of the gross national product of the USSR.

In Russia also there has been an increasing identification of the government with the people and a growth of nationalism in these years, although to a much lesser degree than in Europe. Contemporary Western observers expected Russia to follow the European example fairly promptly once the serfs were emancipated, and indeed in a moment of exuberance the *New York Times* assured its readers that "Russia is on a sure, steady career of progress and reform. With the new provincial bodies, and the spread of common schools and newspapers (of which we hear such encouraging accounts), she will soon educate a mass of intelligent and orderly citizens who will be fully capable of governing themselves."[2] In actual fact, the zemstvos were representative only to a limited extent, and the Constitution of 1906 and the accompanying electoral law made reluctant provision for only a modest degree of representative government at the national level. A system of almost universal representation was prepared in 1917 by the Provisional Government for the elections to the Constituent Assembly, but this proved to be an end rather than a new beginning for representative government in Russia.

The struggle of the national minorities of the Russian empire for autonomy and independence followed a course somewhat parallel to that in the West, and after the revolution of 1905 substantial gains were made in the recognition of local rights. The First World War brought the liberation of some of the principal minorities, although at the end of the Second World War all these except the Poles and the Finns—along with some new territories—were once more annexed. The identification of government and people in the Soviet Union is reflected in the attention devoted to the forms and symbols, as distinct from the substance, of representative government and minorities' rights.

In the economic realm, modernization has meant a rapid increase in production as a result of technical improvements, a parallel growth in capital investments, the division of labor, expansion of trade, and a greater mobility of the factors of production. In general terms Russian economic development fits this pattern, although it has been interrupted by formidable changes in policy. In the periods of most rapid expansion—1890–1900, 1906–1917, and since 1928—the rate of growth of industry has equaled or surpassed that of Russia's rivals. Agriculture and domestic trade, on the other hand, have been relatively neglected. Also, throughout the period the state has played a much more active role in economic life than has been the case in most other societies.

Similarly, in the intellectual sphere Russian developments in the past century have in significant respects followed the course pioneered by the societies that modernized earlier. Scholarship in the humanities and social sciences expanded rapidly in the latter half of the nineteenth century, and Russia became part of the community of Western scholarship. There was an active interchange of ideas with the rest of the learned world, and Russian thought made numerous original contributions. In many aspects of literature and the arts, Russian achievements were unsurpassed. In the natural sciences, applied research was held back by the relatively low level of technology, but in theoretical work Russian scientists were productive. Intellectual activity was to a considerable degree interrupted by the revolution, and after the inauguration of the five-year plans it was increasingly harnessed to the needs of the state as interpreted by the Communist party. Under this policy selected branches of science and technology flourished, and the performing arts were generously provided for; but creative thought in the humanities, in the social sciences, and in some of the natural sciences worked under ever-tighter restrictions and in significant measure lapsed into silence.

Primary and secondary education were less immediately sensitive to changes in policy and grew steadily throughout the period when not interrupted by war or civil strife. Under the empire the government was slow to take up the idea of universal education, and much of the initiative was left to the zemstvos. Very substantial progress was made after 1905, however, and this was continued by the Soviet regime. By 1960, the literacy rate was rapidly approaching that of the most advanced countries, and educational facilities were available for universal primary and secondary education. The content of education was throughout the century subject to political control. Neither Tsarist nor Soviet educational policy favored freedom of thought, although the controls exercised by the latter were immeasurably tighter. With the exception of a decade of experimentation in the immediate postrevolutionary period, since 1861 emphasis has been placed on languages, literature (carefully screened), mathematics, and the natural sciences—the latter particularly stressed in the Soviet period—and on political orthodoxy based largely on the official version of history and on the approved religious or social doctrine. The content of political orthodoxy has of course changed radically as a result of the revolution, but the relationship of state to education, while greatly intensified since 1917, has been a constant theme. To this extent Russian educational policy has resembled in form, but with far greater intensity, that of the Continental European states.

The social structure of Russia has in the past century also evolved in a manner that is in many ways similar to that of the societies which modernized earlier. During the past century what may loosely be called Russia's elite, for want of a better term, has grown in size from perhaps two or three million to some fifteen million and has changed substantially in composition. These changes began in the latter part of the nineteenth century, when a rising generation of professional men and technicians was added to the traditional elite of noble landowners and state officials. This process was greatly accelerated in the first decades of the twentieth century, and at the same time the influence of the nobles declined even though they retained most of their formal privileges. The revolution of 1917 brought an end to these privileges, and perhaps as many as several hundred thousand members of the elite went into exile in the course of the civil wars. The Bolsheviks and their followers were now catapulted into a position of leadership, but many members of the prerevolutionary elite at the level of the bureaucracy and the professions continued to work in their old positions. It took another generation before an essentially new elite, educated under the Soviet regime and greatly enlarged to meet the needs of industrialization, was created. In the meantime the urban population has grown from 12 per cent of the population in 1861 to almost 50 per cent today, reflecting the fundamental impact of industrialization on the way of life of the mass of the population.

The family was much affected by these changes, in Russia as elsewhere. In size it has tended to shrink to the nuclear family, authority within the family has been more equally distributed, and women have gained greater freedom to work outside the home. The family has become more mobile, less bound by traditional social customs, and more closely reflects the values of the state and the developing mass society. There has also been an increasing social mobility as the requirements of industrialization have drawn more and more people into urban and professional life, as well as a gradual reduction in the differences among social strata as to opportunities for general education and technical training.

In the realm of values there has been in Russia, as in other modernizing societies, a gradual adjustment to the new knowledge and to the urban and industrial way of life. A traditional fatalism has given way to the belief that life can be mastered and society transformed. Perhaps because the Russian Orthodox Church was a state institution until 1917, it was slower than most Western churches to adjust to the challenge of modern ideas. In the last decades of the empire this challenge took the form within the church of support on the part of some priests of political liberalism and of reform of the church administration. The Provisional Government, during its brief existence, took the first steps toward separating church and state and curtailing the influence of the church on education. The Soviet government, for its part, has followed a policy of thoroughgoing secularization, undermining the church through a wide variety of indirect attacks and doing its best to win over the younger generation to atheism. At the same time, the Communist Party has recognized the continuing influence of the Russian Orthodox Church and, since its establishment as an autonomous institution in 1943, has employed it increasingly as an instrument of policy at home and abroad. The church has thus regained its formal status to a considerable degree. The government has also been relatively lenient with the Moslem religious bodies, although it has been less compromising in its treatment of the other minority faiths. It seems likely that popular religious feeling has declined somewhat more rapidly in Russia than in other modernizing societies, although it still retains a significant influence even among members of the younger generation.

There has likewise been an increasing attention paid to the welfare of the individual in Russia since 1861. This has been reflected not only in the steady growth of educational facilities, but also in the provisions for public medicine, economic assistance to the poor, and various types of social insurance. Since the latter part of the nineteenth century the Russian state has also been active in regulating the pay and working conditions of industrial labor. Under the empire these measures were taken in part by a paternalistic government and in part by the zemstvos which reflected local needs; in the Soviet period they have been expanded to meet the requirements of the continued growth of industry and adapted to the needs of the Communist Party. There has also been a growing recognition at the level of official policy of the desirability of greater cosmopolitanism in the treatment of national, political, and religious minorities. This trend was reflected especially after 1905 in the easing of the restrictions on public activities on the part of the minorities, and under the Provisional Government and in the Soviet period in the formal legal provisions for civil liberties. At the level of practice, on the other hand, in Russia as elsewhere, the strains of social change have brought to the surface deep-seated tensions—as evidenced by the pogroms under the empire and the extreme forms of political persecution in the Soviet period.

Scarcely less impressive than the development of Russia along the lines suggested above has been the destruction accompanying it. Not only have many customs and techniques become outmoded and left behind, but values and traditions that had stood the test of centuries have been cast aside. Indeed, it is in the realm of human values that the destructiveness of modernization has been most striking. In a manner parallel to that in other societies undergoing social change, but in a more extreme form, material values were deified at the expense of the dignity of the individual. The impulse of the nihilists in the 1860's to reject traditional values in the name of reason proved to be only the beginning of a growing tendency to believe that the goal of building a new world was important enough to justify any sacrifice. This phenomenon of people committing crimes in the name of ideals was one of the central preoccupations of Dostoevsky's thought, and he recognized that Russia was sharing in a widespread occurrence. "This . . . happens not only in our midst but throughout the world," he wrote in 1873; "it has been so from time immemorial, during transitional epochs, at times of violent commotions in people's lives—doubts, negations, scepticism and vacillation regarding the fundamental social convictions. But in our midst it is more possible than elsewhere, and precisely in our day. . . ."[3]

The belief that the end justifies the means formed an important element in the Leninist version of Marxism, which regarded the allegedly inexorable laws of a historically determined destiny as the only guides to action. This attitude had its natural culmination in a political system which did not balk at destroying millions of human lives in the name of "building socialism." As Dostoevsky noted, this attitude is by no means a uniquely Russian phenomenon. "There has been a slipping off of ancient restraints; a real *decivilization* of men's minds," wrote H. G. Wells in 1920,[4] and this is no doubt one of the fateful consequences of modernization. The examples of Nazi Germany and Communist China illustrate the extent to which the deification of a historically rationalized ideology can result in the destruction of human values.

These various ways in which social change in Russia during the past century has paralleled developments in countries that modernized earlier or at about the same time are trends of such a general character that they could hardly have been avoided by any regime in Russia, although they might have been delayed or accelerated in one respect or another. They deserve consideration, however, as the setting for a discussion of the more interesting question of the ways in which the course of Russian modernization has been unique.

III

The question of the role of Russian historical traditions in the course that social change has taken in that country is both simpler and more controversial than that of the relationship of Russian to general modernization. It is simpler because Russian historical traditions differ from those of the West in certain major respects on which there is fairly general agreement; more controversial because it involves seeking out continuities between the Tsarist and Soviet eras which the adherents of both find odious. It is nevertheless an essential exercise, for it is clear that the form a modern society takes is in a substantial measure dependent on the nature of its traditional values and institutions. The things that a society does may change very rapidly, but the way in which they are done continues to bear the imprint of age-old beliefs.

The special character of Russian modernization, which sets it somewhat apart from the Western pattern, can perhaps best be discussed in terms of three interrelated circumstances, not in themselves unique yet scarcely matched elsewhere in this particular combination: the predominant role of the state, Russia's backwardness and defensiveness in relation to the more modern societies, and certain characteristic attitudes and values.

The role of the state is no doubt the most obvious continuing trait of Russian society, and in the century since 1861 it has manifested itself in many ways. Throughout this period the state has had a virtual monopoly of political power, except for brief transitional phases of anarchy. The state has made provision for the organization and regulation of social groups. Through the instrumentality of legal institutions and of the political police it has kept a close control over all social, intellectual, and spiritual activities that might challenge its position. It has taken the primary initiative in economic growth through investment, ownership, supervision, and fiscal policy. Under its auspices, education, scholarship, and the performing arts have been developed. Indeed, it is difficult to point to a significant area of human activity in which the state has not participated throughout the century. The quality and purposes of this participation have of course varied significantly with policy and circumstance, but its existence and acceptance has been a continuing reality.

This dominant role of the state in modern Russia has deep roots and may be explained by a variety of historical circumstances. Geography played its role in giving Russia a land without natural frontiers—at least in its populated areas—and without significant mountains or other internal barriers. External influences also had some effects, for Byzantine autocracy was the principal political model for Russian statesmanship in its formative years, and for over two centuries Mongol rule exerted pressures both direct and indirect which tended to weaken resistance to central authority. In more modern times the poverty of Russia's land and the strength of her neighbors to the West have also played a role, for through the centuries Russian statesmanship has learned that domestic division can only lead to defeat and control by foreigners. After periods of profound civil strife, Vasily II, Ivan IV, and finally the Romanov dynasty emerged with successively increased authority, and a formula of statesmanship was hammered out which gave the tsar and his government authority over all in the realm. While Europe was moving from feudalism through various forms of limited monarchy and enlightened despotism to constitutional and representative government, Russia was evolving a form of autocracy which was in some degree limited only in the turbulent years from 1905 to 1917.

It is not difficult to describe the role that the state has played in Russian affairs, but to explore this role in all of its ramifications would go beyond the limits of this essay. One aspect, and it may indeed be one of the most important, is nevertheless pertinent to our problem. This is the role of the state in protecting a Russia that was backward by comparison with its principal neighbors, and in trying to redress the balance by means of a disproportionate exertion of national effort.

As a relative latecomer, Russia was confronted with the problem of modernizing on the basis of institutions and ideas borrowed from the very Western states with which it was competing and under circumstances in which failure might mean national defeat. Serfdom was one answer, for it served to mobilize the principal source of national wealth on terms considered at the time to be most favorable to the state. Reform of the army, bureaucracy, and nobility was another, for it provided the state with the technical means of playing a successful role in European affairs. Although Russia had one of the lowest per-capita national incomes in Europe, the size of the population and the manner in which its resources were concentrated in the hands of the state provided a solution to Russia's problem during the era in which agriculture and commerce were still the major sources of wealth. The turning point came in the first half of the nineteenth century, and the Russia which had turned back Napoleon was unable forty-three years later to prevent Anglo-French force from seizing Sevastopol. European industrialization is by no means the only explanation of this change in fortune, but from this defeat the conclusion was drawn that serfdom was no longer a sound basis for the autocracy.

Throughout the period since 1861, Russia has been under the pressure of competition felt by all the later modernizers, and the fact that it had a long tradition of national greatness only served to make this pressure more urgent. This position as a latecomer was not an unmitigated disadvantage, for it permitted Russia to import techniques and institutions which had been developed elsewhere as a result of many years of experimentation and at great expense. With the aid of massive infusions of state support, Russia was able to make rapid progress and in isolated fields of endeavor has surpassed its tutors. At the same time, the necessity of borrowing from its rivals has presented the state with a continuing challenge to its security. Alexander II is reported to have remarked that to wait until the serfs liberated themselves from below was the only alternative to liberating them from above, and throughout the century since emancipation the Russian state has felt the hot breath of history upon its neck. The tsar and his bureaucracy themselves undertook to serve as the modernizing elite and up to a point succeeded in maintaining their initiative. But the burden of tradition and of vested interests was too heavy to sustain this initiative, and neither Alexander III nor Nicholas II was capable of playing the role of autocrat-modernizer. Even such conservative and loyal modernizers as Witte and Stolypin came to be regarded as a threat to the autocracy, and the relations between ruler and ruled were strained to the breaking point during the First World War. The various potential heirs of the Tsarist system in 1917 all regarded themselves as modernizers, and after a brief struggle the succession was seized by the leaders best able to harness the popular desire for peace and land reform.

The course of social change in Russia has also been marked by certain characteristic attitudes and values, stemming in part from tradition and in part from the circumstances of modernization itself. Of the traditional attitudes, no doubt the most persistent has been the messianic belief, which can be traced back to the doctrine of the Third Rome formulated in the sixteenth century, in the rightness of Russian values. The belief that the Russians are a "God-fearing" people with attributes of human universality was perhaps most vigorously expressed by Dostoevsky, but it has been shared in one form or another by many Russians of whom the Bolsheviks are only the most recent. No doubt all peoples tend in some measure to become convinced of the universal validity of their views, but the Russian version of messianism has had deeper roots and more powerful political support than most.

Equally deep-rooted and no doubt much more widely held in Russia are the attitudes which seem to spring from the traditional way of life of the Russian peasant patriarchal family. In an era in which many millions of Russians have been transferred within a generation or two from the countryside to all levels of urban life, it can hardly be doubted that the attitudes and values characteristic of the former peasantry continue to have a powerful impact. Their patience and patriotism, their ambivalence with regard to neighbors and foreigners, their submissiveness when confronted by authority despite their frequent hostility to it—elements such as these give the Russian national character its distinctive features. It is indeed as though there were two Russias: the official Russia, powerful and implacable, and the popular Russia, submissive but frequently resentful. When studies have been made of the attitudes characteristic of a wider range of national groups, it will no doubt be possible to identify with greater accuracy the qualities that are peculiarly Russian.

Other attitudes may be traced more directly to Russia's position vis-à-vis the West in modern times, although in some instances these also have a traditional basis. The fear of foreign encirclement, a recurrent theme in Russian official thought, can be found in the writings of Ivan the Terrible. The assertion by Khrushchev that encirclement is a thing of the past, and that the Soviet Union is now becoming the encircler, may properly be regarded as a milestone in the Russian outlook if it proves to be genuine and lasting. The desire to match the West, in technology and productivity if not necessarily in values and institutions, is also a recurrent theme. If the victory over Napoleon gave the Russian government a certain complacency in the era of Nicholas I, his successors turned again to the West with almost the same unrelenting vigor as did the Russia of Peter the Great. This is particularly true of the Communists, who have systematically drawn on the experience of the West and have made "overtake and surpass" a major national slogan. This desire to borrow the technology of the more modern societies while rejecting their political and social values is by no means a purely Russian phenomenon, and indeed the virulently anti-Western modernizer is one of the more common types of leader in the newer states. With the exception of the short-lived Provisional Government, no Russian regime has given serious consideration to reproducing on Russian soil a political culture of a West European type.

Equally characteristic of Russia has been the position of the intelligentsia—deeply attached to their country, profoundly concerned with social problems, and yet in considerable measure alienated from the state. The intelligentsia was in fact defined as that group of intellectuals, the most productive in terms of the public discussion of Russia's problems, who did not have responsible official positions. They relied for their living on their literary and critical skills, if they did not have an inherited income, and not infrequently they lived in Siberian exile or abroad. As is so commonly the case with intellectuals in societies relatively late to modernize, they were torn between the European standards which they had set as their model and the reality which they saw around them. To follow uncompromisingly in the Western path meant in some degree to abandon Russia, and indeed not a few went to Europe to live as distinguished citizens of the world, returning to Russia only occasionally if at all and then usually under police surveillance. To accept Russian reality and to enter public service, on the other hand, meant to become an accomplice in some measure to the policing and censorship of free intellectual inquiry and to work within the relatively narrow framework of officially approved ideas.

If one defines intellectuals as those with higher education—as distinct from the special category of intellectuals known in Russia as the intelligentsia—it must be recognized that many intellectuals achieved distinction and influence in public service in the period of the empire. They also were keen students of the West and, while they did not leave a comparable treasure of creative writing, their memoirs and public documents frequently reflect a profound and responsible concern for the modernization of Russia.

In the Soviet era this dichotomy between the large number of university-educated officials and the small group of independent thinkers has persisted, although the issues are somewhat confused by the Soviet use of the term "intelligentsia" to describe the entire white-collar class which now numbers perhaps fifteen million. If one adheres to the earlier definitions, however, one can distinguish a continuing if limited intelligentsia of free-thinking individuals, critical of officially approved doctrines and standards, irked by the constant harassment of party hacks and security officers, and on occasion willing to take the risk of expressing their views in a variety of ways. The members of this intelligentsia are primarily writers and artists, but there is also evidence of unorthodoxy among natural scientists and other scholars. In many cases they are direct survivors or descendants of the prerevolutionary intelligentsia, but the group is also being replenished from new sources. In the 1920's they had a modicum of freedom, but in the 1930's many ended their days in labor camps. The Communist Party nevertheless values their prestige and skills, and is engaged in a continuous battle of wits and of numerous more or less subtle pressures to keep at least their publicized works within the narrow channel of orthodoxy.

The members of this small intelligentsia appear to have worked out a variety of viable compromises with the state authorities, by whom they are of necessity employed since there is no other source of livelihood except for the few who can be supported by friends and relatives. Their attitudes are not easy to evaluate, however, because little is known of their writings except as they are by chance published abroad or occasionally seen in unpublished form. To this group of free-thinking intellectuals must be added the many distinguished Russians who have sought freedom in exile, in some respects an equally difficult compromise, and who in the course of forty years have stimulated the intellectual life of the Western world with their acute appreciation of both Western and Russian attitudes. These, like their prerevolutionary forerunners, can trace their ancestry back to Prince Kurbsky, who in 1578 from his self-exile in Poland taunted Ivan the Terrible with having "shut up the kingdom of Russia—in other words, free human nature—as in a fortress of hell."[5]

Of the many controversies that have engaged Russian thought in modern times, the one that most concerns us here is the debate over the relationship of Russia to Europe. Was Russia bound to follow in the footsteps of Europe, as the reforms of Peter the Great seemed to imply, or did she have a parallel but distinct destiny? While the arguments in this prolonged debate, which has lasted in one form or another for some four centuries, are too intricate to be summarized here, it is of interest to touch briefly on the main themes as they have developed since 1861.

Of the principal participants in this debate, only the various branches of the liberal movement and the Menshevik wing of the Social Democratic Party can be said to have looked to Europe more or less unconditionally as the model for Russia to follow, although they differed in the theoretical basis of their reasoning. The other participants, again for a variety of reasons, saw Russia developing along its own distinct lines. The Tsarist government expected that the autocracy, supported by a modernizing bureaucratic elite, would continue to rule the masses in a paternalistic fashion. Conservative modernizers regarded Prussia and Japan as possible models. The Populists, and their successors in the Socialist Revolutionary Party, envisaged a modern society arising from a socialized peasantry without an intervening period of free-enterprise industrialization. The Bolsheviks, finally, employed the methods of the extremist wing of the Russian revolutionary movement in implementing what they considered to be a Marxist program. The Soviet state has worked out a formula for modernization that is in many respects quite distinct from European precedents, although it employs in a more drastic form some of the methods of exploiting labor which were characteristic of early capitalism.

In these various ways Russian traditions and attitudes have differed from those of the earlier modernizers and have confounded those who persist in interpreting Russian developments in terms of West European political and social values. These are no doubt only differences of degree, but they nevertheless comprise a distinctive political and social culture. Seen in a world-wide spectrum of modernizing societies, the Russian pattern resembles somewhat that of Turkey, Iran, Japan, and China. As societies with a tradition of vigorous, independent, and relatively centralized governments; modernizing at first defensively but in due course aggressively, and to a marked degree at the initiative of the state; borrowing wholesale from the West, but with a characteristically ambivalent attitude toward Western values and influences—they bear a certain resemblance to each other. This pattern of modernization is distinct not only from that of the West but also from that of the newer states of Asia and Africa.

IV

To say that the modernization of Russia has in very important respects followed the same course as in other societies, but that its style and manner have been significantly affected by certain characteristic Russian institutions and values, does not account for the many specific policies that have marked the course of social change since 1861. These must be explained rather by interests, points of view, and circumstances expressed ultimately through the medium of political leaders, and they may be regarded as contingent influences in the sense that the particular direction and emphasis of policy was the outcome of unpredictable human choices.

That the system of serfdom would at some point have to be changed, for instance, was generally recognized; but the timing and terms of the emancipation were the result of negotiations and decisions not immediately related to broader historical trends. Emancipation had been under discussion for half a century and was given serious consideration by Nicholas I; and the possibility existed of a variety of compromises between landowner and peasant interests. Once the decision was taken, it set the course of social change for a generation or more. The serfs were emancipated, but they were left poorer than before and confined within the communal framework of the mir under circumstances which gave them little mobility. Indeed, the decision to emancipate was not a decision to modernize, although the government soon found it necessary to take further measures which had unforeseen consequences for social change. Once the noble landowners were removed from their traditional responsibilities, new institutions had to be established to take their place, and there ensued a chain reaction of reforms. Organs of local administration were created, the judiciary was reformed, the representative basis of municipal government was broadened, and universal military service was introduced. Public opinion was infused with a new spirit, and most educated Russians felt that their country was finally moving along the trail blazed by Western Europe.

The exhilarating atmosphere of reform was nevertheless deceptive, for thoroughgoing modernization was as yet scarcely under way. The hopes aroused by Alexander II were of West European dimensions, but his performance was quite modest insofar as it affected the mass of the population. Under these circumstances the extremists became increasingly disaffected, and the reign that ushered in a new era was terminated by an assassin's hand. The successors of Alexander II did not have his vision, but they reaped some of the benefits of his reforms and were advised by abler statesmen. The personality of Witte dominates this period, and his skill in using the Ministry of Finance to prime the pump of industrialization marked a new phase in the economic development of the country. The rate of growth of Russian industry was among the highest in the world in the 1890's, and the social consequences of this rapid expansion soon made themselves felt. This dynamic industrial growth, however, was not matched in other spheres. Self-government institutions were increasingly restricted in this period, and harsh censorship stifled public opinion. The decade or two which culminated in the revolution of 1905 were thus marked by a combination of economic boldness and political caution which has few parallels among the societies that modernized earlier, although it resembles rather closely the policies of Japan, Turkey, and perhaps also China in their earlier phases. Here again, the origins of these specific policies must be sought in men rather than in trends and forces.

When the government's authority collapsed as a result of the Japanese victory in 1905, it had to make concessions on a wide front. Once the government regained its equilibrium, however, it worked out a modification of the earlier formula which again sought to provide for economic growth within a traditional framework of autocracy and censorship. The plan of Stolypin to make the transition from communal to independent agriculture was comparable in its implications to the economic measures of Alexander II and Witte, and had it not been for the war it would have had a profound effect on Russian society. The rapid change since the late 1880's was continued in those aspects of society that reflected more or less directly the introduction of modern technology—intellectual ferment, education, industrialization, urbanization, and the erosion of the social traditions based on the peasant patriarchal family—but not in other aspects. In particular, political power remained very largely in the hands of the autocracy, which drew upon itself all the blame for the inequities that seem inevitably to result from rapid social change.

Another emperor, or other advisers, working with the same materials, could have evolved a very different policy. As it is, the political collapse of the empire during the First World War has cast a shadow over all of its policies and has led many to neglect the rapid social change that occurred in Russia in the generation or two before 1917. Indeed, a good case can be made for the proposition that if the rate of change experienced in the later years of the empire had been continued for a generation or so without the burdens of war, revolution, and civil strife, the results might not have differed very greatly from what was actually achieved after 1917. Since no such calculation can be tested, one must satisfy oneself with the realization that Russia was a dynamic society after the 1860's, however different the pattern of change may have been from that of European societies.

The tenure of office of the Provisional Government in 1917 was so brief and stormy, and under such insistent pressure from the Petrograd Soviet, that it is difficult to evaluate its impact on social change. Such influence as it exerted must in fact be judged more as an indication of already existing trends which had been suppressed by the autocracy, or of goals which liberal Russians hoped to achieve, than in terms of its actual accomplishments. The abolition of discrimination on legal and religious grounds, the separation of church and state, and the establishment of electoral procedures for the Constituent Assembly stand as its principal achievements, and its general outlook probably fitted the West European pattern more closely than that of any other Russian government. The measures which the Provisional Government adopted were nevertheless not concerned with the most urgent problems of the moment—peace, land reform, and vigorous administration. It favored a continuation of the war and postponement of land reform until after the war; and it recognized rather helplessly that it had little control over what was going on in the country.

To many, Lenin's victory in 1917 seems to be as much a result of the shortsightedness of his rivals as of his own perspicacity, but few will deny his skill in manipulating the mood of the masses and his grasp of the essentials of politics. As a political event, the Bolshevik seizure of power was as decisive a revolution as has occurred in modern times. In terms of social change, however, it had few immediate results. It was not until 1928 that the 1913 level of production in agriculture and industry was regained, and the trend toward urbanization and a growing working class was in fact temporarily reversed. Modernizing experiments were carried on in education and the arts, but their influence did not extend far beyond a few major urban centers. While efforts were made to educate groups of the population which had hitherto been underprivileged, the quality of general education suffered. The family, youth, public health, intellectual work—all suffered during the first decade after the revolution and recovered only gradually.

By contrast with 1917, 1928 is the dramatic turning point in the Communist program to modernize Russia. The inauguration of the five-year plans, and the use of the vast power at the disposal of the government to mobilize the resources of the country in the drive for industrialization, produced social consequences out of all proportion to those of the political revolution in 1917. No aspect of society was left untouched by this great effort, and in technology and in the aspects of social change directly affected by industrialization Russia again began to move rapidly along the course set by the more modern societies. In many respects the social scene resembled that of the 1890's, although change was now more rapid and more all-embracing. It may seem paradoxical that, in the realm of technology and related matters which were his principal concern, Stalin rather than Lenin should appear as the initiator of the Soviet phase of Russian modernization. This is no doubt more for reasons of circumstance than of policy, for the five-year plans would not have been possible without the preparatory work of the preceding decade. At the same time, it is from 1928 that one must date the purposeful and thoroughgoing totalitarian methods which today characterize the Soviet pattern of social change.

Whether a change of similar significance has occurred since Stalin's death is problematical. As striking as many of the innovations undertaken by Khrushchev are, they are in fact little more than variants of the pattern set a generation earlier. The essentials of the Stalinist formula—emphasis on heavy industry and on those aspects of social change directly related to industrialization, at the expense of almost everything else—have not been altered. The somewhat easier way of life and the relatively relaxed methods of government that have marked Khrushchev's administration seem to be more the result of a need for greater efficiency and of differences in the personalities of the two leaders than of any fundamental change in the philosophy of modernization.

V

In reviewing the ways in which the course of social change in Russia has run parallel to that of societies that modernized earlier or at about the same time, the extent to which traditional social institutions and values peculiar to Russia have influenced its development, and the impact of specific leaders and policies, one is struck by the complexity of this process and impressed by the caution that must be exercised in drawing conclusions and making generalizations.

The comparative study of modernization is still in its infancy, and it will be a long time before an understanding of social change in Russia can overtake (let alone surpass) the level it has reached with regard to West European societies, for instance. Yet even now it seems reasonably safe to make two rather elementary generalizations. The first is that Russian social traditions and values are different from those of Western Europe—certainly only in degree, but in sufficient degree to be significant—and are likely to remain different for the foreseeable future. The pattern of social change set by the early modernizers in the West has had such a powerful influence on men's minds that it has become the standard by which all modernization is judged. Many believe that modernization will have a universally homogenizing effect in creating a more or less uniform world society. Yet the evidence would seem to point in a different direction, toward a uniformity of scientifically verifiable knowledge and of its technological applications but a continued diversity of social institutions and values. Just as a language may become modernized without losing its distinctive features, so also other aspects of group behavior—in varying ways and degrees—are likely to preserve their unique styles and characteristics for some time to come. Apart from the countries of Europe and those settled primarily by Europeans, Russia and Japan are the only ones where social change has gone as far as in the societies that have modernized earlier, and it will therefore be a long time before this generalization can be tested. In any event, the evaluation of social change in Russia must be based on a careful consideration of what is universal and what is relative, and a recognition that there is likely to be significant distortion when one judges Russia (or other societies) only by European standards.

The second generalization is that within the framework of traditional Russian social institutions and values there is a wide range of choice available to the individuals and groups involved in the myriad of decisions that make up social change. The state, for example, is likely to play a predominant role in social change in Russia for a long time to come, but it need not be a totalitarian state. The state is likely to be purposeful and task-oriented, but there is no historical necessity that requires it to place the real income of the average citizen near the bottom of its scale of values. The differences between the policies of Stalin and Khrushchev provide evidence of the range of choice inherent in the Soviet system, and one can imagine many other concessions that could be made to the desire for an easier way of life without significantly affecting the party and state as the source of authority.

NOTES

1. These concluding remarks, not presented at the conference where the papers in this volume were discussed, have drawn so extensively on these papers that it is hardly possible to make separate reference to each obligation. At the same time, the views set forth here differ in some instances from those expressed above and on occasion enter into fields not treated in detail in this volume. Among the wide range of studies one could cite, the following general interpretations are of particular relevance: K. Kocharovsky, *Sotsialnyi stroi Rossii* (Prague, 1926); Nicholas S. Timasheff, *The Great Retreat: The Growth and Decline of Communism in Russia* (New York, 1946); Barrington Moore, Jr., *Soviet Politics—The Dilemma of Power: The Role of Ideas in Social Change* (Cambridge, Mass., 1950); Dinko Tomasic, *The Impact of Russian Culture on Soviet Communism* (Glencoe, 1953); Alex Inkeles, "Social Change in Soviet Russia," in *Freedom and Control in Modern Society*, Morroe Berger, Theodore Abel, and Charles H. Page, eds. (New York, 1954), 242–264; Otto Brunner, *Neue Wege zur Sozialgeschichte* (Göttingen, 1956); Werner Markert, "Marxismus und russisches Erbe im Sowjetsystem," *Tübinger Studien zur Geschichte und Politik*, no. 8 (1956), 53–71; *Soviet Society Today*, A Symposium of the Institute for the Study of the U.S.S.R. (Munich, 1958); and Alex Inkeles and Raymond A. Bauer, *The Soviet Citizen: Daily Life in a Totalitarian Society* (Cambridge, Mass., 1959), especially ch. 16.

2. *New York Times* (March 9, 1865), 4.

3. *The Diary of a Writer*, trans. Boris Brasol (2 vols.; New York, 1949), I, 149.

4. *The Outline of History* (New York, 1930), 1089; italics in original.

5. *The Correspondence Between A. M. Kurbsky and Tsar Ivan IV of Russia, 1564–1579*, ed. and trans. J. L. I. Fennell (Cambridge, Eng., 1955), 215.

CHAPTER 6

Russian History in Japanese Perspective

Chapter 6 leaves a broad comparative framework in order to focus on Russia and Japan. At first glance, the contrasts between these two countries would seem to preclude any meaningful comparison. Russia/USSR is some 60 times larger than Japan in territory and is unusually well endowed with natural resources. On the other hand, it is situated north of 45 degrees latitude and has a long, cold winter and relatively little rainfall. It has also been landlocked for much of its history, and even today most of its warm-water ports are frozen in winter. Japan has a more southern location with plenty of rainfall and easy access to seaborne commerce. However, it is largely lacking in natural resources, apart from water power. Russia/USSR has always been open to invasion, and its history is one of almost constant warfare. Japan has had no foreign invasions between the 13th and 20th centuries.

Despite these differences, Japan and Russia/USSR have much in common in their modern development. They abandoned their Byzantine and Chinese heritages for Western models; they introduced fundamental modern reforms in the 1860s; and there are rather close parallels in their rates of economic growth and social change into the mid-twentieth century. They also had many of the premodern assets that account for the relatively successful transformation of the Western societies. Few later-modernizing societies are likely to do as well as Japan and Russia/USSR. Russia/USSR has usually been regarded as the least developed of the European societies, but in a global context it is associated with the Western countries and Japan as among the most developed. One naturally thinks of China as having similar potentials, despite its slow take-off in the modern era, but that is another story.

Reprinted with permission from *Jahrbücher für Geschichte Osteuropas* 23 (1975), 481–488. An earlier version of this paper was presented at the 88th annual meeting of the American Historical Association in San Francisco, December 28, 1973.

I

Most interpretations of modern Russian history by Westerners have been written from the perspective of the West-European and English-speaking countries; and most judgments of Russia have been implicitly, or more rarely explicitly, comparative. The same may be said of evaluations of their own country by Russians before 1917; by non-Communist Russians since the Revolution; and to a not inconsiderable extent by Communist historians as well. The use of a Western model is explicit in Marxism, and the extensive Marxist-Leninist literature contrasting capitalism and socialism has sought to demonstrate that the USSR overtook the West in political structure in 1917 and is in the process of overtaking and surpassing it in economic and social levels of development as well. In this sense, all of these various interpretations have viewed Russian history from a Western perspective.

The result of looking at Russian history from a Western perspective has been to see it as essentially backward, and as continually falling short of the levels of achievement attained by the West. The consequence has been an evaluation of Russia largely in negative terms, by most Russians as well as by Westerners. In the West, the collapse of the empire in 1917 has been seen as the price paid by the old regime for its failure to move more rapidly toward Western values and institutions; and the hopes invested by many in the Bolshevik regime in the 1920's and 1930's were based on the belief that it might succeed, where earlier leaders had failed, in attaining what were regarded as essentially Western levels of political, economic, and social development.

The purpose of this paper is to explore an appraisal of Russian history from a Japanese rather than a Western perspective.[1] The idea of comparing Japan and Russia arises from an effort to gain a better understanding of the policies a society must pursue if its peoples are to attain the levels of political, economic, and social achievement made possible by the scientific and technological revolution. Societies develop both by converting or adapting their existing institutions to new functions, and by incorporating techniques and structures borrowed from abroad. The Western societies, as the first to take advantage of the opportunities offered by the scientific and technological revolution, had no general models they could follow and hence relied primarily on adaptation by trial and error. As a consequence, it is difficult to distinguish in the Western experience between those patterns that are generally valid for modern development and those that are simply earlier patterns converted to new uses. It is only in the last two or three decades that economists have recognized, for example, that economic growth can take place by means other than those developed in the West; and political scientists are only now beginning to accept the view that the political participation of interest groups may take a much wider range of forms than those provided for in Western constitutions and electoral laws.

One of the main purposes of comparisons such as that between Russia and Japan, and between these two and both more and less developed societies, is to clarify the distinction between the commonalities that reflect underlying policies of change that are widely prevalent, and the variances that reflect differences in political culture, institutional heritage, environment, and leadership. A fuller appreciation of the requirements that all societies must meet in order to attain the levels of political development, economic growth, and social mobilization made possible by the scientific and technological revolution, will lead to a better understanding of the processes of change in the modern era. It may also have a practical value in helping latecomers to decide how their existing institutions can best be converted to new practices, and how to make the difficult choices involved in borrowing foreign techniques and institutions.

The particular attraction of looking at Russia from a Japanese perspective lies in the unusual juxtaposition of similarities and differences that such a comparison affords. Both countries inaugurated their modern reform eras in the 1860's; their per capita levels of economic development were similar throughout the following century; and they are among the very few latecomers to modernization that have in large measure caught up with the West, to the extent that such change can be measured by the available political, economic, and social indicators. Surely these two societies must have employed their skills and resources in a very similar manner to have achieved such a similar result.

The configurations of Russia as seen by comparison with Japan rather than with the West will be considered here in terms of three periods: the premodern era before the great reforms of the 1860's; the rapid transformation from an agrarian and rural to an industrial and urban way of life to the 1940's; and the contemporary era since the Second World War when the two countries face the problems characteristic of highly modernized societies.

II

While it cannot be denied that both Russia and Japan before the 1860's were backward by the Western standards of the nineteenth and twentieth centuries, by which they have usually been judged, a very different picture emerges if they are evaluated by comparison with other premodern societies, including those of the West before the eighteenth and nineteenth centuries.

In no sphere are the distinctive characteristics of Russia and Japan more evident than in that of political culture. In both countries the government had developed an unusual capacity before the modern era to mobilize resources and skills on a national scale. Centralized political coordination and control were exercised more directly in Russia, but more comprehensively in Japan. In both cases, the governments were relatively free from challenges by regional authorities or by interest groups other than those that had been or were being incorporated into the central political authority. The essential instrumentality of this control was a service nobility, although there were significant differences between the two countries in its composition and role. In the early eighteenth century this stratum was at least ten and perhaps twenty times larger in Japan than in Russia, and cultivated values that tended to permeate all other strata.[2] The much smaller Russian elite, by contrast, was both ethnically and ideologically more diverse; and also cultivated values so different from those of other strata that there often seemed to be two Russias.

Among other premodern governments, only those of seventeenth-century Western Europe exercised a comparable degree of coordination and control, and these generally had greater limitations on their power than was the case in Russia or Japan. Since the Western states developed without more advanced rivals that might serve both as threats and models, they were able to maintain relatively pluralistic political systems even in an era of "absolutism." For latecomers like Russia and Japan, however, a high degree of political centralization was probably a prerequisite for survival, and was one of the principal factors that account for their subsequent development.

Among other latecomers, the Chinese and Ottoman empires were also notable for their capacity to mobilize skills and resources, but this capacity did not penetrate to the local level or permit as comprehensive controls as did those in Russia and Japan. Apart from these, no other governments before the modern era possessed a comparable capacity for political coordination and control.

These considerations lead one to question whether the Russian autocracy before the 1860's deserves the opprobrium with which it has more often than not been viewed from the Western vantage point. Seen in the light of the tasks that latecomers to modernization would have to perform in the subsequent course of political development, economic growth, and social mobilization, the capacity for centralized government developed in Muscovite and early imperial Russia, and also in Tokugawa Japan, may well have been an essential precondition to their later capacity to handle problems of institutional adaptation and borrowing. How many other societies, apart from those of Western Europe and their English-speaking offshoots in the New World, have done as well during the past century in responding to the challenge of the scientific and technological revolution?

In the economic realm, Russia and Japan appear to have been among the countries that were the best prepared, apart from those of the West, to adapt to the new technology. It is significant that in Russia the economic activity of almost one-half the present population, and in Japan of about one-fourth, was administered by the national government; and that in these two countries a quarter to a third of agricultural production was absorbed by taxes. In addition, unlike most societies other than the Western, Japan and Russia had relatively high per capita levels of agricultural production. In manufacturing and mining, by contrast, Russia had absorbed much of the advanced European technology before the 1860's, whereas these techniques were still largely unknown in Japan. In domestic commerce, Russia and Japan moved from small periodic markets to a society-wide system of trade at about the same time relatively as England and France, and well in advance of China and most other countries. More generally, even in self-isolated Japan, and particularly in Russia, commerce and manufacturing exhibited a dynamism that was unusual in premodern societies.[3]

In the realm of social mobilization as well, Russia and Japan appear to have attained a level similar to that of the Western countries before the modern era. At the end of the eighteenth century, when Russia, and more particularly Japan, were well behind the West in industrial development, 8 to 9 per cent of the population of Russia was urban as compared with about 16 per cent in France and 16 to 17 per cent in Japan. The population of England, the most advanced country at that time in this and most other respects, was over 30 per cent urban.[4] The unusually high proportion of urban population in Japan tells us a lot about that country both then and now, but to discuss this would take us beyond the limits of this paper.

The Russian level of urbanization, although the lowest in the above comparison, was nevertheless high by the standards of the time. Russia was more urbanized in 1800 than China or the United States, and probably also than most of Europe east of France. Moreover, the proportion of settlements in urban areas is as good an indicator as any of the extent to which a population is moving from the relatively loose assemblage of small communities with few common ties that characterize the less-developed premodern societies toward an integrated, "developed" society capable of making a common effort toward agreed goals.

It is also significant that in the realm of general education and the advancement of knowledge, Russia and Japan before the 1860's were among the most developed apart from the Western countries. In popular education Russia ranked well behind Japan, where general literacy and the circulation of books were virtually at a Western level. In the access of its elite to modern knowledge, however, and in higher education and research, Russia was well ahead of Japan.

Russia and Japan on the eve of the 1860's emerge from such a comparison as relatively dynamic premodern societies. In terms of their receptivity to foreign influence without sacrifice of national identity, the capacity of their political leaders to mobilize skills and resources, and their ability to accumulate savings for investment in social and economic development, and to further education—in these spheres of activity they resembled the vigor of the Western countries at a similar stage of development a century or more earlier, and were matched by few if any other peoples outside the West. Russia had greater capacities than Japan in some realms and less in others, but the capabilities that they shared as premodern societies go a long way to explain their later ability to modernize.

III

The most striking similarity between Russia and Japan during the turbulent four-score years from the 1860's to the 1940's is the extent to which they were able to convert their premodern governmental capacity for mobilizing skills and resources to the needs of economic growth and social mobilization in the modern era. At the same time, as already noted, Japan entered the modern era with a significantly more integrated society, although one still relatively unfamiliar with the scope of modern knowledge and the economic and social uses to which it could be put.

It was because of this relatively weaker hold of government over society in Russia, as compared with Japan, that it experienced a greater incidence of political violence in the forms of both governmental coercion and of popular uprisings. Starting with a much larger political elite, Japan continued to be held together by firm bureaucratic and administrative ties. It has been estimated that between the 1880's and the Second World War, over one-quarter of all civilian cabinet posts were held by military men in Japan, and half of the thirty prime ministers were former generals or admirals. The Japanese are also among the most ethnically homogeneous of peoples, and even today no foreigners are admitted to high positions. The Russian ruling elite was held together by much more tenuous bonds. The nobility filled most governmental positions, to be sure, but also provided much of the leadership of opposition, including the revolutionary movements. Many high officials were Russianized foreigners, or members of minority nationalities. Even the imperial family was Central European in origin; and after 1917 many prominent Bolshevik leaders, including Lenin and Stalin, were at least in part of non-Great Russian ethnic origin. The Russian identity was much less clear than the Japanese, or the English or French, and this was a particular handicap for a society preoccupied with challenges that demanded high levels of mobilization.

Russia and Japan were among the most rapidly industrializing countries in the world by the 1890's, with annual rates of growth in industrial production that equalled or surpassed those of the United States, Sweden, and Germany, the most rapidly growing Western economies.[5] They started from a lower base, of course, and even today their per capita level of development has not reached that of most earlier-modernizing societies. Apart from the West European and English-speaking countries, however, Russia and Japan were among the most effective by the 1940's in converting premodern economic structures to the requirements of industrialization.

Within the framework of this common record of achievement, however, significant differences between them should be noted. Russia began the period of transition in the 1860's with a much larger and technologically more advanced manufacturing establishment, but a relatively smaller reservoir of managers. It would be reasonable to conclude that Russia's social lag, as compared with Japan, held back its economic development; or conversely that Japan's greater social mobilization before the 1860's permitted it to "overtake and surpass" Russia in many respects by the twentieth century. The extent of Russia's social lag is reflected in the fact that the proportions of its labor force devoted to agriculture were 77 per cent in 1897, and still 71 per cent as late as 1926; while the comparable figures for Japan are 65 per cent (1902) in the earlier period, and about 50 in the later period. A related difference is represented by the generally much greater success of Japan in incorporating advanced technology from the West. Although many other factors were involved in the victory of Japan over Russia in 1904–1905, one must recognize as significant among them the relatively greater skill of Japanese managers in the application of modern technology.

In both countries the governments played a large role in the economy as investors and consumers, especially up to 1900, and in the Soviet Union again, of course, after the inauguration of the five-year plans. To those who perceive these countries from a Western viewpoint, this role of government has been seen by some as a "substitute" for that played by entrepreneurs and by the market in the West. As seen from a Russian and Japanese perspective, however, this was a natural pattern of modern development in countries where the government had played a similarly large role before the modern era. This is not a question of "substitution"—

Russia and Japan were facing the same problems as the West, but they started from a different institutional base and therefore followed a separate course.

The advancement of knowledge and the growth of educational opportunities tended to develop from the top down in Russia. The Academy of Sciences (founded in the eighteenth century) and an expanding network of universities supported basic research and training of a West European quality. They produced significant original contributions to knowledge. Russia was slow, however, to achieve universal literacy and general secondary education. Japan moved rather in the opposite direction, extending literacy and education very widely at the popular level, but acquiring relatively late the capacity for basic research.

In both countries the preconditions of modernization were sufficiently well developed before the 1860's to permit them to rely primarily on the conversion of premodern institutions, and the direct borrowing of foreign institutions played a secondary role. In the political realm, for example, central institutions of coordination and control, with policies implemented by professional bureaucracies and with potential sources of competing political power subordinated to the central authority, were well established in the century or two before the 1860's. The bases of organized political leadership were firmly established. The main problem was to convert them, with the aid of significant institutional borrowing from the West, to the needs of urbanizing and industrializing societies. To say this is not to minimize the problems faced by Russian and Japanese leaders in preserving the integrity of national institutions while incorporating the experience of the West. It is rather to note that their earlier history provided them with experience in the mobilization of skills and resources to a degree found in very few societies, in the period before societal transformation, other than those of the West.

IV

Since the Second World War the Soviet Union and Japan, like Italy and the successor states of the Habsburg empire, have gradually approached the high Western levels of modernization. The capabilities that led to rapid change after the 1860's are nevertheless not the same as those called for by the greater complexity of highly modernized societies, and in the early 1970's Japan appears to be the more pragmatic and adaptable of the two in an era in which advanced technology is at least as important as large-scale reallocations of skills and resources. Advanced modernization is accompanied by significant differences in structure and scale from those characterizing societal transformation. Centralized direction and national distinctiveness, necessary during transformation, are generally an obstacle to maintaining high levels of modernization. The benefits of interdependence among societies, of international economies of scale, and of diversity of markets and sources of raw materials, loom larger than those of self-sufficiency.

Yet in the contemporary era the penchant for centralized direction has on the whole been enhanced in the USSR. This may be explained in considerable degree by the victory in the Second World War, which tended to confirm the policies of the 1930's. It was further enhanced by the renewed centralizing role of the Communist Party after Stalin's death, and the momentum of a dogmatically trained bureaucracy whose status has depended on defending time-honored practices. This relatively rigid structure of bureaucratic politics was effective in the 1930's when the first priority was to mobilize skills and resources transferred from the agrarian sector to a relatively few important industrial tasks. Now that economy and society have become much more highly organized and diversified, the centralized power that such a political structure is able to exert tends to be as much an obstacle as an aid to development. As societies become more complex, initiative has to be decentralized for effective management. Of the various forces operative in Soviet society today, the rather slow evolution of generational change seems to be the principal one making for greater flexibility.

Japan, by contrast, approached the problems of highly modernized societies after a dramatic political change. The defeat in the Second World War brought to political power a new generation of leaders not only free from but also critical of the practices of the 1930's, and the pragmatism of these leaders recalls that of the early Meiji period. The search for new and more effective methods was further benefited by freedom from the burdens of national defense, which has continued to absorb some 12 to 14 per cent of the Soviet gross national product. The share of all government civilian and military expenditures in the gross national product (henceforth GNP) of Japan declined from 25 to 9 per cent between 1938 and 1965 permitting a greater diffusion of initiative away from the center, while the comparable share for the USSR remained at about 22–23 per cent.

In the economic realm, this greater Japanese flexibility, including massive infusions of Western technology, led to the economic "miracle" reflected in growth rates of some 12 per cent in manufacturing output in the 1950's and 1960's, and of 8 to 9 per cent in GNP per capita. Despite the setbacks resulting from the current world economic crisis, and the need for greater emphasis on social welfare and on the quality of the environment, the Japanese capacity for sustaining long-term growth does not appear to be substantially diminished.

In the case of the USSR, the growth of GNP per capita in the 1950's and 1960's was at a more modest rate of 4 to 5 per cent, a rate equalled or surpassed by a number of both more and less developed countries, and in the 1970's this rate has declined substantially. Whereas Japan has imported Western technology almost entirely by purchasing or leasing patents, the USSR has turned increasingly to importing whole factories, and has frequently engaged foreign technicians to build them and train the workers. In their mutual trade, Japan now tends to be the exporter, and Russia the importer, of technology and management.

The transfer of the labor force from agriculture to manufacturing and services remains slower in the USSR than in Japan. Agriculture still absorbs 40 per cent of the Soviet labor force, and services only 30 per cent; whereas for Japan corresponding proportions are reversed. The USSR remains well in advance of Japan in its contributions to science, however, and in some aspects of applied science it is unsurpassed in the West. The Soviet government also devotes greater resources per capita to social security and welfare than the Japanese, and exhibits somewhat more concern for environmental planning.

V

The principal conclusion one may draw from this experiment in comparison is that Russia—like Japan—was relatively well developed as a premodern society, and possessed the capability to deal effectively with the challenges both of transformation and of high modernization. While acknowledging the difficulties of diachronic comparisons, it seems both feasible and enlightening to examine Russian development with reference to societies and periods other than the Western countries in modern times.

By comparison with Japan, Russia before the modern era had a more centralized political system, but one that employed a much smaller elite of leaders. This reservoir of leaders and managers was handicapped not only by size, but also by greater divisions of opinion within the dominant Great Russian ethnic group; and in addition a growing population of restless minority peoples. Developing as a European society, Russia was stimulated both by the political and military challenges provided by its Western neighbors and by the opportunity to borrow European knowledge and personnel. Moreover, the continental size of Russia led it to rely on extensive inputs of labor and resources, rather than on careful economic management.

Japan's limitation of size and resources, and also its isolation, led it to employ an intensive rather than an extensive approach to development. That is to say, it sought growth through greater productivity and more careful management rather than relying primarily on greater inputs of labor and resources. This mode of operation became increasingly fruitful as the importance of technology grew, and Japan has now surpassed Russia as a society concerned with mass production and consumption. At the same time, Japan's great spurts of growth have depended more precariously on the outside world as regards both knowledge and resources, and the relative development of the two countries in the foreseeable future depends much on the evolving international context.

The employment of the Western experience as the basis for evaluating Russia, and other latecomers to the modern era, results in serious distortions. The experience of the firstcomers to modernizations was unique—in the freedom from the pressure of more developed neighbors, and in the opportunities for pragmatic adaptation over many decades. All other societies have been under much greater pressure, from within as well as from without.

To view Russia from a Japanese perspective may result in some new distortions, but at least it permits an evaluation of Russia in the light of the experience of other latecomers rather than that of firstcomers to modernization. By this standard, Russia appears as relatively advanced rather than relatively backward. This brief paper has sought to show how Russia compares with Japan in a few selected respects; and by international comparison Russia and Japan emerge together as among very few of some 100 or more latecomers to the modern era that have come close to the achievements of the Western societies in seeking to adapt their societies to the opportunities offered by the scientific and technological revolution.

NOTES

1. The interpretations presented in this paper draw primarily on the forthcoming study of "The Modernization of Japan and Russia" (New York 1975), written collaboratively by Cyril E. Black, Marius B. Jansen, Herbert S. Levine, Marion J. Levy, Jr., Henry Rosovsky, Gilbert Rozman, Henry D. Smith III, and S. Frederick Starr.

2. This comparison of Japanese and Russian elites is based on the research of Gilbert Rozman in his "Urban Networks in Ch'ing China and Tokugawa Japan" (Princeton, N.J. 1973), p. 81, and "Urban Networks in Russia, 1750–1800, and Premodern Periodization" (Princeton, N.J., forthcoming). His findings are summarized in: "The Modernization of Japan and Russia," pp. 77–78.

3. The economic comparisons in this and later sections draw primarily on the work of Angus Maddison, *Economic Growth in Japan and the USSR* (New York 1969), and Kazushi Ohkawa, Henry Rosovsky, *Japanese Economic Growth: Trend Acceleration in the Twentieth Century* (Stanford, Calif. 1973).

4. These comparisons are based on the research of Gilbert Rozman, cited in footnote 2 above, and summarized in: "The Modernization of Japan and Russia," p. 82.

5. See especially Alexander Gerschenkron, "The Rate of Industrial Growth in Russia Since 1885," in: *Tasks of Economic History* 7 (1947), pp. 144–174.

CHAPTER 7

Soviet Society: A Comparative View in 1967

Chapters 7 and 8 resemble each other in that they seek to compare levels of development in the Soviet Union in the postwar period. However, they seek answers to different questions and draw on different sources. The chapter below was written on the fiftieth anniversary of the 1917 revolution with the purpose of determining how the Soviet Union compared with other countries during the half-century in a number of key dimensions. The conclusion that by 1967 the Soviet Union had not overtaken any country that had ranked higher than the Soviet Union in 1900 or 1917, with the possible exception of Italy, is perhaps less interesting than the pattern of achievements and costs. As compared with the more balanced development of the Western countries, Soviet development policy has placed particular emphasis on military power, industrialization, higher education, and science and technology. However, these achievements have been paid for by a relatively lower standard of living, level of consumption, and quality of life, and of course by political oppression.

I. COMPARABILITY AND UNIQUENESS

The central problem of modernizing societies is the adaptation of their institutions to the changes in function that result from the growth of knowledge. This is as explicitly the aim of Soviet as of other modernizing leaders; and one may gauge the pattern of adaptation peculiar to Soviet society in terms of the emphasis on selected aspects at the expense of others, as reflected in differential rates of change. The substance of these changes must be studied in terms of the domestic Soviet scene, drawing on the considerable wealth of information reported and interpreted by Soviet and foreign scholars, but their evaluation

Reprinted with permission from *Prospects for Soviet Society*, ed. by Allen Kassof (New York: Praeger Publishers, 1968), 14–53.

depends in large measure on comparisons with other societies that have grappled with similar problems.

It is one of the rules of the comparative method that entities should be of the same general order of magnitude and should possess certain main characteristics in common if one wishes comparisons to be meaningful. Yet it is not easy to follow this rule in comparing societies, for each is in some significant degree a special case, and the Soviet Union is more nearly unique than most. As the largest country in the world in area, the second largest in gross national product, and the third largest in population, it is in certain important respects comparable only to the relatively few major powers that encompass a similar range of resources and conditions. On a per capita basis, the Soviet Union may also properly be compared to a large number of societies that are reasonably close in levels of political, economic, and social development and in historical experience.

Within these limits, and in those areas where reasonably sound statistical and general information is available, it is possible to estimate the levels of development of the various sectors of Soviet society, the means by which these levels have been achieved, and the rates of change in the past and in the near future. The experience of comparable societies provides the most reliable basis for judging the significance of estimates that evaluate the Soviet program of modernization in terms of achievements and costs. When comparisons are made with societies whose resources and problems are of a very different order from those of the Soviet Union, the results are of interest less as a yardstick than as an illustration of the range of levels and experience that exist among contemporary societies.

Many problems beset the comparison of societies. One is the difficulty of obtaining reliable statistical data. There is now a substantial literature on problems relating to the accuracy of statistics and the difficulty of comparing statistics of societies where different criteria of selection, organizational structure, and purchasing power of currencies must be taken into account. Indeed, no statistics come very close to the degree of accuracy that the untutored layman might expect. It is also difficult to identify satisfactory bases of comparison, for such concepts as "gross national product," "defense," "consumption," "books," "physicians," "engineers," and "students" are all matters of definition that vary from society to society and from specialist to specialist. Even after these discrepancics have been adjusted, it must be borne in mind that no two countries are at the same level of development; no two have identical systems of legislation, education, or values; no two are entirely comparable in their conception of professional, ethnic, or income groups; and no two currencies have the same purchasing power. The best recourse under the circumstances is to use the most accurate statistics that one can find, to describe the problems that may be particularly significant in individual cases, and to bear in mind throughout that the reliability of these comparisons is at best relative.[1]

The statistical comparisons made in this study are drawn from the available specialized sources and prepared by international organizations and by independent scholars in the United States and Western Europe. These, in turn, are based primarily on the official statistics of the various countries, and only occasionally on independent studies made within these countries. In the case of the U.S.S.R., virtually all the evidence is drawn ultimately from official Soviet statistics.

Comparisons with other societies have always played an important role in Soviet official statements and have been cited in numerous works of scholarship and propaganda, but only in very recent years has sophisticated statistical work been published on the problem of comparisons. The appointment in 1961 of a Scientific Council on Economic Competition Between the Two Systems and Problems Facing the Less Developed Countries, under the Academy of Sciences of the U.S.S.R., promises to result in important contributions to this field. Although these new studies are primarily theoretical in their approach, the conclusions reached thus far may be regarded as superseding earlier Soviet studies and are cited where appropriate. As with earlier Soviet studies, the statistical work of the new Scientific Council has concentrated primarily on comparisons of the U.S.S.R. with the United States, and thus has only a limited applicability to the subject of this paper.[2]

II. THE INTERNATIONAL ENVIRONMENT

The problems of comparability and uniqueness should be explored not only in terms of the statistics of domestic development. The formative experiences of the peoples of the Soviet Union— experiences that help to explain the role of the international environment in creating the values and institutions that have prevailed in the twentieth century—should also be taken into account on a comparative basis.

Prominent among these formative experiences have been the unification by the grand dukes of Moscow of the Eastern Slav principalities that came under Mongol rule in the thirteenth century; and the gradual extension of Muscovite rule to include the remaining East Slavs and many other peoples as well in a state that now embraces some fifteen major and almost a hundred minor nationalities. Of similar significance was the establishment and maintenance of a country of imperial dimensions in a setting of initially more powerful countries—Sweden, Poland, and Turkey in the seventeenth and eighteenth centuries; France in the eighteenth and nineteenth; and Germany in the nineteenth and twentieth—that were perceived by Russian leaders as threatening powers seeking to dismember and on occasion to occupy the lands of Russia. There was likewise the difficult problem of integrating a multinational state in which the Great Russians constituted only 44 per cent of the population in 1900 and 55 per cent in 1960, and where the major national minorities lived in borderlands adjacent to rival and often hostile countries. To these formative experiences one should also add a prevailing sense of backwardness in science, technology, and economic development, based on a level of living markedly lower than that of the principal members of the European system, by comparison with which Russia has measured itself.

None of these formative experiences is unique to Russia, when stated generally, but their particular pattern and quality is not reproduced in any other country. Problems of political unification have been faced by all countries, but among those at a similar level of development perhaps only Poland, Germany, Austria-Hungary, and Yugoslavia had comparable difficulties in nation-building. The creation of a state in a hostile environment is also a universal experience; but the fact that Russia is one of the few among the more than 130 sovereign states in existence today with a continuous territorial existence, free from foreign rule in modern times, reflects great stability as a state. England and its overseas heirs and France among the early modernizing societies, and China, Japan, Turkey, and Thailand, and perhaps a few others among those that modernized later, have likewise enjoyed territorial continuity in modern times. All other countries of the world, in one degree or another, have since the eighteenth century been newly established and have undergone extensive reorganizations of territory and foreign occupation for longer or shorter periods of time.

The creation of a modern society characterized by ethnic diversity is perhaps a more unusual experience, for nation-building has more often than not tended toward ethnic uniformity. Among modern multinational states, the Hapsburg and Ottoman empires failed conspicuously; and India and Nigeria, among many in Asia and Africa that are seeking to integrate diverse groups, are still being tested. Yugoslavia, Belgium, Lebanon, and Cyprus have survived several crises in handling their minority problems and may face others in the years ahead. The United Kingdom has achieved such stability that one does not think of it as a multinational state, although it was not so long ago that the Irish question stood high on the world agenda of nationality problems. The ethnic diversity of the countries of the New World is of a different order from those in which ethnic groups live in geographically distinct regions, and involves problems of assimilation rather than federalism.

Russia's position as a latecomer to modernization is of course shared by the great majority of the countries of the world, all of which are seeking to overtake if not surpass those that are more advanced. What is relatively unique about the Russian case, however, is its direct rivalry and participation with the advanced countries in the European political system since the eighteenth century, and the consequent need to exercise power at a European level on the basis of a per capita wealth that has been significantly lower than that of its peers. It is significant in this connection that throughout the twentieth century Russia has ranked highest among the major powers in the proportion of its national income that it has devoted to defense expenditures.[3]

A full delineation of Russia's political personality in world-wide comparison would require a wealth of detail that would go well beyond the limits of this essay, but suffice it to say that the Russian political experience has been significantly different from that of the societies of Western and Central Europe, or of the United States, or of the societies of Latin America, Asia, and Africa, and that comparisons should be based on the assumption of a predominantly different political culture. To categorize Russia as "non-Western" in contrast to "Western," "socialist" rather than "capitalist," "developing" rather than "developed," "totalitarian" rather than "democratic," or—to use Marxist-Leninist terminology —"democratic" in contrast to "imperialist" conceals more than it reveals. These simple dichotomies are not entirely devoid of meaning, but they are so crude and undiscriminating that they have no place in a comparative study.

An evaluation of the effect of these formative experiences is important since the view that Soviet leaders have of their own society is based essentially on a comparison with the advanced societies of Western Europe and the New World. The overarching motivation of Soviet domestic policy has been to "overtake and surpass" the more advanced countries, and in this respect probably only Japan among the major countries of the world has been as strongly motivated. Policy-makers in West European countries have either regarded their rate of development as adequate or, as in the case of Spain and Portugal, have not been seriously concerned with the problem. The countries of Eastern Europe have, by force of circumstance, sought to modernize in close relationship with a major power or group of powers—with the French system in the 1920s, with the German in the 1930s, and with the Soviet since 1945. The countries of Latin America, with a few exceptions (Argentina, Costa Rica, Mexico, and Uruguay, in particular), and the countries of Asia and Africa, Japan again excepted, are still at too early a stage of development to regard overtaking, let alone surpassing, as a practical problem.

The Soviet Union has thus been in the critical position of envisioning the possibility of achieving West European levels of per capita production and consumption, but only after an effort extending into the still distant future and calling for per capita sacrifices significantly greater than those required in the more advanced countries. This effort of economic development was as characteristic of the late empire as of the Soviet period, and there are many continuities in the general line of state policy in this regard since the 1880s.[4]

An important consequence of the adoption of the particular program of modernization that has come to be known as Marxism-Leninism was the ideological isolation of the Soviet Union from countries with which it had customarily maintained normal relations. This isolation was to have profound consequences on domestic policies. The Soviet leaders, like many others, have dealt with other countries on two levels. On one level, they have sought to maintain the security interests that have come to be considered normal by leaders of most nations: stable frontiers, assurance of favorable conditions for economic growth, annexation of territories when justified by national traditions, and participation in alliance systems and international institutions.

At another level, Soviet leaders have sought to maximize for their country what they have considered to be the inevitable consequences of revolutionary developments in world politics. While many countries operate in some degree on two such levels, seeing for themselves a role in world affairs that goes beyond mere maintenance of their security interests, the Soviet Union has carried policies on both levels to greater extremes than most. Probably no country except Germany in the twentieth century has made more drastic demands for territorial change in Eastern Europe, and none since France during its revolutionary phase has sought to make such dramatic use of ideological forces.

In the management of security interests, the Soviet leaders have normally exercised great caution in the use of military power. They have sought to avoid the use of armed forces beyond their frontiers, and have been prepared to compromise when the alternative might lead to war. The series of nonaggression pacts concluded with neighboring countries in the 1920s and which later served to stabilize the European and Asian frontiers of the Soviet Union, and the nonaggression pact with Germany in 1939, had as their essential purpose to avoid involvement in the approaching war.

In their attitude toward the crisis in 1939 the statesmen of the U.S.S.R. showed no more foresight than those of the West European states, and for this they paid an enormous price. The outstanding exception to this rule of restraint was the Soviet attack on Finland in 1939, and it appears likely that the Soviet leaders regarded this as a pre-emptive measure with limited objectives. The occupation of Eastern Europe at the end of World War II occurred in pursuit of an enemy that had attacked the Soviet Union, and the postwar line of demarcation between the spheres of influence of the Soviet Union and the Western democracies has been substantially that which their armed forces reached at the time of Germany's defeat. Since World War II, the principal case of the employment of military power at a distance from Soviet borders has been the attempt to establish missile bases in Cuba. It is still a matter of controversy whether Soviet leaders regarded this as a deliberate act of provocation, or simply misread the rather indecisive American official statements and thought they were undertaking a venture that did not involve great risks. This was in any case an exceptional event in Soviet military policy and one that seasoned foreign observers would not have ventured to predict on the basis of past Soviet behavior.

At the ideological level, Soviet policy has been much bolder and has employed sophisticated methods for taking advantage of the crises of modernization abroad. It has sought to influence, and on occasion dominate, the policies of other countries through the international network of Communist parties. By the mid-1920s these parties had come in large measure under direct Soviet control, and were dominated by well-trained and generally loyal cadres. Associated with this core of organizers, as party members or as fellow-travelers in a variety of front organizations, was a larger group of followers varying in size and influence from country to country. Through these instrumentalities, the Soviet leaders sought to weaken governments that obstructed Soviet policies, turn governments against each other, separate colonies from empires, conduct espionage, and infiltrate the upper levels of bureaucracies. Not infrequently Communist parties sought actively to overthrow governments and to gain power for themselves, either alone or with other parties in coalitions known as "popular fronts."

The fact that the Soviet leaders were able to create such an extensive and influential organization reflects an understanding of the strategic uses of political violence and an awareness of the vulnerabilities of societies in the process of rapid change, but in the perspective of fifty years the costs of this revolutionary policy appear to have outweighed its benefits. Of the other countries that eventually came under Communist rule, the Communist parties gained power without direct intervention by Soviet troops in five—Albania, China, Cuba, North Vietnam, and Yugoslavia. Three of these became active opponents of the Soviet Union within a few years' time, and the remaining two—Cuba and North Vietnam—have not been significantly valuable as Soviet allies. In the remaining eight countries where Communists have come to power, they owe their position primarily to the presence of Soviet armed forces.

Even these governments, since the Stalin era, have been no more cooperative than are the members of other coalitions that operate on the basis of more relaxed principles.

Throughout the period of Soviet rule, the pursuit of ideological objectives has tended to place a great burden both on security interests and on domestic policies of development. The stated policy of supporting revolutionary movements, although not vigorously pursued for long periods, has served to increase the insecurity of other nations and in turn to make them more antagonistic to the Soviet Union. In regard to Germany, the proximity of a revolutionary Russia was one of the main factors in the success of National Socialism, and in due course Germany became Russia's principal enemy. Similarly, the degree of temporary security achieved after World War II with the creation of a bloc of Communist-governed states embracing a third of the world's population must be balanced against the great cost of matching the military power developed by the United States and the NATO coalition in response to what was perceived as a challenge to their security by the Communist bloc.

At the same time, there has been a gradual trend in the course of the half-century of Soviet rule away from a highly ideological view of the world toward one that sees other nations in more restrained and comparative terms. What appears incongruous to observers from the more advanced societies is not the theoretical outlook of Marxism-Leninism, which in its way seeks to describe and harness to Soviet needs the revolutionary implications of the world-wide process of modernization, but rather the view that Russia is in the forefront of this movement and represents a model that all others should follow. In the first years after the seizure of power there appears to have been a genuine belief that "world revolution" was at hand. This belief wore off rapidly in the 1920s, and Stalin was happy to settle for a world in which Russia could devote its attention to domestic development. The theory of world revolution now became more an instrument of foreign policy than an article of faith. As such, it played a vital role after World War II in creating a sense of community for the members of the Soviet bloc and in motivating Soviet attempts to manipulate revolutionary movements when they occurred in other parts of the world. Stalin's successors continued to nurture Marxism-Leninism, and indeed for the first time wove it into a more or less coherent doctrine, but more than ever they gave highest priority in their allocation of resources to Soviet domestic development. Ideology was not weakened, but was rather transformed to serve the needs of a great power seeking prosperity in a relatively stable world. International law and organization, rejected in the early 1920s as "bourgeois," and reluctantly adhered to in the

1930s, were by the 1960s accepted as the normal framework of international relations.

By comparison with its peers, the Soviet Union has been motivated by insecurity to a substantially greater degree—an insecurity stemming both from Russia's formative experiences in history and from the domestic position of a government that has relied heavily on police power. The Soviet leaders have differed from their contemporaries also in their adherence to an ideology significantly lacking in pragmatism. Although they have gained world leadership of a Communist movement, numbering 44 million members in 87 countries in 1966, of whom 41 million were in the fourteen Communist countries,[5] their policies have also greatly heightened the normal tensions of international relations and bore a substantial responsibility for the coming of World War II. The world Communist movement may well have been a burden rather than a benefit to Soviet policy.

By comparison with the Russian Empire in the generation before the Revolution, the Soviet Union isolated itself to a greater extent from the international community. As already suggested, this isolation—with roots in traditional policies, but greatly intensified as a result of the Soviet outlook—had profound consequences for domestic developments: it increased the per capita burden of maintaining national security, and it deprived the country of the economic benefits that would have followed from more normal political and commercial relations. In these respects the Soviet Union stands almost alone among the major countries of the world. Only China, in the 1960s, has carried self-isolation to greater lengths and (excepting as unworthy of comparison the self-defeating nationalism of Germany and Japan in the 1930s) has been guided by an ideology even less sensitive to the complex realities of the world around it. In both cases the domestic costs have been very high.

III. POLITICAL CULTURE: FORMS AND FUNCTIONS

The political culture that informs Soviet policy-making—the heritage of ideas and institutions that Soviet leaders bring to the political process—is deeply rooted in the traditional belief that political authority should be vested in the central government and should be exercised boldly in support of a national policy, with the state predominating over other interests.

Both Soviet and foreign scholars, although they disagree on many points of emphasis, are inclined to stress the central theme in the Russian experience of the consolidation of political authority in response to divisive forces at home and threats from abroad. The continuity between the autocratic power of the emperors and the centralized party in the

U.S.S.R. is one that stands out clearly in contrast to the experience of most other societies in modern times. This historically central role of the state was matched by a corresponding weakness of all other forms of organization: territorial subdivisions, religious bodies, political parties, social and occupational strata, labor unions, cooperatives, and business enterprises. Indeed, one may conjecture whether the Russian polity was not so predisposed to the centralization of authority by the time of World War I that only a group of leaders as single-mindedly devoted to the exercise of political power as the Bolsheviks could have hoped to bring order out of the chaos resulting from Russia's repeated defeats in 1914–17.

The Communist party has greatly intensified and integrated the centralization of authority inherited from the empire, but it has not changed its fundamental character by comparison with other societies. Political scientists sometimes classify the Soviet Union, the other Communist states, National Socialist Germany, and Fascist Italy as "totalitarian." As a simple description of a highly centralized system of controls, a good case can be made for such a classification. But these societies differ greatly as to both traditional heritage and level of development. What is serviceable as a descriptive term is thus markedly lacking in explanatory value. Only in the case of China might one seek a meaningful parallel with Russia in relating a Communist government with totalitarian authority to the heritage of a centralized bureaucratic empire.

The more detailed characteristics that flow from this centralized institutional system may be summarized in terms of the results of a recent cross-polity survey using computer techniques. As reflected in this survey, the U.S.S.R. is one of 32 polities (of 110 studied) that share to a greater or lesser extent a mobilizational style, in the sense that its main purpose is to mobilize resources and skills to meet problems deemed to be of national urgency. It is among 16 polities (of 90) that are totalitarian, in contrast to 23 that are authoritarian, and 51 that are constitutional. It is one of the 22 (of 83) that have enjoyed governmental stability since World War I. It is one of 27 (of 108) where sectional feeling is particularly strong. It is one of 42 (of 80) that have a relatively stable political system. It is one of 6 countries (of 114) in which the federal structure is more formal than effective. It is one of 46 (of 106) in which the horizontal power distribution is negligible.[6]

The Soviet Union is also one of 43 polities (of 98) where the government is not effectively representative even though it is representative in form. Its electoral system is one of 43 (of 82) that are noncompetitive. It is one of 11 (of 99) in which no genuinely autonomous opposition groups are tolerated. It is one of 40 (of 100) in which interest articulation is expressed chiefly by institutional groups rather than by groups outside of the party-state system. It is one of 30 (of 97) where the political leadership may be characterized as elitist, in the sense that party membership is generally a prerequisite to responsible office. It is one of 28 (of 100) where the legislature is wholly ineffective since it is not independent of the party-state. It is one of 31 (of 108) where the military establishment supports the government. It is also one of 66 (of 101) where the police is politically significant.[7]

An interesting quantitative measure of the functioning of the system is provided by comparative statistics on votes in national elections as percentage of voting-age population. The U.S.S.R. ranks highest by this standard, with 99.6 per cent voting in 1958. The achievements of other one-party systems with compulsory voting are almost as high, but Italy also ranked high with 92.9 per cent in 1963 and the Netherlands with 92.1 per cent in 1959. By contrast, 78 per cent voted in the United Kingdom in 1959, 71.2 per cent in Japan, and 64.4 per cent in the United States in 1960, and only 10.4 per cent in South Africa in 1961 and 1.9 per cent in Rhodesia in 1958.[8]

The bureaucracy underlying this political system has been characterized as a party-state bureaucracy, in contrast to representative, military-dominated, ruler-dominated, and ruling bureaucracies.[9] Characteristic is the close control exercised by the party over the bureaucracy through its monopoly of appointments and, at the upper level, through the overlapping of party and state appointments. This coincidence of party and state at the highest level was exemplified by the roles of Stalin and Khrushchev as both General Secretary of the Party and Chairman of the Council of Ministers in 1941–53 and 1958–64, respectively. As a party-state bureaucracy, the Soviet system is similar in general terms to the thirteen other states ruled by Communist parties and to perhaps half a dozen other movement-regimes where a single party exercises a monopoly of political power.

While the Soviet administrative system is thus relatively unique from a structural standpoint, in its functional characteristics it manifests significant similarities to other systems, as reflected in administrative behavior and representation of interest groups. A recent study finds that Soviet administrative behavior is similar to that prevailing in Western Europe in a number of respects. In the realm of industrial production and foreign trade, hierarchical command principles prevail in both cases—although in the administration of welfare, by contrast, Soviet lines of command tend to be blurred by a multiplication of controls. The importance of informal relations among bureaucrats, including persisting associations among former classmates in educational institutions, is considerable in both the Soviet and the West European bureaucracies.

The two systems are also similar in that departures from hierarchical principles usually occur when a staff or functional agency acquires authority by reporting directly to the top of the command structure.

The two systems are significantly different, however, in the realm of communication. Vertical communications are seriously overloaded in the Soviet system because of the practice of requiring many reports to the central authorities and of encouraging lower officials to request permission from their superiors before exercising authority. There is a marked shortage of clerks and stenographers in the Soviet system, and a correspondingly greater reliance on oral communication. There is also a much greater dependence by bureaucrats on relationships with the ruling party, as well as a tendency toward solidarity of the various ethnic groups within the administration.[10]

The Soviet party-state bureaucracy also performs functions similar to those of its counterparts in societies at a similar or more advanced level of development, even though its institutional methods are quite different. Although the Communist party is often thought of as an undifferentiated organ that decides and commands as a single man, it has in fact always been rent by controversies stemming in part from differences over ideology and policy, and in part from the need to reconcile many divergent interests. The Communist party is like the human nervous system in that it has a central organ for receiving and sending messages—the Central Committee, with its Politburo and Secretariat, supported by a staff or "apparatus"—as well as a communications system—the nation-wide network of party officials, with 300,000 primary party organizations as the nerve ends that maintain contact with the functioning organisms of the society.

No less than the administrative svstems in Western Europe and the United States, the Soviet system must in determining policy take into account the interests of heavy industry, light industry, agriculture, the armed forces, the police, science and technology, consumers, and health, education, and welfare. The competition for scarce resources is in fact more intense in the Soviet Union than in other societies at a comparable level of development, and controversy is correspondingly acute. The interests that in a representative bureaucratic system find expression through political parties, labor unions, professional bodies, and organized pressure groups, channeled through elected representatives in legislative and administrative bodies, are in the Soviet Union channeled through the party-state hierarchy until they reach the Central Committee and its Politburo. The staff of the Secretariat of the Central Committee is in fact organized in some twenty departments, most of which specialize in overseeing and communicating with one or more of the major interest groups within the society. Even within the Politburo, comprising in 1967 eleven members and nine alternate members, the roles of the top leaders tend to be functionally specialized with reference to the leading interest groups.

The Soviet party-state system thus performs the function of articulating and aggregating diverse interests, but the means used differ from those in other societies. It has established a hierarchy of interest groups in which heavy industry, science and technology, and the armed forces normally have a privileged status. The perplexities of allocating resources among interest groups are as burdensome in the Soviet Union as in representative systems, and it is probably fair to say that the differences among alternative proposals considered within the politburo are as great or greater than those that divide the Democratic and Republican parties in the United States, the Conservative and Labor parties in the United Kingdom, or the moderate and non-Communist left-wing parties in Western Europe. The pressure to keep these differences behind closed doors is nevertheless very great, and the image presented to the outside world has been one of unanimity punctuated by occasional purges.

Since the Stalin era there has been an increasing tendency for high officials to air policy differences in the press. These public expressions of controversy are still rather veiled, however, and analysts must read the national and provincial press very systematically if they are to gain more than a casual understanding of the issues and participants in these continuing debates. In any event, for those interested in the theory of comparative modernization, the differences between the Soviet and other systems provides one of the best illustrations of the diversity of forms by means of which similar functions can be performed.

IV. MOBILIZATION FOR ECONOMIC DEVELOPMENT

Forms and functions are lifeless without a goal and a program to guide the choice among the options available to a society. In the Soviet Union this goal and program are provided by the ideology of Marxism-Leninism, which maintains that "the creation of the appropriate material and technical basis is the principal link in the chain of economic, cultural, and social tasks that have to be accomplished during the transition to communism."[11] The pursuit of this goal is the common thread that runs through the many twists and turns of Soviet policy over a period of half a century, and the Communist party sees as its principal role the mobilization of Soviet society for economic development.

The comparative position of Soviet society in the economic realm is easier to define than in the political, and its relatively high rate of growth is well documented. The rate of growth of the Soviet Union in net national product for its best periods, 1928–40 and 1950–58, has been estimated at 5.2 per cent per year. This is comparatively quite high, although it has been exceeded over long periods by the United States and Australia in the nineteenth century and by Japan and South Africa in the twentieth. On a per capita basis the growth of the United States and Australia was lower than that of the Soviet Union, however, because of the large influx of population into these countries. That of Japan and South Africa, on the other hand, was higher on a per capita as well as on a net basis.[12]

The estimates of rates of growth for the postwar period alone are 7.2 per cent for gross national product and 6.8 per cent for net national product for the period 1950–58,[13] and 5.7 per cent for gross national product for the period 1950–60.[14] Rates of a similar order of magnitude in the postwar period are found in about a dozen other countries. Some are countries badly damaged by the war, such as Japan, West Germany, Austria, and Burma; others are those receiving extensive foreign aid, such as Greece, Turkey, Jamaica, and Israel. Others yet are countries, such as Venezuela, that could exploit a major national resource.[15] All of them had rates of growth twice or more as great as the more industrialized countries not damaged by the war. On the other hand, countries like Bolivia, Argentina, Paraguay, Morocco, and Syria have had declining rates of growth that went as low as minus 2.2 for Syria.[16]

The growth rate of the Soviet gross national product has been declining since 1958, however, due to a lagging agriculture and to accumulating inefficiencies in industry. The Soviet average annual growth rate in the years 1958–64 has been estimated at 5.3 per cent. This is somewhat above that of the United States (4.4) and the United Kingdom (3.9) in the same period, but below that of other major countries—among which Japan ranks highest at 12.0 per cent.[17]

The evaluation of the economic performance of an economy is a complex matter, since it must be compared with others not only in terms of its over-all purpose but also of the use that it makes of labor, capital, and technology in different branches of the economy. A study comparing the Soviet Union and the United States in this respect reaches the conclusion that in the use of new technology the Soviet Union lagged behind the United States about 25 years in 1963, the lag ranging from 5 to 40 wars in individual indices. It also appears that the more rapid growth of the Soviet national product before 1962 was due primarily to the large Soviet input in fixed business capital. This, in turn, reflects the ability of the Soviet government to keep the standard of living down in the interest of capital formation.[18]

Perhaps more significant as an indication of the Soviet economic effort is the percentage of the gross national product that it has been able to devote to gross domestic capital formation. Although the Soviet

Union is only twentieth in rank among 77 countries for which such information was available in 1955, its percentage of 24.1 ranked relatively high among societies at its level of industrialization. It was surpassed by Yugoslavia (31.2 per cent), East Germany (31.1 per cent), Japan (29.2 per cent), Poland (24.8 per cent), and the Netherlands (24.3 per cent), among others, for varying periods in the 1950s. West Germany, New Zealand, and Switzerland had about the same rate of gross capital formation as the U.S.S.R. in the 1950s. The latter surpassed by a considerable margin, however, the United States (17.8 per cent), and the United Kingdom (15.2 per cent), not to mention the Philippines (8.7 per cent), and Indonesia (5.0 per cent).[19]

International comparisons of gross national product are particularly difficult because of differences in the purchasing power of currencies.[20] On the basis of dollar values at market prices, the U.S.S.R. ranked fifth in 1964 among major countries in per capita gross national product adjusted to market prices, behind the United States, France, Germany, and the United Kingdom. About a dozen other smaller countries in Europe, not included in the study cited, would also rank higher than the Soviet Union on a per capita basis. Italy and Japan, on the other hand, ranked slightly below Russia in this comparison.[21]

The question of the relative standing of the Soviet economy is the subject of a continuing debate, in which the chief protagonists are the Joint Economic Committee of the Congress of the United States and the Scientific Council on Economic Competition Between the Two Systems and Problems Facing the Less Developed Countries, attached to the Soviet Academy of Sciences. The American economists, who have advanced most of the concrete propositions thus far, maintain that in 1964 the Soviet gross national product (in dollar values at market prices) was approximately 47 per cent as large as that of the United States, and that this proportion has not changed significantly since 1958.[22] The Soviet specialists, for their part, maintain that the Soviet national income was 46 per cent of that of the United States in 1955 and over 60 per cent in 1961. Differences in computing national income and rates of growth lie at the heart of these contrasting estimates, and the Soviet economists deny that the rate of growth since 1958 of the Soviet gross national product has been declining.[23]

The burdens resulting from the high Soviet rates of investment and growth are reflected in the drastic decline in the share of household consumption and communal services in the gross national product from an estimated 85 per cent in 1928 to 55.8 per cent in 1950, with only a small rise thereafter. Long-term declines of this type normally accompany industrialization, but in other countries it has been a much more moderate decline of 10 to 20 percentage points over a period of three to eight decades. In the U.S.S.R., by contrast, the decline was 30 points in a little over two decades.[24]

The consequences of this pattern of development are also reflected in estimates that suggest that real wages, net of taxes and bonds, declined drastically between 1928 and 1948; and urban per capita purchases of goods and per capita housing space declined moderately in the same period. Per capita purchases of services and per capita industrial output of consumer goods increased only slightly between 1928 and 1948. Although these trends were certainly affected by the economic effort during World War II, they appear to reflect principally the underlying economic policy of the government. Not until the 1950s did the Soviet level of real wages, per capita purchases, and per capita output of consumer goods rise significantly above the 1928 level.[25] It should be noted in this connection that the 1928 level of the economy was little higher than in 1913. A comparative study that assigns the purchasing power of hourly wages in terms of food in the U.S.S.R. an index number of 100 for 1928 and 1950, estimates that the corresponding indices for Austria were 90 and 200, for France 112 and 221, for Sweden 176 and 450, for Great Britain 200 and 443, and for the United States 370 and 714.[26]

A comparison of patterns of consumption with selected West European countries between 1950 and 1962 finds that Soviet per capita consumption of food, clothing, housing, and durables was generally between 40 and 60 per cent of that in France, Germany, and the United Kingdom, depending on the category, and averaged a little over one-half. By comparison with Italy, Soviet consumption was higher per capita in housing and durables, almost as high in food, and about three-quarters as high in clothing. In the period from 1955 to 1962, Soviet over-all per capita consumption declined somewhat by comparison with France, Germany, and Italy, but rose by comparison with the United Kingdom.[27] A more detailed per capita comparison with the United States, by product and service group for 1955, shows a total consumption of 26.2 per cent of that of the United States, and a total consumption exclusive of health and education services of 23.2 per cent. In individual items, Soviet consumption was much higher in alcoholic beverages and cereal products and potatoes, while it equaled that of the United States in public transportation. Per capita consumption of fish, sugar, and confectionary products, and of health and education services stood at about one-half that of the United States.[28] Similar estimates for 1963 place Soviet per capita consumption at 29 per cent of the United States level.[29]

A critical factor in the Soviet pattern of growth has been the problem of agricultural production. No general comparative studies are available, but a comparison with the United States provides some indications of the dimensions of the Soviet problem. This comparison for 1963 indicates that the Soviet Union has 75 per cent more sown crop land than the United States, and 7.5 times the annual average employment in agriculture. It uses only 31 per cent as many tractors, however, 38 per cent as much commercial fertilizers—or 24 per cent per area sown—and 50 per cent as much electricity. The total Soviet production of major grains in 1963, a poor year for Soviet agriculture, was 47 per cent that of the United States. The average Soviet production of grains for 1955–59, which were good years, was 63 per cent of the American. In livestock commodities, Soviet production was higher than that of the United States in mutton, butter, and wool, but 10 to 56 per cent of the American level in other products. Such a comparison, although it does not take climate and soil fertility into account, highlights the central problem of Soviet agriculture: high input of manpower and land, and low input of technology.[30] The low performance in agriculture may be regarded as a significant part of the price paid for rapid industrialization.

As regards the related question of the distribution of income, on which information is only fragmentary, the general experience that distribution of income is more unequal in less developed than in more developed countries appears to be borne out in the Soviet case. Estimates of distribution of income indicate that in the Soviet Union it is at about the same level of inequality as in other countries where the share of the labor force in agriculture is between 40 and 50 per cent. At the same time it has a greater inequality of income distribution than countries with a similar per capita income.[31]

A major economic mechanism for accumulating savings in the interest of high investment and rapid growth is the tax system. There is no satisfactory comparative study of tax systems, but it is generally recognized that the Soviet tax rate is by a substantial margin the highest among comparable countries. The principal source of revenue is the turnover tax, a form of sales tax that bears particularly heavily on consumer goods. This tax amounted to 36.8 per cent of the retail trade turnover in 1963, and was as high as 77.8 per cent in 1947. Since this is a tax on consumer goods, it especially affects lower income groups and may take as much as fifty per cent of their outlays for certain products. Deductions from the profits of state enterprises is the other major source of revenue. The personal income tax is moderately progressive, but is at a relatively low rate and provides only 7 per cent of state revenues as compared with 38 per cent in the United States.[32]

V. DIMENSIONS OF SOCIAL CHANGE

The most striking feature of Soviet social development has been the many-faceted adjustment to the planned industrialization starting in the late 1920s, which resumed, after a lapse of fifteen years, the process of rapid economic growth and social change that had characterized Russia from the 1880s to World War I.

One of the most profound social consequences of industrialization was the very rapid shift of the labor force from agriculture to industry. It has been estimated that a shift of labor comparable to that which took place in the U.S.S.R. in the twelve years between 1928 and 1940, took from thirty to fifty years in the countries of Western Europe and the English-speaking world that industrialized earlier. Seen in another way, the number of years it took for the share of the agricultural sector in the labor force to decline proportionately as much as in the thirty years between 1928 and 1958 in the U.S.S.R., was over sixty years in the United States, Norway, and Denmark, and fifty to sixty years in Sweden, Canada, and Japan.[33]

This transformation of the labor force is reflected in the rapid annual rate of increase of 0.71 per cent for the period 1926 to 1959 in the population in cities over 20,000. Similar figures for varying but comparable periods indicate that among fifty countries for which figures are available only four, Venezuela, Panama, Poland, and Ireland, had a higher rate of urban growth. A considerable number came close to the Soviet percentage rate, such as Nicaragua (0.70), West Germany (0.67), New Zealand (0.65), Japan (0.64), and Greece (0.61). Others were much further down the scale, such as France (0.24), Italy (0.23), India (0.18), and the United States (0.18). In others yet, such as Belgium, Malta and Gozo, Austria, and Morocco, for a variety of reasons, the percentage of the population in cities over 20,000 declined.[34]

Social mobility is a subject on which sociologists have as yet failed to do much basic research, or to define very adequately the terms and categories on the basis of which comparisons can be made. Indeed, no studies of social mobility have been made within the Soviet Union, and the only empirical evidence we have is based on a study of 765 Soviet emigrés. From this fragmentary data a few comparative judgments may nevertheless be ventured. The U.S.S.R. has a high rate of mobility from manual to nonmanual strata and from manual to elite strata. These two trends are understandable in the light of the rapid industrialization and the role of the Communist Party in destroying and bypassing the traditional elite. Both the United States and France have a comparable, but somewhat lower, rate of mobility from manual to nonmanual strata; and the United States also has a high rate of manual movement into the elite strata. The similarity in these respects of the United States and the U.S.S.R., although for different reasons, is interesting to note. All other societies that have been studied have a substantially lower rate of upward mobility.[35]

The occupational structure that has resulted from the social impact of industrialization is difficult to compare with that of other countries except in a most general way because of lack of adequate statistics. As regards the breakdown between nonmanual and manual occupations, in advanced societies such as the United States, New Zealand, and Sweden, the proportion of employment in nonmanual occupations in 1960–61 was 42.3, 36.7, and 33.2 per cent, respectively. In Japan, which is at about the same level of development as the U.S.S.R., the corresponding percentage is 28.2. In the U.S.S.R., the percentage in nonmanual occupations was 17.7 in 1939 and 20.1 in 1959. As regards the division of the manual category between industry and agriculture, in the advanced societies from about 5 to 15 per cent of the labor force is in agriculture. The corresponding figure is over 30 per cent for the Soviet Union and about the same for Japan.[36]

Instructive comparisons can also be made in the field of education, although these must necessarily be quantitative rather than qualitative. As regards higher education, the total number of students receiving full-time higher education at all levels in 1959–60 per 10,000 population has been estimated at 55 for the U.S.S.R. This is lower than the numbers for Canada (69), Sweden (71), and the United States (126); but it is higher than France (49), New Zealand (48), the Netherlands (47), West Germany (45), Australia (44), and Great Britain (31).[37]

An estimate on a somewhat different basis that compares the number of students enrolled in higher education in 1960, or the closest year for which statistics are available, finds that with 539 students per 100,000 population the U.S.S.R. ranked fifteenth among 105 countries. The fourteen countries with a higher enrollment include Uruguay (541), Japan (750), Argentina (827), Puerto Rico (1,192), the United States (1,983), and many of the countries of Western Europe. Countries with a proportionately smaller enrollment in higher education range from Belgium (536), West Germany (528), the United Kingdom (460), and Czechoslovakia and Switzerland (398), to India (220), China (69), Haiti (29), Ethiopia (5), and Rhodesia and Nyasaland (3). These figures exclude students enrolled in evening and correspondence courses, which comprise about one-half of the students engaged in higher education in the U.S.S.R.[38] It should be noted that comparisons such as these of total numbers of students tend to discriminate against the more efficient educational systems, such as those of Western Europe, where courses of study are tightly organized and students complete them in the normal period with relatively little wastage.[39]

A more accurate basis of comparison is provided by the number of students entering and completing higher education. The percentage of the relevant age group entering higher education in the U.S.S.R. in

1958–59 was 6 per cent for full-time courses and 12 per cent for all levels of higher education. The English-speaking and advanced West European countries all had equivalent or higher rates, ranging as high as 18 and 24 per cent for Canada and 30 and 35 per cent for the United States.[40] Figures for the completion of higher education in 1961–62 in all subjects and at all levels were 8 per cent of the age group in the U.S.S.R., as compared with 9 in Australia, 10 in Great Britain and New Zealand, 15 in Canada, and 17 in the United States. France, Sweden, West Germany, and the Netherlands had lower rates of completion, however, with 7, 7, 5, and 4 per cent of the age group, respectively. In science, engineering, and agriculture alone, however, the U.S.S.R. had the highest rate of completion at 5 per cent of the age group, with the other countries ranging from 2 to 4 per cent.[41]

Comparisons of expenditures for higher education are untrustworthy on account of problems of rates of exchange and national differences in purchasing power as related to the costs of higher education. Estimates of public expenditures on higher education as a percentage of gross national product about 1960 indicate a range between 0.8 per cent for the U.S.S.R., the United States, Great Britain, and Australia, and 0.3 per cent for France.[42] It should be noted in this connection, however, that private (in contrast to public) expenditures on higher education are 6 per cent in France, 10 in Great Britain, 31 in the United States, and 39 per cent in Canada of total expenditures on higher education.[43] Estimates of expenditures on higher education per student that take both public and private expenditures into account do not appear to exist, but from the limited information available it is apparent that Soviet expenditures per student are within the range of those in the English-speaking and advanced West European countries.[44]

An interesting attempt to rank countries according to quantitative indicators of human resource development is the Harbison-Myers scale. In constructing this scale, seventy-five countries were ranked in four groups on the basis of a composite scale based on the arithmetic total of (a) enrollment in secondary education as a percentage of the age group 15 to 19, adjusted for length of schooling, and (b) enrollment in higher education as a percentage of the age groups multiplied by a weight of five. The weighting of higher education reflects the emphasis of this scale on the development of skilled manpower. In this context the U.S.S.R. is in the group of sixteen most advanced countries, with a composite index of 92.6. The higher indices are those of Canada (101.6), France (107.8), Japan (111.4), the United Kingdom (121.6), Belgium (123.6), the Netherlands (133.7), Australia (137.7), New Zealand (147.3), and the United States (261.3). Ranking below the U.S.S.R. in this group of countries are Finland (88.7), West Germany (85.8), Israel (84.9), Argentina (82.0), Sweden (79.2), and Denmark (77.1).[45]

In the realm of research and development efforts, a comparative study has reached some tentative conclusions despite serious problems of comparability. In terms of manpower, the Soviet Union employs about a million people in research and development, as compared with a million and a quarter in the United States and half a million in Western Europe. A comparison of expenditures for research in 1962, taking into account differences in research costs, indicates that Soviet expenditures are about four-fifths of those of the United States and almost twice those of Western Europe. If the comparison were limited to civil research the lag of Western Europe would be much less, since much of the American and Soviet efforts are devoted to military and space research.[46]

As for the percentage of population aged 5 to 19 enrolled in primary and secondary education, the U.S.S.R. ranked thirty-ninth among 124 countries for which information was available in 1960. Its enrollment of 57 per cent of the age group compared with 73 per cent for Japan, 80 for the United Kingdom, 81 for the United States, and 89 for Iceland. Lower rankings included 41 per cent for China, 29 for India, and 2 for Niger.[47] In secondary education alone, however, Soviet enrollments were substantially higher than those of the major West European countries but lower than those in the United States.[48] With respect to literacy of the population aged 15 and over, there were more than twenty countries above the 95 per cent level estimated for the U.S.S.R. in 1959. Literacy in China was estimated at 47.5 per cent of those aged 15 or over in 1950, in India at 19.3 in 1951, and in Mozambique at 1.0 in 1950.[49]

In the realm of communications, the U.S.S.R. in 1960 ranked twenty-sixth in newspaper publication among 125 countries for which information is available, with a daily newspaper circulation of 172 per 1,000 population. The United Kingdom ranked first with 506, Japan sixth with 416, and the United States thirteenth with 326. China, on the other hand, ranked seventy-ninth with a daily circulation of 20 per 1,000, and Upper Volta last with 0.1.[50] In regard to radios, the U.S.S.R. in 1960 ranked twenty-fourth among 118 countries, with 205 sets per 1,000 population. The United States was first with 948, the United Kingdom ninth with 289, Japan fortieth with 106.7, and Upper Volta again last with 0.8.[51] Ranking with respect to television sets was much the same, with the U.S.S.R. twenty-fifth among 69 countries with 27.5 sets per 1,000 population in 1961. The United States was again first with 306.4 sets, Japan in this category was eighth with 98, and India sixty-ninth with 0.001. Cinema attendance in the U.S.S.R. was 17.7 per capita in 1960, giving it a rank of fifth among 104 countries for which such information is available. Countries ranking higher were Israel, Australia,

Lebanon, and Hong Kong, the highest, with an attendance of 22.8 per capita. The United States, often thought of as the home of the cinema, ranked nineteenth with a per capita attendance of 11.8; Japan was twenty-sixth with 9.2, China seventy-third with 2.2, and Laos last with a per capita attendance of 0.4.[52]

The problem of comparing book publication is more complex because of problems of definition. According to Soviet practice, all publications with five pages or more are classified as "books-or-pamphlets." In the United States, on the other hand, publications of forty-nine pages or more are classified as books and those from five to forty-eight pages are classified separately as pamphlets. Another difference is that in the U.S.S.R. unchanged reprintings of old books are counted as new books, which is not the case in the United States and Western Europe. The U.S.S.R. also includes in its book statistics a wide variety of free publications, including administrative instructions, construction plans, and catalogues; this is not the case in other countries. Finally, Soviet statistics include as new titles translations of the same book into its many minority languages.

A discriminating comparison that takes these differences into account reaches the conclusion that in 1961 the U.S.S.R. *produced* 5.55 copies per capita of books and pamphlets of over four pages, and the United States *sold* 6.05 copies per capita of books of over forty-eight pages, not counting municipal, state, federal, and industrial publications. It appears that a number of West European countries do as well or better per capita. The question of the comparative cost of books is also a controversial matter, depending as it does not only on the purchasing power of currency but also on wage and salary levels. A comparison taking these factors into account reaches the conclusion that most categories of books were less expensive in the United States than in the U.S.S.R. in terms of the hours of work required in the two countries to earn the purchasing price.[53]

In matters of public health, the U.S.S.R. ranked thirteenth among 79 countries in 1958–59, with a life expectancy of 72 years for females at birth. Representative higher rankings were Czechoslovakia at 72.3 years, the United States at 73 years, and Sweden, the highest, at 75.2 years. Lower rankings included Japan at 69.9 years, Turkey at 50.4, India at 32.2, and Mali, the lowest, at 26.0.[54] The U.S.S.R. had 35 infant deaths per 1,000 live births in 1960, ranking twentieth after the Netherlands, which had the lowest rate of 16.5 infant deaths in 1960, and thirtieth above India, with 225 infant deaths in 1951. The United States, by comparison, had 26.4 infant deaths per 1,000 live births in 1959, Japan had 37.7 in the same year, and Yugoslavia had 100 in 1958.[55] Interesting figures are also available in regard to inhabitants per physician and per hospital bed. The U.S.S.R. had one physician for every 578 inhabitants in 1959, ranking in this respect second only to Israel with one for 400. By comparison, the United States had one physician for 780 inhabitants, Czechoslovakia ranked third with one for 620, Japan one for 930, India one for 5,200, China one for 8,700, and Ethiopia, the lowest, one for 117,000.[56] In such comparisons the quality of physicians, in terms of length of training and degree of specialization, is not taken into account. In regard to hospital beds, the Soviet ratio of one per 140 inhabitants in 1960 was surpassed by twenty-five countries, including all the English-speaking and advanced West European countries. Ireland ranked highest, with one hospital bed per 70 inhabitants. The ratio in most other countries was much lower, as reflected in one hospital bed per 1,800 inhabitants in China, one per 2,200 in India, and one per 8,100 in Afghanistan.[57]

Comparative estimates relating to the general problem of the changing role of women in society do not seem to be available. This is due in part to the lack of statistics and more particularly to some confusion as to what answers should be sought. Of the many issues involved in the emancipation of women in modern times, those concerning education and professional employment are most amenable to study. Since manual labor has included women in all societies and at all times, the controversial problems have tended to center on the accessibility to women of professional and managerial occupations with compensation equal to that received by men. A unique feature of Soviet society in this regard is the enrollment of women in higher education, which rose from 30 per cent of the students in 1930 to 40 per cent in 1940 and 80 per cent in the mid-1940s, and then declined to 50 per cent in 1950 and about 40 per cent in 1960. This trend was accompanied by an at-work rate of almost 90 per cent in the 1950s for women with a higher education. In the postwar years women have earned about one-quarter of the higher degrees in science and engineering, have occupied some 38 per cent of the faculty positions in Soviet higher institutions, and comprise 36 per cent of all scientific workers and 32 per cent of all engineers. At the same time, very few women have advanced to top positions in scholarship, science, and engineering. This role of Soviet professional women, which surpassed that of any West European country in the period 1930–55, was due principally to war losses and to political purges. Since 1955 the professional role of women in the U.S.S.R. has not been significantly different from that in the advanced countries.[58]

As regards the labor force in general, as distinct from employment in the professions, the underlying fact is that in 1946 it comprised 100.9 million females as compared with 75.1 million males in the U.S.S.R. The surplus of women over men both in the population as a whole and in the working-age population will continue beyond 1980.[59] The U.S.S.R. ranked highest among sixty-nine countries in the proportion of women among wage and salary earners, with 46.7 per cent in 1959. Other countries within ten percentage points were the Barbados, Jamaica, Ecuador, Haiti, and Finland. The United States ranked nineteenth with 30.5 per cent, and Japan twentieth with 30.3 per cent, and the range of the West European countries in general was between 23 and 34 per cent.[60]

Divorce rates, in contrast to many other social indices, tend to correlate more with cultural traditions than with the level of industrialization or urbanization. In 1962, for instance, the Soviet Union had 1.3 final divorce decrees per 1,000 population. This compares with rates of below 1 per 1,000 in England, France, Japan, and Greece, and of over 2 per 1,000 in the United States, Egypt, and Rumania.[61]

It would be interesting to compare, if one could, the prevalence of crime and other forms of social disorganization, but adequate statistical data do not appear to be available. One would expect the U.S.S.R., as a society still half-rural and half-urban, to have a relatively lower incidence of the social problems most characteristic of highly urbanized societies—irrational murder and assault, illegitimacy, homosexuality, suicide, and traffic accidents. At the same time, one might expect somewhat higher rates of murder and assault of relatives and acquaintances, burglary, and other crimes associated with rural and urban communities where people work under conditions of unusual stress and deprivation. In the present state of our knowledge it would doubtless be a mistake to assume a close correlation between social disorganization and urbanization, and a thorough examination of this question on a cross-cultural basis is one of the challenges that still confront students in anthropology, sociology, and social psychology.

If one could, it would also be interesting to compare the use of forced labor in the Soviet Union, where it was widespread from the 1930s to the 1950s, with its use in other countries. The available data do not, however, permit satisfactory comparisons.[62]

VI. A RETROSPECTIVE APPRAISAL, 1917–67

The broad outline of the comparative position of Soviet society that emerges from the available data will not surprise persons knowledgeable about Soviet affairs, but only in recent years have world-wide comparative indices been prepared that permit one to explore in some detail the nuances of the relative standing of the U.S.S.R. in terms of its ranking in regard to other countries, the balance of achievements and costs, and the pattern of modernization represented by Soviet policies.

Rankings

One conclusion that can be drawn is that on a per capita basis the U.S.S.R. ranks in measurable economic and social indices about twentieth among the 130 or more countries for which reasonably adequate information is available. This is more than an impressionistic ranking, for a number of careful calculations have been made in an attempt to compare societies on the basis of composite indices. The Russett scale, for example, ranks 107 societies on the basis of levels of per capita gross national product and then divides them into five groups or stages in such a way as to maximize the consistency of eight variables. These variables are per cent urban population, per cent literacy, higher education per 100,000, inhabitants per physician, radios per 1,000, per cent voting, per cent in military service, and the expenditure of central government, social security, and public enterprise as a percentage of gross national product. According to this scale the most developed group of fourteen countries—in effect the English-speaking and advanced West European countries—are in the stage described as "high mass-consumption" societies. The next level comprises thirty-six identified as "industrial revolution" societies, which includes Czechoslovakia, the U.S.S.R., East Germany, Italy, Poland, and Japan, among others, in that order. The U.S.S.R. ranks sixth from the top in this second group, and twentieth from the top in the entire list of 107 countries.[63] The Central Statistical Administration of the U.S.S.R., on the basis of its own calculations of national income per capita, ranks the Soviet Union fourteenth—placing it ahead of Belgium and the Netherlands, among others.[64]

These indices that rank countries with per capita product or income as a key factor are the simplest to construct, but as a basis of comparison they suffer from all of the distortions that result from differences in purchasing power and rates of exchange when national incomes are converted into U.S. dollars. One attempt to avoid this difficulty is represented by the Niewiaroski scale, which seeks to establish the relative level of living of countries by selecting and weighting items significant to basic living conditions that can be measured in physical quantities. This scale uses nine economic and five social variables, and these are reduced by means of factor analysis to a common component which is expressed in relation to an index number of 100 for the United States. On this basis, the U.S.S.R. ranks twenty-first (of 88) in the economic scale, twenty-fourth in the social scale, and twenty-first in the combined scale, with indices of 46, 43, and 52, respectively. The twenty countries with higher levels of living than the U.S.S.R. include the English-speaking and advanced West European countries, and East Germany, Czechoslovakia, Finland, and Israel. Japan ranks twenty-second, just below the U.S.S.R., in the combined index, with its rank of eighth in the social index compensating for its rank of thirty-first in the economic index. On this scale, India ranks seventy-fifth, and Ethiopia, the lowest.[65]

Another composite index, based on an analysis of the ranking of 95 countries with reference to 43 indices of economic development, ranks the countries in terms of four basic patterns. Of these patterns the first two, technological and economic-demographic, are particularly relevant to our appraisal. In the technological pattern, based on indices of accessibility, transportation, trade, external relations, technology, industrialization, urbanization, national product, and the organization of population, the U.S.S.R. ranks in the second of five groups of 19 countries each. In the economic-demographic pattern, based primarily on birth and death rates, population growth rates, population densities, and population per unit of cultivated land, the U.S.S.R. again ranks in the second of five groups of 19 countries.[66]

This measurement of comparative levels of living may be compared with the Bennett scale, which ranked 31 countries in terms of consumption levels for the period 1934–38. The Bennett scale was constructed by ranking the countries in each of nineteen indicators of physical quantities of consumption, health, communications, and transportation, and then reducing the rankings to a single indicator by scoring countries according to their ranking in the nineteen indicators together and converting this to a percentage of the United States score. On this basis the U.S.S.R. ranked fourteenth (of 31), with a consumption level at 33.6 per cent of that of the United States. By comparison, Argentina, Czechoslovakia, Cuba, and Japan ranked seventh, eighth, ninth, and tenth, respectively.[67]

As regards earlier periods, estimates for eleven advanced countries indicate that in terms of changes of rates of growth per decade Russia was seventh highest in national product before World War I and fifth highest in the period 1913–54; and in rate of growth in per capita product it ranked ninth highest in the prewar period and third highest (after Sweden and Japan) in the period 1913–54. Its change in comparative standing since the beginning of the five year plans is reflected in estimates that it produced 8.1 per cent of world income in 1938 and 11.1 per cent in 1949, and that in the same period its relative income per capita rose from 102 to 133 per cent of the world level. The relative position of the United States, Canada, Australia, and New Zealand improved considerably more in this same period, but that of all other regions declined.[68]

This per capita ranking of about twentieth among the countries of the world in 1967 must, of course, be distinguished from a ranking in gross terms, in view of Russia's position as the largest country in area and the third most populous. In terms of gross industrial production

Russia's world position has risen from fifth to second in rank since 1917. Due to the highly centralized character of the political system, this power is even more impressive in those areas that the government has selected for a special effort. The per capita level of development of a country is only indirectly related to its effectiveness in international relations, in which factors of size and organization are of vital importance. Thus China, with perhaps little more than one-tenth the per capita national income of the Soviet Union, and an even smaller proportion of that of Belgium or Denmark, is nevertheless a world power of great importance. To compare the per capita level of societies is not to deny the importance of gross national income and production in international relations, but rather to stress a related but distinct aspect of development.

In the perspective of fifty years, the comparative ranking of the U.S.S.R. in composite economic and social indices per capita has probably not changed significantly. So far as the rather limited available evidence permits a judgment, the U.S.S.R. has not overtaken or surpassed any country on a per capita basis since 1917 with the possible exception of Italy, and the nineteen or twenty countries that rank higher than Russia today in this regard also ranked higher in 1900 and 1917. The per capita gross national product of Italy, which is just below that of the U.S.S.R. today, was probably somewhat higher fifty years ago.[69]

In significant respects the Soviet Union has at the same time closed the gap separating it from the more advanced countries, although the statistical evidence is again limited. The Soviet gross national product has increased substantially since 1950 by comparison with that of the United States, for instance, although the extent of this increase is still a matter of debate between the economists of the two countries.[70] It is perhaps more pertinent that in certain important individual indices, such as heavy industry and technological education and research, the U.S.S.R. has not only closed the gap but surpassed some of the countries that were well ahead of it in 1917. These significant gains, at the same time, must be balanced against lags in other indices of development. Since all of the more advanced societies have been developing rapidly in the course of the past half-century despite many ups and downs, and a good deal more rapidly than the less-developed societies, it has taken great efforts and sacrifices on the part of the government and peoples of Russia to maintain the ranking of the Soviet Union in this arduous competition. Among the major, later-modernizing societies, probably only Japan has improved its relative standing more markedly than the Soviet Union over a period of half a century.[71]

Achievements and Costs

No less significant than the generalized ranking based on composite indices in the evaluation of Soviet society is an appraisal of the pattern of development reflected in the distinction between those areas where Soviet accomplishment is relatively high, surpassing countries at comparable levels of gross national product per capita, and those where it is relatively low. In making this distinction it is important to recognize that certain of the areas of high achievement are due to the nature of the Soviet political system—such as the high per cent of participation in national elections and the relative stability of the government. Other characteristics, such as the high expenditure on defense, may be attributed to the position of the U.S.S.R. as a great power. The large proportion of women in the labor force also appears to be due more to circumstances of war and revolution than to other factors.

Taking these qualifications into account, there are at the same time significant areas of high per capita ranking that can be attributed primarily to the policies of development adopted by the party-state. The most striking area of achievement is in the rate of economic growth, where the U.S.S.R. ranked ahead of all the major countries in the 1950s except West Germany and Japan. This comparatively high rate of growth is not being maintained, however, in the 1960s.

Closely related to this rapid growth rate is the Soviet pattern of development in the realm of social change. The shift within the labor force from agriculture to industry was twice as rapid as in the English-speaking and advanced West European countries, and the rate of urban growth was among the highest. This was accompanied by one of the highest rates of movement from manual to nonmanual and to elite strata.

The U.S.S.R. also surpasses a number of more advanced countries in enrollment in higher and secondary education, and especially in education devoted to science, technology, and agriculture. It ranks high also in expenditures on higher education per student and on research, and generally in human resource development. It may likewise be noted, although it is not very important, that in cinema attendance per capita the U.S.S.R. ranks among the highest. It no doubt also ranks high in the production and distribution of books, although adequate comparative figures are not available. Similarly, as has been noted, in such aspects of public health as life expectancy and the ratio of physicians to the population, the U.S.S.R. ranks relatively high.

In other respects the U.S.S.R. ranks relatively lower than its general ranking on the basis of gross national product per capita would lead one to expect. It ranks thirty-eighth among 93 countries in the per cent of its labor force in agriculture, and twenty-ninth among 120 in the per cent of its labor force in cities over 20,000. The share of household consumption and communal services dropped much more drastically than in other countries during the period of most rapid growth, and remains relatively low. Real wages also declined rapidly between 1928 and 1948, and only in the 1950s began to rise significantly above the

1928—and hence the 1913—level. The distribution of income within Soviet society has also been significantly more unequal than in countries at a comparable level of development, and lower income groups are taxed more heavily. The growth of purchasing power in hourly wages in terms of food between 1928 and 1950 was much lower than that in any of the English-speaking and advanced West European countries. In enrollment in primary schools the U.S.S.R. ranks relatively low.

These various respects in which the U.S.S.R. ranks relatively low may be considered as the cost of the relatively high rate of industrial growth and of investment in higher education, technology, and public health. In quantitative terms, this cost finds expression in lower wages, higher taxes, poorer housing, and a variety of acute shortages that are familiar to persons acquainted with Soviet life. These costs are borne primarily by the lower-income groups, in contrast to an elite that lives relatively comfortably and free from progressive taxation.

In political terms, the costs of Russian achievements have been reflected in the momentous purges of the 1930s and continued political terrorism into the 1950s. Political oppression of this character has been surpassed among major countries only by Germany in the 1930s and 1940s and China in the 1950s and 1960s. Other countries at a similar or more advanced level have achieved an equivalent or better record of development at a significantly lower cost in human lives and hardship.

The conclusions that one draws from such a balance-sheet of achievements and costs depend on one's goals and values. Those concerned with human welfare and rights will be appalled by the cost. Marxist-Leninists, and technocrats who place a high value on economic development, may admire the ability of the Soviet leaders to hold down the level of living of so many people for so long in the interest of a high rate of growth. Students of comparative modernization, for their part, will note that other societies have achieved similar results at a substantially lower cost, and will seek to discover whether there is something inherent in the Russian traditional heritage and resource base that made these sacrifices necessary.

The Soviet Pattern of Modernization

A comparative appraisal of Soviet society cannot fail to consider in what respects its pattern of development is characteristic of Communist societies in general. It is interesting to note in this connection that few of the characteristics of the Soviet political structure are unique to Communist countries. Thus, to repeat figures given above, although only 14 countries are under Communist rule, the number with totalitarian governments is 16, 28 have legislatures that depend wholly on the state,

30 have an elitist political leadership, 32 have a mobilizational style, 42 have a relatively stable party system, 46 have a negligible distribution of horizontal power, and in 66 the police is politically significant.

The absence of a clear distinction between Soviet and non-Soviet, or more generally Communist and non-Communist, patterns of development raises the question of what political characteristics are in fact unique to Communist societies. Three of these may be distinguished. One is a monopoly of political power by a Communist party. This monopoly undoubtedly lies at the heart of Marxism-Leninism, both in theory and in practice, and one could not regard as Communist a country in which the monopoly was not preserved intact.

The second characteristic is the effort to assert state control over all aspects of economic and social life. One may nevertheless question whether in the economic realm it is not a unique attribute more in form than in substance. Its original role in Marxism was as a means to an end—more equal distribution—rather than as an end in itself. Students of societies that are more industrialized but have maintained the principle of private property, have long since realized that the meaning of ownership in these societies has been greatly changed by the growth in the legal power of the government to restrict use of property. These matters are difficult to compare, but there are significant ways in which governments in free enterprise countries exercise greater control over property—through legal controls other than ownership—than is exercised in the U.S.S.R. and other Communist countries. It is in this sense that ownership of the means of production in the U.S.S.R. may be regarded as more formal than real. Moreover, the fourteen Communist countries vary considerably in the ways in which control of the means of production is exercised in practice. Within the U.S.S.R. itself, the means by which the state exercises its control through ownership has changed significantly in the 1960s, and it is likely that these means will become increasingly pragmatic and diversified in the next decade or two within the framework of an administered society.

The third characteristic of Communist societies is a policy of modernization that places an unusually heavy stress on rapid industrialization and on social factors regarded as essential to economic growth. This characteristic is less distinctively Communist than the monopoly of political power or the ownership of the means of production. A comparable level of mobilization of skills and resources has been achieved by less dramatic means in a number of major countries, including the United States, Sweden, Germany, Australia, and Japan, and by several smaller countries. There is also a considerable diversity among Communist countries in their ability to mobilize skills and resources. China, which has employed as ruthless mobilizational techniques as any Communist society, experienced a virtual stagnation in economic and social development between 1958 and 1962.

The question of the unique attributes of Communist societies is closely related to the question of the distinguishing features of "socialism." This is a term that means different things to different people. Those who are not adherents of Marxism-Leninism generally support one of two definitions: the vesting of ownership and control of the means of production in the community as a whole; or the distribution per capita of the goods produced on the basis of some test of equality, including government policies designed to promote social welfare. Marxist-Leninists, on the other hand, regard common ownership of the means of production as characteristic of both socialism and communism. They consider socialism to be a lower phase of the Communist social formation, in which goods are not produced in sufficient quantity to be distributed according to needs, and distinguish a higher phase—communism proper—in which production will be adequate for such distribution.

The problems involved in comparing ownership and control of means of production in different types of societies have already been noted, and it does not seem possible to compare societies in this regard on any precise basis. As regards distribution of goods, however, the available evidence indicates that there is a more equal distribution in a considerable range of countries, including the English-speaking and advanced West European societies, than in the U.S.S.R. Distribution appears to be a function more of the level of economic development than of the policies of the government, and the degree of equality of distribution is not significantly greater in "socialist" Denmark or Sweden, or in "labor" England, than in "capitalist" United States.[72] Indeed, due to the high rate of investment and the disproportionate emphasis on heavy industry over many years, distribution of goods is in all likelihood more unequal in the U.S.S.R. than in many countries at a comparable level of gross national product per capita, and also more unequal than in Japan, which has a somewhat lower per capita product.

If the U.S.S.R. cannot be considered uniquely "Communist" or "socialist," how can one evaluate the characteristics of its society in a world-wide comparative context? It may be seen as a society whose configuration in 1967 results from a unique heritage of national power and autocratic tradition; a per capita resource base in agriculture that is relatively low by European standards but quite high by Asian or African; and a base in industrial raw materials that was discovered to be quite high once natural resources were fully explored. On the basis of these traditions and resources the Tsarist government achieved a relatively high rate of economic growth and social change in the decades preceding World War I, and this rate was resumed on a more intensified basis after 1928. This second developmental drive was significantly influenced by the theories of Marxism-Leninism, but it was neither as different from the effort before the Revolution nor as closely related to what is usually considered to be "Marxism," "socialism," or "communism," as is commonly thought. In other words, the characteristics peculiar to Soviet society resulting from a unique pattern of resources and inherited traditions are more striking than those that it shares with other societies. As a model, it is useful only to the limited extent that other societies share its attributes.

In concluding this retrospective appraisal of Soviet society, two observations of a more theoretical character are called for. One is that the Soviet Union provides a good example of the role of historically evolved institutions in contemporary affairs. Not only political and social values, but also habits of work and occupational patterns that derive from the resource base of a society, play a profound role in the way in which it develops. The central theoretical issue confronting students of comparative modernization is thus not the one frequently asked of how a given society will move toward a fixed institutional pattern—Western, Soviet, or other, depending on the point of view—but rather how can its own institutions be adapted to the changing functions made possible by the growth of knowledge in modern times.[73]

The second and related observation is that, given the profound influence of historically evolved institutions, the institutional patterns of different societies should not be expected to converge in the foreseeable future. The functions that they perform will converge, but the institutional means by which these are performed are likely to remain significantly different. The United States and the Soviet Union, or Japan and Italy, will converge in the sense that their bureaucratic efficiency, occupational structure, level of education, and per capita consumption of raw materials and energy will become more alike—but their political values, their means of reconciling conflicting interest groups, and their authority patterns in family and social organizations, for example, are likely to remain significantly different.[74]

VII. PROSPECTS

In seeking to envision the configuration of Soviet society as it is likely to evolve in a near future that may be thought of in terms of ten or fifteen years, it is important to make a distinction between those features of the current pattern that appear to be relatively stable and those that seem likely to undergo considerable change.

The international environment, which has played such an important role in the formation of the Soviet pattern of modernization, will in its general outlines be more stable than in the period since the end of World War II. The earlier period from 1945 to 1967 has seen a revolution in the balance of power, the accession to power of Communist parties in twelve other states, including China, and the emergence of no fewer than fifty countries from colonial rule. There has also been a rising incidence of modernizing revolutions and other political convulsions of various types in the countries of Asia, Latin America, and Africa. No changes of comparable significance appear to be in preparation for the near future. There are still some forty colonial territories, most of them very small, but the process by which they gain independence will probably follow the relatively stable pattern already set by their predecessors. In many of the newer states there will be revolutions and coups d'état, probably no fewer than a dozen a year for the foreseeable future, but it does not seem that their consequence will be to add greatly to the world influence of any of the major powers. The proliferation of nuclear weapons will add to the perils that military technology has already contributed, but the degree of consensus already achieved between the United States and the Soviet Union on this issue appears to be adequate to prevent a major catastrophe.

Within the framework of this anticipated relative stability in world politics, there is good reason to believe that the sense of insecurity that has shaped many Russian attitudes both before and since 1917, is giving place to a greater sense of security and assurance. In a technical sense, the turning point in this regard can be placed at 1956 when, as a result of the development of Soviet military technology, Khrushchev declared that war was no longer "fatalistically inevitable" and that the fear of "capitalist encirclement" need not continue to be a central feature of Soviet strategic planning. Increasingly in the past decade, Soviet officials of the younger generation have approached the outside world with greater self-confidence, and in a number of international crises the U.S.S.R. has played a role of mediator. Notable Soviet successes in international relations and in outer space have served to promote a sense of security, and the maturing of the economy has also placed a premium on international stability and on increased foreign trade as necessary for continued Soviet prosperity.

In the realm of domestic politics the prospects for structural change do not appear to be significant. The main features of the party-state bureaucracy appear to be functioning more effectively and rationally than ever before; and as a new generation of officials rises through the ranks, the top leaders are likely to be increasingly less erratic and more concerned with the smooth operation of the administrative apparatus. Within the framework of this institutional structure, however, significant changes may well take place. The Central Committee will probably play a larger role in party affairs, and may even reach the point of electing the members of the Politburo on the basis of competition among candidates. The domination of the party over the state apparatus, however, including the Supreme Soviet, is likely to continue with little change.

The security restrictions on all forms of expression, significantly relieved in their harshness since the 1950s, will probably continue to be lightened within the present framework of party vigilance and state paternalism. There is no indication that the party-state bureaucracy will significantly alter its monopoly of power, or permit the type of criticism that might lead to the organization of centers of opposition within the country. The ideological role of Marxism-Leninism continues to give evidence of vigor, and is indeed becoming more rational in its successive revisions. The abstractions of the doctrine have assumed greater concreteness as Soviet institutions have come to develop stable forms, and there appears to be no reason why Soviet leaders should not continue to regard Marxism-Leninism as the only ideology that corresponds to reality.

Similarly, the characteristic pattern of modernization that places primary emphasis on heavy industry and technology and relegates consumer goods to a secondary position is likely to continue. In the current Five Year Plan (1966–70), expansion is provided for in all sectors of the economy, but the proportion of investments devoted to consumer goods and services is about the same as in earlier plans. Eventually a shift in emphasis to consumer goods and services similar to that in the advanced societies is contemplated, but such a shift is not yet apparent in plans thus far made available.

When one seeks to depict economic and social trends in the near future in greater detail, the essential question concerns the assumptions one should make regarding these developments. The characteristic of projections in this context is that they assume no change in rates of development. Predictions, on the other hand, generally assume changing rates of development. The choice of one method over the other depends on the credibility of the assumptions that one can make regarding rates of change.

A projection of economic growth to 1975 based on the high growth rates of the 1950s, indicates that Soviet gross national product would be $455 billion in 1975 as compared with $121 billion in 1957, but that its position of second in rank would not change. It is interesting to note in this connection that the rank of the United Kingdom would drop from third to sixth, that of West Germany and China would rise from fourth and fifth to third and fourth, respectively, and that of Japan would rise from ninth to fifth. On a per capita basis, the U.S.S.R. would rank fifteenth in 1975 with $1,627, as compared with twenty-first in

1957 with $600. In this period the U.S.S.R. would thus surpass Venezuela, Finland, and the Netherlands. Australia, New Zealand, and Kuwait, ahead of the U.S.S.R. in 1957, are not included in this projection.[75]

Since these projections were made, it has become apparent that Soviet rates of growth in the 1960s are substantially lower than in the 1950s and the above projection must accordingly be discounted. It would appear that in its over-all economy the Soviet Union will continue in the near future to grow at about the same rate as the more advanced countries. The U.S.S.R. may well close some of the gaps, although in the mid-1960s it fell behind slightly in its race to overtake the United States.

The leap from projections to predictions is a big one, and it cannot be said that any predictions have been made that have the credibility of the projections just cited. It is interesting to note that the official Marxist-Leninist doctrine goes so far as to predict unequivocally that "Calculations based on comparing average annual figures of the development of the economies of the U.S.S.R. and the U.S.A. over a long period show that in 1980 the national income per capita in the Soviet Union will exceed the U.S. future national income per capita by at least 50 per cent."[76] Soviet scholars currently working on problems of comparison have made no such predictions, however, and even Soviet propaganda has adopted a much more modest attitude toward this question.

In the social realm, it is estimated that the U.S.S.R. will have 21.4 per cent of its labor force employed in agriculture in 1975 as compared with 48 per cent in 1959, and will rank twentieth instead of twenty-sixth below the country with the smallest labor force in agriculture. As regards inhabitants per hospital beds, the U.S.S.R. will in 1975 be one of nine countries with the highest ratio of one bed per 70 inhabitants, as compared with a ranking of seventeenth in 1960.[77]

The proportion of the age groups 15–19 and 20–24 enrolled in Soviet schools will be substantially higher in 1970 than in the West European countries, but lower than in the United States and Canada. Enrollment for the age group 5–14, however, will still be considerably lower in the Soviet Union. The enrollment ratio for the entire age group 5–24 in 1970 will be about the same in the Soviet Union as in Western Europe.[78] The Soviet Union is likely to retain its predominance in enrollments in higher and secondary education over Western Europe through the 1970s, although it does not appear that it will equal the United States and Canada in this respect.

The near future is also likely to see a further absorption of the various minority peoples of the Soviet Union into the dominant Russian culture. It is a natural process that is probably encouraged but does not need to be enforced. This process in the Soviet Union resembles that in the United Kingdom in earlier periods rather than that in the United States, and, as in the United Kingdom, is likely to lead to the diminution of ethnic differences.

The areas of most rapid change in Soviet society in the near future are likely to be in the institutional adaptation to a more complex industrial society. The methods of economic organization and social control did not change a great deal from the late 1920s to the late 1950s, but the harsh and arbitrary methods that could be made to work in the earlier period are no longer effective. Khrushchev, despite the association of his name with a number of these changes, belonged essentially to the old school of leaders who worked largely by intuition, assumed that the population was rather passive, and tended to equate socialism with rapid industrialization. The demands of agriculture, housing, scientific management, and a consumer-oriented light industry can no longer be neglected despite a continued emphasis on heavy industry, and they introduce complexities not known to the earlier period.

This experimentation with institutional change can now take place in an international environment in which Soviet leaders see their country as a peer among the great powers and no longer isolated in a world of hostile countries. Although the burden of defense expenditures is still very heavy, the relative relaxation of concern regarding national security provides the environment for more permissive domestic policies than in any period since the early 1920s.

At the same time, this process of institutional adaptation will take place within the framework of a system tightly controlled by the party-state bureaucracy, will continue to be oriented primarily toward heavy industry, and will preserve a rather sharp distinction between a university-educated leadership group and a large body of industrial and agricultural workers. The rapid movement from manual to nonmanual labor is likely to diminish, and a greater stability established between leaders and led.

In the world of nations the Soviet Union will be less of a threat and also less of a model. Its leaders will be more concerned with their own problems, and less concerned with ideological abstractions. They will also come to realize that they face major problems in seeking to promote the further development of Soviet society, and that they will be doing very well if over a long period they can maintain the rate of growth of the more advanced countries.

NOTES

1. The range of problems involved in such comparisons is discussed in Richard L. Merritt and Stein Rokkan (eds.), *Comparing Nations: The Use of*

Quantitative Data in Cross-National Research (New Haven: Yale University Press, 1966).

2. Akademiia Nauk SSSR, Nauchnyi Sovet po Kompleksnoi Probleme, "Ekonomicheskoe sorevnovanie dvukh sistem i slaborazvitie strany," *Sorevnovanie dvukh sistem. Problemy ekonomicheskoi nauki* (Moscow, 1963), and *Sorevnovanie dvukh sistem. Ekonomicheskie sopostavleniia* (Moscow, 1965). See also the bibliography on Soviet research on international economic comparisons in Congress of the United States, Joint Economic Committee, *New Directions in the Soviet Economy* (Washington, D.C.: GPO, 1966), pp. 987–88.

3. See the estimates of percentage of national income devoted to defense in 1914, 1921, 1929, and 1937 in Quincy Wright, *A Study of War,* 2 vols. (Chicago: University of Chicago Press, 1942), I, pp. 670–71; and of expenditures on defense as percentage of gross national product in 1955–60 in Bruce M. Russett *et al.*, *World Handbook of Political and Social Indicators* (New Haven: Yale University Press, 1964), pp. 79–80.

4. There is a discussion of this question in Theodore H. Von Laue, "Problems of Modernization," in Ivo J. Lederer (ed.), *Russian Foreign Policy: Essays in Historical Perspective* (New Haven: Yale University Press, 1962), pp. 69–108.

5. U.S. Department of State, *World Strength of the Communist Party Organizations* (Washington, D.C.: GPO, 1966), p. i.

6. These characteristics are discussed in Arthur S. Banks and Robert B. Textor, *A Cross-Polity Survey* (Cambridge, Mass.: Harvard University Press, 1963), pp. 82–84, 88–89, 101, and 106, with detailed analyses in paragraphs 92–100, 112–14, 152–55, and 167–69 of the appended computer printout.

7. Banks and Textor, cited, pp. 85–87, 89–95, 103–4, 110, 113–15, with detailed analyses in paragraphs 101–8, 115–32, 159–61, 174–77, and 184–87 of the computer printout.

8. Russett, cited, pp. 82–87.

9. See Merle Fainsod, "Bureaucracy and Modernization," in Joseph LaPalombara (ed.), *Bureaucracy and Political Development* (Princeton: Princeton University Press, 1963), pp. 233–67, who suggests this typology; also Frederick C. Barghoorn, "Soviet Russia: Orthodoxy and Adaptiveness," in Lucian W. Pye and Sidney Verba (eds.), *Political Culture and Political Development* (Princeton: Princeton University Press, 1965), pp. 450–511; and Robert C. Tucker, "Towards a Comparative Politics of Movement-Regimes," *American Political Science Review,* LV (June 1961), pp. 281–89.

10. John A. Armstrong, "Sources of Administrative Behavior: Some Soviet and Western European Comparisons," *American Political Science Review,* LIX (September 1965), pp. 643–55.

11. *Fundamentals of Marxism-Leninism,* 2nd ed. (Moscow, 1963), p. 645.

12. Simon Kuznets, "A Comparative Appraisal," in Abram Bergson and Simon Kuznets (eds.), *Economic Trends in the Soviet Union* (Cambridge, Mass.: Harvard University Press, 1963), pp. 335–36.

13. Same, p. 337.

14. Russett, cited, p. 160.

15. Kuznets, cited, p. 337.

16. Russett, cited, pp. 160–61.
17. Stanley H. Cohn, "Soviet Growth Retardation: Trends in Resource Availability and Efficiency," *New Directions in the Soviet Economy,* cited, p. 105.
18. Michael Boretsky, "Comparative Progress in Technology, Productivity, and Economic Efficiency: U.S.S.R. versus U.S.A.," *New Directions in the Soviet Economy,* cited, pp. 148–55.
19. Russett, cited, pp. 166–69.
20. On this question see Oskar Morgenstern, *On the Accuracy of Economic Statistics,* 2nd ed. (Princeton: Princeton University Press, 1963); Rolf Wagenführ, *Der internationale wirtschafts- und sozialstatistische Vergleich* (Freiburg-im-Breisgau, 1959), pp. 74–79; Abraham S. Becker, "Comparisons of United States and USSR National Output: Some Rules of the Game," *World Politics,* XIII (October 1960), pp. 99–111; and especially Wilfred Beckerman, *International Comparisons of Real Incomes* (Paris, 1966).
21. Cohn, cited, p. 108.
22. Same, pp. 107–9; see also the discussion in Stanley H. Cohn, "The Soviet Economy: Performance and Growth," *Studies in the Soviet Union,* VI, No. 4 (1967), pp. 24–54.
23. V. M. Kudrov, "Natsionalnyi dokhod SSSR i SShA," *Sorevnovanie dvukh sistem. Ekonomicheskie sopostavleniia,* pp. 101–18, esp. pp. 109–11.
24. Kuznets, cited, pp. 358–64.
25. Janet G. Chapman, *Real Wages in Soviet Russia Since 1928* (Cambridge, Mass.: Harvard University Press, 1963), p. 166.
26. Same, p. 176.
27. Congress of the United States, Joint Economic Committee. *Current Economic Indicators for the U.S.S.R.* (Washington, D.C.: GPO, 1965), p. 122.
28. Same, p. 120.
29. Same, p. 119.
30. Same, pp. 55–61.
31. Simon Kuznets, "Quantitative Aspects of the Economic Growth of Nations: VIII. Distribution of Income by Size," *Economic Development and Cultural Change,* XI, No. 2, Part II (January 1963), pp. 20–23.
32. See especially Franklyn D. Holzman, *Soviet Taxation: The Fiscal and Monetary Problems of a Planned Economy* (Cambridge, Mass.: Harvard University Press, 1955), pp. 275–307; and also Abram Bergson, *The Economics of Soviet Planning* (New Haven: Yale University Press, 1964), pp. 118–26; and Peter J. Pettibone, "The Soviet Turnover Tax," *Public Finance,* XIX (1964), pp. 361–82.
33. Kuznets, cited, pp. 344–47.
34. Russett, cited, pp. 54–55.
35. S. M. Miller, "Comparative Social Mobility," *Current Sociology,* IX, No. 1 (1960), pp. 56–59.
36. U.N., *Demographic Yearbook, 1964* (New York, 1965), pp. 292–335; and G. B. Osipov (ed.), *Sotsiologiia v SSSR,* 2 vols. (Moscow, 1965), I, p. 344. Similar proportions are reflected in comparisons of distribution of employment by economic sector, *New Directions in the Soviet Economy,* cited, p. 111.

37. *Higher Education in Other Countries* (London, 1964), Appendix Five of *Higher Education* (London, 1963), The Report of the Committee on Higher Education (the Robbins Report), p. 16.

38. Russett, cited, pp. 214–16.

39. *Higher Education in Other Countries,* cited, pp. 15–16.

40. Same, p. 9.

41. Same, p. 11.

42. Same, p. 17.

43. Same, p. 18.

44. Same, p. 19.

45. Frederick Harbison and Charles A. Myers, *Education, Manpower, and Economic Growth: Strategies of Human Resource Development* (New York: McGraw-Hill, 1964), pp. 23–34.

46. C. Freeman and A. Young, *The Research and Development Effort in Western Europe, North America and the Soviet Union: An Experimental International Comparison of Research Expenditures and Manpower in 1962* (Paris: OECD, 1965), esp. pp. 11–13, 69–70.

47. Russett, cited, pp. 218–20.

48. *New Directions in the Soviet Economy,* cited, p. 123.

49. Russett, cited, pp. 222–24.

50. Same, pp. 108–10.

51. Same, pp. 120–22.

52. Same, pp. 126–31.

53. *Book Publishing in the U.S.S.R.,* Report of the Delegation of U.S. Book Publishers Visiting the U.S.S.R., August 20–September 17, 1962 (New York, 1963), pp. 27–35.

54. Russett, cited, pp. 197–98.

55. Same, pp. 200–201.

56. Same, pp. 204–6.

57. Same, pp. 208–10.

58. John B. Parrish, "Soviet Womanpower as a Professional Resource," *Quarterly Review of Economics and Business,* IV (Autumn 1964), pp. 55–61.

59. Norton T. Dodge, *Women in the Soviet Economy: Their Role in Economic, Scientific, and Technical Development* (Baltimore: Johns Hopkins Press, 1966), pp. 5–31.

60. Russett, cited, pp. 32–33.

61. U.N., *Demographic Yearbook, 1964* (New York, 1965), pp. 643–46.

62. A pioneering comparative study in this field is International Labour Office, *Report of the Ad Hoc Committee on Forced Labour* (Geneva, 1953), which devoted considerable attention to the U.S.S.R., pp. 82–98, 426–528.

63. Russett, cited, pp. 293–303.

64. Tsentral'noe Statisticheskoe Upravlenie, *Narodnoe khoziaistvo SSSR v 1964 g. Statisticheskii ezhegodnik* (Moscow, 1965), p. 89.

65. Donald H. Niewiaroski, "The Level of Living of Nations: Meaning and Measurement" (Manuscript).

66. Brian J. L. Berry, "Basic Patterns of Economic Development," in Norton Ginsburg (ed.), ***Atlas of Economic Development*** (Chicago: University of Chicago Press, 1961), pp. 110–19.

67. M. K. Bennett, "International Disparities in Consumption Levels," ***American Economic Review,*** XLI (September 1951), pp. 632–49.

68. Simon Kuznets, "Quantitative Aspects of the Economic Growth of Nations: I. Levels and Variability of Rates of Growth," ***Economic Development and Cultural Change,*** V (October 1956), pp. 9–19.

69. Cohn, "Soviet Economic Development in the First Half Century," cited, Table A-1.

70. See references in footnotes 22 and 23 above.

71. ***The Growth of the National Economies of Japan and the Soviet Union*** (Tokyo: Ministry of Foreign Affairs, 1963).

72. This question is discussed in Irving B. Kravis, "International Differences in the Distribution of Income," ***Review of Economics and Statistics,*** XLII (November 1960), pp. 408–16.

73. The adaptation of historically evolved institutions to modern functions is discussed in C. E. Black, ***The Dynamics of Modernization: A Study in Comparative History*** (New York: Harper and Row, 1966).

74. See especially Zbigniew Brzezinski and Samuel P. Huntington, ***Political Power: USA/USSR*** (New York: Viking Press, 1964), pp. 419–36.

75. Russett, cited, pp. 352–55.

76. ***Fundamentals of Marxism-Leninism,*** 2nd ed. (1963), p. 694; it is interesting to note that this prediction does not appear in the 1st edition (1961).

77. Russett, cited, pp. 356–61.

78. Seymour E. Harris (ed.), ***Economic Aspects of Higher Education*** (Paris: OECD, 1964), p. 82.

CHAPTER 8

The Soviet Union as an Advanced Society

Chapter 8 brings the comparative story to the 1980s and is focused on the extent to which the proclaimed stage of "developed socialism" in the Soviet Union compares with advanced modernization in the West. Among the questions raised is whether "socialism" makes any difference. This in turn raises the question of what we mean by socialism. The term is usually used in two senses. The Marxist and Marxist-Leninist view of socialism sees public ownership of the means of production as the necessary prerequisite to the ultimate goal of the equitable distribution of goods and services in a society. The pluralist view of socialism agrees on the goal but not on the means and maintains that a considerable variety of political and economic systems may achieve a more equitable distribution of goods and services. Those concerned with the equitable distribution aspect of social justice should assess the results of social policy rather than the institutional structure or rhetoric of a society. Much depends on one's definition of socialism—an elusive term at best.

Much is being written these days about advanced modernization—referred to sometimes as "the postindustrial society," "the third wave," "advanced industrial society," and in the Soviet Union as "developed socialism," according to the differing ideologies and perspectives of the authors. Although there is considerable agreement as to the characteristics of advanced modernization and the ways in which it differs from the preceding period of societal transformation, it is a relatively new phenomenon, the evidence is still incomplete, and there are numerous unresolved problems. Since Soviet theorists live and think

Reprinted with permission from *The Soviet Polity in the Modern Era,* ed. by Erik P. Hoffmann and Robbin F. Laird (New York: Aldine Publishing Company, 1984), 809–832. This is a revised and expanded version of a paper on "Characteristics of Advanced Modernization Relative to the USSR," presented at the annual meeting of the American Political Science Association in Washington, D.C., August 28, 1980.

in a rather isolated world, it is important to consider the extent to which their conception of "developed" corresponds to the views current in the West—and, more important, how the levels of achievement of the Soviet Union compare with those of other societies insofar as the available indicators permit one to make appropriate comparisons.

THE SOVIET PERSPECTIVE

Soviet theorists today see their country's achievement of a "developed" status as a third stage in its development. The first was that of the establishment of the basic institutions of socialism in the years between the Revolution and the adoption of the 1936 Constitution. This was followed by the period from 1936 to 1967 in which the basic structure of socialism was further consolidated. They see the current stage, since 1967, not coincidentally the fiftieth anniversary of their Revolution, as one which Soviet society is taking advantage of the opportunities offered by the scientific and technological revolution to improve its economic productivity and political and social efficiency. The fourth stage will be the classless and stateless society predicted by Marx.

The characteristics attributed to this current stage of "developed socialism" are in many ways similar to those discussed by students of the advanced industrial societies in Western Europe, Japan, and the New World. These include the application of science and technology to the productive processes, leading to higher productivity and the potential for increasing material prosperity, as well as high levels of education, urbanization, and social welfare. Other characteristics discussed in the Soviet literature are more difficult to compare with those of democratic societies. Much is made, for example, of the new role of the Communist party as embodying the general interest of society now that antagonistic classes and interests allegedly no longer exist, and as aggregating the various nonantagonistic interest groups that compete for influence in decision making. Likewise, the Soviet state is seen as becoming more efficient and also more democratic in the sense of providing for greater public participation in administration.[1]

This conception of *developed socialism,* based on the scientific and technological revolution, evolved in the Soviet Union in the 1950s and 1960s under the influence of developments in Eastern Europe. In these years, a thoroughgoing effort was made in Poland, Czechoslovakia, Hungary, and East Germany to introduce the contemporary Western theory and practice of economics, sociology, and management into the realm of research and policy, which for some two decades had been dominated by a dogmatic Marxism-Leninism. The underlying motivation of this new ideological trend was a desire to reconcile the Marxist-

Leninist doctrinal heritage with the realities of the postwar world. These realities included not only achievements in economic growth and social change but more fundamentally the advances in science and technology—most obviously nuclear power, computers, and automation—that were transforming the advanced industrial societies. This rapid advancement of knowledge was now recognized as underlying modern societal transformation, and the new outlook soon came to be known as "the scientific-technological revolution" (*nauchno-tekhnicheskaia revoliutsiia* in Russian) or STR.[2]

This recognition of the fundamental importance of knowledge ran counter to the accepted Marxist-Leninist teaching that science and technology, including the social sciences, were part of the superstructure of society which was in the final analysis determined by the economic structure which formed its base.[3] This relationship has now been reversed, and in effect, science (which in Slavic languages means *knowledge* generally, not just the natural sciences) and technology (or perhaps more narrowly *technique*) are acknowledged in the final analysis as the base that determines the superstructure of political development, economic growth, and social integration. The closest that commentators seem to have come to an authoritative justification of this fundamental change is a statement by Marx himself, more an aside than a formal assertion, that as societies develop, production will change "from a simple labor process to a scientific process."[4]

As developed by writers in Eastern Europe, the advances in science and technology were seen as representing a revolutionary change in the possibilities for transforming the human condition. These advances lead to radical changes in the process of production, require a large number of highly trained technicians, and will permit a reduction in the differences between mental and manual labor and between urban and rural life. Their effects also include a great increase in the availability of data for use by the social sciences in the solution of complex problems.

One of the early indications of Soviet receptivity to the new trend was the appearance in 1969 of a Russian translation of Jan Szczepanski's *Elementary Principles of Sociology*, originally published in Warsaw in 1965. This was, in effect, a primer of contemporary sociology, predominantly American and West European, which also drew extensively on Polish work since the 1950s. It contained few references to Marx and none to Lenin. Of more general relevance was *Civilization at the Crossroads: Social and Human Implications of the Scientific and Technological Revolution*, published in Prague in 1966 (with an English edition in 1969), by Radovan Richta and his colleagues at the Institute of Philosophy and Sociology of the Czechoslovak Academy of Sciences. This volume cites primarily Western works dating from the 1940s and places no particular emphasis on Marxism-Leninism. It played, incidentally, an important role in the Czechoslovak events of 1968. Although the Prague reform movement was suppressed by the Soviet Union for reasons of national security, the Soviet and Czechoslovak academies of science collaborated 5 years later in publishing ***Man-Science-Technology: A Marxist Analysis of the Scientific-Technological Revolution*** (1973). This was a revised and extended version of ***Civilization at the Crossroads***, which placed more emphasis on relating the new trends to the Marxist-Leninist tradition.

In the meantime, Soviet theorists had since the 1950s been devoting increasing attention to the economic and social significance of the new developments in nuclear power, automation, and computers and a brief reference to this subject appeared in the Communist Party Program of 1961. The STR finally became a dominant official theme when Brezhnev, in his report to the Twenty-Fourth Congress of the CPSU in 1971, stated that "the task we face, comrades, is one of historical importance: ***organically to combine the achievements of the scientific-technological revolution with the advantages of the socialist economic system***, to develop our own, inherently socialist, forms of combining science with production."[5]

In the course of the 1970s, a wide range of views has been expressed in Soviet publications regarding the STR, and there are few areas of activity that have not been challenged to demonstrate that they are achieving the efficiency and productivity made possible by modern techniques.[6] American management and public administration are among the subjects that have attracted most interest, both in the Soviet Union and in the countries of Eastern Europe. Despite the existence of massive central and enterprise bureaucracies in these countries, little systematic attention was devoted before the 1960s to the theory and practice of management. Some specialists were now sent to American business schools for training and research, and in due course, institutions with curricula adapted from American models were established in these countries. A particular problem has been the inefficiency of the highly centralized planning systems and the separation of research and development organizations from the enterprises concerned with production. American business practice has become an important model in the search for more efficient organizational forms.[7] Similarly, in the construction of computers and the adaptation of software to the needs of the users, American technology has been transferred wholesale.[8]

ADVANCED MODERNIZATION: A COMPARATIVE APPROACH

Advanced modernization is the phase in a country's development in which the level of knowledge and of political capacity leads to the application of high technology to a wide range of economic and social processes. A type of society emerges in which specialized education is at a premium, services absorb a larger share of the labor force and of the domestic product than manufacturing and agriculture, and societies become more integrated in a whole series of dimensions. The United States may be said to have entered this phase in the 1930s, the countries of western and central Europe in the 1950s, and Japan and the Soviet Union in the 1960s.

During the preceding period of transformation from relatively non-modernized to relatively modernized societies, these countries have been concerned with two basic problems. One is the conversion of premodern capabilities to modern uses, and the other is the introduction of new techniques and institutions. These latter may either be developed indigenously, in the case of the early modernizers, or borrowed and adopted, in the case of latecomers. This process of transformation involves vast changes in social relationships. Modern knowledge must be accepted as superseding earlier conceptions of the human environment, and in varying degrees of specialization, large segments of the population become involved in the production and distribution of knowledge. This transformation requires a political leadership capable of guiding the development of an economy and society from a predominantly agrarian and rural to a predominantly industrial and urban way of life.

In seeking criteria by which to define and assess levels of "advancement," it is important to recognize that modernization should not be equated with progress. The engine of change in historical times has been the advancement of knowledge resulting from the interaction of human minds—central nervous systems—with each other and with everything else. Modernization results from the enhancement of the human capacity to understand and make use of the environment, and this enhanced capacity can be used for any purpose. It can be used to promote human betterment in terms of health, education, and welfare, or it can be used to destroy all humankind. World wars and holocausts are as characteristic of modernity as are industrialization, urbanization, and high levels of consumption. In this context, we seek here to evaluate levels of advancement in terms of selected intellectual, political, economic, and social indicators.

Intellectual Aspects

One of the main attributes of advanced modernization is the critical importance of theoretical knowledge—in the broad sense that includes the social sciences and humanities as well as the natural sciences—and the application of knowledge to the many areas of technology and public policy that affect human welfare. Whether one associates this development more narrowly, as Marxist-Leninists tend to do, with the scientific-technological revolution since 1945 or more broadly with the rapid advancement of knowledge that can be traced back to the Renaissance, these approaches have a common theme in the importance of applying the new knowledge to human affairs.[9]

One way of assessing the value that a society places on the advancement of knowledge is to measure the resources allocated to research and development. It has been estimated that in the 1970s, the Soviet Union expended an annual average of about 3.5% of its gross national product (GNP) on research and development. This compares with some 2.3% expended by the United States and the Federal Republic of Germany and somewhat less by France and Japan.[10] These are only rough orders of magnitude and do not measure the quality of research, but they indicate that Soviet performance in this area is at least equivalent to that in the developed Western countries and Japan.

Training for professional and technical occupations is a matter of special emphasis in advanced societies, and levels of educational development can be measured by the enrollments at different levels of education. Enrollments in higher education per 1000 of population are reported to range from about 20 to 50 in advanced societies. Available estimates suggest ratios of 52 in the United States, 20 in Japan and 19 in the Soviet Union. This compares with ratios of 10 in Switzerland, 5 in India, and 1 in many developing countries including China.[11] In this case, it should be noted, the high United States ratio would appear to reflect the tendency of the American educational system to delay serious education for many students until after the secondary school level. Many students in American colleges and universities are being taught skills that are learned in secondary schools in many other countries. It would probably be more accurate to reduce the American ratio by one-half. Apart from this correction, these estimates illustrate the wide gap in the resources devoted to higher education that separates the advanced from the less-developed societies.

Comparative indicators are not available to estimate the economic role of knowledge in advanced societies, but it has been estimated that the share in the United States GNP of the production and distribution of knowledge, very broadly defined, was 29% in 1958. The share of the knowledge-producing occupations in the American labor force tripled between 1900 and 1959, reaching some 30% of the labor force in the latter year.[12] Later estimates suggest that these ratios probably reached the 50% level in the 1970s.[13] Although these estimates are only suggestive, it is apparent that advanced societies are knowledge-intensive, in contrast to the capital-intensive nature of societies in the process of transformation and the labor-intensive premodern societies.

Political Aspects

Political development in advanced societies is characterized by an integrated mobilization of skills and resources by central decision-making bodies, whether public or private, and by increasingly complex patterns of interest representation in the formation of policy. In contrast to the earlier phase of societal transformation, which requires a high allocation of resources to investment and is for most citizens an exercise in the postponement of gratification, advanced modernization is characterized by an emphasis on distribution. In the course of societal transformation, the divisive issues concerning the mobilization and allocation of resources are predominantly regional and class-oriented. In advanced societies, politics becomes more concerned with issues facing society as a whole—the industrial, education, urban, welfare, and other consequences of the scientific and technological revolution. This change in orientation has led to the growth of the public sector. In the United States, for example, the federal, state, and local government expenditures as a share of GNP have risen from 2.5% in 1900 to 21% in 1970 and about 35% today. Federal expenditures account for about one-half this total.[14] The corresponding role of the public sector in other advanced societies ranges from 40% (Canada) to 63% (Sweden).[15] There are regrettably no comparable estimates for the Soviet Union.

Advanced societies are also characterized by a growth in the proportion of the population that is able to influence political decisions. The question of how social strata, classes, or interest groups and their changing relations should be defined and interpreted is one of continuing controversy. Most forms of interest representation that influence the formation of public policy are organizational in character, defining organizations broadly to include bureaucracies, legislatures, and political parties, as well as voluntary associations, interest groups, educational, religious, and other social institutions, business and research enterprises, and other corporate bodies.

The role of individuals in policy formation should be viewed in a predominantly organizational context. It is not a question of contrasting individual and organizational participation, since individuals are the only participants in policymaking whether they act alone or through organizations. It is a question rather of making the relevant distinctions between the influence of individuals acting alone and through organizations. The forms taken by political participation depend on the political culture and ideology of a society. In democratic societies, interest representation by organizations interacts with autonomous forms of individual participation, especially the election of representatives to legislative bodies on the basis of universal suffrage under conditions in which freedom of speech, press, and association are guaranteed. In authoritarian societies, interests are represented predominantly through organizations, and individuals exert influence only as members of organizations.

The extent to which organizations may foster or obstruct equity in the representation of interests in advanced societies varies with the nature of the organization and the political culture of the society in which it operates. More often than not, organizations tend to reflect the interests of elites or of selected sectors of a society at the expense of the general interest. Corporate forms of organization such as those currently gaining influence in Western Europe tend in particular to provide a privileged status for selected interests. For this reason, there is greater social equity in democratic than in authoritarian societies. At the same time, members of a society whose interests have been poorly represented during the period of societal transformation more often than not find that the best way to redress their grievances is by organizing. The effectiveness of organizations in representing interests also depends on the extent to which organizations are structured in such a way as to provide an equitable representation of the concerns of its members.[16]

Bureaucratic politics may be considered as a special case of organizational participation and is a form of interest representation by elements of a bureaucracy and their leaders in the intragovernmental decision-making procedures by virtue of the information and administrative skills that they command. In the broadest sense, these decisions involve allocations of resources and responsibility. In most governments, such decisions are taken at least once a year at a general level when national budgets are drawn up and usually more frequently as decisions on specific issues are made. These decisions may affect the size or even the existence of a bureau or department; the influence, programs, and the political future of leading officials; and indirectly the fate of powerful private interests affected by government decisions (e.g., taxpayers, farmers, the armament industry).[17]

How can one assess political participation in the Soviet Union in the context of this general characterization based on the Western experience? One may start by noting that the Soviet administrative vocabulary includes such terms as *interested organizations, interested institutions,* and *interested individuals.* These terms refer to organizations, institutions, and individuals that are represented on the collegial bodies that play an important role at all levels of the Soviet government. Some collegia are decision-making bodies, ranging from the presidium of the Council of Ministers to local executive committees, which are responsible for policy in the areas under their jurisdiction. Others are advisory bodies attached to executive offices, whose role is to monitor the activities of the relevant policy area. In both cases, the role of the collegial bodies is to represent the varied interests relating to a given branch of the administrative system, and the members of these collegia have explicit rights regarding the determination of the agenda of their meetings.[18]

It is not easy to distinguish in the Soviet system between the bureaucracy strictly speaking, together with the interrelated bureaucracy of the Communist party, and the considerable range of institutions that may have sufficient autonomy to be considered as corporatist organizations. Soviet society, like others that are relatively advanced, is made up of a considerable range of organizations with varying strengths and degrees of autonomy that seek to play a role in the mobilization and allocation of skills and resources. The role of these corporatist organizations in the political system is mediated by the Communist party agencies, which are concerned with representing these organizations in dealing with the central authorities as well as with the implementation of the directives that issue from the center. There is a considerable literature documenting the range and nature of this interest group activity as a feature of Soviet politics.[19]

Recent studies of Soviet decision making in such areas as agriculture, education, economic reform, and civil-military relations give evidence of extensive public debates among representatives of the relevant interests. No doubt the degree of autonomy of these organized interests varies considerably, and it is a matter of controversy as to how many of them share the characteristics of the corporatist organizations in Western Europe. The Academy of Sciences is perhaps the best example of a public organization possessing a strong bargaining power with the central authorities. Another type of autonomous organization is the All-Russian Society for the Preservation of Monuments of History and Culture, which has extensive responsibilities in the realm of its special interest and is supported by the dues from its over 10 million members. Coalitions are formed both among autonomous organizations and between them and branches of the party and the bureaucracy, and the role of the central authorities appears to be as much one of forming a consensus out of conflicting views as of dictating policy.[20] There is also evidence that in the case of some controversial issues, such as environmental policy, ad hoc groups of interested individuals may play a significant role. Similarly, individual specialists can participate actively in decision making when they are called in as consultants.[21]

In evaluating the scope of organizational participation in the Soviet Union, it is important to distinguish between the procedures for selecting leaders and the range of organized interests that make an input into policy. The monopoly of political power exercised by the Communist party and the single-candidate electoral system under conditions of severely restricted civil liberties stand out in sharp contrast to democratic multiparty parliamentary systems. There are at the same time significant similarities between the two systems in the extent of organizational participation in policymaking, and these similarities provide an important basis for comparing Soviet politics with that in other political systems.

Economic Aspects

The change from development to distribution involves a basic structural transformation of the economy in the course of which investments and labor force, along with numerous other concurrent trends, are shifted from producer to consumer goods and from manufacturing to services.

Employment of the economically active population is usually classified as primary (agriculture, hunting, fishing, forestry), secondary (mining and quarrying; manufacturing; electricity, gas, water; construction; transportation, storage, communication), and tertiary (wholesale and retail trade, restaurants, and hotels; financing, insurance, real estate, and business services; community, social, and personal services). In the course of societal transformation, the primary sector declines from 80% to 2–3% and the tertiary grows from some 5 to 60%.

Typical proportions for the three sectors in advanced societies in the 1970s are: United States—3.7,35.4,57.9; Sweden—6.1,41.5,52.4; France—10.8, 42.1, 47.1; Japan—12.0, 41.5, 46.6; United Kingdom—2.5, 54.6, 45.4; and the USSR—21.7, 47.2, 31.1. One may characterize societies as advanced that have 20% or less of the economically active population in the primary sector and 30% or more in the tertiary sector.[22] In China, by contrast, the comparable proportions were 85, 6, 9 in 1957 and 77, 11, 12 in 1975.[23]

Like other aspects of advanced modernization, this decline of the primary sector and growth of the tertiary represents an irreversible completion of trends characteristic of societal transformation.

A similar but less clearly defined and verified change takes place in income distribution. Income distribution generally becomes more equal as societies develop, but this trend is affected by social policy as well as by increases in per capita income, and the evidence is by no means clear. It has been estimated that in the course of economic growth, the share of GNP of the lowest 40% of the economically active population is U-shaped (i.e., in the early stages it declines in proportion to other shares and later rises again); and that of the top 20% is ∩-shaped (i.e., first rises proportionately and then declines). The share of the middle 40% rises from 20 to 40%.

The rapidly increasing GNP in advanced societies is allocated more to an increase in income of all groups than to redistribution. Inequality of distribution between the lowest 40%, the middle 40%, and the top 20% in advanced societies ranges from 10,36,52 (France) to 14,42,44 (Sweden) and 20,40,40 (Japan, United States, Canada, Australia, United Kingdom). The conclusion is suggested that the currently advanced societies have not yet confronted the problem of greater inequality and continue to stress equality of opportunity rather than equality of income. The promise of opportunity has taken the form of an increase in all incomes under a stable pattern of distribution. Some Marxist-Leninist countries claim greater equality of distribution than the advanced societies—27,40,33 (Bulgaria, Czechoslovakia)—but the evidence is inconclusive.[24] No adequate comparative figures appear to be available for the Soviet Union.

Social Aspects

Similarly in the social sphere, fundamental changes characteristic of societal transformation appear to approach completion. The best example of such a trend and the most carefully studied is the demographic transition. This transition is completed when societies evolve from high fertility and high mortality before the modern era, through an extended period of high fertility and low mortality—resulting in rapid population growth—to a phase of low fertility and low mortality. The rate of natural increase per 1000 in societies that have completed the demographic transition ranges from −4.1 in the Netherlands, −2.4 in the German Democratic Republic, 0.1 in the United Kingdom, and 0.9 in Sweden, to 3.1 in France, 5.8 in the United States, 9.0 in the USSR, and 10.0 in Japan. The rate of natural increase per 1000 in societies at an earlier stage in the demographic transition ranges from 16.6 in China, 20.0 in India, to 25.0 in Turkey, 29.7 in Iran, and 40.6 in Syria.[25]

Likewise in the case of urbanization, the resettlement from countryside to cities appears to be moving in the direction of an almost entirely urbanized society. The percentage of the population in cities of over 100,000 in advanced societies in the 1970s ranged from 29 (Italy) and 36 (USSR) to 58 (Japan) and 72 (United States). The percentage for less-developed countries ranges from 3 (Tanzania) to 10 (India).[26]

As regards the structure of consumption, in advanced societies the share of expenditures devoted to food and clothing tends to decline in comparison with expenditures for durable goods and services. In the 1970s, the share of consumption devoted to food and clothing was 27% in the United States, 35% in West Germany, 37% in the United Kingdom, and 40% in France, but it was 64.7% in the USSR.[27]

In the realm of health, the USSR has had a record until recently of mortality and life expectancy comparable to that of the Western countries and Japan. It is unique among developed countries, however, in the rise of its death rate in the 1970s. This rise has been particularly high among infants and males aged 20–44. At the end of the 1970s, infant mortality was estimated at 39 per thousand as compared with 12.9 per thousand in the United States. In the ages 20–44, the level of male deaths was 3 to 3.5 times that of females in the same age group. These trends have led to a decline in life expectancy at birth since 1964 of 5 years for males and 2 for females. In this period, the gap between life expectancy for males and females has grown from 4 to 11.6 years. This rise in mortality is due to a variety of causes, among which a decline in health care and a rise in alcoholism loom large. Better reporting is also responsible in part for the higher rates of infant mortality.[28]

HOW ADVANCED IS THE SOVIET UNION?

It is no easy task to compare societies at a given level of development, and on the basis of the foregoing discussion, only a partial answer can be given to the question addressed in this section.

So far as the production and distribution of knowledge is concerned, the Soviet Union is not surpassed by many countries, and the share of GNP allocated to research and development in the Soviet Union is among the highest. In the realm of basic research in the natural sciences, American scientists are inclined to regard their Soviet counterparts as among the most competitive in many areas. In terms of enrollments in higher education per 1000 population, the Soviet Union ranks among the top 10 or 15 countries.

It is an awesome task to evaluate levels of political development, but several statements can be made with some assurance. In terms of the "output" of the political system, the Soviet Union has as specialized and developed a bureaucracy as one could wish. Since we are equating modernity with complexity rather than with progress, one should doubtless accord the Soviet Union a high ranking in the sphere of bureaucratic development.

Comparisons of "inputs" into political systems—the extent to which individuals and groups participate in decision making—depend a great deal on one's point of view. If one uses progress toward democracy as the measure, the Soviet Union as a one-party authoritarian system ranks of course very low. If one evaluates polities in terms of the extent to which organized interests are consulted in decision making, the Soviet Union ranks much higher. The task of the staff of the Central Committee is not only to transmit orders to the multitude of organizations and enterprises that make up Soviet society but also to receive and aggregate their demands. There is much evidence of debate and formation of coalitions among organized interests in their efforts to influence the allocation of skills and resources. Ranking is not possible in this sphere, but in this respect, the differences between authoritarian and democratic political systems are much narrower than is normally assumed in the West.

Comparisons become easier in the economic sphere, where the statistics give at least an appearance of accuracy, and here the Soviet record presents a mixed picture. The course of economic growth as reflected in the shift in the employment of the labor force from agriculture to manufacturing and services has been relatively slow, and the proportion of the labor force in nonagricultural employment is lower by a considerable margin than that of the United States, Sweden, France, Japan, or the United Kingdom. Similarly, in GNP per capita—not discussed in the preceding section—the Soviet Union ranked only thirty-first in 1975 among 131 countries for which information was available.[29]

The information regarding income distribution is most inconclusive. While income distribution tends to become more equal as societies develop, the idiosyncrasies of definition and allocation vary so much among societies that a clear pattern is difficult to discern. In view of the continuing emphasis in the Soviet Union on investment for growth rather than distribution, one is inclined to suspect that income distribution is less equal than in other countries at the same level of economic development.

The indicators of social change are somewhat more serviceable than those relating to the economy, since human beings rather than abstract concepts are being measured, and the Soviet Union comes out rather well in this sphere. The share of the population in cities over 100,000 is above that of Italy and Sweden but considerably below that of Japan and the United States. In the trend of the demographic transition toward low birth and death rates, the Soviet Union ranks between Japan and the United States although behind many West European countries. At the same time, in the late 1970s, there was a significant decline in life expectancy at birth, especially among males, and a marked increase in mortality among infants and among males aged 20–44.

Efforts to aggregate a wide range of economic and social indicators are fraught with problems, but a recent attempt to elaborate an index of development provides a further perspective on the extent to which the USSR may be considered to be advanced. This estimate ranks 43 countries independent since 1869 at 5-year intervals on the basis of an index that aggregates 10 variables. The variables are (1) urbanization per capita, (2) revenue and expenditure per capita, (3) imports and exports per capita, (4) rail mileage per square mile, (5) mail per capita, (6) telephones per capita (since 1889), (7) percentage of work force in agriculture, (8) steel production per capita (since 1930), (9) cement production per capita, and (10) GNP per capita. The fourth variable would seem to place Russia/USSR at a disadvantage due to its vast territory and unevenly distributed population. Apart from this qualification and the caution with which all indicators should be approached, this seems to be a fair basis for comparison. On the basis of this index the USSR is ranked seventeenth in 1973, sixteenth in 1963, seventeenth in 1953, twentieth in 1937, and thirty-fifth in 1927; while the Russian empire ranked twenty-seventh in 1911, twenty-fifth in 1901, thirty-second in 1891, and twenty-fourth in 1871.[30]

In conclusion, insofar as a clear pattern of an "advanced" society can be discerned, the Soviet Union appears to qualify for ranking among the top 20 societies of the world. Whether or not it is "advanced" depends on where one wishes to draw the line in this ranking. Due to distortions in the Soviet development resulting from policies directed toward rapid economic growth with particular emphasis on producer goods and armaments, its pattern of development differs somewhat from that of other advanced societies. Since all aspects of development are in the long run interrelated, however, these differences are in degree rather than in kind.

NOTES

1. Recent general treatments of "developed socialism" include ***Razvitoi sotsialisticheskoe obshchestvo: Sushchnost, kriterii zrelosti, kritika revizionistskikh kontseptsii,*** 2nd ed. (1975); "Razvitoi sotsialisticheskoe obshchestvo," in ***Nauchnyi kommunizm: solvar,*** A. M. Rumiantsev, ed. (1975), pp. 285–289 (It is interesting to note that there is no article on this subject in the 1969 edition of this handbook); Pyotr Fedoseyev, "Developed Socialism: Theoretical Problems," ***Social Sciences*** (Moscow), 8 (Summer 1977), pp. 8–23; Iu. A. Tikhomirov, ***Mekhanizm upravleniia v razvitom sotsialisticheskom obshchestve*** (1978); Ts. A. Stepanian and A. S. Frish, eds., ***Razvitoi sotsializm i aktualnye problemy nauchnogo kommunizma*** (1979); and Erik P. Hoffmann and Robbin F. Laird, ***The Politics of Economic Modernization in the Soviet Union*** (1982).

2. These paragraphs draw on the author's "Changing Mutual Social Science Perceptions: The U.S. and the U.S.S.R. and Eastern Europe," ***A Balance Sheet for East-West Exchanges*** (1980), pp. 9–36. An authoritative Soviet account of the STR is D. M. Gvishiani and S. R. Mikulinskii, "Nauchno-tekhnicheskaia revoliutsiia," ***Bolshaia sovetskaia entsiklopediia,*** 3rd ed., vol. 17 (1974), pp. 341–343. For a general introduction, see Julian M. Cooper, "The Scientific and Technological Revolution in Soviet Theory," ***Technology and Communist Culture,*** ed. by Frederic J. Fleron, Jr. (1977), pp. 146–179; and N. V. Markov, ***Nauchno-tekhnicheskaia revoliutsiia: Analiz, perspektivy, posledstviia*** (1973).

3. See the statement of this proposition cited in A. I. Paskov, "Observations Concerning the Social Sciences in the USSR," *Social Sciences in the USSR*, 2 (1965).

4. Cited in Gvishiani and Mikulinskii, "Nauchno-tekhnicheskaia revoliutsiia," p. 341, from Marx's *Grundrisse der Kritik der politischen Ökonomie*, published for the first time in 1939, in Marx and Engels, *Sochineniia*, 2nd ed., vol. 46, pt. 2, p. 208.

5. *Twenty-fourth Congress of the Communist Party of the Soviet Union, March 30–April 9, 1971* (1971), p. 69, emphasis in original.

6. Erik P. Hoffmann, "Soviet Views of the 'Scientific-Technological Revolution,'" *World Politics* 30 (July 1978), pp. 615–644, reviews some of the principal Soviet treatises on this subject.

7. V. G. Afanasyev, *The Scientific and Technological Revolution—Its Impact on Management and Education* (1975); Robert F. Miller, "The Scientific-Technical Revolution and the Soviet Administrative Debate," *The Dynamics of Soviet Politics*, ed. by Paul Cocks, Robert V. Daniels, and Nancy Whittier Heer (1976), pp. 137–155; D. M. Gvishiani, S. R. Mikulinskii, and S. A. Kugel, eds., *The Scientific Intelligentsia in the USSR: Structure and Dynamics of Personnel* (1976); Paul Cocks, "Rethinking the Organizational Weapon: The Soviet System in a Systems Age," *World Politics* 32 (January 1980), pp. 228–257; and Boris Milner, "Application of Scientific Methods to Management in the Soviet Union," *Academy of Management Review* 2 (October 1977), pp. 554–560.

8. Seymour E. Goodman, "Soviet Computing and Technology Transfer: An Overview," *World Politics* 31 (July 1979), pp. 539–570.

9. Daniel Bell, *The Coming of Post-Industrial Society* (1973), esp. pp. 3–45.

10. National Science Board, *Science Indicators 1980* (Washington, D.C.: National Science Foundation, 1981), p. 210.

11. C. L. Taylor and D. A. Jodice, *World Handbook of Political and Social Indicators*, 3rd ed., 2 vols. (New Haven: Yale University Press, 1983), I, pp. 166–167. The ratio for higher education in China is for 1978, computed from the June 27, 1979 communique of the P.R.C. State Statistical Bureau.

12. Fritz Machlup, *The Production and Distribution of Knowledge in the United States* (1962), chaps. 9 and 10.

13. Fritz Machlup, *Knowledge: Its Creation, Distribution, and Economic Significance*, vol. 1 (1980), pp. xxvi–xxvii.

14. Edward R. Fried *et al.*, *Setting National Priorities* (1973), pp. 8–9.

15. Bank for International Settlements, *Fifty-first Annual Report* (June 1981), p. 24.

16. Cyril E. Black and John P. Burke, "Organizational Participation and Public Policy," *World Politics* 35 (April 1983), pp. 393–425.

17. Mark V. Nadel and Francis E. Rourke, "Bureaucracies," *Handbook of Political Science*, 8 vols. (1975), 5, pp. 373–429; and Graham T. Allison and Morton H. Halperin, "Bureaucratic Politics: A Paradigm and Some Policy Implications," in *Theory and Policy in International Relations*, ed. R. Tanter and R. H. Ullman (1971), pp. 40–79.

18. Ellen Jones, "Committee Decision Making in the Soviet Union," *World Politics* 36 (January 1984), pp. 165–188.

19. The best general treatments of interest group participation in the Soviet Union are H. Gordon Skilling and Franklyn Griffiths, eds., ***Interest Groups in Soviet Politics*** (Princeton: Princeton University Press, 1971); Tatjana Kirstein, ***Die Konsultation von "Aussenstehenden" durch den Partei und Staatsapparat sowie den Obersten Sowjet der UdSSR als stabilisierender Faktor des sowjetischen Herrschaftsystems*** (Berlin: Harrassowitz, 1972); Boris Meissner and George Brunner, eds., ***Gruppeninteressen und Entscheidungsprozess in der Sowjetunion*** (Cologne: Wissenschaft und Politik, 1975); Gerd Meyer, ***Bürokratischer Sozialismus: Eine Analyse des sowjetischen Herrschaftsystems*** (Stuttgart: Frommann-Holzboog, 1977); and Jerry F. Hough and Merle Fainsod, ***How the Soviet Union Is Governed*** (Cambridge: Harvard University Press, 1979), pp. 518–555.

20. Representative studies include Sidney Ploss, ***Conflict and Decision Making in Soviet Russia: A Case Study of Agricultural Policy,*** 1953–1963 (Princeton: Princeton University Press, 1965); Joel J. Schwartz and William R. Keech, "Group Influence and the Policy Process in the Soviet Union," ***American Political Science Review*** 62 (September 1968), pp. 840–851; Philip H. Stewart, "Soviet Interest Groups and the Policy Process: The Repeal of Production Education," ***World Politics*** 22 (October 1969), pp. 29–50; Abraham Katz, ***The Politics of Economic Reform in the Soviet Union*** (New York: Praeger, 1972); Theodore H. Friedgut, "Interest Groups in Soviet Policy Making: The MTS Reform," ***Soviet Studies*** 28 (October 1976), pp. 524–527; Edward L. Warner, III, ***The Military in Contemporary Soviet Politics: An Institutional Analysis*** (New York: Praeger, 1977); Timothy J. Colton, ***Commissars, Commanders, and Civilian Authority: The Structure of Soviet Military Politics*** (Cambridge: Harvard University Press, 1979); Erik P. Hoffmann and Robbin F. Laird, ***The Politics of Economic Modernization in the Soviet Union*** (Ithaca: Cornell University Press, 1982); and Dennis Ross, "Coalition Maintenance in the Soviet Union," ***World Politics*** 32 (January 1980), pp. 258–280. For a critique of this approach, see William E. Odom, "A Dissenting View on the Group Approach to Soviet Politics," ***World Politics*** 29 (July 1976), pp. 542–567.

21. Donald R. Kelley, "Environmental Policy Making in the USSR: The Role of Industrial and Environmental Interest Groups," ***Soviet Studies*** 28 (October 1976), pp. 570–589; Richard B. Remnek, ***Soviet Scholars and Foreign Policy: A Case Study in Soviet Policy Toward India*** (Durham, N.C.: Duke University Press, 1975); and Peter H. Solomon, Jr., ***Soviet Criminologists and Criminal Policy: Specialists in Policy Making*** (New York: Columbia University Press, 1978).

22. International Labour Office, ***Year Book of Labour Statistics, 1977*** (1977), pp. 52–167.

23. Thomas G. Rawski, ***Economic Growth and Employment in China*** (1979), pp. 37–39.

24. Hollis Chenery ***et al., Redistribution with Growth*** (1974), pp. 27–30.

25. United Nations, ***Statistical Yearbook 1977*** (1978), pp. 80–85.

26. Taylor and Jodice, ***World Handbook,*** I, pp. 200–202.

27. Gertrude E. Schroeder and Imogene Edwards, ***Consumption in the USSR: An International Comparison*** (Washington, D.C.: U.S. Congress, Joint Economic Committee, 1981), p. 23.

28. Murray Feshbach, "The Soviet Union: Population Trends and Dilemmas," ***Population Bulletin*** 37 (August 1982), pp. 30–36.

29. Taylor and Jodice, ***World Handbook,*** I, p. 110.

30. Arthur S. Banks, "An Index of Socio-Economic Development, 1869–1975," ***Journal of Politics*** 43 (May 1981), pp. 390–411, and especially pp. 402–407. An evaluation for the 1960s in Cyril E. Black, "Soviet Society: A Comparative View," in ***Prospects for Soviet Society,*** ed. Allen Kassof (1968), pp. 14–53, reached a similar conclusion.

PART THREE

Russia/USSR: How It Relates to the Larger World

The theme of continuity between the Russian empire and the Soviet Union is in most respects as valid in international relations as it is in domestic development. Virtually all the issues of foreign policy that have confronted the Soviet leaders—except, of course, the control of nuclear arms—also preoccupied the diplomats of the empire. Indeed, many of these issues have a history going back several centuries.

In at least one respect, however, there is a distinct discontinuity: the Russian and Soviet leaders' perceptions of their country's relative position as a world power have undergone significant changes. From the early eighteenth century to the 1850s, the Russian autocracy saw itself as an equal and respected member of the European community of nations. The French revolution was certainly a challenge to this self-image, but the defeat of Napoleon and the subsequent peace settlement restored Russia's position as a leading European power. If not used as a model, Russia was generally accepted by the other European governments as a stable society. The defeat in the Crimean War brought an end to this period of complacency. Thenceforth until 1917 the status of the Russian empire was continuously challenged. Most Europeans and much of the educated public within Russia regarded the empire as a society that could not survive without profound transformations.

All this changed after 1917. Lenin and his colleagues, after dispelling doubts as to whether their regime could survive the early turbulent years, saw themselves as being in the forefront of human development. They believed in and propagated the view that all societies were bound by the immutable laws of history to evolve from feudalism and capitalism to socialism and communism. The Soviet Union, as the first socialist state, would lead the way. The propaganda conveying this view scared the wits out of many Westerners in the 1920s. When Stalin turned his attention predominantly to domestic matters in the 1930s, the contrast between the dynamic image of the five-year plans and the years of depression represented a new challenge to the West. Stalin's reign of terror did little to tarnish this image in the 1930s, and the victory in World War II seemed to many to justify the harsh policies of earlier years. This victory, accompanied by annexations, the acquisition of a sphere of influence in Eastern Europe, and many new opportunities to intervene in revolutions in the developing countries, once again highlighted the image of the Soviet Union as a model for others.

Khrushchev himself was fully convinced that the Soviet Union would overtake and surpass the West in economic development within a generation, and in his typically pungent fashion he declared in 1956 at a Kremlin reception for Western ambassadors: "History is on our side. We will bury you." He did not mean kill and bury but simply that capitalism would in due course give way to socialism and communism. Brezhnev was more tactful at the summit meeting in Vienna in June 1979 when, in response to Carter's accusation that the Soviet Union was interfering with national struggles for independence in the Third World, he said: "Why then pin on the Soviet Union the responsibility for the objective course of history and, what is more, use this as a pretext for worsening our relations?"

In the early years of Soviet rule it was assumed that the transformation from capitalism to socialism would take place through military conflicts. Indeed, both world wars were followed by successful revolutions, not the least of which was the Bolshevik seizure of power in 1917. Since 1956, however, the Soviet leaders have recognized that war in the nuclear era is not practicable and have adopted the prevailing doctrine of "peaceful coexistence." This doctrine does not mean that capitalism and socialism should live together in peace, but rather that the transition from capitalism to socialism should take place without a major war.

Many conservatives and liberals in the West continue to be alarmed by this Marxist-Leninist view and see a threat of "world communism" engulfing the earth. It seems to me that one must be a believer in the philosophy of Marx to take this ideological threat seriously. Marx was one of the most perspicacious of the nineteenth-century social thinkers, but his views were naturally limited by the conditions he observed during his lifetime. A century of political, economic, and social change has resulted in developments quite unforeseeable in Marx's day. Since I am not a Marxist, I place little value on the predictions of Marx and on the rather simplified reinterpretations of them that the Soviet leaders seem to believe in. Historical experience in the past century seems to me to lead in a very different direction. To me the Soviet predictions of the ultimate victory of communism, as defined by their theories, are no more of a threat than if they said the world were flat, and they were going to push us off the edge.

CHAPTER 9

The Pattern of Russian and Soviet Objectives

The challenge represented by the Soviet Union today derives not from the ideology of Marxism-Leninism, but from its military power. Chapter 9 argues that this is not a new challenge, except insofar as the Soviet Union has significantly greater military power on a global scale than did the empire. So far as Western and Central Europe are concerned, the empire exerted greater influence from 1815 to 1850 than does the USSR today. It is also interesting to note that the area of the Soviet Union is no greater than that of the empire in 1900. Russian and Soviet perceived national interests and foreign policy objectives reflect very significant elements of continuity. From Central Europe to China and North America and from Ethiopia to the Arctic Circle, Russian armies, explorers, traders, and missionaries were active long before 1917.

This is not to say that the Russian precedents make the Soviet worldwide activities less of a challenge. It is rather to say that any government of Russia/USSR would be inclined to pursue similar interests, and that one should be careful to distinguish between the interests and activities of a great power in the geopolitical position of Russia/USSR and the alleged threat of "world communism." This challenge can be and is being met by the conventional methods of world politics: counterbalancing the military power of the USSR and drawing on the vast resources and skills of the United States and its allies and friends to cope with the variety of problems of political development, economic growth, and social integration faced by the later-modernizing societies around the world.

I

In defining the foreign policy objectives of a country it is useful to make a distinction between those concerned primarily with traditional

Reprinted with permission from *Russian Foreign Policy: Essays in Historical Perspective,* ed. by Ivo J. Lederer (New Haven: Yale University Press, 1962), 3–38.

conceptions of security and those based on broader theoretical considerations. One may think of security objectives as those involving the maintenance and development of a country in a relatively stable evolutionary international political system whose members recognize that each has certain legitimate security requirements. A system of this type may be said to have existed in Europe as a whole, although not in all of its parts, in the century between 1815 and 1914. Objectives based on considerations of a theoretical character, on the other hand, become particularly important at a time when revolutionary changes are occurring in the international political system, and when the welfare or even the existence of a country may depend on the ability of its statesmen to understand the nature and direction of change and to adjust their policies accordingly. The era of the French Revolution and Napoleon, and that of the two world crises of the twentieth century, are typical periods of revolutionary change in which objectives based on considerations of theory attain a special significance.

It is not easy to define in general terms the elements that may properly constitute a nation's security, for much depends on the specific problems it faces. A nation may embrace a continent, or it may have no more than a fragment of territory. Its frontiers may be clearly recognizable and relatively defensible, or they may be drawn across an open plain with no regard to geography. It may be so isolated as to be virtually immune from attack (until the advent of missiles), or it may be surrounded by predatory enemies. It may have a vigorous leadership supported by an advanced population, or it may have a weak government only nominally leading a backward society. It may have a thriving economy favored by geography and resources, or it may be a virtual wasteland barely capable of supporting human life. It may have a population with a strong sense of common history and destiny, or one traditionally divided and uncertain of its future. The peoples considering themselves a nation may live together as a distinct political entity, or they may be divided by serious geographical, political, or cultural barriers.

No two nations have quite the same problems, and no general definition of security can go beyond establishing the central element of survival and ascertaining the essential conditions on which the survival of any nation must depend. Moreover, the question as to what a nation may consider as essential for its security cannot be divorced from the value system of the statesmen who guide its destinies. For some the maintenance of the status quo may be quite adequate, while for others it may represent a great deal less than what is necessary. Assuming the existence of a nation and the desire to maintain its nationhood, it is not necessary to seek explicit statements regarding the essentials of security from its leaders. Their views on this subject are in fact less likely to take the form of statements of policy than of decisions—to wage war, accept peace terms, make budgetary allocations, appoint officials—from which one may infer the scale of values of the decision-makers.

It would doubtless be a mistake to draw too sharp a distinction between considerations based on security and those based on theory in the formulation of foreign policy objectives, for a theoretical approach reflects an understanding on the part of statesmen of the world around them and to this extent informs their concept of their country's security. The definition of the essentials of a country's security is in some degree always a matter of controversy—among contemporary statesmen as well as among chroniclers enjoying the advantages of multidisciplinary hindsight. The concept is nevertheless useful for defining the minimum objectives with which any foreign policy must be concerned. For the achievement of certain objectives involving security a country may rely solely on its own resources, and to this extent it may be able for extended periods to neglect changes in the international political system with which theory is primarily concerned. In so far as a country's security depends on a balance of power and a system of alliances, however, it cannot fail to be concerned with considerations of theory. In revolutionary times, moreover, interpretation of international developments becomes a crucial feature of foreign policy.

In this sense, foreign policy objectives based on theoretical considerations are much more controversial than are those concerned with security. It is difficult enough to get agreement regarding the security interests of a country, but it is much more difficult to determine the nature and course of change in international affairs in revolutionary times. There is nothing more complex in the world of politics than the interrelation of the intellectual, political, economic, and social aspects of change in a world of many societies with diverse cultural traditions and at different stages of development. Indeed, changes of this complexity can never be interpreted with great certainty, and statesmen are frequently inclined to place their reliance on traditional concepts of security rather than to take the risks implicit in a policy that rests on more speculative theoretical considerations. In revolutionary times the dilemma is unavoidable, however, for in such times the underlying assumptions not only of alliance systems but even of the structure of the states comprising the system may be profoundly altered. The evolution of Russian foreign policy offers many examples of the nature of security interests and theoretical considerations, and of the various ways in which they can interact, for within a period of three centuries Russia moved from the periphery to the center of international affairs.

The objectives that may be inferred from the words and deeds of Russian statesmen, whether defined in terms of traditional security and of theoretical considerations as suggested here or in some other fashion, represent only one aspect of the totality of foreign policy. The formulation of policy is a distinct subject of study, including as it does the role of the machinery of government and the influence of domestic interest groups. In this sense foreign policy is the external expression of national life, and everything that goes on in a country is to some extent involved. It is also useful to make a distinction between the formulation of policy and the instruments by which a policy is implemented—the agencies of diplomacy, propaganda, economic relations, and military force which may be employed by a government beyond its frontiers in attempting to carry out its decisions. Finally, there is the implementation of policy itself—the process by which the policy of one country is confronted by those of others in the realm of international relations, and the compromises and adjustments that result from this confrontation. In discussing objectives, it is therefore important to keep in mind the totality of foreign policy of which they form a part. It is proposed here first to present the traditional security objectives of Russian policy, then to discuss the ways in which considerations of theory have been influential, and finally to evaluate the significance of the revolution of 1917 in the determination of Russian objectives.

II

For the sake of conciseness, the objectives of Russian foreign policy that may be said to have been based primarily on considerations of security will be discussed under four somewhat arbitrary general categories: stabilization of frontiers; assurance of favorable conditions for economic growth; unification of territories considered to be Russian by virtue of dynastic, religious, or national claims; and participation in alliance systems and international institutions.

1. "Stabilization of frontiers" may appear to be a rather laconic way of describing the long and bitter struggles in the course of which the boundaries of Russia have been defined. Yet, for a country initially without well-defined goegraphical frontiers, the term stabilization has much to recommend it. The initial problem was that of gaining defensible frontiers, and for the greater portion of Russia's borders this was less a question of geography than of coming to terms with the political power on the other side of the border. Stability could, in most instances, be achieved only by reducing or eliminating the political power of a neighbor through military action, or by establishing pre-emptive political control over relatively uninhabited territories, or by relying primarily on such natural barriers as seas, deserts, and mountains on long stretches of borderland which had relatively little political significance. The

common element in this category of interests is the threat to the security of the population from a major invasion by formidable foes or from disruptive depredations by relatively disorganized nomadic peoples.

This raises the question whether, not infrequently, Russia was not the aggressor rather than the aggrieved; there can be no question but that it has been responsible for its full share of aggressive, preventive, and pre-emptive wars. At the same time, no less in recent years than in earlier centuries when it was relatively weak, it has been subjected to attacks and invasions of such proportions as to give rise to a continuing sense of apprehension and insecurity. Although in general these attacks and invasions were doubtless no more than an effort on the part of Russia's neighbors to stabilize their own frontiers (and indeed the size and strength of Russia have justifiably been regarded as a threat to their own security), the nature of international relations is such that the motives of individual nations may properly be judged in relative terms. One must thus recognize both the fundamental sense of insecurity that Russia's position has aroused in the minds of its statesmen during long and significant periods of its history, and the fear that Russia has frequently inspired on the part of its neighbors and indeed of Europe as a whole.[1]

The oldest Russian frontier of continuing political significance, and for long periods one of the most uneasy, is the Baltic frontier. Here the antecedents of modern Russia maintained a commercial outlet and a small coastline until the defeat of Novgorod by Moscow in the fifteenth century, although the control of the sea and of most of the coastline was in other hands. Thenceforth Russia was to fight a series of wars with the Swedes and the Poles for control of this region, and not until 1721 did it come securely into Russian hands. In 1809 possession of Finland was added to that of the Baltic principalities, and for another century this frontier enjoyed a degree of stability that permitted the peoples on both sides to develop in peace and prosperity. The wars of the twentieth century led to a new period of instability in which Germany was Russia's principal antagonist. The Baltic states enjoyed a temporary independence between the wars, and Finland was able to retain its independence after 1945 although with somewhat reduced frontiers. The settlement in this region after the Second World War placed Russia in a position which resembled, at least in terms of geography, that which existed between 1721 and 1809.[2]

The frontier in Eastern Europe is not as old as that in the Baltic region, but it has offered much thornier problems for Russian statesmanship. Indeed, it would not be too much to say that it has been the most vital frontier and the one that has most accurately reflected Russia's international position. Here Russia has met its principal rivals and fought its greatest battles. It was two centuries after the emergence of a consolidated Russian state in the fifteenth century before a degree of stability was established in this sector of Russia's border, and the course of the struggle depended as much on Poland's fortunes as on Russia's. After the Tatar invasions the Slavic peoples of this region were ruled by Lithuanian and Lithuanian-Polish (1386–1569) princes, and later by the reorganized state of Poland. The long and bitter struggle with Poland was the central preoccupation of Russian foreign policy in the sixteenth and early seventeenth centuries, and a Polish army held Moscow from 1610 to 1612. This event marked the culmination of Polish influence, and a reorganized Russia registered a decisive victory in 1667 in a treaty that marked a turning point in its fortunes. Henceforth, with temporary setbacks, it was Russia's turn to advance.[3]

With the partitions of Poland, Prussia and Austria replaced the dismembered state as Russia's neighbors. Russia now became much more directly involved in the affairs of Europe, an involvement that was accompanied by such dramatic events as the occupation of Moscow by Napoleon and the prominent role of Alexander I in the reorganization of Europe after the French defeat. The frontier changed several times with the fortunes of war, and the line finally established in 1815 marked the greatest extension of Russian power in this area; it remained unchanged for a century as a landmark of the influence of the tsars. In the wars of the twentieth century, as earlier, the fate of this frontier was a sensitive barometer of Russia's national power. The loss of sizeable White Russian and Ukrainian minorities to a reconstituted Poland after the First World War reflected the ravages of war and revolution, and the frontier of 1945 was established after difficult negotiations in which considerations of political power, national feeling, and ideology all played a role.[4]

Further south, in the region of the Black Sea, a different set of factors came into play. In a larger sense the Baltic, Eastern Europe, and the Black Sea have all been part of a single frontier, and in the great crises that have involved Russia with Europe all three have frequently shared a common fate. In the seventeenth and early eighteenth centuries Russia faced Poland, and briefly Sweden, on all three fronts, and at later stages it has been confronted by France and Germany on more than one of these fronts at the same time. Yet the Black Sea region has distinctive geographical and political features that give it a character of its own. Here the initial instability came less from rival powers than from a lack of organized power, and in the seventeenth century the Ukrainians, Cossacks, and Tatars struggled for dominance, subject to indecisive pressure from Poland and Turkey.

Russia became involved in this area both as a protector of the Ukrainians and as a foe of the retreating Tatars. The capture of Kazan in 1552 opened up the region to Russian influence. At about the same time the fertile lands of the lower Dnieper, which had been largely depopulated since the Tatar invasions, began to attract large numbers of settlers. The Cossack settlers, of mixed Slavic, Circassian, and Tatar origin, came initially under Polish protection but soon organized a distinctive form of self-government which permitted them a degree of autonomy and bargaining power. The Cossacks now became a source of conflict between Poland and Russia, and in opting for the latter in the controversial agreement negotiated at Pereiaslavl in 1654 Bohdan Khmelnitskii hoped to retain the autonomy of his peoples. The pressure on the Ukraine from Poles, Turks, and Tatars was nevertheless too great to be resisted successfully by any but a major power, and Russia now entered this region decisively.[5]

The annexation of the Ukraine brought Russia into more direct contact with the Ottoman Empire and its Tatar vassals, in an area which half a millennium earlier had been the main channel of Kievan-Byzantine trade. It was now virtually barren of commerce or production, but the settlement of the surrounding agricultural land was soon to inaugurate a new era of prosperity. In the course of a little over a century (1676–1812) Russia pressed the Turks back in a series of wars and established itself as a Black Sea power. In this period the struggle was essentially between Russia and Turkey, but thenceforth it was to become the "Eastern Question" which vitally affected the European balance of power as one after another of the Balkan peoples came to gain their independence. After 1791 the Russian frontier on the European side of the Black Sea moved only from the Dniester to the Pruth, and even of this small gain a part or all had to be relinquished for considerable periods. Here the combined pressure of European interests has held the Russian frontier with minor changes for a century and a half. This pressure also had the effect after 1841 of closing the Turkish Straits to the warships of foreign states in time of peace, although after 1923 passage of warships was permitted under certain conditions. At this time restrictions were also placed on the right of Turkey to regulate the passage of warships in time of war. The importance of this region to Russia's security was particularly apparent in the Crimean War and in the First World War, when control of the Straits by the enemy permitted it to inflict decisive damage.[6]

In the Caucasus region on the eastern shores of the Black Sea, in the absence of a concentration of countervailing European power, the Georgians and the Armenians relied more fully on Russian assistance against Muslim power than did the Christians of the Balkans. The growth of Russian influence offered them an opportunity to overthrow the oppressive Ottoman and Persian rule. Peter and Catherine were unsuccessful in coping with this region, but by the end of the century conditions had changed, and in a relatively few years (1787–1829) the Russian frontier moved rapidly to the line which has since then been maintained with few alterations. In the case of the frontier with Turkey, the region of Batum and Kars was annexed in 1878, but Kars was lost again after the First World War. The frontier with Iran in the Caucasus has been formally stable since 1828, although after the Second World War—as two centuries earlier (1723–32)—Russia had ambitions to extend the frontier further to the south.[7]

In Central Asia, the instability of the frontier established after the Russian conquest of Siberia stemmed initially from friction with the nomadic Tatars and Bashkirs, and somewhat later the Kazakhs and Kalmyks. This initial friction was overcome in the eighteenth and early nineteenth centuries when Russia expanded systematically across the southern steppes from Orenburg, Orsk, and Omsk to the Aral Sea and the Syr-Daria and Chu rivers. In a second and more rapid expansion (1864–95), the weak khanates of Central Asia were annexed, and the Russian frontier reached the formidable barrier of the Hundu Kush mountains. One may perhaps question whether stabilization against an immediate outside pressure was the primary motive in this last advance. Nevertheless growing British influence in Afghanistan and clashes on the Russian-Afghanistan frontier (1885, 1892–95) convey the impression that, in the absence of Russian interest, Central Asia would not long have remained a great power vacuum. Anglo-Russian friction was also reflected in neighboring Sinkiang, where Russia briefly occupied (1871–81) the Kuldzha region on the Ili River in a move to counter British influence among the restless Chinese Turks.[8]

The frontier with China was of little political significance until the latter half of the nineteenth century, although the two countries had first confronted each other in the 1640s when a Cossack expedition entered the Amur basin. In so doing it touched on Manchu security at a sensitive point, and after almost half a century of minor warfare Russia was forced to retreat in 1689. The long frontier east of Afghanistan gained a certain reality in the eighteenth century when the power of the central Chinese government was extended to its western provinces, and some friction resulted from Russian assistance to Kalmyk and Mongol opponents of Chinese influence. It was not until Russia took a renewed interest in the Amur basin in the 1850s, however, that a real test of strength took place. China was now no longer able to exert a decisive influence on events in this region, and by 1860 the Russian frontier reached the Amur and Ussuri rivers where it has become stabilized despite extensive activity to the south. Not until 1944, with the Russian annexation of Tannu Tuva from Mongolia, was another change made in this long frontier. Russian political influence also became active in the Pacific islands, where the earlier expansion had extended to the northern Kuriles in the eighteenth century and to northern Sakhalin in 1853. Russia exchanged its Kurile possessions with Japan for southern Sakhalin in 1875, but lost the latter to Japan thirty years later. After the Second World War Russia regained these possessions, and for the first time annexed the southern Kuriles as well.[9]

The expansion across Siberia led Russia to the Aleutian Islands and beyond to the Alaskan mainland in the latter half of the eighteenth century, and for a generation after its establishment in 1799 the Russian-American Company maintained an active Russian trading colony in North America. Interest in this region nevertheless waned when trade failed to justify the expense and responsibility of maintaining this distant outpost, and it was sold to the United States in 1867.[10] Siberia also borders on the Arctic Ocean, which was not a political vacuum even though Russia did not face a rival state. Russian activity in this region began in the mid-seventeenth century, about a hundred years after English and Dutch explorers had shown an interest in it, but Russia laid claim to the Arctic islands only during the First World War and not until 1926 did it formally annex them and claim a maritime frontier extending to the North Pole that embraces almost one-half of the entire Arctic area. The development of military technology since the Second World War has given this frontier an importance it never before possessed, although in fact Russian aerial explorations in this region can be traced back to 1914.[11]

2. As a category of security objectives, the stabilization of Russia's frontiers as here defined is no doubt the most comprehensive in time and space and provides a convenient basis for reviewing briefly the range and nature of what have perhaps been Russia's most vital contacts with other states. It is also the least controversial category, in the sense that the wars and treaties affecting the development of Russia's borders are a matter of historic record. It would be a gross oversimplification, however, to think of security primarily in terms of the balance of pressures reflected in frontier changes, for there were other considerations of the stature of major interests that motivated Russian policies. The most generally influential was the desire to assure for Russia favorable conditions for economic growth. On no subject has there been more general agreement among Russian leaders than on the importance of economic strength to national security, although many different views have been expressed as to the nature of economic strength and the best means of achieving it.[12]

The acquisition and maintenance of direct commercial outlets to the open seas has been regarded as one of the basic requirements of Russian economic growth, and of these outlets the Baltic has in modern times been the most important. Until recently the bulk of Russian foreign commerce has been carried by sea and the Baltic ports have during most of this period carried the heaviest share of trade. It is no doubt possible for a landlocked country to engage in active commerce, but the brief periods of crisis in which Russia has had to rely largely on its Arctic ports have only reinforced the conviction that no country in Russia's position can well afford to lose control of its maritime outlets. The various policies pursued by Russia in the Baltic region since 1721 must be understood primarily in the light of its desire to forestall the domination of the region by another great power. This has been accomplished by annexing territories inhabited by non-Russians, by encouraging a policy of neutrality on the part of the states of the region, and by exerting strong pressure on these states when they have allied themselves with other great powers. Russia's interest in seaborne commerce has also been reflected at various times in concern for the maritime rights of neutrals, and in the attention devoted to its navy.[13]

The Black Sea has been second in importance only to the Baltic as an avenue of seaborne commerce, and here again Russia has had to compete not only with other littoral states but also with great powers possessing interests in this region. The commercial rights achieved in 1774 in the Black Sea and its outlets to the Mediterranean were scarcely more than nominal. Before long, however, southern Russia was transformed into a major grain-producing area, and grain was later supplemented and to a considerable degree replaced by the products of the newly developed mines and oil wells. The whole development of this region depended on trade with the Mediterranean, and Russian statesmen regarded their interests here as a matter of highest priority. Russia's first concern was to reduce the influence of the Ottoman Empire—by direct military action in numerous wars, by encouraging the Christians under Turkish rule in the Balkans and the Caucasus to revolt, or by associating itself with Turkey on those few occasions when this appeared to be the most feasible means of exerting influence. In the last analysis, however, the primary obstacle to Russian influence in this region proved to be not the littoral states but the great powers, with whom Russia had eventually to come to terms.

The specific issue on which Russian interest in this region hinged was the passage of commercial shipping through the Turkish Straits—the Bosporus and the Dardanelles. In times of relative strength Russia could exercise (1799–1805, 1833–40) or at least claim (1941–46) the right of partnership with Turkey in control of the Straits. Indeed, the Russian aim of annexing the region of the Straits was officially asserted on numerous occasions. It formed a part of plans to partition Turkey which Russia discussed with the other great powers at various times, and was officially recognized by Great Britain and France in the treaty of 1915, repudiated two years later by the Soviet government. Only in exceptional times could Russia hope for the domination of this region to the exclusion of the other great powers, however, and as a rule the passage of merchant shipping through the Straits has been regulated by hard-headed compromises with the other great powers. The principle of the free passage of the merchant ships of all nations, except in a war in which Turkey itself was a belligerent, was established in a convention concluded in 1841 between Turkey, Russia, and the European powers. In the event of a war in which Turkey was a belligerent, the use of the Straits was to be determined by Turkey itself—a principle that was altered in 1923 to permit the passage of neutral ships in wartime. The Straits can in any event not be used by Russia in time of war except when that country controls the Black Sea, and when the lanes of commerce to the west of the Straits, in the Aegean and the Mediterranean, are in friendly hands.[14]

Russia's other commercial outlets never achieved the significance of those on the Baltic and Black seas, although after the construction of the Trans-Siberian Railway and the subsequent development of eastern Siberia, Vladivostok gained rapidly in importance. It was less constrained than the Baltic and Black Sea ports in that it was on the open ocean, but in practice the presence of Japan had much the same effect as that of Germany and the Scandinavian states in the Baltic and of Turkey and its allies in the eastern Mediterranean. For brief periods (1898–1905, 1945–55), it appeared that Russia might establish itself in the Yellow Sea as a counterweight to both China and Japan through its acquisition of naval and commercial rights at Port Arthur and Dalny, but these bases proved to be too remote to be held in the face of a determined Japan (1904–05) or a powerful China (1950–55).[15]

Russian commerce on the northern coast has increased in importance with the development of Siberia, especially since the organization in 1932 of the Chief Administration of the Northern Sea Route. Trade in the northern seas is almost entirely coastal and domestic, and does not normally enter into considerations of foreign policy. In abnormal periods, however, the northern seas have played an important role. In the period of relative isolation before the eighteenth century, the White Sea ports of Kholmogory and later Arkhangelsk (after 1584) formed the only direct maritime contacts with Europe, and during the two world wars of the twentieth century both the older White Sea outlets and the ice-free port of Murmansk (after 1915) were vital to Russia's economy.

Concern for the security of maritime commerce has probably been the most important continuing economic interest affecting foreign policy, but there have been others that also deserve consideration. From the seventeenth to the early nineteenth centuries the fur trade was of considerable significance, providing perhaps as much as 10 per cent of the income of the state in the seventeenth century, and thereafter continuing to bring in a significant flow of foreign exchange. Since the fur business was from the start conducted under state auspices, it was assured of continuing official protection. The initial penetration of Siberia resulted from the search for furs, but it was primarily in the extension of this search to North America that foreign relations became involved. The support of the Russian-American Company is a good example of the state's concern for an important economic asset, and the withdrawal of this support when the Alaskan fur trade ceased to be profitable illustrates the limited and frequently transitory nature of certain types of interests.[16]

One may also cite the colonization of Siberia as an economic interest whose protection became in some degree a consideration of foreign policy. Although in Siberia itself the Russians met only nomadic peoples, once the Tatar outposts had been overrun, the colonization soon brought them into contact with more settled peoples. Underlying the concern for the Black Sea region was the settlement and development of the Ukraine and the Crimea. Similarly in southern Siberia the pressure of Russian expansion was essentially one of settlement, first by refugees from serfdom and later by colonists who came as part of a considered policy. The economic development of these regions also uncovered mineral resources of vital importance to the national economy. Seen in this light, the entire range of Russia's relations with its southern neighbors from the Pruth to the Yenisei rivers may be interpreted in terms of the protection of an initially unsettled region undergoing agricultural and industrial development.[17]

3. A category of a somewhat different order, but one that has at times aroused more emotional fervor than either the stabilization of the frontiers or the protection of economic interests, is the unification of territories considered to be Russian by virtue of dynastic, religious, or national claims. In the fourteenth and fifteenth centuries the principal concern of the grand princes of Moscow was to unify the territories which had paid tribute to the Tatars. Once this task was achieved, Moscow turned its attention to the Western territories—the former principalities of Smolensk, Polotsk, Chernigov, Kiev, Vladimir, Galich, and others—which had also fallen initially under Tatar rule but had soon been absorbed into the Grand Duchy of Lithuania and later into the Kingdom of Poland.

In the course of this evolution the Orthodox Slavs inhabiting these territories developed separate White Russian and Ukrainian cultures, distinct from each other as well as from that of the Great Russians. They were also divided by religion after 1596, when some of them joined the newly created Uniat church. Other considerations have at various times eclipsed the objective of annexing these territories, but one can trace through the years a definite official concern dating back to the reign of Ivan III. With the partition of Poland a sizable part of the lands inhabited by Orthodox or Uniat Slavs came under Russian rule, but other parts went to the Habsburgs. After the First World War there were very substantial minorities of Orthodox or Uniat Slavs in eastern Poland, in eastern Czechoslovakia, and in the Rumanian provinces of Bessarabia and Bukovina. These peoples came under Russian rule by virtue of the frontiers drawn after the Second World War—along with substantial minorities from the neighboring countries—and for the first time since the thirteenth century all of the eastern Slavs were united under one government. It cannot be maintained that Russian governments have consistently regarded these territories as irredenta whose liberation was a primary aim, let alone that the people concerned were necessarily eager to come under Russian rule. At the same time, the presence on the most disputed and vulnerable sector of the frontier with Europe of territories to which Russia could lay claim—first on dynastic, and later on religious and national grounds—tended to make such claims an important concern of foreign policy.[18]

4. A nation exists not alone but in a community of nations with which it must cooperate in the interest of its own security. Russia's concern through the years for this category of its security interests has been reflected in short-term alliances of opportunity, in alliances reflecting long-term commitments, and in the adherence to formal principles and organizations designed to preserve international security.

Russia has bolstered its security on frequent occasions by short-term alliances with other states. Many of these have been in time of war, such as the early alliances with Denmark against Sweden, participation in the second and third coalitions against France and the grand alliance that finally brought about the defeat of Napoleon, and the mutual assistance pact with Britain concluded in 1941. Other short-term relationships have served to provide temporary assistance in times of peace when Russia was isolated. Thus, for example, the association with France during the Napoleonic wars (1807–12) and more recently (1894–1917, 1935–39) with the German Republic (1922–33) and the Third Reich (1939–41), with Turkey (1925–45), and with China (1924–27, 1937–49) were based not on an inherent ideological sympathy but on the need for assistance in an uncertain world. Similarly the nonaggression pacts concluded in 1932 with Finland, Estonia, Latvia, and Poland—former territories in whole or in part of the Russian Empire—served to temper their animosity at a time when Russia was interested in concentrating on domestic affairs.

Of greater significance are the long-term alliance relationships which were important in maintaining the balance of power but also had deeper significance in reflecting and promoting a common political and social philosophy. The best, and probably the only, examples of this type of relationship have been with the Hohenzollern and Habsburg monarchies in the nineteenth century, and with the Communist states of Europe and Asia after 1945. Russia shared with the German monarchies an outlook that stemmed in part from common problems and in part from a common political heritage derived from the close family ties between the Romanovs and various German dynasties. In the eighteenth century and during the long series of wars with France, Russia found itself more often than not in coalition against one or another of the German states, but there were also periods of close collaboration, as in the partitions of Poland. It was in the nineteenth century that this relationship had its particular significance, however, and from 1813 to 1850 and intermittently thereafter until 1887 the three dynastic states worked out the most durable great power alliance system that modern Europe had known and one that did much to preserve international order. The essence of this order lay in the maintenance of the settlement of 1815 and the preservation of traditional political and social institutions; the unrest characteristic of Europe in this period offered the dynasties frequent opportunities to exhibit a common front. The revolutionary outbreaks in Spain and Italy in the 1820s, in France, Belgium, and Poland in 1830, and particularly the general outbreak of ferment in 1848–50 found the dynasties standing together, and the Russian intervention in Hungary in 1849 was decisive in maintaining Habsburg authority.

In the second half of the century the three dynasties became increasingly divided, first over the issue of German unification and shortly thereafter over the Eastern Question. The problem of Germany was resolved by Bismarck, and in due course Austria and Russia accepted his solution. The Eastern Question led to much more profound differences, affecting as it did major Russian interests and the existence itself of the Habsburg monarchy, and it led eventually to the First World War. These difficulties were foreshadowed by the Russian involvement in the Greek revolution (1821–29), but it was not until the Crimean War that Austria grasped the extent to which Russian policies in southeastern Europe might stimulate the centrifugal forces within the multinational empire. The cooperation of the three emperors was revived in 1873, thanks to

Bismarck's diplomatic skill, and for a decade and a half it survived numerous crises, but Austria finally parted company with Russia in 1887, while Germany did so in 1890. The ideological compatibility of the three dynasties nevertheless survived until 1917 (indeed Germany was probably the principal model for Russian political and economic reforms in these years), but Russia's interests in the Straits outweighed these considerations and it found alternative means of preserving the balance of power.[19]

The Soviet alliance system established after the Second World War also combined ideological and balance of power considerations, and through it Russia has succeeded in forming a grouping of states comprising one-third of the world's population which on many issues is able to speak with one voice. The deeper roots of this alliance system lie in the Communist International (1919–43), and its formation can be traced more immediately to treaties concluded with the Communist states of Europe and Asia after the Second World War. In so far as Communism was imposed by Soviet armies on the states of Eastern Europe—except for Yugoslavia, expelled from the alliance system in 1948, and Albania—one may well question whether it is not a system of satellites rather than of allies, even though its members are accepted by the outside world as independent states. It nevertheless seems clear that at least the Sino-Soviet aspect of the Communist bloc represents an alliance in traditional terms, and that the smaller states are dominated in greater or lesser degree by the two major partners. This alliance system has survived in its present form since 1950, and despite very significant differences of opinion on matters of policy it gives evidence of continued vitality as an instrument of Soviet policy.[20]

Russia has also found it to its interest to adhere to the principles and participate in the organizations designed to preserve international security and to establish an orderly basis of international relations. Russia has accepted the prevailing principles of international law, and as a secondary maritime power has had a particularly active interest in the rights of neutrals. It became a member of most of the functional international organizations established in the nineteenth century and took the initiative in calling the First Hague Peace Conference (1899) which established a permanent court of arbitration. The Soviet government rejected in principle the prevailing international legal system, but in the 1930s for practical reasons it participated increasingly in international bodies and was for a while (1934–40) an active member of the League of Nations. It became one of the founding members of the United Nations in 1945 and has joined most of its specialized agencies and related bodies. There is a significant difference between Tsarist and Soviet participation in the international legal structure, in that the former accepted it as continuing and legitimate whereas the latter has regarded it as an outdated structure bound to be replaced in due course by one based on Communist principles. This difference has thus far been primarily one of theory, however, as Russia has found it to its interest in most matters to abide by conventional rules. It also accepted the unprecedented plan for the internationalization of the Antarctic (1960) and has entertained the possibility of adopting some form of international regulation in outer space.[21]

III

It is useful for purposes of analysis to examine as separate categories the objectives of Russian foreign policy that have been concerned primarily with security interests in the traditional sense. At the same time, it is important to see the interrelationship of these interests in time and space and to examine the ways in which they have been influenced by considerations of a broader theoretical character. Throughout the history of Russia its statesmen have been concerned with the nature and evolution of the international political system, and their theories have at times had a determining influence on foreign policy objectives.

During the formative period of the modern Russian state from the fifteenth century to the middle of the seventeenth, its principal concern in the realm of foreign policy—once the Tatars had been overcome—was to match the power of its western neighbors. Although "overtake and surpass" is relatively new as a formal slogan, it is only more ambitious in degree than the slogans that might have been adopted at an earlier age. The dangers inherent in Russia's position in this earlier phase are graphically illustrated by the events known to history as the Time of Troubles (1604–13). Although this chaotic era of civil strife and foreign intervention was in many respects unique, it was not entirely unprecedented and it resulted from a combination of circumstances that were the continuing concern of Russian statesmen. In this sense foreign policy was seen primarily in defensive terms, and there was a close relationship between the task of consolidating the various Russian principalities under Muscovite leadership and that of standing up to the as yet more powerful neighbors to the west.

By comparison with this problem of self-defense, other interests in this period were secondary. The desire to reclaim the former territories of the Rurik dynasty which had come under Lithuanian and later Polish rule and the need for a Baltic outlet can no doubt be cited as important aims of Russian policy in this period, but they could not be pursued effectively while Russia was still relatively weak and defenseless. Contacts with foreign countries were resumed in the fifteenth century after a hiatus of some two hundred years. Russia was not yet an active member of the European system of states, however, and relied entirely on its own as yet rather limited means except for short-term alliances for specific purposes.[22]

Before the nineteenth century, broader theoretical considerations influenced foreign policy only to the extent that the world view inherited from Byzantium may be said to have had some bearing on Russia's attitude toward Europe. The theory of the Third Rome, set forth on the basis of earlier church writings by the monk Filofei of Pskov early in the sixteenth century, claimed that Moscow was the successor to Rome and Constantinople both as the center of the Christian faith and as the heir of the imperial tradition. Ivan IV apparently took these views seriously and asserted the further claim that he was descended from a brother of Emperor Caesar Augustus. Perhaps this grandiose conception of Moscow's role in history should be held to account in some degree for the vigor of Ivan's offensives against Tatar territories in the east and the Baltic provinces in the west, and also for his matrimonial ambitions, which included a proposal to Queen Elizabeth of England. There are nevertheless other explanations for these policies, including those taking into account the Tsar's psychotic personality, which make it difficult to develop a strong case for theoretical influences at this stage. In any event, this primitive cyclical view of history based on church writings soon lost influence, and in the seventeenth and eighteenth centuries the principal concern of Russian statesmanship was to win a secure place on the fringes of the European political system.[23]

With the acquisition of the territories of the Ukrainian Cossacks in 1654 and the victory over Poland accompanied by significant territorial gains in 1667, Russian foreign policy may be considered to have entered a new phase. In this phase Russia expanded steadily and became involved as a great power in the international relations of Europe, Asia, and North America, and to a limited extent in the affairs of Africa, Oceania, and Antarctica as well. Russia solved the more elemental problems of defense which it had faced before the middle of the seventeenth century, and now approached its foreign relations with a different scale of values. The problem of the stabilization of frontiers persisted, but the pressure was henceforth from Russia rather than from the outside and stemmed from the desire to gain maritime commercial outlets, to protect the new territories to the south and east which were being colonized, and to annex the territories under Polish rule inhabited by Orthodox and Uniat Slavs. Russia also found it increasingly to its interest to participate in the international institutions developed in the course of the eighteenth and nineteenth centuries.

Russia adjusted itself with some success to the European political system of the eighteenth century, but it was poorly equipped to cope with the revolutionary changes inaugurated by the fall of the French monarchy. The eighteenth-century conventions nevertheless remained valid in so far as the wars of the French Revolution and Napoleon were seen from Russia chiefly in terms of the balance of power. After 1815 this remained a central theme of Russian policy in Europe, and when revolutionary situations developed it preferred a multilateral approach which would permit change without upsetting the balance of power. The handling of the Greek question in the 1820s and the subsequent organization of a three-power guarantee of Greece which lasted virtually until 1917 is a classic example of this approach.

Supplementng the balance of power theme Russia now for the first time adopted a broader theoretical conception of its role in the European political system. This conception was embodied in the Quadruple Alliance and in the close cooperation with Prussia and Austria which continued with few interruptions until the Crimean War. It maintained that there was no inherent reason why the structure of the European system should be changed, and that the territorial settlement of 1815 and the legitimate monarchs confirmed by that settlement should be protected from revolution just as one would protect a town from the ravages of fire. There was a brief lapse in this approach between 1828 and 1833, when Russia pursued an independent policy in the Eastern Question, but even in this instance Nicholas I was not prepared to weaken the European system. Indeed, throughout this period, and especially in the twenty years after 1833, Nicholas I sacrificed opportunities for unilateral action that might have brought advantage to Russia in favor of supporting the ideology of conservatism. It must of course be recognized that the theoretical approach in question was one that favored the status quo at the expense of change, and to this extent may be regarded simply as an extension or a rationalization of the balance of power. In the mind of Nicholas I it nevertheless assumed the proportions of an ideology, and thus represents the only clear-cut case before 1917 in which theoretical considerations may be said to have taken precedence at the policy level over traditional security interests.[24]

The Crimean War marked the end of an era in Russian foreign policy, and the very Prussia that had been the most reliable partner in support of conservatism now became the most consistent disturber of the status quo. In this period a new balance of power unadorned by theoretical considerations reasserted itself, and Russia was compelled by its isolation to stand aside while Prussia reorganized Central Europe. The emergence of a powerful Germany and the growing realization that no great power could avoid the revolutionary economic and social changes sweeping

Europe now led to the creation for the first time of an active public opinion deeply concerned with Russia's destiny in the European world. The most striking form taken by this new concern was a vigorous nationalism expressed most characteristically in the doctrines of Panslavism as represented by R. A. Fadeev's *Opinion on the Eastern Question* and N. Ia. Danilevskii's *Russia and Europe*, both published in 1869. The substance of this doctrine was that Russia should take the lead in liberating the Slavic peoples still under Austro-Hungarian and Turkish rule and in creating a federation embracing all the non-German peoples of Eastern and Southeastern Europe up to and including Constantinople.

In the writings of Danilevskii, this ambitious objective was supported by a cyclical theory of history which maintained that Russia was destined to succeed Europe as the eleventh in a series of dominant civilizations of which Egypt was the first. This theory was certainly more sophisticated than that of the Third Rome, although one might have hoped for more progress in this realm of speculation over a period of three and a half centuries. What stimulated Russian opinion was less Danilevskii's rationalization, however, than the image of a Russia participating actively in the reconstruction of Europe along nationalist lines. Panslavism had powerful official representatives in Count Ignat'ev and General Cherniaev, and even Alexander II in a moment of exaltation used the words "our sacred mission" (November 1876) in referring to his country's liberating role in the Balkans. There can be no question that Russian opinion in 1876–78 was inspired by aims that went well beyond those traditionally associated with security interests, and when Russian armies came within sight of Constantinople in the spring of 1878 a new era in Russian policy seemed to be dawning. Almost immediately the European powers sounded a warning, however, and within a few months the realities of the balance of power reasserted themselves.[25]

In justice to Russian policy at this stage it should be noted that Foreign Minister Gorchakov was not himself a Panslav and that he never lost sight of the realities of European politics. In this sense the theories of the Panslavs represented no more than a powerful upsurge of opinion which Gorchakov had to take into account. Indeed, nationalism was less significant as a direct influence on foreign policy than through its impact on the many non-Russian peoples within the empire.

In the course of their expansion in the Baltic and Black Sea regions and in Central Asia, the Great Russians overran numerous peoples who were incorporated into the empire and who presented a continuing problem of domestic and foreign policy. By the end of this period, according to the census of 1897, well over one-half of the population of Russia (56.70 per cent) consisted of peoples other than Great Russians. Except for the Siberian peoples and some of the Tatars, all of these nationalities had become a part of Russia between the 1650s and the 1890s. The largest of these national minorities in terms of native language were the Ukrainians (17.41 per cent), the Poles (6.17 per cent), the White Russians (4.57 per cent), the Jews (3.94 per cent), the Kirghiz (3.18 per cent), and the Tatars (2.91 per cent), and in addition there were some twenty-four other nationalities ranging in size from some 200,000 to well over one million. More striking than their number, however, was their geographical location and political significance. The important minority peoples were located on the periphery of Russia, in areas of great strategic significance in terms of Russian security interests. Moreover, with the exception of the Georgians, they had ties with neighboring countries which were actual or potential rivals of Russia.

In its treatment of these borderland territories, whether they were incorporated directly into the empire or granted initially a degree of autonomy—as was the case with the Ukraine, the Baltic provinces, Finland, and Congress Poland—the Russian government tended at first to respect the local language and institutions. The European minority peoples had a social structure which in most cases—with the notable exception of the Jews—did not differ greatly from that of Russia. The noble landowners, frequently of a different nationality from the common people, retained their traditional rights, as did the cities, and were often assimilated into the Russian ruling class. Many Germans from the Baltic provinces, Swedes from Finland, and Rumanians from Bessarabia found their way to the top of St. Petersburg's bureaucracy and society, as did Georgian princes and Russianized Tatar leaders coming from a somewhat different background. In this respect the Poles were a striking exception, especially after the reign of Alexander I, and in this case the government was inclined to favor the peasants as opposed to the irreconcilable landowners. The treatment of minority nationalities underwent a significant change after the middle of the eighteenth century as the dangers of political separatism and later of nationalism threatened Russian interests in these border regions. From the abolition of Ukrainian autonomy in 1764 to the brief suppression of Finnish rights (1903–05), a policy of centralization and Russification was gradually imposed on the entire empire.[26]

Closely related to the evolution of Russia after the middle of the seventeenth century into a multinational state was the change in its position of relative strength in Europe. Whereas in the mid-seventeenth century the population of Russia (14 million) was little more than one-half that of England and France combined (27 million), by 1800 it was almost as large (36 as compared to 39 million), and by 1900 it was a great deal larger (129 as compared to 79 million). This is certainly only one of the comparisons that could be made, and it should be modified by taking into consideration the colonial empires of Great Britain and France as well as other factors, but it serves to illustrate the change in Russia's relative position in this period. Although Russian society had become relatively static in the first half of the nineteenth century, by the latter part of the century it was undergoing a process of rapid social change in which the development of heavy industry was a major characteristic. Russia's size, population, and economic potential thus made it a great power of the first magnitude, and on at least one occasion—in 1878—the further expansion of Russia seemed likely to upset the balance of power so decisively that all the other major states of Europe joined forces to restrain it. This formidable concentration of power was nevertheless threatened by two interrelated sources of unrest: revolutionary movements that opposed the continuing traditionalism of Tsarist policies, and the disaffection of the minority nationalities that inhabited regions vital to its security interests. These sources of unrest, which still played a minor role at the turn of the century, were to provide a central theme of the policies of the empire in its final years.

The last decades before the First World War were years of weakness and retrenchment in foreign policy. The weakness was no doubt relative, for Russia remained a world power of great potential. In terms of the effective strength in foreign relations that comes from internal stability and technological skill, however, Russia during these years was in a relatively weaker position than it had been for a long time. The underlying sources of this weakness can be traced to the difficulties encountered in making the transition from traditional to modern ideas and institutions. Indeed, in relation to Europe, this period of relative weakness started with the defeat in the Crimea in 1856. In relation to Asia, however, Russia remained relatively progressive until 1905, when Japan's more effective adaptation to modern ways enabled it to seize from Russia the initiative in modernizing Manchuria and Korea. The retrenchment in foreign affairs that started with the loss of southern Sakhalin and of the Manchurian concessions culminated in the unprecedented loss of territory, population, and resources as a result of the First World War.

In discussing the crisis that led to the First World War one must return once more to the relationship between Russia's national minorities and its role in the balance of power. In a country in which more than one-half of the population, living in some of its politically most sensitive areas, consisted of peoples other than the dominant Great Russians, this relationship could not fail to be of central importance. As was amply illustrated in the years of crisis following the revolution of 1905, the leaders of the national minorities not only played a prominent role in the movements advocating rapid social change—for example the Ukrainians, Jews, Georgians, and Armenians; but in some cases were also prepared to secede and even to assist Russia's enemies in time of crisis—for example the Finns, the Baltic peoples, and the Poles.

It is in this context that one must view the crisis in Russia's relations with Austria-Hungary. Both countries had important economic and strategic interests in southeastern Europe, and in addition the balance of power of the two European alliance systems hinged on the outcome of the rivalry. At the same time, each country felt increasingly, especially after the Bosnian Crisis of 1908, that a diplomatic defeat in the Balkans would weaken the authority of its government to such an extent that a general war was preferable to retreat. No doubt the national question was of greater concern to Austria-Hungary, while the social question was more important to Russia, but in both countries these two problems were fatefully related both to each other and to the larger international issues.[27]

The First World War raised once again in a decisive form—for the last time in the case of the empire—the question of Russian objectives. Indeed, not only did the various formulations of war aims reflect the theoretical outlook of the main protagonists in the Russian domestic struggle, but they also became the central political issue in that struggle. The war aims negotiated by the Imperial Government were defined with reasonable clarity only in so far as they concerned the Ottoman Empire, and they left the government free to negotiate a frontier with Germany and Austria-Hungary at the end of the war. Those who supported these aims were not guided by a formal theory of international relations, but their objectives went well beyond what had usually been considered Russia's security interests. They envisaged a Russian frontier expanded to include Turkish Armenia and Kurdistan, as well as parts of Anatolia and European Turkey including Constantinople, and the Straits. They also apparently envisaged an Eastern Europe in which a reunified Poland would remain within Russia as an autonomous province, and a new state of Czechs and Slovaks would be under unilateral Russian protection. Objectives such as these, although not directly inspired by Danilevskii, were clearly in the Panslav spirit and reflected a theory of change that saw a victorious and enlarged Russia replacing Germany as the principal power in Central and Eastern Europe. The proponents of these views were also reluctant to consider the demands of the minority peoples within Russia for a degree of self-government. The more nationalist-minded liberals led by Miliukov supported these aims in the main, although they conceded that a reunified Poland should be granted independence in permanent alliance with Russia and that the autonomy of Finland should be strengthened. The Kerensky socialists and many liberals, on the other hand, were opposed to annexationist war aims. They were prepared to grant independence to both Poland and Finland,

and favored the transformation of the empire into a federal republic. They believed that the prewar frontiers, thus modified, were adequate for the security interests of the country, and they envisaged a European political system based on national self-determination and representative government.[28]

The policies that determined Russian objectives at the end of the war were established not by Nicholas II, Miliukov, or Kerensky, however, but by Lenin. The Bolsheviks had a theory of international relations completely at variance with that of their predecessors, but they were in charge of the same country and faced most of the same problems. The significance of Soviet Marxism lay more in the Bolshevik attitude toward foreign relations than in the actual policies they advocated. Lenin's faith in the ability of his party to maintain itself in power was due mainly to theoretical considerations. When extensive territorial concessions to the Germans proved to be necessary, they were rationalized on the ground that the whole of Europe would soon be socialist. Moreover, his determination to end the war on any terms was one of the principal sources for the domestic support of his regime. Even at the height of ideological fervor, however, the Soviets conceded only those territories they saw no immediate hope of reconquering. The Soviet negotiators at Riga, Rapallo, and Lausanne were no less concerned than their Tsarist predecessors for the security interests of their country.[29]

In the long period from the peace settlement of 1921 to that of 1947, the immediate objectives of Russian foreign policy were determined primarily by security interests. Of the four categories of interests discussed above, only the economic interest represented by seaborne commercial outlets was relatively unaffected by the 1921 peace settlement. The new frontier with Europe was by traditional Russian standards most unstable, since all the border countries were headed by governments hostile to the Soviet Union, and in addition many Ukrainians and White Russians were now under foreign rule. Russia's ability to protect its international security through cooperation with other countries had also been greatly reduced as a result of the revolution, but it was in this sphere that the best opportunities lay for protecting Russian security. The treaties with Germany, China, and Turkey in the 1920s, and with the border states of Poland, Estonia, Latvia, and Finland, as well as with France and Czechoslovakia, in the 1930s, restored some semblance of a balance of power. Russia's brief but dramatic participation in the League of Nations in the 1930s also served a similar purpose. The agreement with Germany in 1939 and the formulation of Russian war aims after 1941 can likewise best be understood in terms of Stalin's desire first to avoid war as long as possible and then to gain frontiers that would protect Russia's security interests as traditionally defined. The Soviet Union gained only a few territories Russia had not possessed before 1914, and since Poland and Finland remained independent the territorial extent of the country today has not yet attained that of the empire.[30]

It was not necessary to abandon Soviet Marxism in order to conduct a defense-oriented policy under the slogan "socialism in one country," for the theory itself made provision for periods of stability in international relations between waves of revolutionary advance. Stalin himself made it perfectly clear that this was only a period of truce since his country was "encircled" by capitalist states, and in a variety of ways theoretical considerations continued to play a role in support of security interests. The Communist movement in other countries was used to advance Soviet policies, and there were innumerable channels for influencing world opinion through national and international functional organizations. Even after the Second World War, when Soviet officials began to refer to a second wave of revolutions and when vigorous support was given to Communism abroad, Stalin was cautious not to over-extend his commitments. He recognized the opportunities for revolutionary advance, but he seems to have advised his clients that they could hope for only such Soviet support as could be granted without unduly antagonizing the Western powers. In Czechoslovakia, China, and North Vietnam, the Communists were successful, but in Iran, Greece, and South Korea they were not. When the Communists did on occasion overextend themselves, this was because the policies of the West were misjudged. This is not surprising, when one considers the manner in which these policies were formulated and expressed. Soviet caution at this stage was no doubt influenced by the fact that Russia's security interests were by no means as yet assured. As a result of the Second World War the frontiers were once again stabilized from the Russian standpoint, conditions were favorable to economic growth, and for the first time since the Kievan era all the eastern Slavs were united in one political system. In these respects Russia had more than regained the ground lost after 1905 and was perhaps more secure than ever.[31]

In one vital respect Russia was less secure, however, for in the immediate postwar years it was confronted by a powerful coalition of states commanding weapons and means of delivery it could not match. The alliance system, which included Eastern Europe and China, might embrace one-third of the world's population, but in military potential it was no match for the NATO coalition. It was not until Russia had perfected its own nuclear weapons and developed means of delivery adequate to deter its rivals that theoretical considerations once again began to assert themselves in foreign policy. Perhaps the most dramatic turning point in this regard was the Twentieth Party Congress in 1956, when Khrushchev asserted that war between "socialism" and "capitalism" should no longer be regarded as inevitable and developed the thesis that Russia was no longer "encircled." The significance of these statements was that they reflected a new confidence in Soviet Marxism and a belief that the tide was now definitely turning in favor of Communism. The policies embraced by the slogan "peaceful coexistence" assumed that Communism would ultimately be victorious without resort to international war and that the process of social change within individual countries could be influenced in such a way as to add new members one by one to the Communist system of states. For the first time since the early years of the Soviet Union attention is again being devoted to the nature and problems of a world Communist state, and the first steps are being taken to lay the foundations of a world-wide political system.[32]

IV

The formulation of objectives in foreign policy must always be related in some measure to an understanding of the international milieu in which states live, and in a rapidly changing world such an understanding is in particular need of a theoretical basis. The establishment of a world Communist state is an objective for Soviet leaders in the sense that they believe that Communism represents the culmination of world-wide social change. It is less a question of wanting to change the world than of assuming the leadership in a process of change that is considered to be inevitable. In this sense the distinctive feature of Russian foreign policy objectives since 1917 has been the conviction of Soviet leaders that they understand the nature of historical change and that their country is in the forefront of this development. For those who hold such a view, security interests represent no more than minimum objectives of a defensive character.

The Soviet leaders are of course not alone in recognizing the revolutionary character of the modern era, and indeed Russia has been well behind the countries of Western and Central Europe and their overseas settlements in developing modern institutions. Modernization in the broadest sense may be seen as a process of change that reflects a revolutionary growth of knowledge unmatched perhaps since the first civilized societies were established in the valleys of the Nile, the Tigris and Euphrates, the Indus, and the Yellow rivers. Its immediate intellectual roots can be traced back to the twelfth century in Western Europe, and its first large-scale political, economic, and social consequences were felt in England, France, and the Lowlands in the seventeenth and eighteenth centuries. In many parts of Asia and Africa modern institutions are only now being introduced, however, and the form that a future modern world may take is still a matter of conjecture to all but Communist theoreticians. It was in fact recognized in the eighteenth century by farsighted theorists that a fundamental revolution in human affairs was occurring, and the great debate—first in the West and more recently throughout the World—has been concerned with the nature and direction of this transformation. It is now a matter of general agreement that all societies are in the process of adopting modern ideas and institutions and that the diverse traditional cultures around the world will have to give way in one degree or another.

Between the French Revolution and the First World War, Europe was the fountainhead of modern ideas and institutions. Russia no less than such countries as the United States, Japan, China, and the Ottoman Empire, which were also undergoing change in one form or another, looked for leadership to the great centers of European civilization. The nineteenth century was a period of rapid change, but the change was dominated by a characteristically European style that reflected the interests and objectives of those leaders who had so successfully placed their stamp on Europe and through it on much of the rest of the world. In so far as Russian statesmen of the nineteenth century were guided by theoretical considerations in their conduct of foreign policy, these were within the framework of this European pattern. Nicholas I associated himself with the most conservative trend which, if it thought of change at all, favored reforms of only the most cautious and gradual character. In the latter part of the nineteenth century Russian foreign policy was under the influence of the prevalent theories of nationalism in a form in which Panslavism was the principal ingredient. Panslavism did not carry much weight in official circles in the 1870s, but by the time of the First World War it had exerted a powerful influence on the Tsarist government and on the more nationalistic liberals in their thinking about Russian objectives upon the achievement of victory. This version of great power nationalism saw Russia, along with a Slavic Eastern Europe under its leadership, in a position similar to Germany's in the generation before the war. These objectives did not differ in their theoretical basis from those of the other Allied countries, or for that matter from those of the Central Powers, before 1917.

By accelerating the trend toward mass societies and by stimulating nationalism in the dynastic and colonial empires, the First World War marked the beginning of the end of the European political system, which had dominated world affairs for a century. The form taken by this transformation in the various countries depended on their specific traditions, problems, and leadership, and it was the destiny of Russia to provide the first decisive evidence that the European system would not survive the war. The call for a new diplomacy was first issued somewhat tentatively by the Kerensky socialists, hampered as they were by the compromises inherent in the situation in which the Provisional Government found itself, and shortly thereafter by Lenin in the more radical form called for by the dilemma of Russia at the end of 1917. These first efforts to revise the war aims were nevertheless too strongly stamped by the peculiarities of the Russian situation to have a universal appeal, and it remained for Wilson to set forth in January 1918 a program that captured the imagination of a war-torn world.[33]

In the years since this great turning point in international affairs it has increasingly been recognized that a new international political system must be evolved to meet the needs of a rapidly modernizing world, and the advent of nuclear missiles has now made imperative the creation of an orderly system of international relations. Wilson's design for such a system is represented today by an evolving United Nations, and that of Lenin survives in the theories and policies of the Soviet government. In Lenin's day confidence in Communism was so great that the Soviet regime was prepared to surrender the traditional security interests of Russia in the expectation of a generalization of the revolutionary situation. It may be questioned whether Communist theory has subsequently been taken quite so literally, but Khrushchev and the leaders of his generation still appear to act in the belief that Communism as it is being developed in the Soviet Union must inevitably serve as the basis of a universal system.

It is possible that the experience of the Soviet government with its Communist allies and the sophistication of a new generation of leaders may lead to the recognition that an acceptable world system must make allowance for a much greater diversity of traditions and cultures than Soviet policy has thus far acknowledged. In any event, theoretical considerations are likely to play an increasing role in the determination of foreign policy objectives in the policies of all the major powers, and those theories will prevail that reflect the best understanding of the modern age.

NOTES

1. This question is debated in O. Halecki, "Imperialism in Slavic and Eastern European History," *American Slavic and East European Review, 11* (Feb. 1952), 1–26, and Nicholas V. Riasanovsky, "Old Russia, the Soviet Union and Eastern Europe," ibid., *11* (Oct. 1952), 171–88.

2. Walther Kirchner, *The Rise of the Baltic Question* (Newark, Del., 1954); G. V. Forsten, *Baltiiskii vopros v XVI i XVII stoletiiakh (1544–1648),* 2 vols. (St. Petersburg, 1893–94); Ia. Ia. Zutis, *Politika tsarizma v Pribaltike v pervoi polovine XVIII v.* (Moscow, 1938).

3. M. K. Liubavskii, *Ocherk istorii Litovsko-Russkago gosudarstva,* 2nd ed. (St. Petersburg, 1915); O. L. Vainshtein, *Rossiia i tridtsatiletniaia voina* (Moscow,

1947); Horst Jablonowski, *Westrussland zwischen Wilna und Moskau* (Leiden, 1955); O. P. Backus, *Motives of West Russian Nobles in Deserting Lithuania for Moscow, 1377–1514* (Lawrence, Kan., 1957).

4. *The Cambridge History of Poland,* 2 vols. (Cambridge, Eng., 1941–50) and Serge Konovalov, ed., *Russo-Polish Relations: An Historical Survey* (Princeton, 1945) provide an introduction to this complex subject.

5. Michael Hrushevsky, *A History of the Ukraine,* ed. O. J. Frederiksen (New Haven, 1941); P. P. Gudzenko and others, eds., *Vossoedinenie Ukrainy s Rossiei: dokumenty i materialy,* 3 vols. (Moscow, 1954).

6. N. A. Smirnov, *Rossiia i Turtsiia v XVI–XVII vv.,* 2 vols. (Moscow, 1946); B. H. Sumner, *Peter the Great and the Ottoman Empire* (Oxford, 1949); Vernon J. Puryear, *England, Russia and the Straits Question, 1844–1856* (Berkeley, 1931); Philip E. Mosely, *Russian Diplomacy and the Opening of the Eastern Question in 1838 and 1839* (Cambridge, Mass., 1934).

7. David M. Lang, *The Last Years of the Georgian Monarchy, 1658–1837* (New York, 1957); Firuz Kazemzadeh, *The Struggle for Transcaucasia, 1917–1921* (New York, 1951); George Lenczowski, *Russia and the West in Iran, 1918–1948: A Study in Big-Power Rivalry* (Ithaca, N.Y., 1949).

8. Richard A. Pierce, *Russian Central Asia, 1867–1917: A Study in Colonial Rule* (Berkeley, 1960); Baymirza Hayit, *Turkestan im XX Jahrhundert* (Darmstadt, 1956).

9. F. A. Golder, *Russian Expansion on the Pacific, 1641–1850* (Cleveland, 1914); David J. Dallin, *The Rise of Russia in Asia* (New Haven, 1949); B. D. Romanov, *Rossiia v Manzhurii* (Leningrad, 1928; Eng. trans., Ann Arbor, 1952).

10. A. I. Andreev, ed., *Russkie otkrytiia v Tikhom Okeane i Severnoi Amerike: Sbornik dokumentov* (Moscow, 1944); *Russian Administration of Alaska and the Status of the Alaskan Natives* (Washington, D.C., 1950); Anatole G. Mazour, "The Prelude to Russia's Departure from America," *Pacific Historical Review, 10* (Sept. 1941), 311–19.

11. T. A. Taracouzio, *Soviets in the Arctic: An Historical, Economic and Political Study of the Soviet Advance into the Arctic* (New York, 1938); Constantin Krypton, *The Northern Sea Route: Its Place in Russian Economic History before 1917* (New York, 1953); Terence Armstrong, *The Northern Sea Route: Soviet Exploitation of the North East Passage* (Cambridge, Eng., 1952).

12. See, for example, T. H. Von Laue, "A Secret Memorandum of Sergei Witte on the Industrialization of Imperial Russia," *Journal of Modern History, 26* (Mar. 1954), 60–74.

13. Erik Brüel, *International Straits,* 2 vols. (Copenhagen, 1947), 2, 11–115; Isabel de Madariaga, *Britain, Russia, and the Armed Neutrality of 1780* (New Haven, 1962), provides a careful study of Catherine's policy of armed neutrality.

14. Mose L. Harvey, "The Development of Russian Commerce on the Black Sea and Its Significance" (Ph.D. Dissertation, University of California, 1938), offers abundant evidence as to the economic significance for Russia of the Turkish Straits; S. N. Goriainov, *Le Bosphore et les Dardanelles: étude historique sur la question des Détroits* (Paris, 1910); André N. Mandelstam, "La politique d'accès à la Méditerranée au XXe siècle," *Recueil des Cours* (Académie de Droit

International), **47** (1934), 603–802; H. N. Howard, ed., *The Problem of the Turkish Straits* (Washington, D.C., 1947); B. A. Dranov, *Chernomorskie prolivy* (Moscow, 1948); Stephen G. Xydis, "The 1945 Crisis over the Turkish Straits," *Balkan Studies, I* (1960), 65–90.

15. N. Nozikov, *Russian Voyages around the World* (London, 1945); A. V. Efimov, *Iz istorii russkikh ekspeditsii na Tikhom Okeane* (Moscow, 1948); John A. Harrison, *Japan's Northern Frontier: A Preliminary Study in Colonization and Expansion with Special Reference to the Relations of Japan and Russia* (Gainesville, Fla., 1953); George A. Lensen, *Russia's Japan Expedition of 1852 to 1855* (Gainesville, Fla., 1955).

16. Raymond H. Fisher, *The Russian Fur Trade, 1550–1700* (Berkeley, 1943); S. B. Okun, *Rossiisko-Amerikanskaia Kompaniia* (Moscow, 1939; Eng. trans., Cambridge, Mass., 1951).

17. G. V. Lantzeff, *Siberia in the Seventeenth Century: A Study in Colonial Administration* (Berkeley, 1943); Roger Portal, *L'Oural au XVIIIe siècle* (Paris, 1950); Marc Raeff, *Siberia and the Reforms of 1822* (Seattle, 1956); Donald W. Treadgold, *The Great Siberian Migration: Government and Peasant in Resettlement from Emancipation to the First World War* (Princeton, 1957).

18. Gotthold Rhode, *Die Ostgrenze Polens: politische Entwicklung, kulturelle Bedeutung und geistige Auswirkung,* I. Band, *Im Mittelalter bis zum Jahre 1401* (Cologne, 1955); Oskar Halecki, *From Florence to Brest, 1439–1596* (Rome, 1958); Robert H. Lord, *The Second Partition of Poland* (Cambridge, Mass., 1915).

19. Hildegard Schaeder, *Die dritte Koalition und die Heilige Allianz* (Königsberg, 1934); S. S. Tatischev, *Vneshniaia politika imperatora Nikolaia I.* (St. Petersburg, 1887); R. A. Averbukh, *Tsarskaia interventsiia v bor'be s vengerskoi revoliutsiei, 1848–1849 gg.* (Moscow, 1935); Evgenii Tarle, *Krymskaia voina,* 2nd ed. 2 vols. (Moscow, 1950); V. G. Revunenkov, *Pol'skoe vosstanie 1863 g. i evropeiskaia diplomatiia* (Leningrad, 1957); S. Skazkin, *Konets avstro-russko-germanskogo soiuza* (Moscow, 1928).

20. Jane Degras, ed., *Soviet Documents on Foreign Policy,* 3 vols. (New York, 1951–53); Leonard Shapiro, ed., *Soviet Treaty Series,* 2 vols. (Washington, D.C., 1950–55); Boris Meissner, ed., *Das Ostpakt-System: Dokumentensammlung,* 2nd ed. (Frankfurt-am-Main, 1955); Robert M. Slusser and Jan F. Triska, eds., *A Calendar of Soviet Treaties, 1917–1957* (Stanford, 1959); Raymond L. Garthoff, "The Concept of the Balance of Power in Soviet Policy-Making," *World Politics,* **4** (Oct. 1951), 85–111.

21. T. A. Taracouzio, *The Soviet Union and International Law* (New York, 1935); L. B. Schapiro, "The Soviet Concept of International Law," *Year Book of World Affairs, 1948* (London, 1948), pp. 272–310; Jean-Yves Calvez, *Droit international et souveraineté en U.R.S.S.* (Paris, 1953). Soviet policy relative to outer space is discussed in Philip C. Jessup and Howard J. Taubenfeld, *Controls for Outer Space and the Antarctic Analogy* (New York, 1959), especially pp. 213–21.

22. Hedwig Fleischhacker, *Die staats- und völkerrechtlichen Grundlagen der moskauischen Aussenpolitik (14.–17. Jahrhundert)* (Breslau, 1938); K. V. Bazilevich, *Vneshniaia politika Russkago tsentralizovannogo gosudarstva vo vtoroi polovine XV veka* (Moscow, 1952).

23. Hildegard Schaeder, *Moskau das dritte Rom: Studien zur Geschichte der politischen Theorien in der slavischen Welt* (Hamburg, 1929); Dmitrij Čiževskij, *History of Russian Literature from the Eleventh Century to the End of the Baroque* (The Hague, 1960), pp. 275–86.

24. Andrei A. Lobanov-Rostovsky, *Russia and Europe, 1789–1825* (Durham, N.C., 1947); Nicholas V. Riasanovsky, *Nicholas I and Official Nationality in Russia, 1825–1855* (Berkeley, 1959), pp. 235–65.

25. Michael B. Petrovich, *The Emergence of Russian Pan-Slavism, 1856–1870* (New York, 1956); B. H. Sumner, *Russia and the Balkans, 1870–1880* (Oxford, 1937), pp. 56–80; C. E. Black, *The Establishment of Constitutional Government in Bulgaria* (Princeton, 1943); W. N. Medlicott, *The Congress of Berlin and After: A Diplomatic History of the Near Eastern Settlement, 1878–1880* (London, 1938).

26. Leonid I. Strakhovsky, "Constitutional Aspects of the Imperial Russian Government's Policy toward National Minorities," *Journal of Modern History, 13* (Dec. 1941), 467–92; Richard Pipes, *The Formation of the Soviet Union: Communism and Nationalism, 1917–1923* (Cambridge, Mass., 1954), pp. 1–113.

27. William L. Langer, *The Franco-Russian Alliance, 1890–1894* (Cambridge, Mass., 1929); Georges Michon, *The Franco-Russian Alliance, 1891–1917* (London, 1929); Rogers P. Churchill, *The Anglo-Russian Convention of 1907* (Cedar Rapids, Ia., 1939); Friederich Stieve, ed., *Isvolsky and the World War* (London, 1926); Serge D. Sazonov, *Fateful Years, 1909–1916* (London, 1928).

28. C. Jay Smith, Jr., *The Russian Struggle for Power, 1914–1917: A Study of Russian Foreign Policy during the First World War* (New York, 1956), provides an introduction to the war aims controversy in Russia; see also Robert P. Browder and Alexander F. Kerensky, eds., *The Russian Provisional Government, 1917: Documents*, 3 vols. (Stanford, 1961).

29. Louis Fischer, *The Soviets in World Affairs: A History of the Relations between the Soviet Union and the Rest of the World, 1917–1929*, 2nd ed. 2 vols. (Princeton, 1951); E. H. Carr, *The Bolshevik Revolution, 1917–1923*, 3 vols. (London, 1951–53).

30. Max Beloff, *The Foreign Policy of Soviet Russia, 1929–1941*, 2 vols. (New York, 1947–49); David J. Dallin, *Soviet Russia's Foreign Policy, 1939–1942* (New Haven, 1942); George F. Kennan, *Russia and the West under Lenin and Stalin* (Boston, 1961); I. F. Ivashin, *Ocherki istorii vneshnei politiki SSSR* (Moscow, 1958).

31. Wladyslaw W. Kulski, *Peaceful Co-existence: An Analysis of Soviet Foreign Policy* (Chicago, 1959); Philip E. Mosely, *The Kremlin and World Politics: Studies in Soviet Policy and Action* (New York, 1960); David J. Dallin, *Soviet Foreign Policy after Stalin* (Philadelphia, 1961).

32. Nikita S. Khrushchev, *For Victory in Peaceful Competition with Capitalism* (New York, 1960); and especially Khrushchev's report of Jan. 6, 1961, published in *Kommunist*, No. 1 (Jan. 1961), 3–37, trans. in *Current Digest of the Soviet Press, 13*, 3 (Feb. 15, 1961), 16–19; *13*, 4 (Feb. 22, 1961), 8–15, 24.

33. Arno J. Mayer, *Political Origins of the New Diplomacy, 1917–1918* (New Haven, 1959), especially pp. 368–93.

CHAPTER 10

Russia/USSR and the Modernization of the Balkans

This chapter is concerned more particularly with the role of Russia/USSR in the process of societal transformation in Southeastern Europe. The chapter illustrates the extent to which Russian/Soviet influence abroad has been a function of the domestic level of development. Apart from its influence on literature and music, and on religion in those areas where the Eastern Orthodox Church predominated, Russia/USSR has exerted decisive influence in the Balkans only when its military power prevailed.

The Soviet Union, no less than other societies, is under constant challenge from the changing international environment. Today, for the first time since 1917, the earlier belief that the Soviet Union was a model for other countries is being questioned by domestic and foreign critics alike. The euphoria of Khrushchev's era continued for several years into Brezhnev's 18-year administration, but by the 1970s the Soviet Union was rapidly losing its relative position through its failure to make use of the achievements of science and technology as it sought to move from an extensive to an intensive strategy of development. The older generation of Brezhnev and Chernenko tended to compare the Soviet Union of the 1980s with the Soviet past and to point out how much things had improved. Their concept of socialism was one in which industry was protected from foreign competition, food prices were subsidized, and both workers and managers were secure in their jobs.

The new generation represented by Gorbachev and his appointees entered politics after the death of Stalin and are more inclined to compare the USSR with the outside world. They are aware that in the 1980s neither the countries under Marxist-Leninist leadership (especially China) nor the countries of the Third World find much in the Soviet Union that they wish to imitate. It remains to be seen

Reprinted with permission from *The Balkans in Transition*, ed. by Charles and Barbara Jelavich (Berkeley, CA: University of California Press, 1963), 145–183.

whether the new generation can free itself from dogma and from bureaucratic lethargy and make their society stand tall again.

THE BALKANS, RUSSIA, AND THE WEST

The transformation of the peoples of the Balkans from oppressed and backward subjects of the Ottoman Empire to citizens in independent national states in the throes of industrialization, is part of a larger story which started in the Middle Ages and is likely to continue for the foreseeable future. The term "modernization" is frequently used to describe this process, by which is meant the entire scope of change accompanying the revolutionary growth in man's control over his environment.

This process started in Western Europe as a revolution in science and technology, but soon became intertwined with political, economic, and social change. Political modernization has taken the form of the consolidation of the authority of national states at the expense of landowners, provincial magnates, the Church, and a variety of local authorities. Where national states already existed, as in England and France, the change was made with relatively little strife; where they did not, as in Germany and Italy, the process of national unification led to extensive upheavals. The movements in ideology and politics which stirred Europe between the fifteenth and eighteenth centuries are familiar enough, and the French Revolution has become a symbol of the dramatic turning point when the proponents of modernization first began to gain decisive victories over the adherents of the traditional regimes on the European continent.

The essential change in economics has been the increase in the per-capita output of human labor as a result of technological innovations. Industrialization is no doubt the most dramatic result of modernization, but the impact of technological change has been scarcely less revolutionary in agriculture, communications, transportation, and in methods of doing business. Economic growth has been accompanied by rapid social change: urbanization, education, the growth of an industrial proletariat and of a professional and political elite, and so on. At the same time, there has been a transformation of popular beliefs from the folklore of rural life to the somewhat more sophisticated outlook of today.

To some extent the entire European world shared in this process, but the initiative was clearly taken by the peoples bordering on the North Atlantic and the new outlook spread only gradually to Central and Eastern Europe, and beyond. In the countries of Southeastern Europe this process has passed through several phases. In the initial phase, during the seventeenth, eighteenth, and nineteenth centuries, modern ideas gained influence and the peoples of this region became convinced that they could and should strive to attain the level of achievement of Western Europe. The Ottoman rulers themselves were influenced by these ideas, and they undertook significant modernizing reforms in their Balkan provinces. These reforms were too limited and too long delayed, however, to capture the imagination of local modernizers. The latter, who before long included practically the entire literate population, were convinced that independence from Ottoman rule was the prerequisite to systematic modernization. Nationalism must thus be regarded as a means to modernization, although it raised political issues of such complexity that for the more short-sighted leaders it became an end in itself to which the larger goals of modernization were subordinated.

National independence nevertheless remains the most convenient point of division between this introductory phase, when traditional political forms predominated, and a second, in which modern-minded leaders gained political control. The central struggle in this second phase was between the leaders interested primarily in national liberation and unification and those who wished to subordinate these traditional goals to economic and social development. This phase may be said to have begun in 1863 in Greece and in 1878 in Rumania, Serbia, and Bulgaria, and it was substantially completed by the end of the First World War. In Albania it did not start until 1912, and it ended in the course of the Second World War. One may also think in terms of a third phase, in which the problems of economic and social development form the central issue. In this phase the main political struggle hinges on the decision which of several alternative programs of modernization should be undertaken. In terms of domestic strife this phase is often the most violent. It is also the one in which the influence of foreign models is greatest. If one thinks of the goal of this third phase as the establishment of stable modern institutions and the achievement of a level of development similar to that of the advanced countries, it is clear that for the Balkan peoples this goal is not yet in sight.

It is within such a framework that one must approach the problem of the political, ideological, economic, and cultural influence of Russia on the modernization of the Balkans. To a significant degree, both Russia and the Balkan countries have turned to the West for ideas, institutions, and technology, and even today the announced goal of the Soviet rulers is to overtake the advanced countries, and at some more distant future time to surpass them. Any discussion of this problem must therefore take for granted the predominance of Western influence. This is not to say, however, that Russian influence was negligible. In an important sense, Russia has served as one of the channels through which Western ideas and institutions reached Southeastern Europe. Moreover, within

Russia the Western heritage was reinterpreted and adapted to Russian traditions and needs, and in this new form was frequently in a position to compete in Southeastern Europe with more direct Western influences.

THE POLITICS OF POWER

The political influence exerted by Russia in the Balkans has reflected the importance of this area to Russian security. Southeastern Europe borders on Russia and has played a key role in the balance of power between Russia and rival great powers. This region also lies across Russia's land route to the Turkish Straits, which for more than a century was one of the vital channels of Russian commerce.

The stabilization of the Russian frontier in the region of the Dniester and Pruth rivers was the culmination of the slow conquest of the Ukrainian steppes from Turkey and Poland in the seventeenth and eighteenth centuries. The annexation of Bessarabia in 1812 kept within reasonable ethnic bounds the territorial expansion of tsarist Russia in Southeastern Europe, although the tsar's troops crossed the Pruth four times after 1812 and for a generation (1856–1878) southern Bessarabia was restored to Turkish sovereignty. The Revolution of 1917 brought no immediate change in Russian objectives in this regard. The loss of Bessarabia to Rumania was never recognized, and the province was reoccupied at a convenient juncture in 1940. In contrast to the reannexation of Bessarabia, the acquisition of northern Bukovina at the same time did represent a new extension of Russian sovereignty in the Balkans. In view of the smallness of the area, however, and the ethnic claim to it which Russia could make, this latter addition of territory did not constitute a substantial departure from Russia's traditional policy of keeping her formal Balkan frontier within general ethnic bounds.

Of much greater significance than the frontier issue has been the Russian aim of asserting a predominant political influence in the Balkans. Possibilities of realizing this objective were seen in the time of Peter the Great, but it was not until the reign of Catherine II that substantial progress was made. The breaking of the Turkish monopoly of the Black Sea and the Straits in the treaty of 1774, the terms of which were to afford Russia in future years many opportunities to intervene in the affairs of the Ottoman Empire, laid the foundations for the extension of Russian influence—achievements which provided a point of departure for Catherine's ambitious but illusory "Greek project" (1782). Henceforth Russia was to exert a steady political pressure in this region, which became an area of intense rivalry with the other great powers, and it was only the combined efforts of the latter that prevented her from completely dominating it. After the Revolution, the desire to exert a predominant political influence remained, although its ideological content was of course radically altered. At the first opportunity, the traditional policy sprang to life again, and after the Second World War Russia's political influence was reestablished under conditions more favorable than before.

A somewhat more complex relationship was that between Russia's policy in the Balkans and her desire to guarantee free passage for her commerce through the Turkish Straits. It was not until the nineteenth century, when the export of grain from southern Russia increased until it constituted from a third to a half of all Russian exports, that Russia's concern regarding the Straits became a major motivating factor in her Balkan policy. Insofar as arrangements regarding the Straits were dependent on negotiations between Russia and Turkey, the exertion by Russia of military and political pressure in the Balkans frequently served as the opening gambit in her efforts to gain concessions from Turkey. Here the Revolution did represent more of a break in Russian policy, for the means used by the Soviet Union to further its interests at the Straits have on the whole had little to do with the Balkans. Even with the revival of Russian influence in that region in 1940, and the subsequent stationing of sizable units of Soviet armed forces within easy striking distance of Constantinople (Istanbul), Russia's interest in the Straits does not appear to play so great a role in her Balkan policy as it did in the century before the Revolution.

Russia has employed various methods to pursue her objectives in the Balkans. Whatever may have been Russia's ambitions at one time or another, the resort to military force has always been a major instrument of policy and the most successful means of extending her political influence in the Balkans and of exerting pressure on Turkey. Of the Balkan states only Albania received its independence without some military assistance from tsarist Russia. When, on the other hand, it was the tsar's policy to oppose popular uprisings, as in the Danubian Principalities in 1848–1849, it took Russian troops to do the job. Similarly, after the Revolution the Soviet regime found no solid basis for its influence before the Red Army arrived, and since that event its influence has been decisive in the areas where its military power has prevailed.

The occupation of important areas in the Balkans has been another serviceable means of attaining Russia's objectives. In her wars with Turkey, Russia has invaded the Balkans about ten times, and her troops have remained in prolonged occupation on eight occasions. Of these, seven were before the Revolution (the Danubian Principalities in 1769–1774, 1787–1792, 1806–1812, 1829–1834, and 1848–1851; the Ionian Islands in 1798–1807; Bulgaria in 1878–1879), and one after the advent of the Soviets (Rumania and Bulgaria after 1944). These periods of occupation have been decisive for the political development of the areas concerned, but they cannot be said to have aroused significant popular support. In the Danubian Principalities, the prolonged periods of Russian occupation before the Revolution were a major factor in giving the Rumanian people the administrative and spiritual unity which were essential prerequisites for the later political unification of Moldavia and Wallachia. The Russian occupation of Bulgaria in 1878–1879 was similarly decisive in the history of that country, for the Constitution of 1879 which Russia sponsored was to provide the framework for the course of the political development of the country for the next several generations.

The Soviet occupation of Rumania and Bulgaria after 1944 was even more decisive than the tsarist ventures. The Soviet authorities were more determined and self-confident than the tsarist, and less restricted by the rival interests of the other great powers. Exercising the rights accorded them in the armistice terms and working largely through local instruments, they used their occupation opportunities to great advantage and with profound results for the future. In Jugoslavia, on the other hand, Russian influence was based on ideology rather than on power, as the Soviet leaders discovered when they failed in their effort to intervene in the domestic affairs of the country. In Greece, Soviet policy supported a large-scale internal war (1944–1949) in an effort to overthrow the government. In all these various forms of political influence, the Soviet Union has drawn heavily on precedents established by tsarist Russia.

Diplomacy has also been an important means of implementing Russian policies in the Balkans and the Straits question. Both tsarist and Soviet Russia have found that the main obstacles to the achievement of their objectives in this region have not been the Turkish armies or Balkan nationalism, but rather the competing interests of the other great powers. Whenever Russia has come up against the great powers in this region she has turned to diplomacy rather than to force although the threat of the latter has always lurked in the background. The periods of greatest Russian influence in the Balkans, from 1815 to 1856 and since 1944, have been times in which the other great powers were unable or unwilling to exert pressure on Russia. Even in its periods of greatest influence, however, Russian policy has been tempered by the need to maintain normal relations with the rest of the world.

IDEOLOGIES OF MODERNIZATION

The study of the influence of Russian ideas as distinct from political power is complicated by the fact that there have often been two and sometimes three "official" policies emanating simultaneously from St.

Petersburg, and later from Moscow. Not infrequently these ideological approaches have been advanced simultaneously or in rapid alternation. There have also been a number of unofficial trends of Russian thought—liberal, radical, populist, Marxist before 1917, and conservative since that date—which have been regarded as subversive by the Russian government but which nevertheless have constituted important Russian ideological influences. Indeed, the range of opinions emanating from Russia has been so wide that at one time or another all major programs of modernization implemented or even discussed in the Balkans have been subjected in some degree to Russian influence. At the risk of oversimplifying, the many trends of policy and thought involved in this process may be summarized in a roughly chronological order under the headings of conservatism, liberalism, and Marxism-Leninism.

From 1774 to 1856, at least, it appeared to be reasonable from the Russian point of view to promote the independence of the Balkan peoples within a framework of conservative domestic policies. In a situation in which Russia and Austria were the dominant European powers in this region, it was quite feasible to support national revolutions without stimulating political liberalism. The germ of weakness in such a policy lay in the growing influence of West European liberalism, which was in due course to become the dominant philosophy of Balkan national leaders. It was only after the Crimean War, however, and indeed not until the Congress of Berlin, that Russian-supported conservatism ceased to exert an influence on the Balkan political scene.

The provinces of Wallachia and Moldavia had the most frequent and direct contact with Russian policy, and here Russian support went initially to the boiars. After Russia's decisive intervention in the Principalities in 1828–1829, the major abuses of the Phanariotes were abolished but the *Réglement Organique* sponsored by Count Kiselev established the basis for a virtual Russian protectorate which lasted until 1856. Similarly, in Greece, though under somewhat different political circumstances, Russian conservative influence was strongly felt. John Capodistrias had been a close associate of Alexander I before 1821, and the regime which he established in Greece was politically conservative even though Greece was a republic. The influence of Russia, as one of the three guaranteeing powers under the treaty terms of 1827, was perhaps even more directly felt during the reign of King Otho (1832–1862). Before his death in 1843 the popular leader Theodore Kolokotronis, who had served briefly in a Russian-led regiment in Corfu, headed the "Russian party" in Athens. In Serbia, Russia joined with the Habsburg monarchy in exercising a conservative influence, and intervened to prevent the adoption of "radical" political ideas on more than one occasion before the establishment of a fully sovereign constitutional government in 1878. In Montenegro, likewise, Russian influences served to support the efforts of the traditional regime to free itself from Turkish rule, in particular after the visit of Prince Nikola to St. Petersburg in 1868. In Bulgaria, the official Russian policy was reflected in the moderate outlook of such leaders as Ivan Seliminsky and Naiden Gerov, who had gone to Russia for their higher education. After the liberation of Bulgaria, under circumstances in which Russia had to work in conjunction with the other great powers, Prince Alexander Battenberg was supported by the tsar on the assumption that he would pursue conservative policies.

The force of Russian conservatism in Balkan politics waned rapidly after 1856, and the renewed Russian participation in Balkan affairs in the 1870's failed to reestablish its former position of influence. It should nevertheless be noted that after 1917 an unofficial version of Russian conservatism reasserted itself briefly, especially in Bulgaria and Jugoslavia, as a result of the influx of Russian refugees. These adherents of tsarism in a number of instances occupied important positions, and exercised some influence on public opinion. Moreover, the fact that King Alexander of Jugoslavia was educated at the imperial court in St. Petersburg no doubt also affected his political outlook.

The impact of official Russia on the liberal programs of modernization which dominated Balkan politics from the 1860's until the 1930's was immeasurably smaller than on the conservative programs of the earlier period. Indeed, there was something incongruous about Russian support in the Balkans of institutions denied to the Russian people themselves, and both during and since the nineteenth century students of the problem have hesitated to believe their sources. Yet it is clear that after the Crimean War it was a vital Russian interest to prevent the domination of the Balkans by another great power, and it was more important to have friends among the Balkan liberal political leaders than to support conservative principles.

It is under these circumstances that Russia came rather hesitantly to the point of supporting liberalism. The most dramatic expression of this policy was the active sponsorship of a draft Bulgarian constitution in 1879 that was advanced by contemporary standards. This draft, after some further liberalization by a Constituent Assembly, was adopted with Russia's blessing and promptly put into operation. The risks of this Russian experiment soon became apparent, however, and it led first to confusion and then to disaster for Russian interests. The initial confusion stemmed from a division of counsels within Russia. Miliutin, the minister of war and a Panslav, calculated that by supporting political liberalism Russia would win the friendship of Bulgarian national leaders and prepare the way for a reassertion of Russian influence in the Balkans at the next opportunity. Indeed, the more ardent Panslavs among his subordinates toyed with the idea of encouraging a new Bulgarian national uprising against the Western powers responsible for the defeat of the San Stefano program. On the other hand Giers, the minister of foreign affairs, supported a policy of moderation designed to keep Bulgarian nationalism in check and to avoid giving offense to Britain and Austria.

While these two divergent policies were reconcilable in the spring of 1879, before Bulgarian political forces had been fully set in motion, the Russian government soon faced some difficult choices. First the liberals were supported against Prince Alexander Battenberg, whose loyalty to Russia was suspect. Then, after the assassination of Alexander II by Russian radicals whose views were suspiciously akin to those of the Bulgarian liberals, Battenberg was permitted to set aside the constitution and rule with the aid of Russian military officials. The latter soon antagonized first the prince and then the liberals, and by 1886 the Russians were forced to abandon Bulgaria, losing most of their friends and influence. Liuben Karavelov set forth concisely the Russian dilemma when he predicted in 1870, in an oft-quoted statement, that "if Russia comes to liberate, she will be received with great sympathy; but if she comes to rule, she will find many enemies." Although one can cite other examples in later decades of Russian support of liberal regimes—support of Geshov in Bulgaria in 1911–1913, Pašić in Serbia throughout the first two decades of the twentieth century, and Bratianu in Rumania in 1916—these were all maneuvers in world politics and were essentially devoid of ideological implications.

The irony of this ideological retreat on the part of official Russia was that to some degree the Balkan liberalism dominant after 1878 had been nurtured under the influence of unofficial Russian ideologies. If one interprets liberalism broadly to include the radical and populist strains of thought, one can trace the process by which the utilitarianism, romanticism, utopian socialism, liberalism, and nationalism prevalent in Western Europe were absorbed and adapted by the Russian radicals and passed on through their writings and political movements to Balkan public opinion. The difficulties of tracing this type of influence are many, for the Russian radicals were familiar with a wide range of Western thought and the Balkan radicals in turn studied both Western and Russian writings. If one considers also that both the Russian and the Balkan radicals were less concerned with a discriminating analysis of these ideas than with their applicability to the political and social problems of their respective countries, one can see how difficult it is to distinguish between specifically Russian and specifically Western influences. At the same time the difficulties of this task should not be exaggerated, for there is considerable evidence of direct Russian influence.

The first wave of unofficial Russian liberal and radical influences may be traced to the Decembrists. The Society of United Slavs of Kiev, in particular, included among its aims the liberation of all Slavic peoples and the establishment of democratic governments united in a federation. The Decembrists established a branch of their movement in Kishinev and were in touch with the Philike Hetaeria in Odessa. It is significant that Tudor Vladimirescu, as an officer of the Russian army and through his contacts with the Philike Hetaeria, was familiar with the views of the Decembrists. Alexander Ypsilanti and his colleagues in the Philike Hetaeria were also acquainted with advanced thought in Russia, although the aims and methods of their own organization were so misconceived that it is difficult to distinguish a recognizable ideology in their abortive efforts.

A second generation of Balkan liberals and radicals, most of whom were engaged primarily in revolutionary activity, but never reached the point of holding public office, received their education in Russia or came into close contact with Russian radicalism. It has been estimated that approximately five hundred Bulgarians were educated in Russia between 1856 and 1878, apart from the members of the substantial Bulgarian colony in Odessa, and an unknown number of Serbs and Rumanians also went to Russia for their higher education. Although some of these students no doubt returned to their countries as loyal admirers of the Russian government, most appear to have been inspired by Western liberalism and socialism as reflected in the writings of Pisarev, Chernyshevsky, Herzen, Dobroliubov, Bakunin, and Nechaev.

No doubt the most typical representative of this generation was Svetozar Marković. He studied in St. Petersburg in the 1860's, at a time when the influence of radicalism was in full blossom. Later, in Zürich, he met Bakunin on a number of occasions but did not become a member of the Bakuninist clique of Serbian students. Despite this exposure to Russian radicalism, Marković's philosophy drew primarily on West European progressive thought. In Bulgaria, such prominent leaders of the revolutionary movement as Liuben Karavelov and Khristo Botev also studied in Russia, and in their writings the Russian radical influence probably plays a proportionately larger role than in Marković. Their relations with the Russian radicals were frequently direct. Karavelov was personally acquainted with Herzen, Ogarev, Bakunin, and Nechaev, and his colleagues in the Bulgarian revolutionary movement were all familiar with their writings. Moreover the substantial number of Bulgarians who emigrated to such centers as Bucharest, Braila, and Odessa in the first half of the nineteenth century, came more or less directly into contact with the prevailing currents of Russian thought. In Rumania the radicals of this period drew much more directly on French thought, whereas in Greece and Albania there is even less evidence of Russian influence.

A later generation, in experience if not in years, is formed by radicals of the 1860's and 1870's who survived to become liberal statesmen later in the century. Of these, Nikola Pašić is doubtless the best known. Like Marković, he met Bakunin as a student in Zürich, and he was nurtured in his early years on Russian radicalism as well as on West European socialism and liberalism. In his later career as a statesman it was nevertheless these latter influences that predominated. He served as his country's diplomatic representative in St. Petersburg in 1893–1894, and as prime minister of his country in the prewar era he counted tsarist Russia as an ally, but under the circumstances this coexistence of an early admiration for Russian radicalism and a later reliance on the friendship of Russian tsarism is not so incongruous as it might seem. Similarly Petko Karavelov and Stefan Stambolov, who spent their student years in Russia and whose outlook reflected a characteristic blend of Western liberalism and Russian radicalism, went on to become liberal statesmen who looked primarily to the West for their political inspiration. These few examples are only the best known of an entire generation of Serbian and Bulgarian leaders who gained a significant share of their ideas about the modern world through the writings of the Russian radicals.

In the latter part of the nineteenth century the influence of Russian populism was much less prominent. In Rumania, where the agrarian situation somewhat resembled that in Russia, the Russian populist tradition had only a few representatives. Zemfiri K. Ralli-Arbore studied in Russia and later was intimate with Bakunin and Nechaev in Zürich. He exercised only a negligible influence in his home country, however. More prominent was Constantin Stere, a Bessarabian boiar who had served a term of exile in Siberia. He became one of the principal theorists of the Rumanian Peasant party in the early years of the twentieth century, and some characteristic aspects of Russian thought were reflected in his views. Two Russian populists emigrated to Bulgaria, Vladimir K. Debogori-Mokrievich and Boris Mintses, but they did not become prominent in the affairs of that country. Among Bulgarian political writers, Todor G. Vlaikov and Petko Todorov in particular were influenced by Russian populism, but the organized agrarian movement in Bulgaria gained its principal inspiration from the West. Alexander Stambolisky received his higher education in Germany, and the references in his principal theoretical work are exclusively to Western authorities. Stjepan Radić, on the other hand, studied in Russia and throughout his life combined a characteristic Croatian Russophilism with his peasantist ideology. He visited Russia in the 1890's, and again in 1923, but the problems of the Croatian peasantry were very different from those in Russia, and it cannot be said that the solutions proposed by the Croatian Peasant party relied significantly on Russian models.

The Socialist movements which developed in the Balkan countries at the end of the nineteenth century had deep roots in the earlier radicalism, but were distinguished from it by their formal party structure and their concern for organized political action. These movements developed in three stages: from the founding of the Social Democratic parties to 1917, from 1917 to 1944, and since the latter date. From the start, Russian influence was significant. Serbian social democracy was strongly influenced by the legacy of Marković and, of its more prominent leaders, Vasa Pelagić, Mihailo Ilić, and Dragutin Popović had lived and studied in Russia and were close to the Socialist movement in that country. The leading Rumanian theorist of socialism was a Russian radical named M. I. Kats, who emigrated to Rumania in the 1870's and became prominent under the pseudonym of Constantin Dobrogeanu-Gherea. Even more prominent was Christian G. Rakovsky, who was the guiding spirit of the Rumanian Social Democratic party founded in 1893 and also played an active role in Bulgarian socialism. After 1917 he went on to play a leading role in Soviet affairs.

More extensive yet was the Russian influence on the Bulgarian Socialists whose leader for many years, Dimitur Blagoev, studied in Russia from 1878 to 1885 and is credited with establishing the first Social Democratic group in that country in 1884. He founded the Bulgarian Social Democratic party in 1891, and headed its Narrow wing until his death in 1924. Many of his fellow Socialists also had close Russian connections: Yanko Sakuzov who, as leader of the Broad wing after 1903, became Blagoev's chief rival; as well as Georgi Bakalov, Khristo Kabakchiev, and Vasil Kolarov, who were all closely associated with the Russian Socialist movement. Georgi Dimitrov was the only Bulgarian Socialist prominent before 1917 who did not have close Russian associations, and he made up for this by spending much of his long period of exile (1923–1946) in the Soviet Union. In Croatia, Slovenia, and Bosnia-Hercegovina, by contrast, the Social Democratic movement received its inspiration from Central Europe, and this was true to almost the same degree in Serbia and Greece.

In the two or three years following the Bolshevik Revolution, the Left wings of the various Social Democratic parties in Bulgaria (1919), Serbia (1919), Rumania (1921), and Greece (1924) became the nuclei of new Communist parties and henceforth had close relations with the U.S.S.R. All the more prominent leaders visited Russia at one time or another, and many lived there for long periods. Many also served as agents of the Comintern in various international activities, and particularly in the Spanish Civil War. A few rose to international prominence in the interwar period. The influence of communism within the Balkan countries was based primarily on its role of claiming to speak for the oppressed and discontented. Whereas the trade unionists were predominantly Social Democrats, the Communists drew their support from a wide variety of sources. The Magyars, Jews, and Slavs in Rumania; the Macedonians, Montenegrins, and Bosnians in Jugoslavia; the Macedonians in Bulgaria; and in Greece the new immigrants from Russia and Turkey—all these tended to find in the Communist party an outlet for grievances ignored or suppressed by the traditional parties. In all these countries there was also a substantial population of semiskilled workers on the border between village and urban life, and various categories of migrant and seasonal workers, to whom the Communists could appeal.

The electoral strength of the Communists was never great, except in the Jugoslav election of 1920 when they won 58 of 419 seats in the National Assembly. As parties under constant persecution they had limited opportunities for political maneuver. In 1936 the small Communist party in Greece held the parliamentary balance between the Royalists and the Liberals, but this was exceptional. The Communists also had some success in winning over splinter groups from the Socialist and Agrarian parties as a result of united-front tactics. They likewise exerted influence through the organization of strikes and revolts, and especially in the 1920's contributed substantially to the already considerable hazards of Balkan politics.

Perhaps the greatest impression made by Communist policy was in international relations. In an era of bitter enmities among the Balkan peoples, the idea of peace and friendship was attractive, and the Communist proposals for Balkan federation held out hope for resolving such controversial issues as the Macedonian question. The key to such influence as the Communists exerted nevertheless lay in the Soviet Union. In the 1920's the Soviet Union had little to offer the Balkan peoples. Its domestic system was neither stable nor prosperous enough to attract admirers, and in international relations it was regarded chiefly as a source of aggression and disturbance. At the same time, the radical transformation which Russia was undergoing doubtless served in some degree as a challenge to traditional political leaders in the Balkans, leading them in some instances to undertake reforms which they might not otherwise have considered.

This picture changed somewhat in the early 1930's, when the growing political stability and economic purposefulness of the Soviet government coincided with a period of depression and retrenchment in the West. The role of the Soviet Union in the League of Nations also relieved tension, and diplomatic relations were restored with Rumania and

Bulgaria in 1934. Relations had been established with Albania as early as 1924, but were not renewed with Jugoslavia until 1940 and with Greece until 1941. These events did not greatly benefit the local Communist parties, however, and they were soon offset by the purge trials in the Soviet Union, and the German economic drive. On the eve of the Second World War, it could not be said that either the Soviet Union or the local Communist parties exerted any considerable ideological influence in these countries.

The events of the Second World War and after do not need to be recounted, but the relationship between Soviet military force and the influence of the Communist ideology deserves brief attention. In Rumania and Bulgaria it seems clear that the establishment of Communist regimes was entirely dependent on the presence of Soviet military power. In neither country did the Communist parties wield any considerable influence over centers of political power, or in the countryside through guerrilla operations, although they were substantially stronger in Bulgaria than in Rumania. In Jugoslavia and Albania, on the other hand, their strength was developed as a result of guerrilla operations and initially without Soviet assistance. In Jugoslavia, Tito's cadres proved to be sufficiently strong to withstand Soviet infiltration. The clumsy Soviet effort in 1948 to oust the Jugoslav Communist leadership proved to be a total failure, and Tito survived with aid from the West to implement his own version of national communism. In Greece a strong guerrilla position was established by the Communists during the war, but in the absence of Soviet military support it was unable to retain its influence after the war despite persistent efforts.

Russian ideological influence in Rumania, Bulgaria, and Albania is now unrivaled, and all policies and institutions have been remodeled along Soviet lines. To the extent that this process is not yet completed, it is due to local conditions which can only be changed over a period of time. This is not to say that public opinion has been won over, however, and it may be questioned to what extent even the younger generation educated since 1944 is ideologically loyal. In the absence of an effective alternative, however, opposition to communism is limited to local efforts. In Jugoslavia the situation is more complex. The Communist party had primarily Soviet models in mind when it established its new institutions immediately after the war. Since the break with the Cominform, however, there has been considerable experimentation with alternative forms of administration as well as frequent consultation with West European Socialists. As a result, a peculiarly Jugoslav form of communism has been developed which combines highly centralized controls with some local administrative autonomy. In Greece, on the other hand, Communist influence has survived in the form of the

Communist-sponsored Union of the Democratic Left, which won a quarter of the seats in the Greek parliament in 1958. It thus represents an important force to be reckoned with, and attracts the support of a variety of disaffected groups.

In reviewing the record since the beginning of the nineteenth century, one may conclude that until 1944 there was relatively little Russian influence on the ideologies of modernization actually implemented in the Balkans. During the first half of the nineteenth century Russian influence supported governments in the Danubian Principalities, Serbia, Montenegro, and Greece which were opposed to fundamental social change. Between the Crimean War and the First World War Russian radicals and Socialists had considerable influence on progressive thought in Bulgaria and Serbia, and to a lesser extent in Rumania, but this had only a negligible impact on government policies. This influence was chiefly as an interpreter of Western ideas, which also came to these countries in a more influential and effective form directly from the West. Even among the southern Slavs of the Habsburg Empire, where Russian sympathies were particularly strong, neither radical nor official Russia had much to offer in the way of programs of social and economic change. In the interwar period government policy in the Balkans paid little attention to Soviet models, and only after 1944 did these exert a determining influence north of Greece.

ECONOMIC GROWTH

In many respects the most direct and impressive aspect of modernization as a general phenomenon has been in the realm of economic growth. The Balkan countries have shared in this process, although in a rather modest way, and all branches of their economies have undergone a fundamental change. The peasant agriculture and handicrafts of the mid-nineteenth century have been supplanted to a considerable degree by modern technology. This transformation was brought about in part by free enterprise and in part by state initiative, and in both foreign capital played a significant role. The underlying social significance of this transformation has been the possibility of increased per-capita consumption along with the social and cultural benefits of a higher standard of living.

In this process Russia played almost no role until after the Second World War. The programs and technology of economic growth, as well as the bulk of the foreign capital, came from Western and Central Europe. Throughout this period Russia was a capital-importing country and, except for relatively modest financial operations in Turkey, Persia, and Mongolia, did not undertake foreign investments. Its financial operations in the Balkans were in fact limited to a few loans with a political aim: the financing of wars of liberation against the Ottoman Empire. Thus in 1830 Russia advanced 3,000,000 francs to Greece. Two years later Russia joined with the United Kingdom and France to guarantee a larger loan to the new Greek state, but no Russian capital was involved. Between 1867 and 1878 Russia advanced some 8,700,000 dinars to the Serbian government, in addition to military assistance. Russia also gave extensive assistance in the form of military supplies to Bulgaria in 1877–1878, but under the Treaty of Berlin that country was required to assume the costs of the Russian occupation and, after 1885, of the expenses of the Russian army in Eastern Rumelia as well. These costs amounted to 56,300,000 francs, and Bulgaria continued payments on this debt until the First World War.

Apart from these limited financial operations, Russia appears to have had little direct share in the economic growth of this region. There was some effort by Russian banking concerns in the early 1880's to participate in the construction of railroads in Serbia and Bulgaria, but these efforts were not supported by the Russian government and they came to nothing. To this one may add several instances in which Russian economic institutions served as a model for those in this region. Thus it is clear that Prince Cuza, in promulgating the land reform of 1864, was influenced by the Russian emancipation of 1861. In Bulgaria, the fiscal system established after the liberation was based on the Russian model, and other examples of this type of influence could be cited. Yet by comparison with the extensive adaptation of institutions and methods in the economic sphere from European societies, Russia's role in this regard was small.

The relative absence of Russia from the Balkan economic scene before the Second World War is also reflected in its small share of the foreign trade of these countries. The following table reflects this situation, as well as the dramatic change which occurred after the Second World War.

Since 1944 Russia has played a major economic role in Rumania and Bulgaria, in Jugoslavia up to 1948, and in Albania since that date. The first impact of Soviet economic policy took the form of the removal of capital goods from Bulgaria and Rumania in compensation for war losses. In Bulgaria this amounted to relatively small enforced shipments of foodstuffs, but from Rumania capital goods valued at some $2,000,000,000 were removed by 1948. Both countries also had to pay occupation costs. In addition, sixteen Soviet-Rumanian and five Soviet-Bulgarian joint companies were established. These enjoyed various tax privileges, and turned over one-half of their earnings to the U.S.S.R. The Soviet share in these companies consisted of confiscated German assets, which in turn included the assets of other European countries

Table 10.1 Russia's share in the Balkans trade
(in percent of total trade)

	1909-1912	1938	1957	Soviet bloc 1957
Albania	---	import 0.0 export 0.0	import 67.6 export 54.2	import 86.4 export 79.2
Bulgaria	import 3.9 export 0.2	import 0.0 export 0.0	import 55.4 export 57.2	import 72.7 export 78.8
Greece	import 19.4 export 2.0	import 2.0 export 0.3	import 2.0 export 4.1	import 4.6 export 8.5
Rumania	import 2.7 export 1.0	import --- export ---	import 55.9 export 50.5	import 70.8 export 66.3
Jugoslavia	---	import 0.1 export 0.0	import 10.4 export 12.3	import 20.4 export 24.0

NOTE: --- = negligible, less than 0.1.

Sources: Bulgaria, Rumania, and Serbia for 1909-1912, from A. Zaleski, Les courants commerciaux de l'Europe danubienne au cours de la premiere moitie du XIX siecle (Paris, 1952), p. 48; Greece for 1909-1912, from M. Dorizas, The Foreign Trade of Greece (Philadelphia, 1925), p. 124; remaining figures from United Nations, Direction of International Trade, annual issue (New York, 1959), passim.

which Germany had confiscated earlier in the war. The total removal of capital under these and various other operations has not been estimated, and perhaps cannot be, but in the first postwar decade it clearly amounted to several billion dollars in value, and by far the greater share was from Rumania.

The joint companies in Bulgaria and Rumania were dissolved between 1954 and 1956, with compensation for the U.S.S.R., and after the events of the latter year a new Soviet approach was attempted. The debts of Rumania ($717,000,000) and Albania ($105,500,000) were canceled. At the same time, Russia extended loans and credits in the amount of $47,700,000 to Albania, $192,500,000 to Bulgaria, and $100,500,000 to Rumania. Simultaneously, the terms of Soviet trade with these three countries reflect a significant and continuing price discrimination against them.

The net loss to Rumania and Bulgaria since the Second World War would appear to be considerable, although it cannot be estimated without more complete information. Albania is exceptional, as it was in fact a dependency of Jugoslavia until 1948 and received from its northern neighbor substantial economic assistance. Since that date, the task of supporting the Albanian economy has been shared by the Soviet Union and the people's democracies. Jugoslavia also is exceptional, as its economic relations with the U.S.S.R. and the Soviet bloc have for political reasons fluctuated so greatly. In the period up to 1948, the Soviet Union failed to gain any substantial hold on the Jugoslav economy, although about one-half of Jugoslav foreign trade was with the Soviet bloc. Trade relations were resumed, and Soviet credits extended, during the brief period of reconciliation between 1955 and 1957. More recently, however, economic relations between Jugoslavia and the Soviet bloc have again reached a low ebb.

In the aims and methods of their economic policies since the war, Albania, Bulgaria, and Rumania have followed closely the Soviet pattern. Industry, capital, and trade have been brought under state control. A high percentage of the national income is invested each year in industry, where production has increased rapidly. At the same time agriculture, which still employs the bulk of the population, and also consumer goods, have been neglected. The burden on private consumption resulting from this investment pattern is well known, and it may be questioned whether disposable income per capita has yet attained the prewar level. The new managerial elite, on the other hand, takes care of itself and enjoys many of the perquisites of power. There are also significant variations within the overall pattern. Bulgaria has hewn most closely to the Soviet line, and has even undertaken an economic reorganization á la Khrushchev despite the fact that the entire country is not much bigger than one of the larger Soviet *sovnarkhozy*. In Rumania the pace has been somewhat more relaxed. Albania, on the other hand, is a generation or two behind its neighbors in economic development and is in many respects unable to meet the requirements of the Soviet model.

The question of Russian economic influence on Tito's Jugoslavia is more subtle. Although the Jugoslav economy still resembles the Soviet pattern, it has evolved some unique solutions to the problems of a socialist economy. The similarity to the Soviet system lies in the degree of state ownership and control, the reliance on planning, the emphasis on producer goods at the expense of consumer goods and agriculture, and the creation of a small privileged group of managers in the environment of a generally low level of per-capita consumption. The differences, however, are also striking. The new economic system developed since 1950 has aimed at a significant decentralization of planning, participation of workers in factory management, reliance on a monetary rather than an administrative regulation of prices, and on market incentives instead of collectivization in agriculture. It is also significant that from the start Jugoslav economic policies have been independent of direct Soviet pressures, and also that some of Khrushchev's reforms in industrial and agricultural production resemble (no doubt unconsciously) those of Tito in significant respects.

CULTURE AND INSTITUTIONS

Russia and the Balkans were equally indebted to the West in literature, the arts, education, and other institutions. At the same time, in these as in other fields, Russia played in some measure the role of mediator between the West and the Balkans. Two important distinctions must nevertheless be noted. In literature, music, and the performing arts, Russia became a major contributor to world culture, widely admired and imitated. In these matters Russia was not only an equal but also a teacher of the West in a significant sense. At the same time, the common link of religion with the great majority of the Balkan peoples, and of language with the southern Slavs, gave Russia a particular advantage as compared with the West.

Ecclesiastical relations may in fact be traced back to the early years of the Turkish conquest, when the only substantial contacts were those between the Russian Orthodox Church and the monasteries and clergy in this region. These contacts were supplemented by the intermittent diplomatic relations between Moscow and Constantinople after 1495. By the eighteenth century there was a recognition on the part of leaders of opinion, especially among the southern Slavs, that Russia was one of the principal enemies of the Ottoman Empire and to this extent a potential ally against Turkish oppression. The cultural relations among the monasteries of Moldavia, Wallachia, Bulgaria, and Serbia, and between these and the Russian church, served to keep alive this idea of a Russian presence. Nevertheless this was a political rather than an ideological influence, and neither Father Paisii nor Dositej Obradović, for example, drew significantly on Russian inspiration for their ideas, although the latter was friendly to Russia and headed the Serbian mission to Russian army headquarters in Wallachia in 1806–1810.

During the years of struggle against Turkish rule, Russian Orthodoxy was no doubt an active force assisting in the process of national liberation and guiding it along conservative lines. In some measure it served as a branch of the Russian government, but it could also act independently, as in the crisis of 1875–1878, to provide both moral and material support for the southern Slavs. After the Balkan peoples gained their independence, it is difficult to discern any substantial influence emanating from the Russian church apart from the normal maintenance of ecclesiastical relations.

The doctrine that Slavic culture was distinct from that of Western Europe, and should be preserved from contamination, was actively preached in Russia in the middle years of the nineteenth century. It was nevertheless an idea that had relatively little appeal even to the Serbs and Bulgarians, in competition with Western ideas and institutions, and to the Rumanians, Greeks, and Albanians it was meaningless. Panslavism, as the political aspect of Slavophilism, no doubt had its greatest influence in Croatia. In its formulation by Juraj Križanić, as publicized in the mid-nineteenth century, and in its espousal by such leaders as Ljudevit Gaj and Bishop Strossmayer, it represented the brightest hope for liberation from Habsburg rule. Their plans envisaged the union of the Catholic and Orthodox churches, however, and this idea never attracted Russian support. Panslavism also had a brief and dramatic period of influence among the Slavic peoples under Turkish rule in the 1870's and 1880's. Characteristic of the strengths and weaknesses of this movement was the activity of General Cherniaev in Serbia in 1876–1878. Apart from its temporary political significance, however, Panslavism had no more to offer than Slavophilism and remained an essentially sterile doctrine. It was nevertheless a source of considerable apprehension on the part of the Greeks, and served to exacerbate relations between them and the Slavic peoples to the north.

Although this particular effort to export Slavic traditions proved to be ineffectual and even self-defeating, the true greatness of Russian culture as expressed in literature had widespread influence in the Balkans. The Russian literary classics were translated into the Balkan languages, widely read by the educated public, and studied by writers. Russian plays and operas were frequently performed, and Russian music was also popular. Of particular relevance was the preoccupation of Russian writers with the social and moral questions peculiar to an era of rapid change. The problems were confronted in the Balkans about a generation later than in Russia, and the works of Turgenev and Dostoevsky, Chekhov and Gorky, undoubtedly held a special significance apart from their literary merit. Russian literature was perhaps most widely appreciated in Bulgaria, where similarities of language as well as a sense of cultural kinship were strongest. Among the leading writers, Petko R. Slaveikov, Ivan Vazov, Pencho Slaveikov, Aleko Konstantinov, and Elin Pelin in particular turned to Russia for inspiration. At the same time, much of Western literature also came to Bulgaria first in the form of Russian translations. In Serbia, one may cite the influence of Chernyshevsky and Turgenev on Laza Lazarević, of Gogol on Jakov Ignjatović, and of Lermontov on Jovan Jovanović Zmaj. In Croatia, there were translations of Tolstoy and Shevchenko by Avgust Harambašić, and influences of Turgenev in the work of Ljubomir Babić.

In the non-Slavic countries Russian literature played a lesser role, but it was by no means unimportant. Rumanian writers from Bessarabia were particularly subject to Russian influence. Constantin Stamati gained prominence as a translator and imitator of Derzhavin, Zhukovsky, Pushkin, and Lermontov. Bogdan Hasdeu wrote his early works in

Russian, and Costache Negruzzi decided to undertake a literary career after meeting Pushkin during the latter's Bessarabian exile. After the middle of the nineteenth century Western literary models predominated in Rumania, but the influence of the Russian classics was never absent. In Greece one may cite the influence of Tolstoy on Kostis Palamas, of Turgenev on Gregorios Xenopoulos, and of Tolstoy and Dostoevsky on Constantine Theotokis.

Other Russian cultural influences must be sought primarily among the Slavic peoples, and date from the early eighteenth century. In 1724, Peter the Great sent to Serbia what would now be called a technical-assistance mission, headed by Maksim Suvorov, which established the first schools and initiated the study of grammar and language. In the nineteenth century, Vuk Karadžić maintained close relations with Russian scholars, although his own contributions were primarily of Western inspiration. In Bulgaria, the initiative of Vasil Evstatiev Aprilov in founding the first secondary school in 1835 was due to the influence of the Ukrainian scholar Venelin. The leading creators of the modern Bulgarian language, Naiden Gerov and Ivan Andreev Bogorov, relied extensively on Russian scholarship.

In noting briefly these influences on culture and institutions, which were significant primarily for Bulgaria and Serbia, it should not be forgotten that in these as in other matters the Balkan people looked primarily to the West. French and German were the foreign languages most widely studied throughout the Balkans, and education, scholarship, law, the press, literature and the arts, and political and social institutions were based primarily on European rather than Russian models. This was a reflection not of any lack of respect for Russian institutions, but rather of the recognition that it was in most respects Europe that set the standards in these matters for the whole world.

Russian influence on Balkan culture and institutions declined significantly after 1917. This was due in part to political reasons, as contacts between Russia and the Balkans were in considerable measure cut off between the wars, but it was due also to the fact that Soviet institutions were still in the process of formation and not yet ready for export. Since the Second World War, under very different circumstances, Russian culture and institutions have of course exerted a very pervasive influence in Albania, Bulgaria, and Rumania. Political and social institutions, as well as education, scholarship, literature, and the arts, have been extensively remodeled along Russian lines. A lively program of cultural interchange is maintained, with many Soviet specialists visiting these countries, and many students going to Soviet universities. Jugoslavia followed the same course until 1948, and probably went further than its neighbors in sending students to Russia and modeling its institutions after those in the U.S.S.R. Many of these institutions have remained unchanged since 1948, but the West has now replaced Russia as the principal source of inspiration. Jugoslav students and technicians now study in Central and Western Europe and in the United States, and Western books, plays, and motion pictures are preferred. Even in the field of ideology, Soviet influence is no longer prominent.

In Greece, Soviet culture and institutions have relatively few admirers. Indeed, the constitution adopted in 1952 goes out of its way to provide that all teaching in elementary and intermediate schools should be "on the basis of the ideological principles of Greek Christian civilization" (Art. 16, para. 2). Greece's cultural contacts have always been more cosmopolitan than those of its Balkan neighbors, and for most Greeks the bitter experiences in the wars of the twentieth century outweigh the memories of Russian assistance in the struggle for liberation. The range and intensity of Greek feelings on this subject are sensitively reflected in the novels of Nikos Kazantzakis, who spent two years in Russia as head of the mission in charge of evacuating Greek refugees after the First World War.

EXTENT AND NATURE OF RUSSIAN INFLUENCE

The relationship of Russia to the Balkans reflects, in microcosm, patterns that are characteristic of many other parts of the world. Every society tends to modernize in its own way, adopting the ideas and institutions essential to all social change but investing them with a spirit based on its own traditions and values. Political power aside, societies will tend to borrow from those who seem best able to meet their needs. But political power is in fact never absent, and it frequently tends to distort the natural flow of nonpolitical influences. It is therefore relevant to suggest answers to two questions raised by the role of Russia in the modernization of the Balkans. How has the relative influence in this region of Russia and of the countries of Western and Central Europe been affected by social change? What has been the relative role in Russian influence of forcible imposition and voluntary borrowing?

Throughout the period since Turkish rule, the extent and nature of Russian influence has depended on the balance of power, which in turn has reflected in a marked fashion the differing effects of social change within each of the powers. From the latter part of the eighteenth century, when Russia emerged as a major factor in Balkan affairs, until the Crimean War, Russia was the bulwark of the dynastic conservatism which still predominated in most of Europe and did not consider itself to be behind the times. Europe was not the static world which Nicholas I imagined it to be, however, and the ineluctable pressures of social change soon brought an end to the dynastic system which appeared to have survived so successfully the crisis of 1848–1850. Once again in 1876–1878 Russian troops were able to dominate the Balkans, but the political consequences of this war soon revealed the changes wrought by the unification of Germany and the beginnings of Austrian disintegration. Russia was now faced by a new Europe, with which it could compete neither in power nor in ideas. From 1856 to 1917 the official Russia of tsarist policy exerted less influence in the Balkans than the unofficial Russia of radical thought and of a literature concerned with social change.

Between the wars both Europe and Russia were in the throes of social readjustment, and the Balkan countries experimented with many half-solutions which met with little success. Neither the French system of the 1920's nor the German system of the 1930's offered a stable program for modernization, although if Europe had been led by competent statesmen a constructive program embracing Western, Central, and Southeastern Europe might well have been evolved. In Russia the unrest was even greater, marked by social experiments purchased at the cost of millions of lives and a political system held together by purges and labor camps. Not until after the Second World War was the Soviet system generally accepted as a viable alternative to the European approach to modernization, and by then it had to compete with a Europe that was again dynamic.

The social change characteristic of the modern world has had a twofold effect on Russian influence: it has affected Russia's relative power position, as well as her ability to make a substantive contribution to the modernization of Southeastern Europe. In terms of power, the effects of social change led to the relative decline of Russia as compared with Western and Central Europe between 1856 and 1944. Despite the strength of Russia's position in this region in terms of size, proximity, and historic relationships, she was unable to retain her influence because of the more rapid modernization of the rival powers. With the reconstruction of Russia after the Second World War, after a period of rapid if interrupted social change dating from the 1880's, Russia's relative strength again approximates that of the first half of the nineteenth century.

As a contributor to social change in Southeastern Europe, the delayed modernization of Russia deprived her of much of the influence which she could otherwise have exerted. Only in a few fields, such as literature and the performing arts, did Russian influence transcend the role of reinterpreting European achievements to an audience limited primarily to the southern Slavs. In such vital matters as political institutions, programs of economic growth, and technology, Russia made only a limited contribution before 1944. Since the Second World War, the significance of this contribution has grown as the gap between Russia and the West is closing.

A somewhat different question is that of the relative role of forcible imposition and voluntary borrowing in Russian influence in this region, although it is a reflection of the same forces of social change. Certainly there are significant aspects of Russian influence which are difficult to imagine in the absence of Russian power. The entire role of Russia as the liberator of Balkan peoples from Turkish rule was essentially a military proposition, implementing political programs which originated elsewhere. The generally conservative trend of Balkan governments in the first half of the nineteenth century, and most characteristically the support given to the boiars in Moldavia and Wallachia, was also a consequence of military power. Similarly, the degree of Russian influence in Bulgaria and Rumania since 1944, and in Albania since 1948, can be explained only by the unchallenged presence of Soviet power.

At the same time it is clear that some influences have also depended significantly on the unimposed example of Russia. Indeed, some of the most salient features of Russian influence in the latter half of the nineteenth century came from the unofficial Russia, not the Russia that controlled the armies. Although the national traditions and values of Russia differ significantly from those of the Balkan peoples, she has been confronted with many of the same problems of social change. In addition, the similarity of language and culture go a long way to explain Russia's special influence in Serbia and Bulgaria.

At the least, the Russian radicals served as intermediaries of European progressive thought, restating its conclusions in a manner that was frequently more relevant to Balkan problems. Many southern Slavs, in particular, first learned of Western thought from Russian writers, and then went on to study the originals. This may account for the apparent paradox that such leaders as Nikola Pašić and Stefan Stambolov, who were so imbued with Russian radicalism in their youth, went on to become bulwarks of stable government. It was not so much that they became conservative with age, as that the Russian radicals introduced them to the Western thought and institutions which guided them throughout their careers.

It was also no doubt natural, in view of the profound frustrations encountered by the Balkan peoples in their efforts to modernize, that Marxism—and more particularly its Leninist version—should have had a following among them. The idea that state socialism could provide a solution to their problems had particular influence after the solutions sponsored by Western Europe ended in a great depression and that of Central Europe in the Second World War. That the strength of communism reflected domestic discontents rather than Soviet pressure is illustrated by the fact that it achieved its greatest successes in war-ravaged Jugoslavia and Greece at a time when Russian power was temporarily in eclipse. Indeed, it is interesting to speculate whether communism would have as much support today in either Rumania or Bulgaria, were it not for the Soviet presence, as in Greece. Throughout the interwar period, Jugoslavia and Greece were the two countries in this region which were burdened with the most difficult social problems and at the same time with the most ineffectual and unimaginative governments. Jugoslavia, like other Communist states, also illustrates the fact that even so aggressive an ideology as communism cannot obliterate traditional attitudes and ways of doing things, and that there is such a thing as national communism which can evolve independently of and even in resistance to Soviet influence.

In the category of influences independent of politics one must also include literature and the arts, education, science, technology, and economic relations. Influences in this category may follow the flag, as they have in Rumania and Bulgaria since 1944, but they also move in the free market of ideas and interests. Where contributions of universal significance have originated in Russia, they have found as ready a reception in the Balkans as elsewhere. If such contributions were limited in the nineteenth century primarily to ideas, literature, and the arts, by the mid-twentieth they have increasingly included much more varied fields of knowledge and branches of technology.

The prospects for long-term Russian influence in the Balkans, apart from that which can be imposed by force, lie in the ability of the Soviet system to evolve original solutions to the myriad of problems confronted by societies undergoing modernization.

BIBLIOGRAPHY

There are no general accounts of Russian influence in the Balkans, treating all aspects of the subject for the entire period since Turkish rule. Even for briefer periods, or individual countries, few general works exist. Of these, the most important is B. H. Sumner, ***Russia and the Balkans, 1870–1880*** (Oxford, 1937), a pioneering achievement which sets a high standard for all work in this field. A valuable brief interpretation is Ivo J. Lederer, "Russia and the Balkans," in Ivo J. Lederer, ed., ***Russian Foreign Policy: Essays in Historical Perspective*** (New Haven, 1962), 417–451. The recent revival of Soviet interest in Balkan history is reflected in the numerous articles which have appeared in recent years in the ***Uchenye zapiski*** [***Studies***] and the ***Kratkii soobshcheniia*** [***Brief Communications***] of the Institute of Slavistics of the Academy of Sciences of the USSR, and in handbooks and symposia such as F. N. Petrov, ed., ***Balkanskie Strany*** [***The Balkan Countries***], (Moscow, 1946); V. Picheta, ed., ***Slavianskii sbornik*** [***Slavic Symposium***], (Moscow, 1947); S. M. Stetskevich, ed., ***Ocherki istorii iuzhnykh i zapadnykh*** *slavian [Essays on the History of the Southern and Western Slavs]*, (Leningrad, 1957); S. A. Nikitin and L. B. Valev, eds., *Obshchestvenno-politicheskie i kulturnye sviazi narodov SSSR i Iugoslavii [Social, Political and Cultural Bonds Between the Peoples of the USSR and Jugoslavia]*, (Moscow, 1957); and L. B. Valev, V. N. Kondratyeva, and S. A. Nikitin, eds., *Iz istorii russko-bolgarskikh otnoshenii [From the History of Russian-Bulgarian Relations]*, (Moscow, 1958).

Among the relatively few general treatments of individual countries and regions, Charles Jelavich, *Tsarist Russia and Balkan Nationalism: Russian Influence in the Internal Affairs of Bulgaria and Serbia, 1879–1886* (Berkeley and Los Angeles, 1958), covers a broad range of political, ideological, and economic questions. A brief, but reasonably comprehensive, Soviet interpretation of Russian-Jugoslav relations is provided by V. G. Karasaev, *Istoricheskie sviazi narodov Sovetskogo soiuza i Iugoslavii [Historical Bonds of the Peoples of the Soviet Union and Jugoslavia]*, (Moscow, 1956). Guides to bibliography and historiography should be sought in the standard reference works, but two items of particular relevance should be noted: A. Pogodin, *Ruskasrpska bibliografia 1800–1925 [Russian-Serbian Bibliography, 1800–1925]*, (Belgrade, 1932–1936), 2 vols.; and Stephen A. Fischer-Galati, "Slavic-Romanian Relations in Modern Romanian Historiography," Mid-European Studies Center, Mimeographed Series, No. 8 (New York, 1953).

The scarcity of general works is largely compensated for by the number of special studies available. Apart from the extensive literature dealing with the history of Southeastern Europe, the Eastern Question, Russian foreign policy, and related subjects, much has been written on specific aspects of Russian political and ideological influence in the Balkans. Less has been done, however, in the realm of economic and cultural influences. Much of this work is by Balkan scholars, particularly those of Bulgaria, Serbia, and Croatia. This work has produced many contributions to scholarship, even though it has been strongly influenced by the prevailing nationalist (and, more recently, Communist) bias. Russian research in this field is concentrated primarily in the latter part of the nineteenth century, in the 1920's, and in the period since the Second World War. Although these productive phases have tended to coincide with active Russian interest in the Balkans, the Russian publications include much valuable scholarship.

Useful work has also been done by European and American students of this subject. On the whole this work benefits from a relative freedom from immediate political concerns, apart from a general tendency to favor Balkan resistance to Russian political controls, and has produced some penetrating analyses of the Russian-Balkan relationship. If one may venture to criticize this body of scholarship as a whole, it would be essentially from two points of view. First, there has been a strong tendency to dwell on political and ideological influences to the exclusion of social, economic, and cultural. This can no doubt be explained by the difficult problems of sources and method, but every effort should be made to go beyond the traditional two-dimensional approach. Second, there is a tendency in many of these studies to ignore the larger context of Balkan relations with Europe as a whole, and to treat Russian-Balkan affairs as though they existed in isolation.

What follows is a limited review of the work of particular significance for the subject of the preceding essay. The limitations in my knowledge of Balkan languages has prevented me from making use of works in Albanian, Greek, and Rumanian.

Political Influences

The story of Russian political and military policies in the Balkans is told in the general accounts and monographs dealing with Russian foreign affairs during the century and a half under consideration, too numerous to cite here. Attention should be called, however, to several recent contributions dealing with the latter half of the nineteenth century, the period that has attracted the most active interest on the part of historians: Charles and Barbara Jelavich, ***Russia in the East, 1876–1880*** (Leiden, 1959), a documentary study based on the papers of Giers, and their "The Danubian Principalities and Bulgaria under Russian Protectorship," ***Jahrbücher für Geschichte Osteuropas,*** IX (October, 1961), 349–366; Melvin C. Wren, "Pobedonostsev and Russian Influence in the Balkans, 1881–1888," ***Journal of Modern History,*** XIX (June, 1947), 130–141; and three studies by S. A. Nikitin, the leading Soviet student of Russian-Balkan relations: "Diplomaticheskie otnosheniia Rossii s iuzhnymi slavianami v 60–kh godakh XIX v." ["The Diplomatic Relations of Russia with the Southern Slavs in the 1860's"], ***Slavianskii sbornik [Slavic Symposium]***, (Moscow, 1947), 262–290; "Podlozhnye dokumenty o russkoi politike na Balkanakh v 70–e gg. XIX v." ["Spurious Documents Concerning Russian Policy in the Balkans in the 1870's"], ***Isvestiia Akademiia nauk SSSR. Seriia istorii i filosofii [Bulletin of the Academy of Sciences of USSR.*** Series of History and Philosophy] III (1946), 87–91; and his valuable ***Slavianskie komitety v Rossii 1856–1876 [The Slavic Committees in Russia, 1856–1876]***, (Moscow, 1960), based on extensive use of Russian archives. Of the various accounts of Soviet policy in Eastern Europe since the Second World War, Zbigniew K. Brzezinski, ***The Soviet Bloc: Unity and Conflict*** (Cambridge, Mass., 1960) is the most valuable.

Of the available studies of Russian political influence in Rumania, the most comprehensive is Nicolas Iorga, ***Histoire des relations russo-roumaines*** (Jassy, 1917), which takes the story to the end of the nineteenth century. Individual periods and problems are discussed in I. Cheban, "O vzaimootnosheniiakh Moldavii s Moskovskom gosudarstvom v XV–XVIII vekakh" ["On the Relations of Moldavia with the Muscovite State from the Fifteenth to the Eighteenth Centuries"], ***Voprosy istorii [Problems of History]***, No. 2 (Feb., 1945), 50–71; Jean C. Filitti, ***Les Principautés roumaines sous l'occupation russe (1828–1834)***, (Bucharest, 1904); Barbara Jelavich, ***Russia and the Rumanian National Cause 1858–1859*** (Bloomington, 1959); S. Graur, ***Les relations entre la Roumanie et l'U.R.S.S. depuis le traité de Versailles*** (Paris, 1936); V. Fedorov, "Russkaia voennaia missiia v Romynii vo vremia mirovoi voiny 1914–1918 godov" ["The Russian Military Mission in Rumania during the World War of 1914–1918"], ***Voprosy istorii [Problems of History]***, No. 8 (Aug., 1947), 94–99; and C. G. Rakovsky, ***Roumania and Bessarabia*** (London, 1925).

There is no general study of Russian-Bulgarian relations, although the *Istoriia na Bulgariia* [*History of Bulgaria*], (Sofia, 1954–1955), 2 vols., by the Bulgarian Academy of Sciences, devotes much attention to this subject from the Communist point of view. Dimitŭr Iotsov, *Rusiia i Bulgaria (vchera, dnes i utre), Diplomaticheski studii* [*Russia and Bulgaria (Yesterday, Today, and Tomorrow), Diplomatic Studies*], (Sofia, 1940) discusses selected problems in the diplomatic relations of the two countries. General accounts of briefer scope include James F. Clarke, "Russia and Bulgaria, 1878–1944," *Journal of Central European Affairs,* V (January, 1946), 394–398; E. Grimm, "K istorii russko-bolgarskikh otnoshenii" ["Concerning the History of Russian-Bulgarian Relations"], *Novyi vostok* [*The New East*], V (1924), 68–85; and I. N. Shabatin, "Iz istorii velikoi russko-bolgarskoi druzhby" ["From the History of the Great Russian-Bulgarian Friendship"], *Zhurnal moskovskoi Patriarkhii* [*Journal of the Moscow Patriarchate*], No. 12 (Dec., 1948), 45–56. A number of special studies deal with the events following the war of 1878; N. R. Ovsianyi, *Russkoe upravlenie v Bolgarii v 1877–78–79 gg.* [*The Russian Administration in Bulgaria in 1877–78–79*], (St. Petersburg, 1906); P. Pavlovich, ed., *Avantiury russkogo tsarizma v Bolgarii: Sbornik dokumentov* [*Adventures of Russian Tsarism in Bulgaria: Collection of Documents*], (Moscow, 1935); Khristo N. Gandev, "K izucheniiu deiatelnosti russkogo okupatsionnago upravleniia v Vostochnoi Rumelii 1878–1879 g.g." ["Toward the Study of the Activity of the Russian Occupation Administration in Eastern Rumelia in 1878–1879"], *Zapiski nauchno-izsledovatelskago obedineniia pri russkii svobodnyi universitet v Prage* [*Reports of the Scientific Research Association of the Russian Free University in Prague*], VI (1938), 43–86; S. Sidelnikov, "Avantiura russkogo tsarizma v Bolgariia, 1878–1896 gg." ["The Adventure of Russian Tsarism in Bulgaria, 1878–1896"], *Uchenyi zapiski Leningradskogo gosudarstvennago universiteta. Seriia istoricheskikh nauk* [*Studies of the Leningrad State University. Historical Science Series*], No. 36, issue 3 (1939), 145–80; J. J. Mikkola, "Einige Bemerkungen über die Tätigkeit General Casimir Ehrnrooths als Bulgarischer Staatsmann," *Sbornik v pamet na Profesor Petr Nikov* [*Symposium in Memory of Professor Peter Nikov*], (Sofia 1939), 301–307; C. E. Black, *The Establishment of Constitutional Government in Bulgaria* (Princeton, 1943); P. K. Fortunatov, *Voina 1877–1878 gg. i osvobozhdenie Bolgarii* [*The War of 1877–1878 and the Liberation of Bulgaria*], (Moscow, 1950); V. Konobeev, "Russko-bolgarskoe boevoe sodruzhestvo v voine 1875–1877 godov" ["Russian-Bulgarian Military Collaboration in the War of 1875–1877"], *Voprosy istorii* [*Problems of History*], No. 10 (Oct., 1951), 42–64; L. B. Valev, S. A. Nikitin, and P. N. Tretiakov, eds., *Osvobozhedenie Bolgarii ot turetskogo iga: Sbornik statei* [*The Liberation of Bulgaria from the Turkish Yoke: Collection of Articles*], (Moscow, 1953); and S. A. Nikitin and others, eds., *Osvobozhdenie Bolgarii ot turetskogo iga* [*The Liberation of Bulgaria from the Turkish Yoke*], Vol. I (Moscow, 1961), of a projected three-volume series. Valuable treatments of other topics include Charles Jelavich, "Russo-Bulgarian Relations, 1892–1896: With Particular Reference to the Problem of the Bulgarian Succession," *Journal of Modern History,* XXIV (Dec., 1952), 341–351; and James F. Clarke, "The Russian Bible Society and the Bulgarians," *Harvard Slavic Studies,* III (1957), 67–104.

The most comprehensive study of Russian-Serbian relations deals with the first half of the nineteenth century: Nil Popov, *Rossiia i Serbiia: istoricheskii ocherk russkago pokrovitelstva Servii s 1806 po 1856 god* [*Russia and Serbia: A Historical Account of the Russian Protectorship of Serbia from 1806 to 1856*], (2 vols.; Moscow, 1869). There are also a number of studies limited to special periods: S. K. Bogoiavlensky, "Iz russkoserbskikh otnoshenii pri Petre Pervom" ["From Russian-Serbian Relations in the Time of Peter I"], *Voprosy istorii* [*Problems of History*], No. 8–9 (Aug.–Sept., 1946), 19–24; S. K. Bogoiavlenskii, "Sviazi mezhdu russkimi i serbami v XVII–XVIII vv." ["Relations between Russians and Serbs in the Seventeenth and Eighteenth Centuries"], *Slavianskii sbornik* [*Slavic Symposium*], (Moscow, 1947), 241–261; Vaso Trivanovitch, "Serbia, Russia, and Austria during the Rule of Milan Obrenovich, 1868–78," *Journal of Modern History*, III (Sept., 1931), 414–440; Wayne S. Vucinich, *Serbia Between East and West: The Events of 1903–1908* (Stanford, 1954); Illija Jovanović, Stevan Rajković, and Beljko Ribar, *Jugoslovenški dobrovoljački korpus u Rosiji: prilog istoriji dobrovoljačkog pokreta 1914–1918* [*The Jugoslav Volunteer Corps in Russia: Contribution to the History of the Volunteer Movement 1914–1918*], (Belgrade, 1954). On the controversial question of Soviet-Jugoslav relations since 1945, several useful monographs and collections of documents are available: Royal Institute of International Affairs, *The Soviet-Yugoslav Dispute: Text of the Published Correspondence* (New York, 1949); Milovan Djilas, "Yugoslav-Soviet Relations," *International Affairs*, XXVII (1951), 167–175; Adam B. Ulam, *Titoism and the Cominform* (Cambridge, Mass., 1952); Robert B. Farrell, *Jugoslavia and the Soviet Union, 1948–1956* (Hamden, Conn., 1956); and Vaclav L. Benes, Robert F. Byrnes, and Nicolas Spulber, eds., *The Second Soviet-Yugoslav Dispute: Full Text of Main Documents, April–June, 1958, With An Introductory Analysis* (Bloomington, 1959).

Russian political influence in Greece does not appear to have received much separate attention, although it is extensively treated in general works on diplomatic history and the Eastern Question. O. Shparo, "Rol Rossii v borbe Gretsii za nezavisimost" ["The Role of Russia in the Struggle of Greece for Independence"], *Voprosy istorii* [*Problems of History*], No. 8 (Aug., 1949), 52–73; and A. M. Stanislavskaia, "Rossiia i Gretsiia v kontse XVIII—nachale XIX v Iz istorii politiki Rossii na Ionicheskikh Ostrovakh (1798–1807)" ["Russia and Greece at the End of the Eighteenth and the Beginning of the Nineteenth Centuries. From the History of Russian Policy in the Ionian Islands (1798–1807)"], *Istoriia SSSR* [*History of the USSR*], (Jan.–Feb., 1960), 59–76, may be cited as examples of recent Soviet treatments of this problem. See also Barbara Jelavich, "Russia, Bavaria and the Greek Revolution of 1862/1863," *Balkan Studies*, II (July, 1961), 125–150. E. Adamov, *Evropeiskie derzhavy i Gretsiia v epokhu mirovoi voiny* [*The European States and Greece in the Period of the World War*], (Moscow, 1922), is based on the archives of the Russian foreign office. On Albania, in this as in other matters, Stavro Skendi, ed., *Albania* (New York, 1946) is the best guide.

Ideological Influences

In the Balkans, as in Russia, the question as to what program of modernization should be adopted has been the subject of an extensive literature throughout the period under consideration. Of particular interest were such questions as how the peoples of the Balkans should attempt to match the achievements of

Central and Western Europe, and what was the relevance of the Russian experience in this regard. In discussing these issues it is not easy to draw a clear line between ideological and political influences, but the attempt has been made in this essay to restrict the latter to the establishment and control of political power. This leaves to the realm of ideology not only abstract speculation but also the programs of those in office and in opposition.

The three principal aspects of Russian ideological influence in the Balkans—conservative, liberal, and Marxist-Leninist—have received unequal treatment. The conservative influences which predominated in the earlier part of the nineteenth century have been the subject of relatively little separate attention as they have concerned the Balkans, despite the extensive literature on the more general aspects of the subject. The Russian setting in this influence has been treated most recently in the chapter on foreign policy in Nicholas Riasanovsky, *Nicholas I and Official Nationality in Russia, 1825–1855* (Berkeley and Los Angeles, 1959), 235–265; and for the later period in Michael B. Petrovich, *The Emergence of Russian Panslavism, 1856–1870* (New York, 1956). Two recent articles discuss the significance of Križanić, about whom a large literature exists: Michael B. Petrovich, "Juraj Križanić; A Precursor of Pan-Slavism," *American Slavic and East Europe Review*, VI (Dec., 1947), 75–92; and V. I. Picheta, "Iurii Krizhanich i ego otnoshenie k Russkomu gosudarstvu (1618–1683 gg.)" ["Juraj Križanić and His Relationship with the Russian State, 1618–1683], *Slavianskii sbornik* [*Slavic Symposium*], (Moscow, 1947), 202–240. There are also studies of the popular Bulgarian tradition of respect for Russia: I. Trifonov, "Istoricheskо obiasnenie na verata v deda Ivan (Rusiia) u Bŭlgariskii narod" ["A Historical Explanation of the Belief in Grandfather Ivan (Russia) on the Part of the Bulgarian People"], *Biblioteka na Slavianska beseda* [*Library of the Slavic Society*], III (1908), 26–56; and of the general problem of the influence of Russian absolutism on the southern Slavs: N. S. Derzhavin, "Russkii absoliutizm i iuzhnoe slavianstvo" ["Russian Absolutism and Southern Slavdom"], *Izvestiia Leningradskogo gosudarstvennogo universiteta* [*Bulletin of the Leningrad State University*], I (1928), 43–82. Conservative as well as liberal influences are discussed in two useful general interpretations of Bulgarian and Serbian thought in the nineteenth century: B. Mintses, "Dŭrzhavnopravnite i sotsialno-stopanskite idei v bŭlgarskata doosvoboditelna literature" ["Constitutional, Social, and Economic Ideas in Bulgarian Pre-Liberation Literature"], *Sbornik na narodni umotvoreniia, nauka, i knizhnina* [*Journal of Folklore, Education, and Literature*], XVI–XVII (1900), 3–58; and Traian Stoianovich, "The Pattern of Serbian Intellectual Evolution, 1830–1880," *Comparative Studies in Society and History*, I (March, 1959), 242–272; and a recent anthology of Croatian writings about Russia spans a considerable range of opinion: Josip Badalić, ed., *Hrvatska svjedočanstva o Rusiji* [*Croatian Accounts of Russia*], (Zagreb, 1945).

The earliest liberal influences from Russia may be traced to the Decembrists, whose plans for the Balkans are discussed in B. E. Syroechkovsky, "Balkanskaia problema v politicheskikh planakh Dekabristov" ["The Balkan Problem in the Political Plans of the Decembrists"], in N. M. Druzhinin and B. E. Syroechkovsky, eds., *Ocherki iz istorii dvizheniia Dekabristov: sbornik statei* [*Essays in the History of the Decembrist Movement: Collection of Articles*], (Moscow, 1954), 186–275. The direct impact of the Decembrists in Rumania is discussed in S. Vianu, "Quelques aspects de l'influence exercée par la pensée progressiste russe sur la société roumaine de la fin du XVIIIe siècle," *Nouvelles études d'histoire* (Bucharest, 1955), 285–297; S. Stirbu, "Les rapports de collaboration entre Tudor Vladimirescu et les movements de libération des pays de l'Est européen," *Nouvelles études d'histoire* (Bucharest, 1955), 313–339; and Alfred Roth, *Theodor Vladimirescu und die Orientpolitik: Der Beginn nationalrumänischer Entwicklung und die Haltung der Anrainergrossmächte Russland, Österreich und Türkei 1821–22* (Leipzig, 1943). Russian influences in Bulgaria in this period are treated in James F. Clarke, "Serbia and the Bulgarian Revival (1762–1872)," *American Slavic and East European Review*, IV (Dec., 1945), 141–162; and S. S. Bernshtein, "Stranitsa iz istorii bolgarskoi immigratsii v Rossiiu vo vremia russko-turetskoi voiny 1828–1829 gg." ["A Page from the History of the Bulgarian Immigration in Russia at the Time of the Russian-Turkish War of 1828–1829"], *Uchenye zapiski instituta slavianovedeniia Akademiia nauk SSSR* [*Studies of the Institute of Slavistics of the Academy of Sciences of the USSR*], I (1949), 327–341.

The influences on the southern Slavs of Russian populism and radicalism has been the subject of much study. The principal problem of interpretation is whether one is to regard this influence as an aspect of Western liberalism, joining with more powerful direct influences from the West to make up the characteristic Southern Slav liberalism of the latter part of the nineteenth century, or as a more distinctive and exclusive Russian influence foreshadowing the advent of Marxism-Leninism. The present essay shares the former view, but most of the work in this field has been done by Russian or Balkan scholars who favor the latter interpretation. The evolution of this latter view through the years is reflected in V. Bogucharsky [Iakovlev], "Revoliutsionnoe dvizhenie sredi balkanskikh slavian, russko-turetskaia voina i otnoshenie k etim sobytiiam russkikh sotsialistov" ["The Revolutionary Movement among the Balkan Slavs, the Russian-Turkish War, and the Attitude to These Events of the Russian Socialists"], Chap. IX in his *Aktivnoe narodnichestvo semidesiatykh godov* [*Active Populism in the 1870's*], (Moscow, 1912), 262–294; K. A. Pushkarevich, "Balkanskie slaviane i russkie 'osvoboditeli.' (Slavianskie komitety i sobytiia na Balkanakh pered russko-turetskoi voinoi 1877–1878 gg.)" ["The Balkan Slavs and the Russian 'Liberators,' (The Slavic Committees and the Events in the Balkans before the Russian-Turkish War of 1877–1878)"], *Trudy instituta slavianovedeniia Akademiia nauk SSSR* [*Transactions of the Institute of Slavistics of the Academy of Sciences of the USSR*], II (1934), 189–229; L. Erikhonov, *Russkie revoliutsionnye demokraty i obshchestvennaia mysl iuzhnykh slavian v 60–70kh godakh XIX veka* [*The Russian Revolutionary Democrats and the Social Thought of the Southern Slavs in the 1860's and 1870's*], (Moscow, 1950); and S. A. Nikitin, "Iuzhnoslavianskie sviazy russkoi narodnicheskoi pechati 60–kh godov XIX veka" ["South Slav Relations of the Russian Populist Press in the 1860's"], *Uchenye zapiski instituta slavianovedeniia Akademiia nauk SSSR* [*Studies of the Institute of Slavistics of the Academy of Sciences of the USSR*], VI (1952), 89–122.

As regards Bulgaria, the general subject of Russian liberal influences is discussed in C. E. Black, *The Establishment of Constitutional Government in*

Bulgaria (Princeton, 1943). A number of other studies complement and revise this treatment: D. Sheludko, "Liuben Karavelov i Ukraina" ["Liuben Karavelov and the Ukraine"], *Sbornik v chest na Profesor Iv. D. Shishmanov [Symposium in Honor of Professor Ivan D. Shishmanov]*, (Sofia, 1920), 158–170; G. Bakalov, "Russkaia revoliutsionnaia emigratsiia sredi bolgar" ["The Russian Emigré Revolutionaries in Bulgaria"], *Katorga i ssylka [Penal Servitude and Exile]*, LXIII (1930), 114–137, LXIV (1930), 105–120; G. Bakalov, "Chernyshevskii na Balkanakh" ["Chernyshevsky in the Balkans"], *Katorga i ssylka [Penal Servitude and Exile]*, CXIII (1934), 22–32; L. B. Valev, "Sotsialno-politicheskie vozzrennia Khristo Boteva" ["The Social and Political Views of Khristo Botev"], *Uchenye zapiski instituta slavianovedeniia Akademiia nauk SSSR [Studies of the Institute of Slavistics of the Academy of Sciences of the USSR]*, II (1950), 95–105; and I. V. Kozmenko, "Peterburgskii proekt Tyrnovskoi konstitutsii 1879 goda" ["The St. Petersburg Draft of the Tirnovo Constitution of 1879"], *Istoricheskii arkhiv [Historical Archive]*, IV (1949), 184–324. Russian populist influence in later years is discussed in Vivian Pinto, "The Civic and Aesthetic Ideals of Bulgarian Narodnik Writers," *Slavonic and East European Review*, XXXII (June, 1954), 344–366, which draws on the same author's doctoral dissertation on "The Narodnik Movement of Bulgarian Literature and the Influence on that Movement of Russian Thought" (University of London, 1952).

The best brief account for Serbia is the recent article by Professor Traian Stoianovich cited above. Those wishing to probe the subject further should turn to the extensive literature on Svetozar Marković and Serbian socialism. Four recent articles of particular relevance may be cited: Jean Mousset, "Le socialisme serbe a la croisée des chemins: Bakuninisme ou Marxisme?" *Revue des études slaves*, XXIII (1947), 102–119; E. N. Kusheva, "Iz russko-serbskikh revoliutsionnykh sviazei 1870–kh godov" ["Russian-Serbian Revolutionary Relations in the 1980's"], *Uchenye zapiski instituta slavianovedeniia Akademiia nauk SSSR [Studies of the Institute of Slavistics of the Academy of Sciences of the USSR]*, I (1949), 343–358; I. D. Ivanov, "Dokumenty o russko-serbskikh revoliutsionnykh sviaziakh 80-kh godov XIX v." ["Documents on Russian-Serbian Revolutionary Relations in the 1880's"], *Kratkie soobshcheniia instituta slavianovedeniia Akademiia nauk SSSR [Brief Communications of the Institute of Slavistics of the Academy of Sciences of the USSR]*, XIX (1956), 64–77; V. G. Karasev, "D. I. Pisarev i Svetozar Marković" ["D. I. Pisarev and Svetozar Marković"], *Kratkie soobshcheniia instituta slavianovedeniia Akademiia Nauk SSSR [Brief Communications of the Institute of Slavistics of the Academy of Sciences of the USSR]*, IX (1952), 24–33.

Marxist-Leninist influences have been the subject of much writing in recent years, principally by Soviet and Balkan scholars. Rather than citing examples of this literature, it seems best to refer to appropriate guides. The literature on Bulgaria is discussed in meticulous detail in Joseph Rothschild, *The Communist Party of Bulgaria: Origins and Development, 1883–1936* (New York, 1959). The fullest guide to recent Jugoslav work in this field is Jorjo Tadić, ed., *Ten Years of Yugoslav Historiography, 1945–1955* (Belgrade, 1955). On Greece, Dimitrios G. Kousoulas, *The Greek Communist Party since 1918* (unpublished doctoral dissertation, Syracuse University, 1957) provides a valuable introduction. Useful bibliographies are also available in the handbooks prepared by the Mid-European Studies Center: Stavro Skendi, ed., ***Albania*** (New York, 1956), Stephen Fischer-Galati, ed., ***Romania*** (New York, 1957), L. A. D. Dellin, ed., ***Bulgaria*** (New York, 1957), and Robert F. Byrnes, ed., ***Yugoslavia*** (New York, 1957).

Economic Influence

Russian economic influence in the Balkans before the Second World War was slight, and the literature on the subject is correspondingly small. Indeed, there appears to be no special study of this subject. The most useful references to Russian activity are in several studies of more general aspects of Balkan economic life: Radoslave M. Dimtschoff, ***Das Eisenbahnwesen auf der Balkan-Halbinsel. Eine politisch-wirtschaftliche Studie*** (Bamberg, 1894); Mirko Lamer. "Die Wandlungen der ausländischen Kapitalanlagen auf dem Balkan," ***Weltwirtschaftliches Archiv,*** XLVIII (Nov., 1938), 470–524; John A. Levandis, ***The Greek Foreign Debt and the Great Powers, 1821–1898*** (New York, 1944); E. Zaleski, ***Les courants commerciaux de l'Europe danubienne au cours de la première moitié du XIXe siècle*** (Paris, 1952); and Nicolas Spulber, "The Role of the State in Economic Growth in Eastern Europe since 1860," in Hugh G. J. Aitken, ed., ***The State and Economic Growth*** (New York, 1959), 255–286.

Much has been written, on the other hand, about Russia economic influences since 1944. This literature can best be followed in three recent general studies of Eastern Europe: Nicolas Spulber. ***The Economics of Communist Eastern Europe*** (New York, 1957); Irwin T. Sanders, ed., ***Collectivization of Agriculture in Eastern Europe*** (Lexington, 1958); and Jan Wszelaki, ***Communist Economic Strategy: The Role of East-Central Europe*** (Washington, D.C., 1959): which cite the extensive Soviet and Balkan literature in this field. The question of the terms of Soviet-Balkan trade has been explored recently in two articles by Horst Mendershausen, "Terms of Trade between the Soviet Union and Smaller Communist Countries, 1955–1957," and "The Terms of Soviet-Satellite Trade: a Broadened Analysis," in ***Review of Economics and Statistics,*** XLI (May, 1959), 106–118, and XLII (May, 1960), 152–163, respectively; and by Jan Wszelaki, "Soviet Price Discrimination in Export to East-Central Europe," ***Assembly of Captive European Nations,*** Doc. 207 (VI) Econ. (June 7, 1960).

Cultural Influences

General treatments of Russian cultural influence in the Balkans in modern times are scarce, although if one may judge from the papers on Russian influence on the South Slav literatures summarized in ***IV Mezhdunarodnyi s'ezd slavistov [Fourth International Congress of Slavists]***, (Moscow, 1962), I, 79–469, special studies of specific authors and topics are now sufficiently numerous to permit the elaboration of a general interpretation. Suffice it here to cite a few titles that were found useful for this essay. For Rumania: Euphrosine Dvoičenko-Markoff, "L'influence de la littérature russe sur la littérature roumaine," ***Communications et Rapports. IIIème Congrès International des Slavistes*** (Belgrade, 1939), 92–96; Eufrosina Dvoichenko-Markoff, "Pušhin and the Rumanian Historical

Legend," *American Slavic and East European Review,* VII (April, 1948), 144–149; and Sergiu Farcasan, "Constantin Dobrogeanu-Gherea: A Prominent Representative of Rumanian Literary Criticism," *Rumanian Review,* IX (Fall, 1955), 57–73. Russian literary influences in Bulgaria are extensively discussed in Nicolai Dontcheff, *Influences étrangères dans la littérature bulgare* (Sofia, 1934), 9–79; and more generally in N. S. Derzhavin, *Plemenni i kulturni vruzki mezhdu Bulgarskiia i Ruskiia narod* [Ethnic and Cultural Ties between the Bulgarian and Russian Peoples], (Sofia, 1945); and in D. F. Markov, "Problema genezisa sotsialisticheskogo realizma v bolgarskoi literature" ["The Problem of the Genesis of Socialist Realism in Bulgarian Literature"], *Issledovaniia po slavianskomu literaturovedeniiu i stilistike [Studies in Slavic Literary Scholarship and Stylistics],* (Moscow, 1960), 338–375. In regard to Jugoslavia, two valuable articles by M. N. Speransky are: "K istorii vzaimnootnoshenii russkoi i iugoslavianskikh literatur" ["On the Interrelations Between the Russian and the South Slav Literatures"], *Izvestiia otdeleniia russkogo iazyka i slovesnosti [Proceedings of the Department of Russian Language and Letters],* XXVI (1921), 143–206; and "K voprosu o russkom vliianii v serbskoi leterature XVIII veka" ["On the Question of Russian Influences in Serbian Literature in the Eighteenth Century"], *Trudy instituta slavianovedeniia AN SSSR [Transactions of the Institute of Slavistics of the Academy of Sciences of the USSR],* II (1934), 24–33. One may also cite N. I. Kravtsov, "Gogol i bolgarskaia literatura" ["Gogol and Bulgarian Literature"], *Kratkie soobshcheniia institut slavianovedeniia Akademiia Nauk USSR [Brief Communications of the Institute of Slavistics of the Academy of Sciences of the USSR],* VIII (1952), 22–42; D. F. Markov, "Maiakovskii i bolgarskaia revoliutsionnaia poeziia" ["Maiakovsky and Bulgarian Revolutionary Poetry"], *Kratkie soobshchennia instituta slavianovedeniia Akademiia nauk SSSR [Brief Communications of the Institute of Slavistics of the Academy of Sciences of the USSR],* I (1951), 9–28; J. Badalić, "Der Einfluss Tolstojs auf die kroatische dramatische literatur," *Festschrift für Dmytro Čyževskij* (Berlin, 1954), 59–68; and E. D. Goy, "The attitude of the Serbs to Turgenev's works in the nineteenth century," *Slavonic and East European Review,* XXXVI (Dec., 1957), 123–49; as examples of Soviet and Western literary scholarship relating to individual authors. Russian influences in Greek literature are treated briefly in D. C. Hesseling, *Histoire de la littérature Grecque moderne* (Paris, 1924).

CHAPTER 11

The Origins of the Cold War: The View from Bulgaria

Chapters 11 and 12 provide insights into Soviet relations with the outside world that are based on my own personal experience. As a member of the U.S. section of the Allied Control Commission in Bulgaria in 1944–45, I had the opportunity to observe and play a small role in the U.S. conflict of interest with the Soviet Union that later came to be known as "the origins of the Cold War." This experience involved not only the rivalry between the two allies but also included the process by which the Bulgarian Communist Party—with the essential assistance of the Soviet troops of occupation—transferred authority into their own hands from the popular front government that had seized power at the end of the war.

In discussing the origins of the Cold War in Bulgaria, it is important to keep in mind the background of the high American hopes for a postwar settlement and the limited capabilities for the exertion of U.S. influence under the interim surrender and occupation arrangements that were concluded in the autumn of 1944. Inter-Allied relations in the course of 1944–45 evolved in terms of three main issues: American and British participation in the Allied Control Commission; the election crisis of August 1945; and the Ethridge mission.

My own experience with these events extended from the planning of postwar policy in the Department of State in 1943–44 through the first year (1944–45) of American participation in the implementation of the Bulgarian armistice.

HIGH HOPES AND LOW CAPABILITIES

American policy proposals relating to the negotiation of a postwar settlement evolved along essentially separate lines from those concerning

Reprinted with permission from ***Witnesses to the Origins of the Cold War***, ed. by Thomas T. Hammond (Seattle, WA: University of Washington Press, 1982), 60–97.

interim problems of surrender and occupation. Plans for the postwar reconstruction of Europe and for a new international organization were the responsibility of the State Department's Office of Special Political Affairs, as it was known in 1944 after several reorganizations. Interim policies in regard to surrender and occupation were developed by the State Department in consultation with the Joint Chiefs of Staff, with which it communicated in the last instance through Adm. William D. Leahy at the White House, in his capacity as chief of staff to the commander-in-chief of the Army and Navy, that is, President Roosevelt. These policies were coordinated with the two major U.S. allies through the European Advisory Commission (EAC) in London.[1] Although both interim and postwar policies were in the last analysis determined by the president, they were not treated as part of a single policy process. Questions of surrender and occupation were seen as essentially military matters to be determined on a short-term, pragmatic basis. Negotiation of a European peace settlement was seen as a postwar problem, and one that was subordinated in the president's thinking to achieving a consensus on the new international organization.

From where I sat, virtually at the bottom of the bureaucratic pyramid, after leaving my teaching duties at Princeton University in January 1943, the prevailing view among the department's postwar planning staff was that the political structure of Europe after the war would have a democratic character similar to that anticipated after the First World War. The states of Europe to the west of the Soviet Union would have independent and representative governments as these terms were generally understood in the United States, and would participate in the solution of common problems within the framework of the new international organization.

This view of postwar Europe reflected the goal of "freedom of speech and expression everywhere in the world" set forth by President Roosevelt in his speech on the Four Freedoms (January 1941) and in the pledge of the United Kingdom and the United States in the Atlantic Charter (August 1941) to "respect the right of all countries to choose the form of government under which they will live. . . ." The Soviet Union expressed agreement with the charter in the following month, on the understanding that "the practical application of these principles will necessarily adapt itself to the circumstances, needs, and historic peculiarities of particular countries. . . ."[2] The degree of agreement achieved by the Big Three in the wartime conferences at Moscow (October 19–30, 1943), Tehran (November 28-December 1, 1943), and Dumbarton Oaks (August 21–September 28, 1944), led to an American expectation that cooperation on postwar problems would continue in the same spirit.

The Department of State's research staff was concerned with studying the background of territorial and political problems that the policy makers were likely to face after the termination of hostilities, and with proposing alternative solutions for the consideration of the policy makers. The precedent for this work was the Inquiry organized by Col. Edward M. House on behalf of President Wilson in preparation for the Versailles peace conference, and consideration was given to the entire range of problems that might come up at the anticipated peace settlement. The only recommendations of the research staff that reached a policy level in 1944 were those formulated in October in a report of the department's policy committee on American interests and policies in Eastern Europe, with a separate statement regarding Bulgaria.[3]

The aims set forth in this report included the right of peoples to choose the political, economic, and social systems they preferred without outside interference; equality of opportunity and freedom to negotiate in commerce, trade, and transit; the right of access of all countries in matters of press and public information; freedom of activity for American philanthropic and educational organizations; and protection of American citizens and their legitimate economic rights. The recommendations for Bulgaria specifically included withdrawal from occupied Greek and Yugoslav territory, with the subsequent possibility of free port facilities on the Aegean; and American access to Bulgarian tobacco on the basis of free enterprise. This report was not a summary of U.S. policy, but simply a recommendation to the secretary of state based on the views current in 1944 within the department. It clearly assumed the predominance of Anglo-American rather than Soviet influence in Bulgaria.

The work of the research staff reflected an awareness of differences among the allies in outlook and national interests, but the predominant disposition was to anticipate the resolution of these differences by means of multilateral consultation. Thus in preparing recommendations on the creation of representative governments after the termination of hostilities for discussion at the Yalta Conference, it was proposed in January 1945 that an Emergency High Commission for Liberated Europe be established. This body would be an agency of the four governments (now including France) "acting together to assist in establishing popular governments and in facilitating the solution of emergency economic problems in the former occupied and satellite states of Europe." The proposal was accompanied by the text of a Declaration on Liberated Europe, couched in terms of the principles of the Atlantic Charter.

On the eve of the Yalta Conference (February 4–11, 1945), President Roosevelt and his immediate advisers reviewed the proposal and rejected the idea of an emergency high commission. Only the declaration was presented to the conference, and it was adopted with minor revisions. The proposed high commission was rejected in part because of dissatisfaction with the way in which the European Advisory Commission had worked, and in part because of the fear that it might prejudice acceptance of the proposed United Nations organization, which was the president's primary concern at Yalta. The president preferred to have questions regarding the liberated areas handled directly by the foreign ministers.[4]

It is clear that the president was also concerned that the proposed high commission might involve the United States in responsibilities in Eastern Europe that it did not wish to assume. There are numerous indications of the president's views. In September 1943, for example, Archbishop Francis Spellman reported that in a long private conversation on postwar prospects the president had expressed the view that the world would be divided into spheres of influence. Britain and the Soviet Union would take the responsibility for Europe and Africa, and the United States would concentrate on the Pacific.[5] In a note to Acting Secretary of State Edward R. Stettinius, Jr., in February 1944, the president stated more explicitly that "I do not want the United States to have the post-war burden of reconstituting France, Italy and the Balkans. This is not our natural task at a distance of 3,500 miles or more."[6] In this case he referred to Britain alone as the interested and responsible party. Pursuant to the president's views, the plans of the Operations Division of the U.S. Army in the summer of 1944 provided that the American political role in Europe should be limited to measures strictly necessary for the defeat of Germany. In the case of Austria, Hungary, Bulgaria, and Romania, no U.S. forces were expected to be used for occupational duty, nor would civil affairs or relief and rehabilitation responsibilities be undertaken.[7]

It was in the context of this restricted view of the U.S. role in southeastern Europe that the question of the Bulgarian surrender arose in the summer of 1944. Bulgaria had been at war with the United States and the United Kingdom, but not with the USSR, and armistice terms became a matter for negotiation between the two Western allies and between them and representatives of the indecisive Bulgarian governments headed by Dobri Bozhilov (September 14, 1943–June 1, 1944), and Ivan Bagrianov (June 1-September 2, 1944). Bulgaria had as a member of the Tripartite Pact occupied the territories of Macedonia and Thrace, to which it had long laid claim in neighboring Yugoslavia and Greece, while avoiding military action and remaining at peace with the USSR. Apart from the Allied bombing of Sofia and other cities in the winter of 1943–44, Bulgaria had suffered little from the war. Bagrianov had hoped to secede from the Tripartite Pact and adopt a policy of neutrality, while keeping the occupied territories. The allies pressed for a declaration of war on Germany and withdrawal from these territories. When the Soviet armies launched their offensive against Romania, the

Bulgarian government announced on August 26 its withdrawal from the alliance with Germany and the adoption of a policy of neutrality. This gesture was rejected as inadequate by both the Western allies and the USSR, however, and within a week Soviet troops had reached the Danube.

Bagrianov now resigned, and on September 2 a pro-Western cabinet headed by Konstantin Muraviev took office. It was composed of moderate Agrarians and Democrats who had opposed the alliance with Germany, but it did not include members of the more radical Fatherland Front coalition. These latter did not join because they expected to seize power themselves in a few days. Muraviev's government finally decided on September 5 to break relations with Germany. On the same day it also discussed the possibility of declaring war on Germany, but apparently decided to delay the decision at the request of the minister of war, Gen. Ivan Marinov. Marinov has since stated that he found the military situation in a state of disarray, and that it took him until September 7 to reorganize the general staff, and to prepare the Bulgarian forces to take action against the German troops that had not yet been disarmed and interned.[8]

Meanwhile, on September 5, the Soviet government took the initiative by declaring war on Bulgaria, without previous consultation with its allies and giving them only an hour's notice. It seems likely that the USSR took this action on very short notice, fearing that otherwise it would be left out of the armistice negotiations that would follow a Bulgarian declaration of war on Germany. The fact that General Marinov was later awarded an ambassadorship while his colleagues in the Muraviev government received prison sentences as war criminals, has led many observers to conclude that the general had played a key role in this Soviet maneuver by delaying a declaration of war until the Soviets were ready to move and by assisting the takeover by the Fatherland Front. Bulgaria finally declared war on Germany on the same day that Soviet troops began to occupy Bulgaria, September 8, and thus was briefly at war with both Germany and the USSR as well as with the United States and the United Kingdom. That evening the Soviet government agreed to a cease-fire, and the following day the Muraviev government was overthrown by the Fatherland Front.[9]

Armistice negotiations were now resumed with active Soviet participation, on the basis of the precedents established in Italy and Romania. In 1943 an Allied Control Commission (ACC) had been established in Italy under joint American and British command and with no formal participation by the USSR. An Allied Advisory Commission for Italy was also established, with Soviet participation, but it had no executive authority. These arrangements in Italy, which reflected the view that occupation policy was the exclusive prerogative of the governments exercising military control, served as the precedent for the armistice terms in Eastern Europe, and later for the unilateral U.S. control of Japan. In September 1944 the United States and the United Kingdom agreed to armistice terms with Romania in which the Soviet representative on the ACC was to exercise exclusive executive authority. It was explicitly understood that, by analogy with the Soviet status in Italy, the role of the American and British representatives in Romania would be limited to maintaining liaison between the ACC and their governments.[10]

In the Bulgarian case, particular attention was given to Article 18, which dealt with the respective roles of the three allies on the ACC. As negotiated by British Foreign Secretary Anthony Eden and Soviet Foreign Minister V. M. Molotov in Moscow on October 12, this article provided that for the whole period of the armistice the ACC would be under the chairmanship of the Soviet representative with the "participation" of the British and American representatives. The term "participation" was not defined, but it was understood to mean no more than liaison, as in Romania. The execution of the armistice terms would be under the general direction of the Soviet high command.[11]

In the days immediately following this agreement, Eden and Molotov had several oral and written exchanges in which the former sought to increase the role of the British and American representatives after the defeat of Germany. The only concession that Molotov would make, on October 15, was that in this second period the role of the Soviet high command would be "to some extent restricted in favor of British and American representatives."[12]

Eden finally accepted this Soviet position, feeling that Soviet military occupation of the country prevented the British and American representatives from insisting on a more influential role. Perhaps the best explanation of these events is that of U.S. Ambassador John G. Winant, reporting from London on October 12: "A casual evaluation of the conversations in regard to Bulgarian armistice terms, on the evidence I have seen, might suggest that our friend Eden was having his pants traded off. But when you stop to realize the advance of Russian troops into Yugoslavia, it is clear that the primary British purpose was to continue their relationship with Greece and to maintain a sufficient degree of control in Yugoslavia to protect British Mediterranean interests."[13]

It is significant that the armistice terms for Bulgaria were considered in Moscow only a few days after Churchill's famous percentage deal with Stalin of October 9, in which the USSR was assigned a 75 percent interest in Bulgaria and "the others" 25 percent. This agreement was revised on the following day by Eden and Molotov to give the USSR an 80 percent interest. To be sure, this agreement, like the armistice itself, was applicable only to the period up to the conclusion of peace, and did not signify a postwar division into spheres of influence. Yet the attitudes reflected by these arrangements were bound to cast a long shadow into the future. It is also significant that in the case of both Churchill's negotiations with Stalin and Eden's with Molotov, the United States was not represented and U.S. Ambassador W. Averell Harriman participated only as an observer at some of the meetings. President Roosevelt was opposed to bilateral British-Soviet talks, not wishing to be committed to any agreements that Churchill and Stalin might reach, and preferring to regard their talks as preliminary to agreements to be reached later by all three heads of state.[14] Whatever the president's motives, it seems most likely that Stalin and Molotov gained the impression that the United States was not particularly concerned with developments in southeastern Europe and was leaving these matters to its British and Soviet allies. The State Department, for its part, was not fully informed about the details of the British-Soviet agreements at the time and did not regard them as binding on the United States.

The negotiations on the Bulgarian armistice terms now reverted to London and were concluded in the EAC on October 18. In its final form, Article 18 provided that, during the period prior to the conclusion of hostilities against Germany, the Allied Control Commission would be under the general direction of the Allied (Soviet) high command, as it was called. This was generally understood to mean that the Soviet commander would have unrestricted authority, as in Romania. The arrangements for the second period, from the termination of hostilities to the conclusion of peace, were left vague. So far as the British and Soviet governments were concerned, the arrangement giving the Soviet commander continuing but somewhat modified authority during the second period had already been agreed to in Moscow on October 15. The U.S. government, however, did not accept this agreement as binding. In a formal letter to its two allies on October 22, it restated its position that the three governments should have an equal role on the ACC during the second period, and reserved its right to raise the issue again at a later date. The armistice was finally signed in Moscow on October 28, by Marshal F. I. Tolbukhin and Lt. Gen. J. A. H. Gammel of the British Mediterranean Command, the latter signing also on behalf of the United States. On the same day, Molotov rejected the American interpretation of Article 18, and reasserted the Soviet view that since only Soviet troops were on the territory of Bulgaria, the Soviet high command should preserve its leading role in the second period, although in a somewhat modified form.[15]

THE ALLIED CONTROL COMMISSION

This is how matters stood when the American officials arrived in Sofia. Maj. Gen. John A. Crane, who had served as military attaché in Istanbul and Sofia before the war, was chief of the United States military representation on the Allied Control Commission. Maynard B. Barnes, with the personal rank of minister, was head of the American mission as American representative in Bulgaria. He had served in Bulgaria in 1930–34 and was well acquainted with the local political scene.

Their assignments in Bulgaria in the 1930s had overlapped, and Barnes had urged the War Department to assign Crane to Bulgaria in 1944 so as to be assured of a congenial colleague. Under Soviet and British practice, the military representatives on the ACC had full authority and the political representatives served as their advisers. In the case of the United States, however, the president had issued an executive order in 1942 placing all American representatives in a foreign country under the political representation. As this applied to the ACC in Bulgaria, General Crane took the initiative only in matters relating strictly to the armistice terms, while Barnes spoke for the United States on political matters. This arrangement gave Barnes much more authority than his Soviet and British counterparts, and accounts for some of the initiatives that he was able to take.[16]

I left the United States with Barnes on November 4 and arrived in Sofia ahead of him on November 14, having hitched a ride from Italy on the plane of Brig. Gen. Egmont F. Koenig. Koenig was chief of the American delegation on the Allied Joint Military Mission for Bulgaria, and had the task of verifying the withdrawal of Bulgarian armed forces from Macedonia and Thrace. His mission was easily accomplished, and on November 25 he joined his signature to those of his Soviet and British colleagues to the protocol declaring that Bulgaria had complied with all prearmistice requirements. This particular inter-Allied task was of a purely technical character. It did not involve any contention for influence, and was carried out without controversy. In the meantime, Barnes arrived on November 19 and Crane joined him a few days later.

The terms of the armistice agreement gave full authority to thc Soviet Commander, Marshal F. I. Tolbukhin, represented locally by Col. Gen. S. S. Biriuzov and his deputy Maj. Gen. A. I. Cherepanov. Lacking clear instructions, as well as any knowledge of the British-Soviet negotiations in Moscow, it was difficult for Barnes and Crane to believe that they should not at least be informed of major decisions of the ACC and be given an opportunity to comment on them. Not only were there no provisions for such minimal participation apparent when they arrived, but their personal movement was restricted to the city limits of Sofia.

They could not go beyond these limits without a Soviet officer accompanying them—and it often took a day or more before such an officer was made available. Since the airport was outside these limits, and severe restrictions were placed on the movements of personnel, supplies, and even mail pouches from Italy, their resulting frustration where they represented the victorious powers in a defeated country can be readily imagined.

More significant than these relatively minor inconveniences was that important decisions were relayed to the Bulgarian government in the name of the ACC without the knowledge of the American and British members. By November the ACC had military representatives in all district administrative centers and in the main seaports, who worked in close support of the local Fatherland Front committees. They brought the Soviet garrisons to the assistance of local Communist efforts "to liquidate fascism," to use the then current euphemism, by suppressing all opposition to Communist influence and by organizing demonstrations. More often than not we learned of such activities only from the press or from members of the Bulgarian government. This was humiliating enough in dealing with officials of what was an occupied enemy country. It was all the more frustrating when such decisions of the ACC were directed against the political self-determination that the United States was trying to foster.

The initial frustrations were somewhat relieved as a result of an extended dinner meeting on December 26 attended by Biriuzov and Cherepanov as guests of Barnes and Crane. Biriuzov confirmed the American conjecture that the restrictions imposed by the ACC on the Western Allies were primarily directed against the British, whom at this point they tended to suspect as the inspirers of all anti-Communist activity in Bulgaria. In the ensuing months these matters were handled more subtly. A greater effort was now made to communicate with the British and American members of the ACC although without in any way restricting Soviet authority.

The outlook of General Biriuzov and his colleagues was that Soviet influence in Bulgaria could best be implemented by a government dominated by the Communist party (known officially as the Bulgarian Workers party) in coalition with Agrarian and Socialist elements that fully supported Communist policies within the framework of the Fatherland Front that had come to power on September 9. He saw the current political situation as a conflict between "popular-democratic" forces (i.e., those groups adhering to Communist policies) and "bourgeois" forces (in effect, all others), which he regarded as "reactionary" and aiming at the restoration of "fascism." As he later wrote in his memoirs, "We did not have the right to withhold assistance to the efforts of the

Bulgarian people to crush this reptile." And, with reference to his American and British colleagues on the ACC, "We had no doubt that they would try to interfere with the establishment of a democratic order in Bulgaria. We had to strike from the hand of our 'partners' the spoke which they were constantly trying to put in the wheel of history."[17]

An important role in these plans was played by the series of trials organized by the new government, as least nominally in implementation of the provision of the armistice terms that "Bulgaria will cooperate in the apprehension and trial of persons accused of war crimes." No article of the armistice was implemented with greater enthusiasm. Many hundreds of individuals around the country were sentenced to death by local people's courts, in what was probably the most extensive postwar purge of any of the European countries. The crucial trial was that of the heads of previous governments that opened in Sofia on December 21. The defendants included the three former regents (Prince Kiril, brother of the late King Boris III; Bogdan Filov, the leading pro-German political figure; and Gen. Nikola Mihov), and all of the cabinet members, royal counselors, and members of the National Assembly from 1941 to September 9, 1944.

The public prosecutor asked for fifty-two death penalties, and on February 1 the defendants prepared to hear the sentences standing in a square in the courtroom surrounded by armed militiamen. The prince looked haughty and defiant, Filov was restless and uneasy, and the others talked and joked nervously with each other while waiting for the judges to appear. The clerk read the sentence in a loud and clear voice: death for twenty-five regents and ministers, eight counselors, and sixty-seven members of the National Assembly—a round one hundred. They were shot that evening in batches of twenty.

Light prison sentences were meted out to members of the pro-Western government of Konstantin Muraviev, which had come to power on September 2 in an effort to conclude peace with the United States and the United Kingdom. Muraviev had in fact decided to break relations with Germany on September 5 but, as already noted, the Soviet Union had declared war on Bulgaria on the same day so that the opportunity for Bulgaria to negotiate with the Western Allies was preempted. Muraviev's government was overthrown on September 9 by the Fatherland Front, which arranged a cessation of hostilities with the Soviet Union on the same day.

The one-hundred death sentences, almost twice the number that the public prosecutor had demanded, were generally regarded as an arbitrary figure designed to strike terror into the hearts of all who might contemplate further opposition to the new government. The lighter sentences handed out to the Muraviev government served to eliminate from the political scene the centrist parties, including the moderate Agrarians and the Democrats. Their only war crime had been their refusal to join the Fatherland Front in the course of 1944. This trial is as good an example as any of how the Soviet high command, through the ACC and in implementation of the armistice terms, could clear the way for the the eventual elimination of all rivals to the Communists.

There remained now the Fatherland Front itself. The government that took power on September 9 was headed by Kimon Georgiev, who, along with Damian Velchev (minister of war) and Petko Stainov (minister of foreign affairs), led the Zveno National Union. Zveno was an elite group of antidynastic officers and technocrats who saw it as their role to form a link (*zveno*) uniting the diverse parties and interest groups. They had strong influence in the army and the bureaucracy, but little general support. There were in addition two nonparty cabinet members, known in the contemporary jargon as "independent intellectuals."

A much more important component of the Fatherland Front government was formed by the representatives of the radical Agrarians and the Social Democrats. The radical Agrarians—or more accurately the Pladne Agrarians from their newspaper *Pladne* (Noonday) founded in 1928—were distinguished from the moderate or Vrabcha I Agrarians, from their street address, who were led by Dimitur Gichev and Konstantin Muraviev. The radical Agrarians within the Fatherland Front government were led by Nikola Petkov, who had headed the party throughout the war, and three other cabinet members. The principal leader of the party was Dr. G. M. Dimitrov, who returned to Bulgaria from exile on September 23, 1944, and was elected secretary-general of the party on October 15. The broad popular support of the radical Agrarians was reflected in the large public meetings they held in Sofia, Lovech, Stara Zagora, and Plovdiv in the autumn of 1944. The Social Democrats had a much more limited following among trade union members and civil servants. They were led by Grigor Cheshmedjiev until his death (of natural causes) in September 1945, and thereafter by Konstantin Lulchev.

The Communists themselves were represented by Anton Yugov (minister of interior, controlling the militia, the ubiquitous police force), Mincho Neichev (minister of justice, administering the courts), and two other members. The National Committee of the Fatherland Front, headed by Tsola Dragoicheva, was more openly dominated by the Communists at this time than the government. Traicho Kostov, secretary-general of the party, and most of his colleagues, remained outside the government. The veteran Communist leaders Georgi M. Dimitrov and Vasil Kolarov remained in the USSR for the time being, either hesitating to return until their party's position was more firmly consolidated, or more likely restrained by the Soviet government for fear of alarming their allies.[18]

A new council of regency was also appointed, including one Communist, one member of Zveno, and one independent. The council of regency had been established when King Boris III died in August 1943 and was succeeded by his six-year-old son Simeon II. Its original members, as already noted, were arrested in September 1944 and executed in February of the following year. The new regents remained in office until September 1946, when Bulgaria was declared a republic and the young king and his family went into exile.

When it came to power, the Fatherland Front could properly be said to have represented a solid majority of the politically active population, in view of the wide popular support of the radical Agrarians and Social Democrats and the narrower but substantial support of the Communists among urban workers and some minority groups. Ten days after taking office, the government announced a program of reforms that included further socialization of the already extensively socialized economy and society, legalization of trade unions and civil marriages, credits for the peasants, and guarantees of civil liberties. This was essentially the established Agrarian program, and it was well received by the general public so far as one could gather in the confused situation existing at the time. Bulgaria also became a cobelligerent with the Russians, but this status was not recognized by the United States or the United Kingdom. In the course of the winter its armed forces lost some 32,000 lives fighting with the Soviet armies from Bulgaria to Hungary—the farthest from its borders that a Bulgarian army had ever ventured.

At the same time, the Communists from the beginning controlled the police and the courts directly. The Bulgarian army was fully counterbalanced by the Soviet occupation forces. Some sixteen general officers of Bulgarian origin who had served with the Soviet armed forces were appointed to leading positions in the army, one of them becoming chief of staff. Suspect officers were soon purged, and the Zveno minister of war was effectively isolated—his adjutant was killed, it being rumored that he was found in his office one morning with his skull crushed, as a gentle reminder to the minister that he should not meddle in army affairs.

By February 1945 there remained as potential opponents of Communist control only the radical Agrarians and the Social Democrats. They had worked closely with the Communists in the Fatherland Front opposition group during the war, in contrast to the moderate Agrarians and other centrist parties who had preferred a Western connection, and Nikola Petkov in particular had been confident in the early weeks after September 9 that the Agrarians would be able to share power with the Communists and the Social Democrats. All three parties had a heritage of independent and frequently conflicting policies dating back to the early 1900s; but since 1923, and especially during the war, they had shared the common experience of being in opposition to prevailing government policies. The task confronting the Communists in the spring of 1945 was thus to consolidate their exclusive control of the government, while keeping up the appearance of collaboration with the radical Agrarians and Social Democrats.

During the early months of the occupation Barnes and Crane were working on the assumption that Biriuzov and his colleagues were overstepping their rights in promoting extensive political changes within the country without reference to their allies on the ACC. The moment of truth finally came on January 18, when Barnes and Crane learned for the first time from their British colleagues of the Eden-Molotov negotiations of October 12–15, which limited the role of the American and British members of the ACC in effect to that of liaison. The State Department responded to Barnes's queries rather ambiguously, by asserting that the Eden-Molotov deal was not binding on the United States and urging Crane to press for frequent meetings of the ACC with prior information about important decisions; and at the same time acknowledging that the Soviets would have full authority in the first period. For the second period, after the conclusion of its hostilities with Germany, the department noted that it had reserved its rights to press for a more active role.[19]

The question of the American and British roles on the ACC continued to be a matter of active concern. There were extended messages from Barnes and Crane documenting the limitations under which they were working, and equally eloquent responses from the department expressing its concern and determination. Yet the defeat of Germany on May 8 came and went with no change in the situation, despite new communications from Barnes and Crane that were in due course brought to the attention of President Truman.[20] After the Potsdam Conference, the Soviet government proposed some alterations in ACC procedures, but these did not change matters substantially. The principal change was that Westen journalists were now admitted to Bulgaria, with the result that the election crisis received wide publicity.

THE ELECTION CRISIS

The Yalta Declaration on Liberated Europe (February 11, 1945) had come at a time when the Fatherland Front was beginning to prepare for elections. Within the country the issue of free elections centered on the Communist insistence that the candidates of the four parties in the Fatherland Front run on a single government list, and that other candidates could run only as individuals. In other words, the Communists would use their control of the police and the courts to bargain before the elections for a larger share of the candidates than they could expect to win if they ran in competition with the other parties. At the same time they sought to split their two main competitors, the radical Agrarians and the Social Democrats, by isolating their leaders and limiting participation in the Fatherland Front to splinter elements of these parties. On January 20, 1945, the leader of the radical Agrarians, Dr. G. M. Dimitrov who had returned to the country from Cairo in September, was forced to resign his position, and on April 23 he was placed under house arrest. His close relations with the British both before and during the war made him particularly vulnerable in Soviet eyes. Nikola Petkov, who had led the radical Agrarians during the war and was at this time considered by the Communists to be more amenable to their influence, again became head of the party.

After the publication of the Yalta declaration in the Bulgarian press, Barnes queried the department: "Does the U.S. really intend to make its influence felt in this part of the world and, in particular, will it actually seek to assure a free expression of Bulgarian opinion in the forthcoming elections?"[21] The department responded to this query that it expected "to see with respect to the former Axis satellite countries full implementation of the Crimea Declaration on Liberated Europe, announcing mutual agreement among the three principal allies to concert their policies in helping these former enemy states . . . to form interim governmental authorities broadly representative of the democratic elements."[22]

Pursuant to this policy, Ambassador Harriman was instructed at the end of March to inform the Soviet government of American concern about Bulgaria's electoral plans and to propose that the parties forming the Fatherland Front have full freedom to present separate lists of candidates to the electorate. The proposal was also made that this procedure be supervised by a tripartite commission in Sofia, independent of the ACC, composed of the Soviet, British, and American political representatives.[23] Molotov was not attracted to this idea, however, replying that he had no information about Bulgarian elections in the near future, that foreign intervention in eventual elections would not be justified, and that successful elections had been conducted in Finland without foreign interference.[24]

While the forthcoming elections had for some time been the main political topic in Bulgaria, Molotov's reply was correct in the technical sense that the date for elections had not yet been set. In the Finnish elections, held on March 18, the People's Democratic party, formed by the Communists running on a single ticket with the Farmers' party and dissident Social Democrats (a grouping analogous to the Fatherland

Front) had won a quarter of the seats in the assembly. The Social Democrats, running independently, had won another quarter, with the balance going to the Agrarians and other parties. The government resulting from this election was recognized by the United States after the Potsdam Conference as broadly representative of the democratic forces in the country.

In Bulgaria, the radical Agrarians and the Social Democrats were becoming increasingly aware that if the elections were carried out as planned the two parties would very shortly be shorn of all political influence. In this context the dramatic escape of Dr. G. M. Dimitrov from house arrest sharpened the issue of political freedom and of the American role in supporting representative government. Dr. Dimitrov escaped from house arrest on May 23 and sought asylum with a member of the British mission. The British representatives, after communicating with London, informed him that they could not offer him asylum. Barnes agreed to take him in, pending instructions from the U.S. government, and at 4:00 A.M. on May 24 he was driven to Barnes's residence about four miles outside Sofia.[25]

Dr. Dimitrov was now under American protection. Foreign Minister Stainov and other high officials were out of town celebrating a national holiday, so Barnes spent the day consulting Exarch Stefan, head of the Bulgarian Orthodox church, and several political leaders, as to the legal and political aspects of his problem. In the afternoon Barnes finally got in touch with the Senior Regent Venelin Ganev and Prime Minister Georgiev, and discovered that neither of them had yet been informed of Dr. Dimitrov's escape. The prime minister agreed that the police search— now proceeding full force—should be called off, and promised that the government would take no action until Barnes had received instructions from the United States. In the evening, Barnes had another long session with the prime minister and Minister of Interior Yugov. The latter agreed to withdraw the large militia detachments that had been thrown around Barnes's villa, and said he would leave only a few unobtrusive agents to guard the place.

In the meantime I spent the evening of May 24 alone with Dr. Dimitrov at the villa. Not knowing what Washington might decide to do, or what sudden steps the militia or the Soviet authorities might take, he was not a little nervous. We closed all the downstairs shutters as soon as it got dark, and then after dinner went upstairs to be out of sight of militia who might enter the grounds. We talked until twelve-thirty, when Barnes finally returned from Sofia with the news that the situation was at least for the time being under control.

In the course of the first two days of negotiations Barnes did not know what Washington's response to this incident would be. Finally, on the morning of the 26th, we received the cable that gave the department's view. "Your action," it said, "has the Department's entire approval. We consider that through your prompt notification to the Bulgarian authorities and your action in obtaining their declaration of intention to work out a solution for Dimitrov's safety you have kept within reasonable limits as regards the application of the principle of asylum, and at the same time have placed the ultimate responsibility for the protection of Bulgarian political leaders on the Bulgarian Government where it belongs."[26] Barnes replied on the following day: "I don't believe any more welcome telegram has ever been received in the history of the Service."[27]

In the course of these developments, we learned that Mrs. Dimitrov had been arrested, and severely beaten while under interrogation.When her plight became known, the British made a strong protest, and in about two weeks she was released and interned in her husband's native village with her two children and her mother. The fate of Mara Racheva was more tragic. She had been the private secretary of Dr. Dimitrov, and subsequently of Nikola Petkov, and it was to her apartment that Dr. Dimitrov went first before seeking refuge with a member of the British mission. She was apprehended as soon as his escape was discovered, and was severely tortured. Her death four days later was attributed by the police to suicide by jumping out of a prison window. When her remains were returned to her parents for burial, however, the results of extensive mutilation were quite evident. Apart from the personal tragedy, this incident contributed further to the prevailing atmosphere of terror.

The situation on May 29 could be described roughly as follows: The U.S. view was that (1) the security of Dr. Dimitrov must be guaranteed; (2) Barnes was authorized to take such steps as he saw fit to assure Dr. Dimitrov's security; (3) the matter was considered to be one for negotiation primarily between the United States and Bulgaria; (4) no pledge given by the Bulgarian government for Dr. Dimitrov's safety would be respected; and (5) a decision of the Allied Control Commission would be accepted only if it were reached on a tripartite basis.

The Bulgarian view was that (1) Dr. Dimitrov should be surrendered to the Bulgarian government; (2) if the United States desired to negotiate directly with Bulgaria, then the ordinary rules of international law should apply, and these required the United States to return Dimitrov; and (3) if the United States desired to negotiate with Bulgaria as an occupied country, then the matter should be handled by the Allied Control Commission.

The Russian position was that (1) Dr. Dimitrov was a "defeatist" and that the official Bulgarian position was justified; (2) this was primarily a matter for negotiation between the U. S. and Bulgarian governments; and (3) the Allied Control Commission remained under Soviet authority and could not make decisions on a tripartite basis.

The British mission in Sofia—headed by Maj. Gen. Walter H. Oxley, with William E. Houstoun-Boswall as political representative, reflecting the spirit of the October negotiations in Moscow and aware of the analogous British position in neighboring Greece—was reluctant to challenge Soviet authority and was prepared to accept the single electoral list of the Fatherland Front. The British felt that any approach to the Bulgarian government through the ACC would have to be on a tripartite basis, and that the Soviet representative would clearly not cooperate. London's refusal to grant asylum to Dr. Dimitrov was consistent with this policy.

The issue remained deadlocked at this point throughout June and July and into August. Dr. Dimitrov remained in Barnes's villa, in good health and excellent spirits considering his situation. Barnes frequently had visitors for drinks or meals, and Dr. Dimitrov participated as a permanent guest—like "the man who came to dinner," or rather "to breakfast" in this case.

Meanwhile in May, the Communists had undercut Petkov's leadership of the radical Agrarians by organizing a splinter party led by Alexander Obbov as the officially recognized radical Agrarians. They similarly set up a splinter Social Democratic party under Dimiter Neikov, replacing Cheshmedjiev, who refused to accept Communist predominance. Obbov and Neikov were induced to accept Communist control by a combination of bribes and threats that depended for their effectiveness on the pervasive employment of terror against opponents of exclusive Communist controls.

The single Fatherland Front electoral list remained the central issue, since it guaranteed a plebiscitary form of elections based on a representation of parties negotiated in advance on Communist terms. Announced in early July, the list made provision for ninety-five Communists, ninety-five Agrarians, forty-six members of Zveno, thirty-one Social Democrats, and nine independents, which was a clear enough indication that the Communists expected to do much less well in a free competition. Apart from this basic limitation on free elections, throughout the summer of 1945 opposition political workers, especially Agrarians, were continually harassed by restrictions on newsprint and printing facilities, and by beatings and arrests.

In the midst of these developments, it became clear that the main Soviet objective at this time was to obtain American and British recognition of postwar governments in Romania, Bulgaria, and Hungary. Stalin sent a forceful note in May to Truman and Churchill urging recognition, and pursued the subject vigorously at the Potsdam Conference (July 17–August 2). Truman and Byrnes, for their part, sought during several extended confrontations at Potsdam to press for more open electoral procedures and also for a larger role for the American and British representatives on the ACC now that hostilities with Germany were concluded. These issues remained essentially deadlocked at Potsdam, however, and the only significant Soviet concession was agreement to lift restrictions on the access of Western journalists.[28]

Petkov now emerged as the leader of the opposition within the Fatherland Front, and on July 26 he wrote a letter to the prime minister urging postponement of the elections until they could be held on a more democratic basis under Allied control.[29] He was forthwith forced to resign from the cabinet, and in mid-August he was soon followed by the remaining independent Agrarians and Social Democrats in the Fatherland Front. For Petkov this was a critical step. Both his father and his brother had been prominent political leaders who had lost their lives by assassination. Perhaps because of his family history, he himself had not been noted for aggressive leadership. In 1944 he had been convinced that cooperation with the Communists would be possible without sacrificing Agrarian independence, but during the winter of 1944–45 he reached the conclusion that this would not be possible. When on May 9 the Communists replaced him with Obbov as leader of the radical Agrarians (as they had replaced Dimitrov with Petkov in January), he felt that he had no choice but to oppose Communist policies. Thenceforth, until his execution in September 1947, he used all the resources at his disposal to prevent unilateral domination by the Communists.

Events moved rapidly as the election day approached. On August 13, Secretary of State James F. Byrnes instructed Barnes to convey the American criticisms of the electoral procedure to the Bulgarian government, and on August 18 Byrnes issued a public statement to the same effect. It asserted that the United States was prepared to establish diplomatic relations "with a provisional government which would be representative of all important elements of democratic opinion," but added that it was not satisfied that the elections being prepared would ensure effective participation of all democratic elements.[30] The British now took a similar position, and pressure was exerted on the Soviet authorities by the regents and by influential Bulgarians outside the government to postpone the elections. On August 14 the USSR had strengthened its support of the Fatherland Front by granting diplomatic recognition to the Bulgarian government. On August 22, however, Foreign Minister Stainov held a press conference at which he stated that it was up to the ACC to determine whether the elections should be postponed. Taking advantage of this hint, Crane and Oxley pressed successfully for a meeting of the ACC on the following day, at which they presented a comprehensive proposal outlining the conditions under which acceptable postponed elections might be held. The political representatives then joined the generals from midnight to 5:15 A.M. After repeated statements of their opposing positions, the meeting ended in a deadlock and Biriuzov said that he would have to consult Moscow.

At midnight on August 24, Barnes was able to telegraph Washington that the "battle of elections" had been won. The decision was doubtless made in Moscow, but the form it took was a request from the Bulgarian government to the Allied Control Commission for permission to postpone elections. Barnes now recommended that the United States award Biriuzov a decoration, and that arrangements be completed for a Bulgarian political representative to be sent to the United States. The Bulgarian government was now in a state of sufficient shock that it agreed to let Dr. Dimitrov leave the country, and on September 5 he departed with his wife for Italy. Their two children were left behind with their maternal grandmother.

It is ironic that on the same August 24 on which the elections were postponed, Washington informed Barnes that it was not making representations to Moscow in regard to the elections and could not support the proposals for postponement that Crane and Barnes had made to the Allied Control Commission. The department had not contemplated requesting postponement of the elections, and felt that "the formation of a representative democratic government in Bulgaria is a matter for Bulgarians to undertake in absence of pertinent provisions in armistice not for consideration by ACC." It added that Barnes had exceeded his authority, and should have consulted the department before proposing postponement.[31] This was certainly a sharp reprimand, and in his reply Barnes referred to it as a "censure." He explained his action on the ground that postponement had seemed to him to follow from the logic of his instructions, and that "obviously the purpose of expressing the view of the U.S. government was to forestall rigged elections and formation of a government that [the] U.S. could not recognize."[32] This telegram again crossed with one expressing the department's gratification at the postponement of elections and authorizing Barnes to convey to the Bulgarian government the American hope that this decision "When appropriately implemented . . . will ensure to the Bulgarian people full freedom of choice in the establishment of a representative government."[33]

THE ETHRIDGE MISSION

The postponement of the elections scheduled for August 26 revealed to the Communist party in Bulgaria that Soviet support had its limits, and it now recognized that some concessions would have to be made to the American position. New elections were scheduled for November 18, and the electoral procedure was revised to permit opposition candidates to run on separate party lists. Greater freedom was also permitted to the opposition press, although the government retained its monopoly of the radio.

Meanwhile the Council of Foreign Ministers had held its first meeting in London (September 11 to October 3, 1945), and reached a deadlock on the question of implementing the Yalta declaration in Bulgaria and Romania.[34] In the course of these discussions Molotov maintained that Byrnes was not well informed about conditions in these countries. Byrnes also apparently felt that American public opinion was insufficiently informed to give him the support he would need if recognition were to become a major issue. He therefore announced the appointment on October 10 of Mark Ethridge, publisher of the *Louisville Courier-Journal* and a liberal Democrat, to make a fresh appraisal in Bulgaria and Romania of the extent to which the conditions of the Yalta declaration were being met. Ethridge had no knowledge of southeastern Europe, but with his journalistic experience and keen mind he soon proved to be an able investigator. He never mispronounced a name once he heard it, and he quickly grasped the frequently subtle differences between groups and individuals. As a publisher he had had long experience in negotiating with labor unions, and he had a sympathetic understanding of left-wing attitudes.

I had left Bulgaria with Barnes and Dimitrov on September 5, and was on the point of resuming my academic career at Princeton University. When the State Department asked me to delay my resignation and accompany Ethridge on his mission, however, it looked like an offer that I could not refuse. We covered 13,000 miles between October 18 and December 3, spending two weeks in Bulgaria, one in the Soviet Union, and ten days in Romania. In Bulgaria, Ethridge talked with some forty-five political leaders, and with the Soviet and British representatives. The inteviews were freely conducted, and included all the leading members of the government and the opposition. The opposition leaders reported the extensive use of violence by the militia in the recent electoral campaign, and also the methods that might be used in a future election to stuff the ballot boxes.

In two lengthy talks, Nikola Petkov defended his position that he would not participate in elections unless the Fatherland Front parties could run on separate lists. He also insisted that the Communists relinquish the Ministries of Interior and Justice in a reconstructed government before the elections. He did not believe that the Communists would be able to govern the country without the independent participation of the other Fatherland Front parties. He based this view partly on the international situation, no doubt influenced by the recent postponement of elections, and also on his belief that the Communists did not have enough popular support to govern the country alone. Petkov recognized, at the same time, that the United States did not intend to press for the postponement of the new elections scheduled for November 18. Since there was no chance of the Communists meeting his conditions, he would not compete in the new elections.

Prime Minister Georgiev, for his part, pointed out in his talks with Ethridge that the electoral procedure had been revised since the postponed elections to permit opposition parties, instead of individual opposition candidates, to run on separate tickets—although the Fatherland Front itself would run again on a single ticket, including the dissident Agrarians and Social Democrats. The prime minister felt that he had achieved some success in getting the Communists to take their governmental responsibilities more seriously, and implied that his efforts would be jeopardized if Petkov and the other Fatherland Front leaders insisted on challenging the government rather than helping him exert constant pressure on it from within. He acknowledged that Petkov was an exceptional personality in Bulgarian politics because of his great integrity, but he strongly disagreed with his tactics. Other Zveno leaders also advocated a policy of gradualism in containing the Communists, and seemed to feel that this goal could be achieved better by administrative means than through an elected parliament.

In some ways the most interesting talk was with the veteran Communist leader Georgi Dimitrov. He returned to Bulgaria on the eve of November 7, 1945, the twenty-eighth anniversary of the Russian Revolution, for his first visit since 1923. In the course of the past year he had been sending instructions to his Bulgarian colleagues by telegram, some of which were published in the press, and had come to be known as "Telegram George." He was reported to be in poor health, and indeed his color seemed very high. He looked like an aging actor at the end of a long performance, who had not yet had time to remove his makeup. He was accompanied by an unidentified individual who never left his side. We assumed that he was a Soviet watchdog.

Dimitrov maintained firmly that he considered one area of discussion closed. There could be no further postponement of elections, and no reorganization of the Fatherland Front government before the currently scheduled elections were held. He foresaw the possibility, however, that when the government was reorganized after the forthcoming elections the admission of opposition Agrarians and Social Democrats might be discussed. Under such circumstances, however, the opposition would have to come to terms with the government rather than vice versa. In reviewing the recent history of the Fatherland Front, Dimitrov also sought to assure Ethridge that the Communists had no intention of monopolizing political power and wished instead to cooperate with the other parties within the framework of the Fatherland Front. Ethridge, for his part, reiterated the conclusion he had reached in the course of his visit that the Fatherland Front was no longer representative in the sense that it had been in September 1944, and that the forthcoming elections were not likely to change the situation.

Among the numerous social events in the course of the mission was a lunch tendered by Mr. and Mrs. Barnes for Generals Biriuzov and Cherepanov, Prime Minister Georgiev, Foreign Minister Stainov, Soviet Political Representative Kirsanov, and their spouses. This event was notable not only for its relaxed and friendly atmosphere, but also for a menu that included two roast suckling pigs sent to Barnes by peasants from the Pleven district in gratitude for his efforts on behalf of Dr. Dimitrov.

In the meantime the electoral campaign was proceeding without the participation of the radical Agrarians and Social Democrats. It was clear that it would not result in a government that the United States could recognize if it continued to be guided by the Yalta formula of one that was "broadly representative of all democratic elements of the population." Adherence to this formula called for reorganization of the Fatherland Front government, either as a result of elections or by negotiation, to include the radical Agrarian and Social Democratic leaders who had resigned in August.

It was clear that the local situation was now firmly deadlocked, and that no change was likely without an initiative from Moscow. Barnes now came up with the suggestion that Ethridge himself go to Moscow to report his findings to the Soviet government. Secretary Byrnes gave his approval to this idea, and instructed Ethridge to recommend that the Yalta powers "take appropriate steps immediately (1) to provide for the submission to the electorate of lists of opposition candidates, postponing the election scheduled for Nov. 18, for sufficient time to accomplish this purpose, and (2) in the meantime to reorganize the Government by the inclusion of opposition representatives. A necessary condition for the achievement of a basis for this course would appear to be the reorganization of the militia to preclude its use as an instrument of force and intimidation."[35]

Ethridge flew to Moscow on November 11, and two days later had a long talk with Andrei Vyshinsky, vice-commissar of foreign affairs. Ambassador Harriman accompanied us, and the interpreter on the American side was Robert C. Tucker of the embassy staff—with whom I had studied Russian at Harvard University before the war and who was later to become my colleague at Princeton. The exchange was pleasant enough, but it did not bring the two sides any closer together. After listening to Ethridge's extensive report on the ways in which representative government was being restricted in Bulgaria, Vyshinsky replied that the reports he had received presented a different picture. He had no reason to believe that the Fatherland Front was not representative or that the elections would not be free. In response to a direct question, Vyshinsky replied that postponement of the elections would be an unjustifiable intervention in Bulgarian affairs. If the Bulgarian government should ask for Soviet advice on this question, however, the matter would be considered in the light of existing circumstances.[36]

Ethridge now recommended that the State Department issue another statement such as that of August 18, expressing the view that there was no reason to believe that elections held under existing conditions would represent the free expression of the popular will, and this was done on November 14.[37] This time the elections were held as planned, and the Fatherland Front won the overwhelming victory that was anticipated in view of the absence of opposition candidates. In the meantime Ethridge made a further recommendation from Moscow on November 14, along lines already discussed with Barnes, that in the event the elections were held, the United States should press for a reorganization of the government to include the leaders who had resigned in the course of the spring, neutralization of the Ministries of Interior and Justice, and the holding of new elections with single or separate lists as the parties might wish. He also suggested that the national assembly issuing from the November 18 elections should have a limited competence pending the reorganization of the government.[38] It is perhaps significant that Ethridge's trip from Sofia to Moscow had been in a plush Soviet plane, but he was sent back to Bucharest via Odessa in a crowded bucket-seat transport plane.

After ten days in Romania we returned to Washington on December 4 to report to Byrnes. My own direct participation in these events came to an end shortly thereafter. I stayed on in the department's Division of Southeastern European Affairs into February, when I resumed my teaching position at Princeton.

Ethridge's report to Byrnes included separate accounts of the developments in the two countries he had visited, a "Summary Report on Soviet Policy in Rumania and Bulgaria," dated December 7, and a briefer letter to Byrnes, dated the following day, intended for publication.[39] Ethridge had a lengthy talk with Byrnes on December 8 and on the following day received a phone call from the secretary to explain that he had decided not to publish the letter but instead would take it with him to the forthcoming meeting of the Council of Foreign Ministers in Moscow. Ethridge agreed to this change in plans.

The subsequent development of events can best be understood in terms of Bulgaria's relation to the changing international context. When he became secretary of state in July 1945, Byrnes had inherited a situation arising from the adoption of two related but conflicting policies during the preceding months. One was the short-term policy, initiated by the United States and the United Kingdom in Italy, favoring the administration of liberated satellite states by the armies of the countries that occupied them at the end of the war. The other was the longer term policy of a tripartite sponsorship of free elections leading to representative governments along the lines of the Yalta formula. The conflict between these two policies, in view of the differences in ideology and interests between the USSR and the Western democracies, were in the early postwar months treated as isolated episodes subject to local settlement. With the termination of hostilities in the Pacific, however, political leaders felt increasing pressure to conclude the peace treaties and move on to postwar reconstruction.

In this atmosphere the difficulties experienced with tripartite cooperation made the alternative of compromise by division into spheres of influence more attractive. In the course of the American-Soviet negotiations preparatory to the December meeting of the Council of Foreign Ministers, the USSR had demanded a more active role in the control arrangements for occupied Japan and this question became linked to that of Romania and Bulgaria. The USSR could not very well be excluded completely from a voice in occupation policy in Japan in view of American complaints about ACC procedures in Romania and Bulgaria, but on the other hand there was no need to give them greater voice than we had received in the Balkan countries. This linkage argued for accepting Russian dominance in the Balkans in return for a similar U.S. role in Japan.[40]

A policy of compromise in the Balkans was strongly urged at this time by the British. The view was advanced by Sir Orme G. Sargent, British deputy undersecretary for foreign affairs, that the best approach to breaking the stalemate in Romania and Bulgaria would be a negotiated "dilution" of the existing governments. Further freedom within these countries might then be achieved by "nagging" to a point where recognition would be possible. Once peace treaties were signed, Soviet troops would be withdrawn and this in turn might lead to a relaxation of Communist controls.[41]

Reorganization of the Bulgarian government had already been broached, as an alternative to or in connection with new elections with separate lists, as a solution to the stalemate. Byrnes now seized on this device. Publication of the Ethridge report would have made such a compromise more difficult, so instead he took it to Moscow to show to Molotov and Stalin.

Byrnes's position was made all the more difficult by the division within the American foreign policy establishment between the advocates of compromise and firmness. Those who advocated compromise were the heirs of the New Deal and Atlantic Charter themes of Roosevelt's policies. For them cooperation with the Russians, especially in view of the forthcoming first meeting of the United Nations General Assembly scheduled for January 1946, was a higher priority than the form of government in the countries bordering Russia in southeastern Europe. In this view Byrnes was strongly supported by his principal assistant Benjamin V. Cohen, now serving as counselor of the Department of State, by Joseph E. Davies, former ambassador to the USSR, and by other New Deal liberals. The liberal branch of the establishment found it difficult to believe that Russia was interfering in Balkan affairs to the detriment of free elections. While still in Washington, Ethridge was invited by Eugene Meyer to meet with a group of liberals, including Walter Lippmann, Lyndon Johnson, and Estes Kefauver. They found his account of his findings quite contrary to their expectations, and seemed to wonder if the liberal editor had not turned into a red-baiter.[42]

The policy of firmness—of resisting Soviet pressure on specific issues of principle—was favored by President Truman and had as its strongest supporter Admiral Leahy, who had continued in his role as chief of staff to the commander in chief. This view was also held by Dean Acheson, undersecretary of state, by career Foreign Service officers with Soviet experience, by a substantial majority of leaders in the Congress, and by most of the press.[43]

In preparing for the December meeting of the Council of Foreign Ministers, the department's Office of European Affairs proposed terms for Bulgaria essentially along the lines of Ethridge's telegram from Moscow of November 14. This proposal was watered down by the secretary, however, before presentation to the conference. He proposed that a reorganization of the Bulgarian government be "suggested" by the three powers; that the reorganized government be pledged to hold free elections within six months; and that the national assembly elected in November should adopt a restricted legislative program pending the new elections. If these conditions were met, the United States would agree to recognize the reorganized government before the elections were held. There was no mention of neutralizing the Ministries of Interior and Justice and, more striking, no reference to the Yalta declaration.[44]

This proposal was further diluted in the course of Byrnes's direct negotiations in Moscow with Molotov and Stalin, to whom he showed the Ethridge report as a means of conveying American objections to recognition. The final compromise reached on December 27, at the very end of the conference, provided that the Soviet government alone would give "friendly advice" to the Bulgarian government regarding the desirability of including in the Fatherland Front cabinet "two representatives of other democratic groups, who (a) are truly representative of the groups of the parties that are not participating in the government, and (b) are really suitable and will work loyally with the Government." When the United States and the United Kingdom were convinced that this had been accomplished, they would recognize the reorganized government.[45] At the same time, among many other issues decided at the conference, the USSR agreed to accept no more than a nominal role in the occupation arrangements for Japan.

Most of Byrnes's advisers at Moscow were opposed to the extent of the concessions involved, and in Washington it was widely regarded as a sellout. President Truman himself was deeply disturbed by this outcome. While this negotiation was only one of many issues that divided the president and his secretary of state, it played its role in the replacement of Byrnes by George C. Marshall a year later. Among Byrnes's few supporters, interestingly enough, was Ethridge, who wrote in the *Louisville Courier Journal* on January 2 that if the Bulgarian government followed through on the Soviet advice in good faith it would lead to a more representative government.[46]

As it turned out, the Moscow compromise proved to be impossible to implement. Petkov and his colleagues in opposition refused to accept positions in the government unless the Ministries of Interior and Justice were removed from Communist control, new elections were held with separate party lists, and other steps were taken to relieve the political repression. Byrnes flirted for a while with a proposal to recognize the Bulgarian government if it simply pledged to hold new elections, with no other conditions attached. He was dissuaded from this by his advisers, however, and U.S. policy now reverted to its pre-Moscow position of simply withholding recognition.[47]

A reorganization of the Fatherland Front government in March 1946 strengthened the influence of the Communists, and in September a republic was proclaimed after a referendum. New elections were held in October, and this time the combined opposition ran on a separate ticket and won 101 of the 465 seats in the new assembly. Considering the control exercised by the Communists over all aspects of electoral procedure, and Georgi Dimitrov's announcement on the eve of the elections that all those who voted for the opposition would be regarded as traitors, this was a remarkable achievement. Petkov and his colleagues now continued their attacks on the government as members of the assembly under the protection of their parliamentary immunity, but with a government now headed by Dimitrov himself the Communists were prepared to make no further concessions to improve their chances for recognition.

Byrnes now became reconciled to recognition of the existing government, and went ahead with the negotiation of the peace treaties with Italy, Romania, Bulgaria, Hungary, and Finland. He resigned as secretary of state on January 7, and was succeeded by George C. Marshall. The Peace treaties were signed in February 1947, and on June 5 they were ratified by the U.S. Senate. On the following day Petkov was arrested, following removal of his parliamentary immunity, and charged with plotting to overthrow the government.

Meanwhile Barnes had returned to Washington in April. Upon learning on June 9 of the final decision of Secretary Marshall to recognize the Bulgarian government following the coming into force of the Peace treaty and to deny Barnes's request that he return to Bulgaria to work for the release of Petkov, Barnes decided to resign from the Foreign Service.[48] Petkov's trial lasted from August 5 to 15, and he received a death sentence, which he appealed. The Bulgarian Peace treaty came into force on September 15. On September 19 the United States informed Bulgaria of its intention to establish diplomatic relations. On September 23 Petkov was executed after his appeal had been denied. On October 1 the United States granted formal recognition.[49]

RETROSPECTIVE REAPPRAISAL

The foregoing has been written essentially as the events appeared at the time, on the basis of personal recollections enriched by the subsequent publication of contemporary documents. There has been no mention of the Cold War because the term was not used by us at the time, and no one suspected that we were involved in "the origins of the Cold War."

With the benefit of hindsight, some of the controversial issues relating to these events now deserve our attention: (1) Did the United States use "atomic diplomacy" in Bulgaria? (2) Did the American representatives in Bulgaria misrepresent the local political situation in their reports to Washington? (3) Did American officials, especially Barnes, conspire with Nikola Petkov in a counterrevolutionary policy against the Fatherland Front? (4) What was the United States seeking to accomplish in Bulgaria, and why did it fail? (5) How did the Cold War originate, as seen from the Bulgarian experience?

(1) It has been alleged that the United States resorted to "atomic diplomacy" in 1945 and that, more specifically, the successful use of atomic bombs against Japan in early August gave Truman and Byrnes

new confidence and encouraged them to demand the postponement of the Bulgarian elections. This view has been presented in its most direct form by Gar Alperovitz, who notes that Byrnes's communication of August 13 to Bulgarian political leaders criticizing the electoral procedures (but not demanding postponement of the elections, as Alperovitz asserts) occurred four days after the bombing of Nagasaki.[50] Alperovitz concludes his account of the events leading to the postponement of the elections scheduled for August 26 with the comment that the atomic bomb represented "a threat." The American success in getting the elections postponed, he says, "could only be attributed to the atomic bomb." He argues further that the atomic bomb "determined much of Truman's shift to a tough policy aimed at forcing Soviet acquiescence to American plans for Eastern and Central Europe."[51]

The only evidence that Alperovitz cites to support his allegation that the atomic bomb brought the postponement of the elections is the timing of the note of August 13. To the best of my recollection, the atom bomb played no role in United States policy toward Bulgaria, and the timing of this and other communications in the course of the election crisis was not related to the deployment of the nuclear weapons against Japan.

A more balanced view of the role of nuclear weapons in American policy at this time is represented by the work of Martin J. Sherwin, based on recently declassified documents. It is his conclusion that news of the successful test on July 16 made President Truman more self-confident and assertive at the Potsdam Conference. The president and his colleagues anticipated the U.S. possession of the bomb would influence Soviet policy, and were surprised when it had no perceptible effect. At no time, however, was there any intention of using the bomb as a "threat."[52]

Barnes reported on August 24 that "we are not afraid of atomic bomb" was one of the electoral slogans employed by the Fatherland Front,[53] but I have seen no evidence that U.S. possession of the bomb had any influence on Bulgarian or Soviet thinking. Subsequent accounts of these events published in Bulgaria and the USSR make no mention of a nuclear "threat." As already noted, U.S. bargaining power at this time was based not on the bomb but on the withholding of diplomatic recognition.

(2) It has also been alleged, as part of a general criticism of American postwar diplomatic reporting, that Barnes misrepresented the political situation by portraying the "Agrarian party" as devoted to civil liberties and the Communist party as the enemy of democracy.[54] Apart from the fact that there was no "Agrarian party," but numerous Agrarian factions, only the most radical of which was included in the Fatherland Front,

readers of the foregoing account will recognize that this allegation greatly distorts the situation.

What is significant in this context is that Barnes and the rest of the U.S. government did accept the political groups included in the Fatherland Front when it seized power in September 1944 as "broadly representative of all democratic elements of the population." Indeed, U.S. policy might well have been criticized for not including in its definition of "all democratic elements" the members of the pro-Western Muraviev government of September 2–9, 1944, who were more traditionally "bourgeois" (if one wishes to use that term) than the more populist followers of Petkov. The issue to which Barnes's dispatches and Ethridge's report were addressed was not whether the Fatherland Front as originally constituted was representative, but whether the prevailing electoral procedures would permit a free choice among its constituent parties.

Barnes was certainly more of an activist than most American diplomats. He had been appointed as vice-consul in Patras a few months after graduating from Grinnell College in 1919, and he had served in Smyrna during the Greek-Turkish war, and at the Lausanne Conference, as well as in Sofia in 1930–34. Strongly anti-German and pro-French, it had been his sad duty to close the American embassy in Paris in May 1941, and he was critical of his government's support of the Vichy government. He believed that the Yalta declaration meant what it said, and pressed for nothing more than a government representing the political forces that had joined together to form the Fatherland Front coalition in 1944. He was in agreement with Washington when the decision was finally made in the winter of 1946–47 to recognize Bulgaria upon the negotiation of the peace treaty. He saw this not as a surrender, but as an opportunity under changed conditions to continue to press for a more liberal political regime in Bulgaria. He also hoped that Bulgaria's need for economic aid might be used as bargaining power.[55] Only in the summer of 1947, when the State Department decided not to alter its timetable of recognition despite the arrest of Petkov, did Barnes come to feel that pragmatism had been carried too far.

Barnes set forth his views in a lecture at the National War College in June 1947, in which he emphasized that under existing conditions Bulgarian foreign policy should be "closely integrated" with that of the USSR. "It is also clear," he added, ". . . that any government in which the Communists did not play an important part could not possibly last." At the same time, he argued, since most Bulgarians did not support the Communists, the United States should seek to bring about a state of affairs in which the Communists and other Fatherland Front parties could coexist in what would in effect be a coalition government.[56] It was toward this end that he urged American support for Petkov and his colleagues.

There is evidence that Secretary of State Byrnes was distrustful of professional diplomats generally and that both he and Benjamin V. Cohen, his principal personal assistant in these matters, thought that Barnes was too sympathetic to the dissident members of the Fatherland Front.[57] Indeed, one of the reasons for sending Ethridge to the Balkans was to make an independent evaluation of the situation there. Byrnes accepted Ethridge's findings, however, and the compromises he finally agreed to were based not on doubts about the facts, but on the pressures he felt to conclude the peace treaties and to reach an accommodation with the USSR on the larger issues of postwar policy.

(3) Did American officials, especially Barnes, conspire with Nikola Petkov in a counterrevolutionary policy against the Fatherland Front?

When Petkov was brought to trial in 1947, he was accused of organizing a conspiracy that aimed at overthrowing the Fatherland Front government and handing over power to a Petkov government.[58] The accounts of these events published in Bulgaria in recent years continue to describe Petkov and other defectors from the Fatherland Front with such epithets as "anti-democratic," "anti-revolutionary," "fascist remnants," and "traitors" working in collaboration with the United States and the United Kingdom.[59]

Certainly Petkov and his colleagues expected support from the American and British members of the ACC in their efforts to get free elections—that is, elections free from police terror and permitting parties to run on separate lists. They counted on this support in 1945, however, not as the result of personal commitments from the American representatives in Sofia but because of the goals set forth in the Yalta declaration and such indications of U.S. determination to achieve these goals as were reflected in its refusal to accept the Fatherland Front's electoral procedures and the protection it afforded to Dr. Dimitrov.

Petkov broke with the Fatherland Front in July 1945 because he came to realize that the Communists were intent on preventing him and his colleagues from exerting any influence on government policy. During the Second World War, Petkov had been one of the principal Agrarian advocates of cooperation with the Communists, and he was closely associated with them and Zveno leaders in the seizure of power in September 1944. Throughout 1945 he believed that Western pressure on the USSR, and popular support within the country, would make it possible for him to seek an independent position for the Agrarians within the Fatherland Front coalition. The Zveno members of the Fatherland Front, as noted earlier, thought that Petkov had made a mistake in resigning and that Communist influence could best be limited by pressure from within the government.

In reflecting on these developments it is important to recall how the balance of influence between the U.S. and the USSR appeared in 1945. From the perspective of Soviet policy, the postponement of the elections in August reflected their interest in gaining American and British recognition of the Bulgarian government. The essential American bargaining power at this point was the threat of withholding recognition. The USSR was willing to compromise in some measure to achieve recognition.

This was not the first time, from the information then available to us, that the Soviet authorities had shown themselves sensitive to British and American pressure in regard to Bulgaria. When the Soviet troops first entered Bulgaria in September 1944, General Biriuzov had advised the Bulgarian army to remain in the occupied Greek territory of Thrace, but Moscow later ordered withdrawal at British and American insistence. Bulgaria and Yugoslavia had made plans in January 1945 for federation, and later for alliance, but the Soviet government vetoed these plans as unacceptable to the United States and the United Kingdom.[60] When Dr. Dimitrov sought asylum, the Soviet authorities were unwilling to take him by force from Barnes's villa. Biriuzov did suggest to the Bulgarian government that it request such action, but the latter declined to take the initiative, likewise for fear of antagonizing the United States.

After the announcement of the Moscow compromise in December 1945 it was clear that American and British policy was seeking to retreat from the objectives set forth at Yalta, but Petkov's refusal to enter the Fatherland Front government on its terms led to the failure of this effort. In the course of a meeting with Byrnes in January 1946, Vyshinsky charged specifically that Barnes was advising the opposition in Bulgaria not to accept the Moscow compromise. He added that his government "found it difficult to understand why a U.S. representative should endeavor to sabotage an agreement that had been reached bv the Secretary of State in Moscow. . . ."[61] Byrnes replied that he would look into the matter, but in fact he supported Barnes in not seeking to bring pressure on Petkov and his colleagues. In a personal message to Barnes shortly thereafter, the secretary said that "we do not regard the decision at Moscow as requiring us to urge the abandonment of the opposition's principles."[62] At this point not only Byrnes but also President Truman and most of those concerned with foreign policy in Washington were firmly opposed to recognition.

(4) This brings us to the fourth question: what was the United States seeking to accomplish in Bulgaria, and why did it fail?

The remarks of Barnes in 1947 are as clear a statement as one is likely to find in the contemporary record of American aims in Bulgaria: a government that took into account the priority of Soviet security interests and the related role of the Communist party, but that also provided for the freely elected representation of other parties. Of the countries bordering on the USSR, Finland is the only one in which such a state of affairs was brought about. The compromise reached in Finland was not an achievement of American policy, but it provides evidence that the type of solution sought by the United States in Bulgaria was at least theoretically within the realm of possibility.

There was a dramatic reduction in American objectives in Bulgaria during the period under consideration—from the goal of "the earliest possible establishment through free elections of governments responsive to the will of the people," as enunciated in the Yalta declaration in February 1945, to the granting of diplomatic recognition in October 1947 to a government fully dominated by the Communist party.

In the case of the Yalta declaration, one need not assume either that Roosevelt did not intend it to have any practical effect or that he expected it to be literally implemented. Like other declarations of this kind, it was intended not as a formal commitment but as a statement of goals that policy makers should seek to achieve. It is quite clear that at no time did Roosevelt believe that the United States should take direct responsibility for its implementation. He left the main burden of the final negotiation of the Bulgarian armistice to the United Kingdom and the USSR, and he let a British officer sign it on behalf of the United States.

In the course of preparing for the Yalta conference Roosevelt, as noted above, explicitly rejected the proposal that a four-power High Commission for Liberated Europe be established to implement the Yalta declaration. After his death in March 1945, changing American official attitudes toward the Yalta declaration reflected the prevailing political confusion and uncertainty. In the first three months of his administration, Truman was inclined to view the Yalta declaration as a contract that should be fulfilled to the letter. Byrnes, following his appointment as secretary of state in June, sought to implement what he and his New Deal associates believed to be Roosevelt's policy of accommodation with the USSR. A further turning point came in the spring of 1946, when a series of confrontations with the USSR led to a general consensus in the American foreign policy establishment that accommodation was not feasible. The issue now was no longer one of implementing the Yalta declaration but of building a barrier to what was perceived as an aggressive Soviet threat to Greece, Turkey, and Iran.

By this time, U.S. policy was in effect prepared to trade what remained of its influence in Bulgaria, and also in Romania and Hungary, for a predominant role in Italy and Japan. When the question of Japan was raised at Potsdam and at the meeting of the Council of Foreign Ministers in Moscow in December 1945, Byrnes had found it difficult to insist on a strong position in Bulgaria while seeking to limit severely the Soviet role in Japan.

The main goal of U.S. policy in southeastern Europe by 1946 was to contain what was perceived as an expansionist Soviet policy, and it was generally agreed that the best place to take a stand was at the line separating Anglo-American and Soviet occupation forces at the end of the war. The main reason advanced for Senate ratification of the Bulgarian peace treaty in June 1947 was the security of the eastern Mediterranean. The treaty required the withdrawal of Soviet troops from Bulgaria within ninety days, and to this extent the pressure on Greece would be relieved.[63] The United States had by now assumed the role in Greece originally allotted to the United Kingdom, and the spheres of influence that Roosevelt had rejected when negotiated by Churchill and Stalin in October 1944 as a short-term accommodation were now accepted by American policy, in practice if not in theory for an indefinite term.

(5) Finally, what light do these Bulgarian events shed on the origins of the Cold War? The foregoing suggests the conclusion that the Cold War arose from the long-term differences in the ideology and national interest of the United States and its Western Allies, and of the USSR.

The view that the USSR started the Cold War rests on the assumption that at Yalta the Western Allies and the USSR negotiated a binding agreement, in effect a treaty, the terms of which were clearly understood by both parties; and that the USSR subsequently violated the agreement. But this is not what happened. In the case of Bulgaria, the USSR certainly violated the Yalta declaration if one regards it as a binding agreement and interprets "democratic elections" from a Western point of view. There is no reason to believe, however, that Stalin any more than Roosevelt or Churchill regarded it as a formal contract, or that he accepted the Western view of democracy. The Yalta declaration was in fact quite casually adopted and no effort was made to negotiate a clear understanding as to its meaning.

The view that the United States started the Cold War rests on the assumption that it wished for political and economic reasons to exert a predominant influence in the countries of Eastern Europe, and pressed for the adoption of the Yalta declaration in the expectation that free elections would bring pro-Western governments to power. In fact, a lack of carefully considered long-term policies in regard to Eastern Europe was the dominant feature of the American posture in 1945. The available evidence supports the view that neither Roosevelt nor Truman wished to become involved in any significant way in political and economic developments in these countries. At best, U.S. policy in Eastern Europe was one of moderating exclusive Soviet influence to the extent possible with limited means, mainly by withholding recognition. At worst, it was simply a "nonpolicy," an exercise in "*word* politics."

There remains the third alternative: the Cold War arose as a result of long-term differences in ideology and national interest, rather than being "started" by either side. It is true that in Finland, and eventually in Austria, solutions were found that satisfied both Soviet security concerns and Western political values. In both of these cases, however, the solutions were primarily an achievement of the two countries concerned. One can imagine conditions under which similar conditions might have been achieved in Czechoslovakia, and possibly also Hungary. It is very difficult to imagine compromises of this type being reached in Poland, Romania, or Bulgaria. Britain had harbored no illusions about sharing political influence in this region with the USSR, and from the start had favored a division into separate spheres. It did not take the United States more than a couple of years to accept this as the only workable solution. In particular, exclusive American influence in Japan soon came to be regarded as adequate compensation for exclusion from Bulgaria and Romania.

The differences in values and interests reflected in the Cold War go far beyond the early postwar problems of Bulgaria and the other countries of Eastern Europe. These differences can be overcome only as the contending parties come to recognize that their common interest in a stable world order is a matter of higher national priority than exclusive spheres of influence. In the perspective of thirty-five years since the Yalta declaration, only modest progress has been made in the reorientation of values and interests from Cold War to world order.

NOTES

1. The organization, scope, and development of this work are described in U.S. Department of State, ***Postwar Foreign Policy Preparation, 1939–1945,*** Publication 3580, General Foreign Policy Series 15 (Washington: Government Printing Office, 1949).

2. ***Postwar Foreign Policy Preparations,*** p. 51.

3. U.S. Department of State, ***Foreign Relations of the United States*** (hereafter cited as ***FRUS) 1945*** (Washington: Government Printing Office, 1968), 4: 143, nn. 26, 27.

4. ***Postwar Foreign Policy Preparation,*** pp. 372–73; 394–95; the texts of the proposal and of the final declaration are on pp. 655–57 and 663–64.

5. Robert I. Gannon, ***The Cardinal Spellman Story*** (New York: Doubleday, 1962), p. 222.

6. Maurice Matloff, ***Strategic Planning for Coalition Warfare, 1943–1944*** (Washington: Department of the Army, 1959), p. 491.

7. Matloff, ***Strategic Planning,*** pp. 504–6.

8. Ivan Marinov, "Pet dni v pravitelstvoto na K. Muraviev" [Five days in the government of K. Muraviev], ***Istoricheski pregled*** 24 (May–June 1968):81–102.

9. Developments in Bulgaria in the summer and autumn of 1944 are discussed in Marshall Lee Miller, ***Bulgaria during the Second World War*** (Stanford: Stanford University Press, 1975), pp. 174–205. The most recent Bulgarian account is Vitka Toshkova, Bulgaria i Tretiiat Raikh, 1941–1944 (Bulgaria and the Third Reich, 1941–1944] (Sofia: Nauka i Izkustvo, 1975), pp. 182–234. The U.S. role in the armistice negotiations is covered in ***FRUS, 1944,*** 3:300–395.

10. ***FRUS, 1944,*** 4:230.

11. Ibid., 3:449–50.

12. Ibid., p. 463.

13. Ibid., p. 452.

14. Llewellyn Woodward, ***British Foreign Policy in the Second World War*** (London: H. M. Stationery Office, 1962), pp. 307–8; and Albert Resis, "The Churchill-Stalin Secret 'Percentages' Agreement on the Balkans, Moscow, October, 1944," ***American Historical Review*** 83 (April 1978):268–87. On the U.S. role, see W. Averell Harriman and Elie Abel, ***Special Envoy to Churchill and Stalin, 1941–46*** (New York: Random House, 1975), p. 354; Vojtech Mastny, ***Russia's Road to the Cold War*** (New York: Columbia University Press, 1979), pp. 207–12; and ***FRUS, 1944*** 3:455.

15. ***FRUS, 1944*** 3:396–479; and Miller, ***Bulgaria during the Second World War,*** pp. 204–20.

16. Maynard B. Barnes, "The Current Situation in Bulgaria," Lecture, National War College, Washington, D.C. (June 3, 1947), p. 11.

17. S. S. Biriuzov, ***Surovye gody*** [Bitter years] (Moscow: Nauka, 1966), p. 486. See also pp. 522–30. On the domestic activities of the ACC, see Stoyan Tanev, "Pomoshtta na suvetskoto voenno komanduvane za politicheskoto ukrepvane na narodnodemokratichnata vlast v Bulgariia (Septemvri 1944–1947 g.)" [The assistance of the Soviet military command in political support of the national democratic power in Bulgaria (September 1944–1947)], ***Voennoistoricheski sbornik*** 40 (July–August, 1971):65–81.

18. The political situation in Bulgaria in late 1944 and early 1945 is discussed in Nissan Oren, ***Revolution Administered: Agrarianism and Communism in Bulgaria*** (Baltimore: Johns Hopkins University Press, 1973), pp. 79–102. On the role of the radical Agrarians, see also Charles A. Moser, ***Dimitrov of Bulgaria: A Political Biography of Dr. Georgi M. Dimitrov*** (Ottawa, Ill.: Caroline House, 1979), pp. 187–203. Both the Agrarian and the Communist leaders were named Georgi M. Dimitrov—with middle names of Mihov and Mihailov, respectively. Since the Agrarian was a physician by training, he was generally known as Dr. G. M. Dimitrov. His political nickname was "Gemeto"—literally, "the G. M."

19. *FRUS, 1945,* 4:144–54.
20. Ibid., pp. 191–211.
21. Ibid., p. 163.
22. Ibid., p. 169.
23. Ibid., pp. 179–81.
24. Ibid., p. 186.
25. Moser, *Dimitrov,* pp. 215–48, provides a full account of Dimitrov's escape and subsequent events.
26. *FRUS, 1945,* 4:224.
27. Ibid., pp. 230–31.
28. Curtis H. Martin, "United States Diplomacy and the Issue of Representative Government in the Former German Satellite States 1943–1946: A Study of Foreign Policy and the Foreign Policy Process" (Ph.D. diss., Tufts University, 1974), pp. 234–311, provides a detailed account of the discussion at Potsdam of the complementary issues of free elections and recognition.
29. The text of Petkov's letter is in *FRUS, Conference of Berlin (Potsdam), 1945* (Washington: Government Printing Office, 1960), 2:724–25; and for related comments see pp. 722–23, 728–32.
30. Ibid., 4:284–94, 302–6.
31. Ibid., pp. 308–9.
32. Ibid., pp. 311–12.
33. Ibid., pp. 312–13.
34. The London meeting and its aftermath are discussed in Martin, *United States Diplomacy,* pp. 365–449.
35. *FRUS, 1945,* 4:364.
36. Ibid,. pp. 374–75.
37. Ibid., pp. 376–77.
38. Ibid., pp. 377–78.
39. The latter two documents are published in ibid., 5:633–41; see also Mark Ethridge and C. E. Black, "Negotiating on the Balkans, 1945–1947," in *Negotiating with the Russians,* ed. R. Dennett and J. E. Johnson (Boston: World Peace Foundation, 1951), pp. 171–206, for a more general account of the mission.
40. Martin, *United States Diplomacy,* p. 480.
41. *FRUS, 1945,* 4:405–6, 409–10.
42. Letter from Ethridge to author, Februry, 13, 1951.
43. Martin, *United States Diplomacy,* pp. 489–504.
44. *FRUS, 1945,* 2:700–701.
45. Ibid., p. 822; a full account of the Moscow negotiations is available in Martin, *United States Diplomacy,* pp. 539–65.
46. Martin, *United States Diplomacy,* pp. 567–72.
47. Ibid., pp. 591–609.
48. *FRUS, 1947,* 4:163–64.
49. *The Trial of Nikola D. Petkov* (Sofia: Ministry of Information and Arts, 1947), is an official record of the proceedings. Dr. G. M. Dimitrov published an appraisal of his Agrarian colleague in "Bravest Democrat of All," *Saturday Evening Post* 220 (December 6, 1947):28–29, 208–10. See also the account of

these events by the acting American representative in Sofia during Barnes's absence, John E. Horner, "The Ordeal of Nikola Petkov and the Consolidation of Communist Rule in Bulgaria," *Survey* 20 (Winter 1947):75–83; and Michael Padev, *Dimitrov Wastes No Bullets. Nikola Petkov: The Test Case* (London: Eyre and Spottiswoode, 1948).

50. Gar Alperovitz, *Atomic Diplomacy: Hiroshima and Potsdam* (New York: Random House, 1965), pp. 211–12.

51. Ibid., pp. 216, 13.

52. Martin J. Sherwin, *A World Destroyed: The Atomic Bomb and the Grand Alliance* (New York: Knopf, 1975), chaps. 8 and 9.

53. *FRUS, 1945,* 4:308.

54. Ernest R. May, *"Lessons" of the Past: The Use and Misuse of History in American Foreign Policy* (New York: Oxford, 1973), pp. 27–29; and more recently Martin Weil, *A Pretty Good Club: The Founding Fathers and the U.S. Foreign Service* (New York: Norton, 1978), pp. 195–97.

55. *FRUS, 1947,* 4:145–48.

56. Barnes, "Current Situation in Bulgaria," pp. 8–9.

57. Martin, *United States Diplomacy,* pp. 225, 230.

58. *Trial of Nikola D. Petkov,* p. 40.

59. Voin Bozhinov, *Zashtitata na natsionalnata nezavisimost na Bulgaria, 1944–1947* [The defense of the national independence of Bulgaria, 1944–1947] (Sofia: Bulgarian Academy of Sciences, 1962); K. Kukov, *Razgrom na burzhuaznata opozitsiia, 1944–1947* [The rout of the bourgeois opposition, 1944–1947] (Sofia: Bulgarian Communist party, 1966); Ilcho Dimitrov, *Godini na prelom: Tri ocherka iz nai-novata bulgarska istoriia* [Years of crisis: Three sketches from contemporary Bulgarian history] (Sofia: Dimitrov Communist Youth League, 1969); and Mito Isusov, "Otechestveniiat Front i opitite za deformirane na novata parlamentarna sistema v Bulgariia, 1945–1946" [The Fatherland Front and the efforts to undermine the new parliamentary system in Bulgaria, 1945–1946], *Istoricheski Pregled* 30 (July–August 1974):160–88.

60. *FRUS, 1945,* 4:250–51.

61. *FRUS, 1946,* 6:60–61.

62. Ibid., p. 66.

63. *Executive Sessions of the Senate Foreign Relations Committee,* vol. 1, *Eightieth Congress, First and Second Sessions, 1947-1948* (Washington, D.C., 1976), p. 45.

CHAPTER 12

An Interview with Mr. Khrushchev

The interview with Mr. Khrushchev presented in this chapter offers particularly interesting insights into his thinking. The interview took place in 1958 at the end of a visit by a three-man delegation, of which I was one, to observe the elections to the Supreme Soviet. We were summoned for the interview on the day after the elections, and I had the opportunity to ask Mr. Khrushchev about his conception of the future world socialist society as envisioned by Marxist-Leninist theory. He did not know in advance that he would be asked this question, and he clearly groped for an appropriate answer. He may well not have given much thought to this issue, and he certainly did not have a ready-made answer. He recognized the significance and appropriateness of the question, however, and the spontaneity of his response—reflecting as it did his boundless faith in the success of the Soviet Union—conveyed the impression that he meant what he said.

The Soviet Union will always be ahead of the United States in education, Khrushchev told me in Moscow in 1958. It is not because Russians are more clever, he added, but because they have a better system. These and other opinionated statements were accompanied by a cheerful grin, and if I did not find them convincing, they at least served to clarify my understanding of the Soviet Union and its energetic leader.

The occasion for these remarks was the visit of a three-man U.S. team sent to observe the elections to the Supreme Soviet, the bicameral legislative body of the U.S.S.R., on March 16, 1958. My colleages were Richard M. Scammon, director of elections research for the Governmental Affairs Institute in Washington, and Hedley Donovan, of Time Inc. We were returning the visit of a Soviet team which observed our national elections in 1956, and the trip was conducted in the spirit of reciprocal

Reprinted with permission from the *Princeton Alumni Weekly* (January 29, 1960), 10–11, 17, 20.

exchanges which has developed since the summit meeting at Geneva in 1955.

On the national level, these exchanges involve such massive operations as our brilliant exhibition in Moscow last summer and Khrushchev's spectacular visit to this country in September. But amidst this clamor there have also been many trips by smaller groups and individuals, and in quite a number of cases even our little community in Princeton has been affected: In this particular instance, the impressions and opinions gleaned from a two-week trip serve to enrich the teaching of Russian history. They make it possible to convey a sense of personal contact with the Russian scene which is lacking in the assigned readings, and relieve somewhat the rather ponderous and impersonal generalizations which tend to roll forth from the lecture platform.

Since this was an official visit, we received very hospitable treatment. For the greater part of the trip we had our own plush two-engined plane, which carried us and our Soviet hosts from Leningrad to Kharkov, Kiev, Tiflis, Stalingrad, Baku, and Tashkent, whence we returned to Moscow on the regularly scheduled jet airliner. We were accompanied by a representative of our Embassy and by Max Frankel of the *New York Times*. Although our principal job was to observe electoral procedures, we also had an opportunity to learn about other aspects of the Soviet system. In the course of the trip we talked with some fifty or sixty relatively high officials, including half a dozen members of the Central Committee of the Communist Party.

Several times a day we would be ushered into the office of the head of a local electoral commission, the director of a steel plant or a textile mill, the chairman of a collective, a local Communist Party secretary, a mayor of a large city, or a leader of the Communist youth organization. Their offices were generally arranged in conference-room style, and we would soon be seated around a table provided with bottles of soda water and lemonade, cigarets, and occasionally fruit, as well as pads and pencils. On one occasion the pencils bore the inscription of the Sacco and Vanzetti Factory but, since none of us was from Massachusetts, we did not take it as a personal affront. Yet it did seem odd to us, coming from a country where no more than a handful of political extremists have been executed in the past generation or two, to observe this commemorative gesture in a country where as a matter of principle many hundreds of thousands of persons suspected of opposition have been shot in recent decades.

Normally our host would open these sessions by giving a brief account of his area of responsibility—electoral, industrial, agricultural, political—and he would then invite questions which usually covered a wide range of subjects. These exchanges were frequently pointed, but always friendly, and were usually followed by a tour of the premises and a more substantial and stimulating repast than that offered at the conference table. We also attended a number of election meetings, and on the day of the election we observed the proceedings in several Moscow precincts and early on the following morning sat in on a tally of votes. This made for a rather strenuous schedule, usually from 8:00 a.m. until midnight or after, but we were able to fit in half a dozen performances of the ballet, opera, and folk dancing which the Russians do so well.

II

Our observations on political and economic topics have already been published elsewhere,[1] and suffice it to note here that Russian elections are rather different from ours. There is only one candidate for each of the 1,378 seats in the Supreme Soviet, so the voters had no choice and hence there was no contest. This greatly simplified matters for all concerned. The election campaign was reasonably vigorous in terms of public meetings and newspaper articles, but it was of course rather one-sided. When the great day came, the voter simply received a ballot with the name of his candidate printed on it, and deposited it in the nearby ballot box. There were curtained booths where voters could in privacy cross out the name of the candidate, but they could not substitute another name. Of the 133,836,325 eligible voters, less than one-half of one per cent expressed their discontent in this fashion, according to the official statistics. "The elections were very well organized," is the phrase I am proud to have coined when asked my impressions of this procedure. Not only is this an accurate statement, but it left all parties happy.

Indeed, the organizational job involved was not inconsiderable. To arrange for the registration of these millions of voters a month or more before the election, to appoint and organize the 1,200,000 members of the electoral commissions which supervised the election, to arrange for the nomination of 1,378 candidates, and then on election day to see to it that all the registered voters went to the polls (only 0.03% failed to vote, according to the official report) and that they all (or at least over 99.5%) voted the right way—all this took some doing and must have kept the Communist Party very busy. If it was not an electoral campaign in the sense of providing the voters with a choice of candidates, it was certainly an organizational exercise of massive proportions. The Party would certainly not go to all this trouble if it did not think it worthwhile, and after some speculation we concluded that Soviet elections serve important political purposes. They offer a special opportunity for widespread propaganda on major themes (and there is nothing subliminal about this campaign); they give the voter a sense of participating in the political process; they establish through the election of deputies to the Supreme Soviet a transmission belt for the conveyance of Party policies to the "masses" (as the Russian people are called by their leaders); and they also provide a rigorous test of the efficiency and reliability of the Party organization. Apart from this, there is also some question whether the Party has ever considered the possibility of not having elections. For a century or more elections have come to be accepted as a part of modern government, as neckties are a part of modern dress, and it is a question of making them serve a useful purpose rather than of doing without them.

III

At breakfast on Monday, March 17th, the day after the elections, we were informed that Mr. Khrushchev would see us at noon. At the start of the trip we had asked to see one or more of the political leaders of the Soviet Union, since they were the leading candidates in the election which we were to observe, but we had not had any response to our request until this time. We were accompanied by our official host, Mr. L. N. Solovyev, deputy chairman of the All-Union Council of Trade Unions; Mr. G. A. Zhukov, Chairman of the State Committee on Cultural Relations With Foreign Countries (the cabinet-level body in charge of exchanges); and Mr. Yu. I. Pavlov, the very able interpreter from the Foreign Office. We made no preparation for the interview, beyond agreeing not to take up the time with obvious questions offering opportunities for long harangues that might be used for Soviet propaganda (Example: Q. "What is the difference between Soviet and American elections?" A. "Soviet elections are democratic, whereas in the U.S. they are controlled by Wall Street, etc., etc."). While we did not avoid harangues entirely, we at least avoided the publication of anti-American propaganda using us as straight men—although it is possible that the Soviets withheld publication because they did not think that either the questions or the answers were of much significance. Let the reader be the judge. Both Hedley Donovan and I took notes during the interview (as did Mr. Zhukov, although we did not get to see them), and we were later told that we could use the notes as we saw fit. What follows is therefore a reasonably full, but not a verbatim, statement of Mr. Khrushchev's views, omitting some of the discussion of electoral details.

Humorous Repartee

Mr. Khrushchev received us promptly at noon in his office at the headquarters of the Central Committee of the Communist Party in No.

2 Staraya Ploshchad (Old Square), and while we were being photographed we exchanged jokes about our relative size. Our little delegation was reasonably ponderous, ranging from my 200 pounds and 6'3", with Donovan about the same size, to Scammon who was 100 pounds heavier and a couple of inches taller. The Russians by contrast were (physically) relative lightweights. I cannot expect, Mr. Khrushchev asserted later on in the interview, to convince you with my arguments, as the U.S. government has no doubt sent a well-armored delegation. It will not melt away. If it did, one of us replied, it might flood the Central Committee building. This is a serious danger, our host concluded. This note of rather heavy humor ran through the interview, but when answering serious questions the Soviet leader took on an air of intense concentration.

After thanking Mr. Khrushchev for receiving us, we asked him whether it would be correct to say that in the last analysis no final decision is taken as to the selection of electoral candidates without consultation with the Communist Party organs at the appropriate level. Candidates are nominated at district pre-electoral meetings by trustworthy people, he replied. Several candidates are selected at the initiative of public organizations (trade unions, factories, etc.). You are quite right in noting that the Party organization plays a major role in selecting candidates, he added. We then asked him what other tasks the Party has in the electoral process after the nomination of candidates? The Communist Party is like all parties, he asserted, in that it wishes to see its candidates succeed. It therefore strives to employ all spiritual and material resources at its command to make sure that its candidates are victorious.

Foreigners often do not understand why we have only one party, Mr. Khrushchev continued. They misunderstand the Soviet system. It is not surprising that we have only one Party, because we have only the interest of the people to represent. In capitalist countries there are many classes and vested interests, and each has its own press and political party. In Russia there are only the workers and the peasants, as well as the intelligentsia who serve their interests. In the U.S. there are the antagonistic interests of employers and workers. In Russia there are no antagonistic interests, the Party is the vanguard of the peasants and workers.

At this point we noted that there were different interpretations of this matter. There are many functional similarities between our societies despite the differences. We also have a different point of view regarding class structure, but this was not the place to argue these points. I agree, he replied.

Rate of Growth

On several occasions our conversation returned to the differences between our two countries. When we told Mr. Khrushchev how impressed we were by the seriousness of the Soviet aim of overtaking and surpassing the United States, he replied that he did not know why the American people did not take this slogan seriously. It is a perfectly logical aim from the Soviet point of view, he said. Our rate of growth is three to four times higher than yours [the rate of growth of gross national product in 1959 was about 2% in the U.S. and 6% in the U.S.S.R.], despite the fact that the volume of your production is greater. I do not know when it will take place, but the lines are bound to cross. We are all convinced that we will overtake you. And this is not simply a matter of theory, it can be supported by facts. The figures are available in my 40th anniversary speech in October, 1957, and in my speech of March 14, 1958.

We replied that it was good for us to know this. It helped us to evaluate his country. We welcomed this competition. Mr. Khrushchev then added: We are not threatening the United States with this competition. We have set the task to overtake and surpass the high United States level of production. We hope all peoples will reach this level. There is enough raw material in the world to do this. There is only a need for peace, therefore we struggle to prevent war.

When discussion turned to longer-range goals, the inevitable comparison with the United States recurred. There will be shorter working hours with much more free time, Mr. Khrushchev explained. People will work three or four hours a day, and there will be enough to supply all material needs. All our people will have at least a secondary education. I do not wish to appear fantastic, but I hope that 25%, 30%, perhaps 50% of all people will have a higher education. There will be time for enriching their spiritual powers, and more time for gaining knowledge of engineering, literature, art, astronomy, and the theater. It will be possible to use this wealth and time rationally.

We do not think that we are wiser than you in the United States, he continued. We recognize that at present you create more material wealth in your country than we do, but much of your wealth is expended wastefully and irrationally. At present you have six or seven million unemployed able-bodied people eager to work [the number of unemployed at this time was 5.2 million], an enormous waste of human resources. If we had your economic potential and five or six million men to spare we would have reduced our working day to four or five hours and give people a fuller share of public life. I myself suffered poverty. I am of an age to have experienced unemployment. I understand the sentiments of Mr. Meany. (Speech of March 11, 1958, citing unemployment figures). We will publish his speech so that our young people will appreciate American reality. They will know that these are not the words of Mr. Khrushchev, who is a well known anti-capitalist, but of Mr. Meany, who supports the capitalist system.

Mr. Khrushchev was then asked whether he would publish an article by Donovan explaining the capitalist system. If Donovan could explain it better than we can, he replied, we would publish his article; but if we are able to do it, it would not be necessary, because we know our readers better and we would not need to borrow his article. We then suggested that it might be good for the capitalist system to learn about Russia. What about an exchange of articles? This is not a bad idea, he acknowledged, provided the articles are of a scholarly character and not slander. A good discussion and exchange of ideas could be organized. If the recent treaty on exchanges between our two countries is properly implemented it will serve a useful purpose. We will not agree on many issues, but it will help the two countries to understand each other.

A little later he added, in this connection, that he did not consider men of literature as class enemies. Now they are serving capitalist society, he asserted, but this will change. You do not believe now that capitalism will change to socialism, but you will see. You have only a small group of exploiters in the United States. Our system tries to work for the people, while capitalists are only interested in their profits. Is this propaganda?—YES! we chorused.

Future Society

Mr. Khrushchev was then asked to comment on a rather theoretical topic, which is not often discussed by high Soviet officials. It was our understanding, we said, that according to the doctrine of the Communist Party the Marxist principles of society as developed in the U.S.S.R. would in due course be adopted throughout the world. Could he tell us about the proposed form of government, economy, languages and organizational arrangements of this future society?

It is too early to state what form these will take, he replied. When we come to that point, we will find the appropriate means and forms. It is still a field for fantasy and it is impossible to describe the organizational arrangements in any detail. It would be a fantasy. The general principles are set forth in the doctrines of Marx, Engels, and Lenin. We believe that not only the victory of socialism is required, but that it is also necessary to raise the living standards of peoples so as to equalize conditions of life all over the world. Say that socialism (by which he meant the Soviet form of Communism) wins in the U.S.A.: if the wealth of the U.S. were distributed all over the world the American people would not accept it. The first step is to raise living standards.

As to governmental forms—I cannot answer this question, he continued. War is a result of capitalism, and with the victory of socialism economic resources would no longer be needed for armed forces and defense which now consume much material wealth. If these resources are freed it will facilitate the development of mankind and its well-being—clothing, housing, and political and spiritual needs.

As for other matters, we will preserve the languages of all countries. All countries will be allowed to preserve their native languages. Russian, English, and Chinese will be world languages. Perhaps a common language will eventually be arrived at. I cannot say how long it will take before socialism is established all over the world, but the important thing is to raise living standards before the transition to Communism.

But you are saying, look at Khrushchev—he has been convinced by others of these theories. You are all laughing at him. You disagree with me now. You are cultured, well-educated people. After the transition to Communism, you will serve the people's interests. But we will have our differences for some time. What we need is peaceful coexistence.

When we concluded the interview by congratulating him on his re-election (the results had not yet been announced, but could not be in doubt), he took the opportunity for a parting shot: Here all capable people can develop their talents. In the U.S. you must have means and money. There, seeds of talents fall on sterile soil. In Russia we have a proverb: "He who laughs last, laughs best" [a very old Russian proverb]. We have a population of 200 million as a basis from which to choose, but you only have capitalists and servants of capitalism. Think it over before it is too late.

IV

With this challenge ringing in our ears we returned to our hotel, and the comforts of vodka, caviar, and rye bread. The interview speaks for itself as a brief glimpse of Mr. Khrushchev's views and personality, but perhaps a few concluding remarks are in order.

In talking with the Soviet leader, and from observing other aspects of Russian life, one gets the impression that the Soviet elite has only a limited understanding of the outside world. Mr. Khrushchev has a very practical approach to the domestic problems of his country, but he still seems to view the outside world, or at least the West, through the red-tinted glasses manufactured by Marx. The Soviet system resembles a good deal that of an army, with a clear-cut chain of command in all walks of life and a well-defined slot for everyone. From the vantage point of such a system, American society seems very disorganized. Who makes decisions? Who does the planning? Who is responsible for what? It is pretty much a mystery to them, and the attribution of all direction to "Wall Street" is a very feeble substitute for understanding. I do not think Mr. Khrushchev has any clear idea how we get things done in this country, and I doubt whether his visit last fall helped much.

What interested me in particular was the Soviet leader's belief, which he reiterated in a variety of ways, that the Soviet form of socialism—Communism—is the best system and will inevitably win out around the world. He seemed to think that this would happen only after the standard of living in Asia and Africa approximated that in the West, which the Soviets seem to think will take a generation or more—say, by about 1984. While due allowance must be made for the propaganda aspects of Soviet statements—including those which Mr. Khrushchev made to us—they seem to be sincere in the belief that world Communism is not more than a generation or two away. They believe that they have found the best way to modernize, that Communism is steadily expanding, and that it will inevitably triumph. The talk of "peaceful coexistence" which we hear these days must be understood in this light. At best, it means to them that this ultimate victory will take place, gradually and without a major war. At worst, it is intended to lull us to sleep while they prepare for war.

NOTE

1. Richard M. Scammon, "Why the Russians Bother With Elections," *New York Times Magazine* (April 6, 1958), 14, 63–64; Hedley Donovan, "How the Russian People Vote—and Why," *Life* (April 21, 1958), 55–56, 59–60; Cyril E. Black, "Soviet Political Life Today," *Foreign Affairs* (July, 1958), 569–81.

Other Publications by the Author

BOOKS

The Establishment of Constitutional Government in Bulgaria, Princeton: Princeton University Press 1944; reprint ed., New York: Johnson Reprint Co. 1970.

Twentieth Century Europe: A History (with Ernst C. Helmreich), New York: Knopf 1950; 2nd ed., 1959; 3rd ed., 1966; 4th ed., 1972.

Challenge in Eastern Europe (Editor and Coauthor), New Brunswick: Rutgers University Press 1954; Spanish ed., trans. by J. M. Claramunda Bes, Barcelona: Hispano Europea 1956.

Rewriting Russian History: Soviet Interpretations of Russia's Past (Editor and Coauthor), New York: Praeger 1956; 2nd ed., New York: Vintage 1962; Spanish ed., trans. by Adriana T. Bo, Buenos Aires: Hobbs 1965.

American Teaching About Russia (Coeditor and Coauthor, with John M. Thompson), Bloomington: Indiana University Press 1959.

The Transformation of Russian Society: Aspects of Social Change Since 1861 (Editor and Coauthor), Cambridge: Harvard University Press 1960.

Our World Today (Consulting Editor and Coauthor), Boston: Ginn 1960.

Communism and Revolution: The Strategic Uses of Political Violence (Coeditor and Coauthor, with Thomas P. Thornton), Princeton: Princeton University Press 1964; Marathi ed., trans. by Nana Joshi, Bombay: Janpad Prakashan 1968; Spanish ed., trans. by Emilio M. Sierra, Buenos Aires: Troquel 1968; Bengali ed., trans. by Sushil Mukherjea, Calcutta: Sarkar 1968; Japanese ed., trans. by Seijiro Nakazawa, Tokyo: Keio Tsushin 1969.

The Dynamics of Modernization: A Study in Comparative History, New York: Harper and Row 1966; Japanese ed., trans. by Hideo Uchiyama and Ichio Ishikawa, Tokyo: Keio Tsushin 1968; Portuguese ed., trans. by Celia Maria G. de Stewart, Rio de Janeiro: APEC 1971; Italian ed., trans. by Lisa Occhetto Baruffi, Milan: Instituto Librario Internazaionale 1971; Vietnamese ed., trans. by Bui Quang Khanh, Saigon: Hien Dai 1972; Dutch ed., trans. by G. A. Isarin-Smit, Alphen aan den Rijn: Samson 1972; Chinese ed., trans. by Kuo Cheng-chao, Chang Chung-ping, and Chou Yü-hua, Taipei: Shu-yu 1972, 2nd printing 1974; Turkish ed., trans. by Fatih Gümüs, Ankara: Türkiye Is Bankasi Kültür Yayinlari 1986.

Neutralization in World Politics (with Richard A. Falk, Klaus Knorr, and Oran R. Young), Princeton: Princeton University Press 1968.

The Future of the International Legal Order (Coeditor and Coauthor, with Richard A. Falk), Vol. I, *Trends and Patterns;* Vol. II, *Wealth and Resources;* Vol. III,

Conflict Management; Vol. IV, *The Structure of the International Environment* (Princeton: Princeton University Press 1969–72).

The Modernization of Japan and Russia (with Marius B. Jansen, Herbert S. Levine, Marion J. Levy, Jr., Henry Rosovsky, Gilbert Rozman, Henry D. Smith, II, and S. Frederick Starr), New York: Free Press 1975; Chinese ed., Beijing: Shangwu yin shuguan 1984.

The Modernization of China (Coauthor), ed. by Gilbert Rozman, New York: Free Press 1981.

ARTICLES AND CHAPTERS

"The Russo-Bulgarian Military Convention of 1902" (with E. C. Helmreich), *Journal of Modern History,* 9 (December, 1937), 471–482.

"The Influence of Western Political Thought in Bulgaria, 1850–1885," *American Historical Review,* 48 (April, 1943), 507–520.

"The Greek Crisis—Its Constitutional Background," *Review of Politics,* 10 (January, 1948), 84–99.

"Poznan and Europe in 1848," *Journal of Central European Affairs,* 8 (July, 1948), 191–206.

"Greece and the United Nations," *Political Science Quarterly,* 63 (December, 1948), 551–568.

"Constitutional Trends in Eastern Europe, 1945–48," *Review of Politics,* 9 (April, 1949), 196–207; trans. in "Tendencias constitucionales de Europa oriental 1945–48," *Hechos e Ideas,* 10 (February, 1950), 141–154.

"Negotiating on the Balkans" (with Mark Ethridge), *Negotiating With the Russians,* ed. by R. Dennett and J. E. Johnson (Boston: World Peace Foundation, 1951), 171–206.

"The People's Democracies of Eastern Europe," *European Political Systems,* ed. by Taylor Cole (New York: Knopf, 1953), 188–265; 2nd ed. (with Randolph L. Braham) (1959), 741–837.

"Soviet Political Life Today," *Foreign Affairs,* 36 (July, 1958), 569–581; reprinted in *Soviet Society: A Book of Readings,* ed. by Alex Inkeles and Kent Geiger (Boston: Houghton Mifflin 1961), 182–189.

"An Appraisal of Russian Studies in the United States" (with John M. Thompson and others), *American Slavic and East European Review* (October, 1959), 417–441; trans. in *Soren Mondai* 18 (Tokyo), 4 (April, 1960), 78–90.

"The Nature of Imperial Russian Society," *Slavic Review,* 20 (December, 1961), 565–588; reprinted in *The Development of the USSR,* ed. by Donald W. Treadgold (Seattle, 1964), 173–208; *Imperial Russia After 1861: Peaceful Modernization or Revolution?* ed. by Arthur E. Adams (Lexington, Mass.: Heath 1965), 90–96; *Revolution: A Reader,* ed. by Bruce Mazlish, Arthur D. Kaledin, and David B. Ralson (New York: Macmillan 1971), 99–114.

"Political Modernization in Russia and China: Suggestions for a Comparative Evaluation," *Unity and Contradiction: Major Aspects of Sino-Soviet Relations,* ed. by Kurt L. London (New York: Praeger, 1962), 3–18.

"The Pattern of Russian Objectives," *Russian Foreign Policy,* ed. by Ivo J. Lederer (New Haven: Yale University Press, 1962), 3–38.

"Russia and the Modernization of the Balkans," *The Transformation of Balkan Society,* ed. by Charles Jelavich (Berkeley: University of California Press, 1963), 145–183.

"Russia and Eastern Europe," *New Perspectives in World History,* ed. by Shirley H. Engle (Washington, D.C., 1964), 304–331.

"Change as a Condition of Modern Life," *Modernization: The Dynamics of Growth,* ed. by Myron Weiner (New York: Basic Books, 1966), 17–27.

"Soviet Society: A Comparative View," *The Prospects for Soviet Society,* ed. by Allen Kassof (New York: Praeger 1968), 14–53.

"Government-Sponsored Research in International Studies" *World Politics,* 22 (July 1970), 582–596.

"Hikaku kindaika no shiten" [Viewpoints of Comparative Modernization], *Hikaku kindaika ron* [Theories of Comparative Modernization], ed. by Kiyoko Takeda (Tokyo: Miraisha 1970), 5–33.

"Diachronic and Synchronic Comparisons in the Study of Modernization in Southern Asia," *Essays on the Modernization of Underdeveloped Societies,* ed. by A. R. Desai (2 vols.; Bombay 1971), I, 40–52.

"Theories of Political Development and American Foreign Policy," *The Role of Ideas in American Foreign Policy,* ed. by Gene M. Lyons (Hanover, N.H.: University Press of New England 1971), 47–65.

"Russian Interpretations of World History," *The Analysis of International Politics,* ed. by James N. Rosenau, Vincent Davis, and Maurice A. East (New York: Free Press 1971), 371–390.

"The United States in the Arena of Modernizing Revolutions," *American Foreign Policy and Revolutionary Change,* ed. by Jack B. Sabbert (Pullman, Wash.: Washington State University Press 1968), 1–11.

"Neutralization of South Vietnam: Pros and Cons" (with Oran R. Young), *The Vietnam War and International Law,* ed. by Richard A. Falk (3 vols.: Princeton: Princeton University Press 1970–72), III, 811–823.

"The Relevance of Theories of Modernization for Normative and Institutional Efforts at the Control of Intervention," *Law and Civil War in the Modern World,* ed. by John Norton Moore (Baltimore: Johns Hopkins University Press 1974), 53–69.

"Eastern Europe in the Context of Comparative Modernization," *The Politics of Modernization in Eastern Europe,* ed. by Charles Gati (New York: Praeger 1974), 22–39.

"Military Leadership and National Development," *The Military and Society,* ed. by David MacIsaac (Washington, D.C.: GPO 1975), 16–35.

"World Orders: Old and New," *Occasional Papers,* World Order Studies Program, Center of International Studies, Princeton University, No. 1 (1975), 1–13.

"The Great Society in a Little America? Political and Social Values and Institutions," *Isolation or Interdependence? Today's Choices for Tomorrow's World,* ed. by Morton A. Kaplan (New York: Free Press 1975), 81–102.

"Russian History in Japanese Perspective: An Experiment in Comparison," *Jahrbücher für Geschichte Osteuropas,* 23 (December 1975), 481–488.

"The Process of Modernization: The Bulgarian Case," ***Bulgaria, Past and Present,*** ed. by Thomas Butler (Columbus, Ohio: American Association for the Advancement of Slavic Studies 1976), 111–131.

"Rushton Coulborn's Contribution to Civilizational Studies" (with Joseph R. Strayer), ***Comparative Civilizations Bulletin,*** 6 (Summer 1977), 4–8.

"Japan and Russia: Bureaucratic Politics in a Comparative Context," ***Social Science History,*** 2 (Summer 1978), 414–426.

"New Soviet Thinking," ***New York Times*** (November 24, 1978), A27; reprinted in ***International Herald-Tribune*** (November 26–27, 1978), 6.

"The Evolving Political System," ***Perceptions: Relations Between the United States and the Soviet Union,*** Committee on Foreign Relations, United States Senate (Washington, D.C., 1978), 103–106.

"The Start of the Cold War in Bulgaria: A Personal View," ***Review of Politics,*** 41 (April 1979), 163–202.

"The Impact of U.S.-Soviet Trade on Soviet Society," ***Common Sense in U.S.-Soviet Trade,*** ed. by Willard C. Matthias (Washington, D.C.: American Committee on East-West Accord, 1979), 107–112.

"Changing Mutual Social Science Perceptions: The U.S. and the U.S.S.R. and Eastern Europe," ***A Balance Sheet for East-West Exchanges*** (New York: IREX 1980), 9–36.

"A Comparative Approach to the Preconditions of Ottoman Modernization," ***International Journal of Turkish Studies,*** 1 (Autumn 1980), 25–37.

"The Concept of International Regimes as an Approach to Settlement," ***The Iraq-Iran War: Issues of Conflict and Prospects for Settlement,*** ed. by Ali E. Hillal Dessouki (Princeton University: Center of International Studies, Policy Memorandum no. 40, 1981), 60–65.

"The View from Bulgaria," ***Witnesses to the Origins of the Cold War,*** ed. by Thomas T. Hammond (Seattle: University of Washington Press 1982), 60–97.

"Russian and Soviet Entrepreneurship in a Comparative Context," ***Entrepreneurship in Imperial Russia and the Soviet Union,*** ed. by Gregory Guroff and Fred V. Carstensen (Princeton 1983), 3–10.

(with John P. Burke), "Organizational Participation and Public Policy," ***World Politics,*** 35 (April 1983), 393–425.

(with Robbin F. Laird), "The Impact on Soviet Society," ***Common Sense in U.S.-Soviet Trade,*** ed. by Carl Marcy and Margaret Chapman (Washington, D.C.: American Committee on East-West Accord 1983), 61–66.

"The Soviet Union as an Advanced Society," ***The Soviet Polity in the Modern Era,*** ed. by Erik P. Hoffmann and Robbin F. Laird (Chicago: Aldine 1984), 809–823.

"The American Revolution in Comparative Perspective," ***Humanitas,*** 1 (1984), 3–6.

"An Introduction to Modernization Studies," "Periodization in Modernization Studies," "Preconditions: Russia," "Transformation: Russia," and "Advanced Modernization," in Michio Nagai, ed., ***Development in the Non-Western World*** [Eng. ed. of ***Hi-seiyo shakai ni okero kaihatsu***] (Tokyo: University of Tokyo Press, 1984), 124–129, 130–132, 141–148, 161–169, 196–224.

"The Soviet Union and Arms Control," ***The Nuclear Arms Debate: Ethical and Political Implications***, ed. by Robert C. Johansen, World Order Studies Program Occasional Papers no. 12 (Princeton: Center of International Studies 1984), 101–126.
"Roots of Modernism: Russia and Japan," ***United Nations University: Work in Progress***, 9 (July 1985), 11.

Publications of the Center of International Studies

BOOKS (available from publishers)

Gabriel A. Almond, *The Appeals of Communism* (Princeton University Press 1954)
William W. Kaufmann, ed., *Military Policy and National Security* (Princeton University Press 1956)
Klaus Knorr, *The War Potential of Nations* (Princeton University Press 1956)
Lucian W. Pye, *Guerrilla Communism in Malaya* (Princeton University Press 1956)
Charles De Visscher, *Theory and Reality in Public International Law*, trans. by P. E. Corbett (Princeton University Press 1957; rev. ed. 1968)
Bernard C. Cohen, *The Political Process and Foreign Policy: The Making of the Japanese Peace Settlement* (Princeton University Press 1957)
Myron Weiner, *Party Politics in India: The Development of a Multi-Party System* (Princeton University Press 1957)
Percy E. Corbett, *Law in Diplomacy* (Princeton University Press 1959)
Rolf Sannwald and Jacques Stohler, *Economic Integration: Theoretical Assumptions and Consequences of European Unification*, trans. by Herman Karreman (Princeton University Press 1959)
Klaus Knorr, ed., *NATO and American Security* (Princeton University Press 1959)
Gabriel A. Almond and James S. Coleman, eds., *The Politics of the Developing Areas* (Princeton University Press 1960)
Herman Kahn, *On Thermonuclear War* (Princeton University Press 1960)
Sidney Verba, *Small Groups and Political Behavior: A Study of Leadership* (Princeton University Press 1961)
Robert J. C. Butow, *Tojo and the Coming of the War* (Princeton University Press 1961)
Glenn H. Snyder, *Deterrence and Defense: Toward a Theory of National Security* (Princeton University Press 1961)
Klaus Knorr and Sidney Verba, eds., *The International System: Theoretical Essays* (Princeton University Press 1961)
Peter Paret and John W. Shy, *Guerrillas in the 1960's* (Praeger 1962)
George Modelski, *A Theory of Foreign Policy* (Praeger 1962)
Klaus Knorr and Thornton Read, eds., *Limited Strategic War* (Praeger 1963)
Frederick S. Dunn, *Peace-Making and the Settlement with Japan* (Princeton University Press 1963)
Arthur L. Burns and Nina Heathcote, *Peace-Keeping by United Nations Forces* (Praeger 1963)

Richard A. Falk, *Law, Morality, and War in the Contemporary World* (Praeger 1963)
James N. Rosenau, *National Leadership and Foreign Policy: A Case Study in the Mobilization of Public Support* (Princeton University Press 1963)
Gabriel A. Almond and Sidney Verba, *The Civic Culture: Political Attitudes and Democracy in Five Nations* (Princeton University Press 1963)
Bernard C. Cohen, *The Press and Foreign Policy* (Princeton University Press 1963)
Richard L. Sklar, *Nigerian Political Parties: Power in an Emergent African Nation* (Princeton University Press 1963)
Peter Paret, *French Revolutionary Warfare from Indochina to Algeria: The Analysis of a Political and Military Doctrine* (Praeger 1964)
Harry Eckstein, ed., *Internal War: Problems and Approaches* (Free Press 1964)
Cyril E. Black and Thomas P. Thornton, eds., *Communism and Revolution: The Strategic Uses of Political Violence* (Princeton University Press 1964)
Miriam Camps, *Britain and the European Community 1955–1963* (Princeton University Press 1964)
Thomas P. Thornton, ed., *The Third World in Soviet Perspective: Studies by Soviet Writers on the Developing Areas* (Princeton University Press 1964)
James N. Rosenau, ed., *International Aspects of Civil Strife* (Princeton University Press 1964)
Sidney I. Ploss, *Conflict and Decision-Making in Soviet Russia: A Case Study of Agricultural Policy, 1953–1963* (Princeton University Press 1965)
Richard A. Falk and Richard J. Barnet, eds., *Security in Disarmament* (Princeton University Press 1965)
Karl von Vorys, *Political Development in Pakistan* (Princeton University Press 1965)
Harold and Margaret Sprout, *The Ecological Perspective on Human Affairs, With Special Reference to International Politics* (Princeton University Press 1965)
Klaus Knorr, *On the Uses of Military Power in the Nuclear Age* (Princeton University Press 1966)
Harry Eckstein, *Division and Cohesion in Democracy; A Study of Norway* (Princeton University Press 1966)
Cyril E. Black, *The Dynamics of Modernization: A Study in Comparative History* (Harper and Row 1966)
Peter Kunstadter, ed., *Southeast Asian Tribes, Minorities, and Nations* (Princeton University Press 1967)
E. Victor Wolfenstein, *The Revolutionary Personality: Lenin, Trotsky, Gandhi* (Princeton University Press 1967)
Leon Gordenker, *The UN Secretary-General and the Maintenance of Peace* (Columbia University Press 1967)
Oran R. Young, *The Intermediaries: Third Parties in International Crises* (Princeton University Press 1967)
James N. Rosenau, ed., *Domestic Sources of Foreign Policy* (Free Press 1967)
Richard F. Hamilton, *Affluence and the French Worker in the Fourth Republic* (Princeton University Press 1967)
Linda B. Miller, *World Order and Local Disorder: The United Nations and Internal Conflicts* (Princeton University Press 1967)

Henry Bienen, *Tanzania: Party Transformation and Economic Development* (Princeton University Press 1967)

Wolfram F. Hanrieder, *West German Foreign Policy, 1949–1963: International Pressures and Domestic Response* (Stanford University Press 1967)

Richard H. Ullman, *Britain and the Russian Civil War: November 1918–February 1920* (Princeton University Press 1968)

Robert Gilpin, *France in the Age of the Scientific State* (Princeton University Press 1968)

William B. Bader, *The United States and the Spread of Nuclear Weapons* (Pegasus 1968)

Richard A. Falk, *Legal Order in a Violent World* (Princeton University Press 1968)

Cyril E. Black, Richard A. Falk, Klaus Knorr and Oran R. Young, *Neutralization and World Politics* (Princeton University Press 1968)

Oran R. Young, *The Politics of Force: Bargaining During International Crises* (Princeton University Press 1969)

Klaus Knorr and James N. Rosenau, eds., *Contending Approaches to International Politics* (Princeton University Press 1969)

James N. Rosenau, ed., *Linkage Politics: Essays on the Convergence of National and International Systems* (Free Press 1969)

John T. McAlister, Jr., *Viet Nam: The Origins of Revolution* (Knopf, 1969)

Jean Edward Smith, *Germany Beyond the Wall: People, Politics and Prosperity* (Little, Brown 1969)

James Barros, *Betrayal from Within: Joseph Avenol, Secretary-General of the League of Nations, 1933–1940* (Uale University Press 1969)

Charles Hermann, *Crises in Foreign Policy: A Simulation Analysis* (Bobbs-Merrill 1969)

Robert C. Tucker, *The Marxian Revolutionary Idea: Essays on Marxist Thought and Its Impact on Radical Movements* (W.W. Norton 1969)

Harvey Waterman, *Political Change in Contemporary France: The Politics of an Industrial Democracy* (Charles E. Merrill 1969)

Cyril E. Black and Richard A. Falk, eds., *The Future of the International Legal Order.* Vol. I: *Trends and Patterns* (Princeton University Press 1969)

Ted Robert Gurr, *Why Men Rebel* (Princeton University Press 1969)

C. Sylvester Whitaker, *The Politics of Tradition: Continuity and Change in Northern Nigeria 1946–1966* (Princeton University Press 1970)

Richard A. Falk, *The Status of Law in International Society* (Princeton University Press 1970)

John T. McAlister, Jr., and Paul Mus, *The Vietnamese and Their Revolution* (Harper & Row 1970)

Klaus Knorr, *Military Power and Potential* (D.C. Heath 1970)

Cyril E. Black and Richard A. Falk, eds., *The Future of the International Legal Order.* Vol. II: *Wealth and Resources* (Princeton University Press 1970)

Leon Gordenker, ed., *The United Nations in International Politics* (Princeton University Press 1971)

Cyril E. Black and Richard A. Falk, eds., *The Future of the International Legal Order.* Vol. III: *Conflict Management* (Princeton University Press 1971)

Francine R. Frankel, *India's Green Revolution: Political Costs of Economic Growth* (Princeton University Press 1971)
Harold and Margaret Sprout, *Toward a Politics of the Planet Earth* (Van Nostrand Reinhold 1971)
Cyril E. Black and Richard A. Falk, eds., *The Future of the International Legal Order.* Vol. IV: *The Structure of the International Environment* (Princeton University Press 1972)
Gerald Garvey, *Energy, Ecology, Economy* (W.W. Norton 1972)
Richard Ullman, *The Anglo-Soviet Accord* (Princeton University Press 1973)
Klaus Knorr, *Power and Wealth: The Political Economy of International Power* (Basic Books 1973)
Anton Bebler, *Military Role in Africa: Dahomey, Ghana, Sierra Leone, and Mali* (Praeger Publishers 1973)
Robert C. Tucker, *Stalin as Revolutionary 1879–1929: A Study in History and Personality* (W.W. Norton 1973)
Edward L. Morse, *Foreign Policy and Interdependence in Gaullist France* (Princeton University Press 1973)
Henry Bienen, *Kenya: The Politics of Participation and Control* (Princeton University Press 1974)
Gregory J. Massell, *The Surrogate Proletariat: Moslem Women and Revolutionary Strategies in Soviet Central Asia, 1919–1929* (Princeton University Press 1974)
James N. Rosenau, *Citizenship Between Elections: An Inquiry Into the Mobilizable American* (Free Press 1974)
Ervin Laszlo, *A Strategy For the Future: The Systems Approach to World Order* (Braziller 1974)
John R. Vincent, *Nonintervention and International Order* (Princeton University Press 1974)
Jan H. Kalicki, *The Pattern of Sino-American Crises: Political-Military Interactions in the 1950s* (Cambridge University Press 1975)
Klaus Knorr, *The Power of Nations: The Political Economy of International Relations* (Basic Books Inc., 1975)
James P. Sewell, *UNESCO and World Politics: Engaging in International Relations* (Princeton University Press 1975)
Richard A. Falk, *A Global Approach to National Policy* (Harvard University Press 1975)
Harry Eckstein and Ted Robert Gurr, *Patterns of Authority: A Structural Basis for Political Inquiry* (John Wiley & Sons 1975)
Cyril E. Black, Marius B. Jansen, Herbert S. Levin, Marion J. Levy, Jr., Henry Rosovsky, Gilbert Rozman, Henry D. Smith, II, and S. Frederick Starr, *The Modernization of Japan and Russia* (Free Press 1975)
Leon Gordenker, *International Aid and National Decisions: Development Programs in Malawi, Tanzania, and Zambia* (Princeton University Press 1976)
Carl Von Clausewitz, *On War,* edited and translated by Michael Howard and Peter Paret (Princeton University Press 1976)
Gerald Garvey and Lou Ann Garvey, eds., *International Resource Flows* (D.C. Heath 1977)

Walter F. Murphy and Joseph Tanenhaus, *Comparative Constitutional Law Cases and Commentaries* (St. Martin's Press 1977)

Gerald Garvey, *Nuclear Power and Social Planning: The City of the Second Sun* (D.C. Heath 1977)

Richard E. Bissell, *Apartheid and International Organizations* (Westview Press 1977)

David P. Forsythe, *Humanitarian Politics: The International Committee of the Red Cross* (Johns Hopkins University Press 1977)

Paul E. Sigmund, *The Overthrow of Allende and the Politics of Chile, 1964–1976* (University of Pittsburgh Press 1977)

Henry S. Bienen, *Armies and Parties in Africa* (Holmes and Meier 1978)

Harold and Margaret Sprout, *The Context of Environmental Politics* (The University Press of Kentucky 1978)

Samuel S. Kim, *China, the United Nations, and World Order* (Princeton University Press 1979)

S. Basheer Ahmed, *Nuclear Fuel and Energy Policy* (D.C. Heath 1979)

Robert C. Johansen, *The National Interest and the Human Interest: An Analysis of U.S. Foreign Policy* (Princeton University Press 1980)

Richard A. Falk and Samuel S. Kim, eds., *The War System: An Interdisciplinary Approach* (Westview Press 1980)

James H. Billington, *Fire in the Minds of Men: Origins of the Revolutionary Faith* (Basic Books, Inc. 1980)

Bennett Ramberg, *Destruction of Nuclear Energy Facilities in War: The Problem and the Implications* (D.C. Heath 1980)

Gregory T. Kruglak, *The Politics of United States Decision-Making in United Nations Specialized Agencies: The Case of the International Labor Organization* (University Press of America 1980)

W. P. Davison and Leon Gordenker, eds., *Resolving Nationality Conflicts: The Role of Public Opinion Research* (Praeger Publishers 1980)

James C. Hsiung and Samuel S. Kim, eds., *China in the Global Community* (Praeger Publishers 1980)

Douglas Kinnard, *The Secretary of Defense* (The University Press of Kentucky 1980)

Richard Falk, *Human Rights and State Sovereignty* (Holmes & Meier 1981)

James H. Mittelman, *Underdevelopment and the Transition to Socialism: Mozambique and Tanzania* (Academic Press 1981)

Gilbert Rozman, ed., *The Modernization of China* (The Free Press 1981; paperback edition 1982)

Robert C. Tucker, *Politics as Leadership*. The Paul Anthony Brick Lectures. Eleventh Series (University of Missouri Press 1981)

Robert Gilpin, *War and Change in World Politics* (Cambridge University Press 1981)

Nicholas G. Onuf, ed., *Law-Making in the Global Community* (Carolina Academic Press 1982)

Ali E. Hillal Dessouki, ed., *Islamic Resurgence in the Arab World* (Praeger Publishers 1982)

Richard Falk, *The End of World Order* (Holmes & Meier 1983)
Klaus Knorr, ed., *Power, Strategy and Security* (Princeton University Press 1983)
Finn Laursen, *Superpower At Sea* (Praeger Publishers 1983)
Samuel S. Kim, *The Quest for a Just World Order* (Westview Press 1984)
Gerald Garvey, *Strategy and the Defense Dilemma* (D.C. Heath and Co. 1984)
Peter R. Baehr and Leon Gordenker, *The United Nations: Reality and Ideal* (Praeger Publishers 1984)
Joseph M. Grieco, *Between Dependency and Autonomy: India's Experience With the International Computer Industry* (University of California Press 1984)
Jan Hallenberg, *Foreign Policy Change: United States Foreign Policy Toward the Soviet Union and the People's Republic of China, 1961–1980* (University of Stockholm 1984)
Michael Krepon, *Strategic Stalemate: Nuclear Weapons and Arms Control in American Politics* (Macmillan 1984)
Gilbert Rozman, *A Mirror for Socialism: Soviet Criticisms of China* (Princeton University Press 1985)
Henry Bienen, *Political Conflict and Economic Change in Nigeria* (London: Frank Cass 1985)

Index

For Product Safety Concerns and Information please contact our EU representative GPSR@taylorandfrancis.com Taylor & Francis Verlag GmbH, Kaufingerstraße 24, 80331 München, Germany

Batch number: 10725879

Printed by Printforce, the Netherlands